The Republican Hero

The Republican Hero

From Homer to Batman

MICHAEL LUSZTIG

Published by State University of New York Press, Albany

© 2023 State University of New York

All rights reserved

Printed in the United States of America

No part of this book may be used or reproduced in any manner whatsoever without written permission. No part of this book may be stored in a retrieval system or transmitted in any form or by any means including electronic, electrostatic, magnetic tape, mechanical, photocopying, recording, or otherwise without the prior permission in writing of the publisher.

For information, contact State University of New York Press, Albany, NY
www.sunypress.edu

Library of Congress Cataloging-in-Publication Data

Name: Lusztig, Michael, 1962– author.
Title: The republican hero : from Homer to Batman / Michael Lusztig.
Description: Albany : State University of New York Press, [2023] | Includes bibliographical references and index.
Identifiers: LCCN 2023009084 | ISBN 9781438495378 (hardcover : alk. paper) | ISBN 9781438495385 (ebook) | ISBN 9781438495361 (pbk. : alk. paper)
Subjects: LCSH: Heroes—Political aspects. | Heroes in literature. | Republicanism.
Classification: LCC BJ1533.H47 L87 2023 | DDC 170/.44—dc23/eng/20230705
LC record available at https://lccn.loc.gov/2023009084

10 9 8 7 6 5 4 3 2 1

For my family

Contents

Acknowledgments		ix
Preface		xi
Introduction: Heroes and Republicans		1
Chapter 1	The Epic Hero and the Roots of Republican Governance	37
Chapter 2	Justice, Magnanimity, and the Republic	53
Chapter 3	Rome and the Limits of Heroic Magnanimity: The Great, the Greatly Good, and the Not So Good	77
Chapter 4	The Christian Hero in the Orders of Nature and Grace	93
Chapter 5	Romanticism: The Egotistical Sublime and Moral Agency	115
Chapter 6	God, Godliness, and the Birth of the Common Hero	141
Chapter 7	The American Common Hero	167
Conclusion: What Is a Republican Hero?		193
Notes		215
Works Cited		227
Index		255

Acknowledgments

As with any book, this one could not have been written without the support of friends, colleagues, family, and financial assistance. I would therefore like to thank Gianna Englert, Cal Jillson, Joe Kobylka, Gavin Rudman, and Matthew Wilson for their help in reading and/or talking through portions of the manuscript. I am grateful to acquisitions editor Michael Rinella, who provided guidance and support throughout the review process. In addition, three anonymous reviewers for SUNY Press took a great deal of time to improve the book with detailed and insightful comments. Institutionally, I am benefited from course relief provided by Dedman College at Southern Methodist University. Finally, I thank my wife, Christine Carberry, for her patience and support. In addition to reading multiple drafts of the manuscript with the keen eye of a copy editor, she cheerfully undertook the always underappreciated task of indexing the book.

Preface

ANDREA: "Unhappy the land that has no heroes."

GALILEO: "No, Andrea, unhappy the land that is in need of heroes."

—Bertolt Brecht, *The Life of Galileo*

This is a book about heroes. More specifically, it is about whether or not heroes matter in the successful construction of republican government. The perspective is both empirical and normative. That is, I want to know if we are living in a postheroic age and, regardless of the answer, whether or not we should be. Certainly, the profanity and vulgarity of the modern age tempt the belief that modern society is postheroic and none the better for it. From this perspective, heroism is a relic of more meaningful and less secular times; when humans elevated their moral horizons above their own immediacy; when God or immanent mortals loomed larger than they themselves; when a spiritual order took precedence over the natural one. There is plentiful evidence for this perspective. One only need to pick up a magazine or tune in to one of the nightly television shows dedicated to Hollywood hagiography to gain appreciation for the vacuity of modern "hero" worship.

Excoriation of the modern age is reasonable. Look around, and you can find something to complain about. We pollute the environment, potentially beyond the state of sustainability. Scientific evolution has brought us to the brink of nuclear holocaust. There is too little faith in the world and too much radical theology. Try as we might, we cannot perfect human nature beyond the primitive plateau on which it has always operated. Jeremiads, secular and theological, are ubiquitous. The covenant is broken, Robert Bellah (1975) tells us. Our moral compass is failing, warns

William Bennett (1992). And we are slouching towards Gomorrah, Robert Bork (1997) chimes in. The subtext of such modern postheroism is tinged with a regressive eschatology of mediocrity in which humanity becomes so self-absorbed as to fail to recognize what is meaningful about their lives.

And yet, there is something not quite believable about the idea that so much has changed so fast; about the implicit suggestion that vacuity and nihilism are recent importations to the human condition, and that, somehow, rationalism, scientism, and cultural embourgeoisement have fundamentally altered the timeless practice of elevating heroes above their fellows. Indeed, we need to remind ourselves that nihilistic despair is not new. History has boasted any number of golden ages to which nostalgic social critics can point. Once an age has been elevated to an ideal, any (inevitable) social changes constitute evidence of decline (Morley 2004, 578). Writing almost three thousand years ago, Hesiod bemoans the moral failure of his time, contrasting his race of iron with the hero-men who once populated the earth. Polybius and Livy and Sallust and Cicero all diagnose republican Rome's perilous condition in terms of dissipation of the traditional customs that long had infused Rome with moral goodness. Christian theology is grounded in postlapsarian departure from a state of grace. And so it goes through history.

Do republican heroes matter, and do we live in a postheroic age? The short answers are respectively, yes and no. Yes, republican heroes matter, insofar as the heroic currencies of greatness and goodness are essential to protection, promotion, and preservation of republican virtue. Republican heroes inspire citizens to live better lives than they otherwise might think themselves capable of living. No, we do not live in a postheroic age. The argument here is that while it is true, earlier times were characterized by singular heroes, the modern age is more complete in its heroism. It enjoys the residual benefits of four types of republican hero. The hero types are not all equal in relevance. Epic and magnanimous heroes do not enjoy the same prominence today as they did in less egalitarian times. Yet, the legacy of each hero type persists. Their heroic qualities conspire in creation of a complete, unified if you prefer, republican heroism for the modern age. Complementary, these qualities temper one another's excesses. They persist in the cosmic justice—the justice implicit in just condition, just balance, and just agency—that has characterized republican values from the time of pre-Socratic natural philosophy.

Ultimately, a defense of republican heroism amounts to a conservative justification of republican values. Yet the argument here speaks to an institutionally dynamic conservatism, evolving with the progressive perfection of social and political institutions. It eschews the lamentations of those who desire the return to a better age. Instead, it is an apology for the times, the republican values that continue to sustain it, and the robustness of those forces despite the immutable weakness of human nature. Mostly, it confirms that, as ever, the ancients had it right—that temperate balance is more just, if less exhilarating, than the pomp and pageantry that historically has attached to heroic singularity. Modern republican heroes are no longer warrior progeny of divinity. Nor are they philosopher kings or noble lords or saints or chivalric knights. They do not slay dragons. They are not steeped in the immanence that past heroes enjoyed. They do not rule with an imperious hand in the name of social order and public welfare. But even as we move into a cultural sense of modern humanity's moral self-sufficiency, we have not lost primeval recognition that there are others, mortals and gods, to encourage us to be better than we are.

The Book

In addition to being a justification for the heroism of the age, this book explores heroes' relevance to the evolution of republicanism through the lens of philosophy, theology, history, literature, and cinema. Chronologically, it takes us from the early Hellenic masterpieces of Homer and Hesiod to the modern superhero. Looking at history from the perspective of republican heroism permits analysis of the triumphs and failures of the heroic ideal and a greater understanding of the values that continue to underscore republican government. Thus, the book is not about discrete heroes—although discussion of them is unavoidable—but illustration of the historical preeminence of one hero type or another and the political ramifications of that preeminence.

The organizing principle is roughly chronological, not because heroism undergoes some sort of secular soteriological progression, but because republicanism does. In addition to the heroic narrative, then, the book traces the evolution of republican governance, from its emergence in the socially stratified Archaic Greek city states, to its present manifestation in egalitarian liberal democracies. Chapter 1 begins the process with a discussion of Homer's prototypical epic heroic archetype, concerned chiefly with honor and immortality through posterity. Politically, Homeric heroism played two fundamentally important roles in pre-Classical Greece. First, Homeric heroes created a schematic sense of the aristocratic ideal of physical excellence in legitimation of wealth, power, and authority. Second, in provoking violent response from commoners chafing under aristocratic dominance, the institutional framework balancing the interests of the great and the many was devised by Solon in mitigation of social conflict. The chapter concludes with a brief discussion of the changing ideal of epic heroism from one in which goodness was tangential or incidental, to one that insisted upon at least some degree of moral competence.

If chapter 1 chronicles the institutional antecedents of republicanism in ancient Greece, chapter 2 explores the metaphysics in the context of heroic magnanimity. The story begins with another poet, Hesiod, who is interested in humanity's place in the cosmic order, the imperative for justice, and the effects of human depravity—themes that would become central to republican philosophy and Christian theology. The chapter continues with a discussion of the preeminent philosophers of Classical Athens, with particular attention paid to Socrates's prototypical philosopher king and Aristotle's more ambiguously heroic great-souled man. Finally, it explores magnanimous heroism in the counterfactual, with a discussion of the tragedy that attaches—particularly in the *Hecuba* and the *Antigone*—to a failure of heroic magnanimity. Greek tragedy plays another important role as well, speaking to the imperative for balance between the cosmic and positive laws.

Chapter 3 examines the quintessential case of the land unhappy for want of heroes. The Roman Republic enjoyed a long tradition of heroes great and good. During the Late Republican period, as foreign wars became less significant for Rome's survival, the lions who had once safeguarded Rome against hostile forces abroad began to turn on Rome itself. The Roman case, in which no real heroes are discussed in depth, illustrates the perils of assuming the natural conflation of greatness with goodness, as well as the consequences for a regime whose greatest citizens were not good. Indeed, it was Republican Rome that, centuries after its demise, would cause modern republicans to reevaluate the efficacy of civic humanism in general, and epic and magnanimous heroism in particular.

The next chapter explores heroic greatness—epic and magnanimous—through the lens of Christian republicanism. The subtext is the tension between two elements of cosmic justice—condition and balance—in construction of the Christianized republic. The primacy of just condition is represented by Augustinian and orthodox Calvinist insistence upon the hegemony of the spiritual order—the order of grace—over the natural (or worldly) order. Just balance, by contrast, reflects Christian humanists' insistence upon realizing the golden mean between divine and terrene authority. A number of heroic archetypes reflect this tension. The most prominent standard bearers for the supremacy of the spiritual order are the Puritan saints, insistent upon social stratification and a millennialist republic deferential to Christian teleology. More reflective of equilibrium are chivalric knights, balancing obligation to lord and lady (the latter in proxy for God). Patriots (or country gentlemen), heirs to gallant cavaliers, assume importance for a number of reasons. First, in oppositional alliance with Puritan divines against royal absolutism and the intolerance of the English High Church, they helped usher in the sweeping changes wrought by the English Civil War and subsequent Glorious Revolution. Second, in their self-sufficiency and vestigial pastoralism lay the harbingers of Romanticism. Finally, and more immediately, in breaking with the saints over the nature of the Christianized republic, they stimulated the Whiggish liberalism institutionalized in the wake of the Glorious Revolution.

The ascendance of the order of nature during the Enlightenment indirectly gave rise to the Romantic hero, who occupies our attention in chapter 5. Romantics' reimagining of the good society in terms of natural (as opposed to biblical) spirituality created a more humanist dynamic in promotion of human dignity through liberty, equality, and social identity. The most nuanced part of the chapter defines what a Romantic hero actually is. Neither necessarily great nor good, facially self-absorbed, the Romantic appears to be no-one's idea of a hero or even of a republican. The first task of the chapter, then, is to make the case for Romantic heroism through the conduct of an authentic life and the exhortation to others to live a similarly transcendent life. The danger is that fidelity to self overwhelms the social and cosmic obligations that (also) characterize republican virtue. Thus, the second part of the chapter is dedicated to articulating a theory of social and cosmic obligation within Romanticism. Finally, the chapter concludes with a discussion of the political effects of contemporary Romantic heroism in the context of the new social movements that have increasingly influenced the sociopolitical landscape in modern republics since the 1960s.

The Enlightenment represented the celebration of innate moral agency that informs the American common hero discussed in chapters 6 and 7.

Chapter 6 explores the bases of the common hero's just agency. Rather than cognition or affect, the chapter makes the case for common heroism grounded in intuitive reasoning. We look at two manifestations. The first is commonsense moral reasoning, legitimated through the Scottish Enlightenment and, more proximately, Protestant evangelism. Manifesting in the aftermath of two great spiritual awakenings, the efficacy of the individual armed with common sense stimulated both American independence and legitimation of the new republic. The second manifestation of common just agency was American transcendentalism and the imperative to heed the imperatives of the super-sensual over-soul, as Emerson styles it, in challenging social convention through the celebration of moral intuition.

Having established requisite capacity for common heroism in chapter 6, chapter 7 represents an exploration of the archetypical American common hero. The subtext tying all together is the dialectic of the primitive and civilized. Prototypical common American heroes were Hector St. John de Crevecoeur's idealized yeoman farmer Andrew the Hebridean, and the new American burgher as personified by Royall Tyler's Henry Manly and Mr. Van Rough. More enduring was the rugged individualism of the hero of the sylvan frontier. From the backwoodsman, the American common hero progressed to the Old West gunslinger, illustrating even more clearly the ambient tension between purity in nature and the social imperative for civilization. With the passing of the Old West, two new archetypes emerged in the twentieth century. The first, more dystopian, was the hard-boiled detective, typified by Carroll John Daly's Race Williams, Dashiell Hammett's Continental Op and Sam Spade, and Raymond Chandler's Philip Marlowe. Verging on the antiheroic, the hard-boiled character was soon replaced by the enduring superhero, epic in her powers, but common in her exhortation of the efficacious everyman.

I conclude the book with the suggestion that the most complete heroic age—the one that best balances the composite dimensions of republican heroism—is the modern one. The problem is that heroic completeness does not lend itself easily to singularity. The closest we might come is the superhero, whose manifest epic powers are more subtly joined with magnanimity, Romanticism, and common heroic citizenship. Of course, if the heroic incarnation of such completeness is fictional insect men and women parading around in garish spandex tights, the relevance is suspect. Indeed, the paucity of equally singular real-life heroic analogues is grist for the mill of those lamenting the passage of heroism.

Yet this need not concern us much. From Homer through the Caped Crusader, the arts have always reflected the values of their times by mythologizing heroes in ways that few would confuse with reality. Mythology demands efficient packaging—requisite virtues coalescing theatrically in singular individuals. Reality, on the other hand, is less efficient. Heroic virtues typically do not congregate in unlikely clusters. As such, the relevant virtues that comprise a balanced composite republican heroism tend toward broad distribution throughout society. Such distribution makes for poor hagiography. It is suboptimal for hero worship and mythology. Harnessed, aggregated, and properly appreciated, however, the argument here is that the distribution of heroic virtues in the modern age is no less politically relevant for its lack of efficiency and singularity. More forcefully, in appreciating and balancing the broadest range of virtues relevant to the good society and the transcendent life, the case can be made that modern age reflects the epitome of republican heroism.

Introduction

Heroes and Republicans

It is difficult to define what is meant by heroes; the word enjoys enormous elasticity. Heroes manifest in all realms of social interaction. The name attaches to men and women who accomplish extraordinary feats, who prevail in contests against the worthiest rivals, who transcend misfortune or treachery, or who prevail in prolonged quests (Klapp 1949). Heroes possess rare capabilities, such as courage, wisdom, piety, imagination, or even self-confidence. They present as the incarnation of societal values, serve as role models, exist in fulfillment of vicarious success or experience, or epitomize an ideal self-image (Sullivan and Venter 2010; Wolf and Zuckerman 2012, 644). We find heroes in mythology and spirituality, in high culture and pulp fiction, in all forms of human communication. Often, they are the stuff of folklore; often, they represent the foundation of political or spiritual authority (Klapp 1949). Heroes entertain, they teach, and they reflect the moral parameters of the good society (see Wright 2001). They are social benefactors, leaders, protectors, inspirers, avengers, and sages. They are gods and mortals, fictive or real (Raglan 1934; Ruebel 1991; Porpora 1996; Miller 2002; Allison and Goethals 2011).

The elevation of iconic heroes—divine or apotheotic beings set apart and held up for admiration or reverence—is a sociological constant. It exists in legend and myth across such diverse ancient cultures as the Babylonian, Egyptian, Greek, Hebrew, Hindu, Persian, Roman, Asian, African, Christian, European, and Aboriginal American, bespeaking an elemental sociopsychological imperative (Rank 1914, 1, 4–11). The *variable* is how these heroes manifest historically. The hero "bears with him the ethos of the age, the unspoken assumptions, the philosophical presuppositions in the context of which his existence becomes meaningful" (Thorslev 1962, 19; also Plutarch 1920; Carlyle 1841; Emerson *Rep.*). From the primeval emergence of Western civilization, Homeric heroes were godlike, realizing their exaltation in posterity. Retrospectively at least, Greece made heroic figures of philosophers. In ancient Rome, heroism was manifest in acts of public virtue. Medieval Christianity reprised the supernaturalism of the Homeric hero, albeit not as god-men but *God's* men and women (Fishwick 1969, 5). The hero of the late Middle Ages was the chivalric knight. In the Renaissance, heroism was reborn as well-roundedness and self-mastery. The Romantics grounded heroism in authenticity. In more modern times, it is the common individual who has acquired volitional heroic qualities through innate cognitive or intuitive capacities.

This book has four main purposes. First, it explores the hero's role in the evolution of republican regimes and values, from the classical hierarchically structured form of mixed government, to the Christianized city, to modern liberal democracies. Second, it demonstrates the means by which republics have managed to protect themselves, sustain themselves, and redeem themselves through the cultivation of heroic figures, real or mythological. Informing the political values of the republic, the republican hero speaks to the values requisite to the good human life as it was understood in her time. Bringing such abstractions to life, she provides justification and legitimation—to say nothing of a *face*—to the metaphysical basis of republican social organization. Third, the book identifies and illustrates four different types of republican hero—epic, magnanimous, Romantic, and common—defined in terms of the presence or absence of the heroic currencies of greatness and goodness. Finally, the fourth mandate of the book is to rebut the premise that we live in a postheroic age. In assessing the republican hero's political relevance, her historical manifestations, her place in the orders of nature and grace, her posterity and her evolution, the book seeks to demonstrate the republican hero's continued existence in the modern age. Indeed, the argument here is that the modern age is not only heroic, but it is arguably the most *justly* heroic age, at least as it pertains to republican heroism.[1] In order to make the case, we will need to establish a few points. To start, we need to know what republicanism is and how it has evolved, what republican heroes do, what makes a (republican) hero, what types of republican hero exist, what others have said about heroes in a social or political context, and whether or not republican heroes still matter. These issues will occupy the rest of this chapter.

What Is Republicanism and How Has It Evolved?

John Adams reportedly lamented of republicanism, there "is not a more unintelligible word in the English language" (quoted in Rodgers 1992, 38). He had a point. Classical republicanism was sufficiently complex. Its evolution did little to simplify things.[2] Since "republicanism" defies universal specification, let us start by defining classical republicanism here in terms of both structure and values. Central to both is the pre-Socratic ideal of cosmic justice (e.g., Vlastos 1946; 1947; Engmann 1991). As I portray it here, such cosmic justice—natural, philosophical, spiritual, aesthetic, and institutional—is determined by three things. The first is *just balance*. The nullification of extremes, just balance represents a temperate mean. We can think of just balance in the way that dialectical forces maintain the constancy of a thing (such as the pull of gravity that keeps the earth in constant orbit). More pertinent is the mixed government that gives republicanism its defining institutional structure. Occupying a medial position between two of Aristotle's pure forms of government—aristocracy and polity—republicanism annexes best qualities of both, each countering the excesses and supplementing the deficiencies of the other. Indeed, it is in such just balance that republicanism represents a brake on the cycle of regimes that, Aristotle famously maintains in the *Politics*, causes each pure regime type (monarchy, aristocracy, and polity) to be corrupted and subsequently displaced in its turn (Aristotle *Pol.* Bk V; also Fink 1945, ch. 1; Pocock 1975, 79).

The second determining element is *just condition*, or the fidelity of a thing to the purpose for which it was created. The underlying assumption here is that the universe did not unfold as a series of random events, but rather according to some sort of discernable rational pattern, with every element of the cosmos having its own proper function. In consequence, everything—humans and animals, natural phenomena and social constructs included—can be thought to exist in just or unjust condition. To take an example from the Greek poet-statesman Solon, the sea is just in condition when, placid and navigable, it is in harmony with its proper function (2008, fr. W12; Vlastos 1946). By contrast, it is unjust, when, roiled by wind and storm, it works against its cosmic purpose. What is true of the sea is true of the republic, the purpose of which, classical and modern republicans tell us alike, is to aid citizens in fulfillment of a fully human life—one that realizes the *human* condition of which we will have more to say in a moment.

The final determining element of cosmic justice is *just agency*, or acting justly. Foundational to republican values, just agency is a means to just balance and just condition. For Aristotle, just agency manifests as temperance, or habitually selecting the medial position between excess and deficiency of a quality within the context in which that quality is operative (*N.E.* 1106b, 36—1107a, 26). The just agent is courageous in battle, for example, when she chooses the mean between recklessness and cowardice. More profoundly, it is the relationship between just agency on the one hand, and just balance and condition on the other, that Socrates is at pains to illustrate in the *Republic*. Socrates conceives just agency as action reflecting the supremacy of reason over appetite. The seat of just agency is the soul. Where the soul is governed by its appetites—whether for material goods, power, or honor—Socrates conceives the soul as more bestial than human. Single-minded in its quest for appetitive gratification, the host can never be sated. Its desires constitute the metaphorical leaky jar that can never be filled. Because there will never be *enough* wealth or power or glory, the host becomes ever more extreme—unjust—in seeking fulfillment (Plato *Gorg.*, esp. 493a-d). By contrast, where reason prevails, the appetites will be more temperate—more balanced. Moreover, it finds fulfillment in realization of the human condition, the cosmic purpose for which humanity exists.

Another way of looking at Socrates's primacy of reason is agency governed by the imperative for what republicans call *virtue*—another conceptually ambitious term. Distinct from discrete virtues (or excellences), let us think of *virtue* itself as a tripartite obligation to self (to live a life just in balance and condition), society (to share in the stewardship of the just republic), and cosmological design (to live in accordance with the objective moral principles that we will continue to call *the good*). These obligations are indivisible; fulfillment of one is fulfillment of all. Even so, in order to illustrate a fairly nuanced point, let us talk about each obligation individually as a means of getting a better sense of the obligations that govern just agency.

As noted, obligation to the self is to fulfill the human condition. Unlike plants and animals, humans do not naturally realize just condition. Instead, as we have already seen with Socrates, human beings have a natural inclination to be governed by their appetites. Just condition therefore demands transcendence of the slavery to the appetites, or overcoming what Charles Taylor calls the *ordinary life* of production and reproduction (1989, 211). (Henceforth we will contrast this ordinary life to the transcendent life—a balanced life, governed by just agency in realization of just [or the human] condition.)

Classical republicans start from the premise that humans are incapable of self-transcendence. Rather, they must be socialized—educated and habituated—into lives just in condition. Indeed, it is only when one is taught to be reflexive in her justice—preferring the just over the pleasurable as *second* nature—that one can be said to fulfill her obligation to herself (e.g., Aristotle *N.E.* 1102a, 14—1104b, 4). The mandate for socializing individuals to live transcendent lives falls to the just republic. Because the *res publica* (public thing) exists for the good of all, implicit is a corporate responsibility to aid others in fulfillment of such just condition.

As such, the second—*social*—obligation inherent in republican virtue demands that each citizen do her share to contribute to the effective functioning of the just republic. Such civic virtue, as it is also known, attaches most readily to military or public service. It might extend to production of goods and services—an economic contribution to the common weal. It is manifest in social benevolence, the creation of knowledge, and even the arts. Most fundamentally for most republicans, though, social obligation is civic contribution to the quality of laws. Ideally, each citizen will bring her talents to bear in the construction of just laws. Inherent is virtuous recursivity: just laws make just people, and just people make just laws.

The idea of just laws leads us to the third obligation constitutive of virtue, obligation to cosmological design. We can think of this third component as obligation to the way things were meant to be. Albeit conceived in manifold ways, classical republicans conceived this third obligation as fidelity to an inductively discernable entity that we have already called the good. There are two relevant elements—*knowledge* of the good and action in *accordance* with the good. Classically, both were governed intellectively. For Socrates, knowledge of the good is the province of the philosopher. Manifesting as wisdom, it entails understanding the first principles of goodness through an ontological process of inquiry and contemplation (e.g., Plato *Rep.*, 590c–590d; *Meno*, 87a–89c). Action in *accordance* with the good, by contrast, is governed intellectively by prudence, or good judgment in the conduct of life. In keeping with the prevailing duality, the two elements of goodness conform to two elements central to the making of law in a republic: the sagacity inherent in the proposition of good law and the mechanics inherent in deliberation or ratification. In the classical republican division of labor, proposition of good laws falls to sagacious knowers of the good. Ratification is the prerogative of the good citizen.[3] This differentiation between knowing and acting endowed classical republicanism with its institutional logic, classical republicanism representing balance between the expertise implicit in the wisdom of the best (*aristoi*) and the contextual practical judgment that derives from the aggregated virtues of the masses (*demos*).

The Changing Face of Republicanism

Starting roughly with the late Italian Renaissance, the face of republicanism began to change (esp. Pocock 1975). Two fundamental differences, both relating to just agency, are noteworthy. The first is the debunking of the mythical exclusivity of moral sagacity; the second is movement away from the primacy of cognition in the conceptualization of just agency. As to the first, one of the great effects of the Enlightenment was the conviction that humans enjoy innate capacity to comprehend the first principles of goodness requisite to realization of the human condition. The attendant dispensation of the distinction between the knower and the actor was no small shift in perspective. If comprehension of first moral principles was no longer the exclusive preserve of the philosopher, the aristocrat, the divine, or her immanent analogue, then the social stratification of ancient republics was unjustifiable. The upshot of this transformative assumption is that while modern republics retain the institutional balance that attaches to mixed government, they reject the political division of labor that once stratified the great and the many. In this more egalitarian guise, modern republicanism is far more *liberal*. It places greater emphasis on (negative) liberty—the imperative for morally self-sufficient individuals to be free from unreasonable external constraint in the conduct of their lives. This fundamentally alters the nature of obligation to self. If humans are indeed self-sufficient in the capacity to live fully human lives, then the function of the good republic shifts from compulsion (to coerce individuals to live justly), to support (provision of requisite social resources for individuals to pursue their own best lives).

The second fundamental shift that distinguishes modern republicanism from its classical counterpart was away from the supremacy of cognition. Inherent in the Scottish Enlightenment and the later Idealist, *Sturm und Drang*, and Romantic movements, was a greater emphasis on affect, or sentiment, as the basis of endogenous moral capacity. Certainly, it is true that ancient philosophers appreciated the complementarity of aesthetics to ethics, but it was cognition rather than affect that enjoyed pride-of-place as the driver of the just agency. Later on, as we shall see in examining the American transcendentalist movement of the mid-nineteenth century, mystical moral intuition—staking a liminal position between cognition and affect—also assumed importance as source of the innate capacity for what we will call *moral agency* (which is a handier way of saying self-sufficiency in the just agency requisite to realization of the human condition). The evolutionary understanding of moral agency, and the concomitant change in the makeup of the republican hero, is a central theme in the chapters to follow.

What Do Republican Heroes Do?

Republican heroes, individual or archetypal, are emissaries of virtue. They promote and protect environments conducive to human transcendence of the ordinary life. Their political impact is institutional or cultural. Institutionally, republican heroes are integral to the context—the good republic—in which human transcendence occurs. Practically, they fulfill this by protection, preservation, or reparation of the good republic. In the language employed in this book, they are *defenders, stewards,* or *redeemers* of republics. Culturally, republican heroes reflect the values and ambitions of their times. Helping to craft good citizens, they are civic *exemplars*, inspirational and aspirational. They are also *nation builders*, articulators of social identity, archetypes of usness, symbols of what it means to be "people like us."

Some general rules and qualifications apply. Typically, institutional impact is direct, the prerogative of real-life heroes. The more diffuse cultural impact, on the other hand, is relatively insensitive to whether or not a hero is real or fictional. There are manifest perils, of course, in drawing too sharp a distinction between the institutional and cultural and between the real and the fictional. A hero may directly affect the fate of the republic in her time, and culturally affect posterity. Moreover, the just noted roles of republican heroes are often complementary and not always easy to differentiate (as with stewardship and redemption, for example). Heroes may perform multiple roles simultaneously, or may perform different roles at different times. However, collectively, these functions speak to the political impact of republican heroes as discussed in this book. Finally, whether fictional or real, a reality-distorting mythology tends to attach to heroism. Even if a hero herself once lived and breathed, heroic acts are often embellished or exaggerated to the point where the heroic impact itself is more creditable to fiction than reality.

The Institutional Impact of Heroes

Prototypical republican heroes are extraordinary *defenders*, apotheotic warriors, protectors of the realm, risking their lives in pursuit of worthy objectives. Physically heroic, their martial skills and courage exceed the ordinary. The role is atavistic. In tracing the etiology of heroism, Smirnov and his colleagues (2007) find that martial heroism was requisite to the primitive bands, tribes, chiefdoms, and other clan-based entities of the distant past that found themselves frequently at war for their very survival.[4] Speaking purely in evolutionary terms, martial capacity, including the sacrifices often inherent in military heroism, was central to group survival (Smirnov et al. 2007). For this reason, ancient societies tended to attach tangible rewards to military heroism. Often, this was as simple as permitting warriors to retain their plunder, although frequently rewards extended to the privilege of exercising political power. Indeed, as we will see in chapter 1, in the Homeric Dark Ages, absent formal structures of government, tribal chieftains earned their legitimating status as great warrior-defenders (see Finley 1954, esp. 128–133; Donlan 1982, 140; Whitley 1991, 349–51; Trepavlov 1995, 41–42; Kelly and Dunbar 2001, 90; Mitchell 2013, 36). By the same token, qualification for Roman heroism (chapter 3) typically demanded proficiency in the manly arts (*virilis virtus*) of horsemanship and warfare, both in aid of defending Rome and consolidating the ever-expanding republican empire.[5] In a spiritual context, heroic defenders of the faith were fundamental to the preservation of visible institutions (chapter 4). Physical defense also occurs within republics, and explains the heroism of what we will later call common heroes, as crime-fighting upholders of civility and justice (chapter 7).

Somewhere between defense and redemption, *stewardship* manifests in perpetuation of the republic through promotion of virtue at the expense of corruption, becoming heroic by dint of extraordinary dedication to that end. Stewards occupy the center of what Porpora calls the world of moral space—a place of sacred/civil order distinct from the profane environment that surrounds it (1996, 210–11). Equally, heroic stewards are trustees of the monomyth, as Campbell (2004) calls it, that constitutes the social bedrock of shared history and tradition. Manifesting as public servants, stewards privilege the common weal ahead of personal interests that conflict with the greater good. As such, we find stewardship associated with good or magnanimous leadership. Heroic stewardship does not necessarily rely on the formal power of the state, however, as can be seen in such archetypal figures as chivalric knights and (at least in the American context) Puritan saints dedicated to the synthesis of gospel and law (chapter 4). We even find heroic stewardship in common citizens—ordinary individuals made extraordinary in their public service through nothing more than volitional employment of innate human moral agency (chapters 6 and 7).

The relevance of stewardship is most observable in the breach, in the breakdown of magnanimous leadership, where leaders place their private interests (what Cicero calls *utile*) ahead of their public responsibilities (*honestum*). We see this, for example, in the clientelism that augured the demise of the Roman Republic (chapter 3). Failure of moral leadership destabilizes regimes, inviting the prospect of rebellion or revolution. Indeed, we can understand the Puritan Revolution—and the roles of country gentlemen and Puritan visible saints—in terms of the failed stewardship of king and bishop (chapter 4). To the Romantics of the late eighteenth and early nineteenth centuries (chapter 5), the French Revolution also had its genesis in failed stewardship.

In cases of failed stewardship, the erstwhile good republic finds itself in need of social *redemption*. The conceptual distinction between heroic stewards perfecting the moral order and heroic redeemers is more continuum than dichotomy. Here I operationalize redemption as fundamentally altering regime trajectory through reformation of the relationship between government and civil society. Emerging in response to social or institutional pathologies that threaten the goodness of the republic, redemptive heroes are proxies for the Eleatic Stranger's divine pilot, their mandate to rescue civil societies from the rot of corruption that has insinuated itself into the institutional structure and common mores of society as a whole.[6] Inherent is the re-establishment of a (cosmically) just order. William and Mary—symbols of the Glorious Revolution, for example—were integral to the settlement of the monarchy question in seventeenth-century England that had driven that country to civil war. An analogous case can be made for Abraham Lincoln's (partial) settlement of the racial question in America. Catherine the Great's revitalization of the laws, economy and culture of the Russian Empire is another prime example of heroic redemption (Van der Leeuw 1938, 571, 651; O'Connell 1962, 67; Barnes 1978; Johnson 1992; Ramati 2001; Broder 2008).

Redemptive heroes, and sometimes the absence of them, are important players in this book. Solon's heroic redemption of Athens from the violent class conflict that threatened to tear it apart (chapter 1) became the institutional template for republican mixed government. The fall of the Roman Republic (chapter 3) speaks to the counterfactual, the absence of redemptive heroes (as well as the peril of reliance upon them as an alternative to strong republican institutions). Spiritual and social redemption is a persistent theme in chapter 4. In this context, we identify English country gentlemen and Puritan saints as redemptive archetypes. The aforementioned Romantic hero also plays a redemptive role through aesthetic reimagination of the good republic. Such Romantic reimagination covers a broad range of heroes, including Prometheus, Satan, Byron's Manfred, Frankenstein's monster, and even civil rights leaders such as Rosa Parks and Martin Luther King and feminist leaders like Betty Friedan and Gloria Steinem (chapter 5). Less aesthetically, hard-boiled detectives and superheroes play a redemptive role in seeking to rescue America's foundational values—such staples of human dignity as liberty, equality and civic responsibility—from the evil designs of the criminal and corrupt (chapter 7).

The Cultural Impact of Heroes

In a more diffuse sense, we can think of heroic function in terms of the cultural manifestation of heroic defenders, stewards or redeemers, heroes serving to inspire superior civic values and practices. A central question is one of causality: whether heroes impact cultures or exist merely in reflection of extant mores and values. Certainly the latter must be true; to become culturally relevant is to strike a chord, to be an iconic symbol with which people can identify. There also has to be a degree of recursivity. Even if heroes emerge as reflections of extant cultural values, they tend to survive their generations. That is, they persist in maintaining an inter-generational cultural affinity that reinforces bonds of community.

Whether metaphorical chicken or egg, heroes persist as *exemplars*, didactic role models, serving as the incarnate representation of the principles for which the good republic and its citizens stand, or should stand. Heroic exemplars represent what Marcus (1961, 237) calls the "fulcrum of the value system for [their] followers," reflecting the moral values of a religion—spiritual or civil—such that a people comes to understand those values as not just definitional, but aspirational. As exemplars, heroes are most likely to be represented as archetypes. Actual or fictional, their exploits find voice through artistic celebration. Going all the way back to ancient Greece, we see this in Homeric warriors (chapter 1) and in Greek tragedy (chapter 2). We find it in chivalric knights (chapter 4) and any number of

Romantic figures portrayed in exhortation of aesthetic moral agency (Prometheus, Satan, Rameau's Nephew, Werther, Manfred and even the leaders of new social movements noted earlier) (chapter 5). Self-reliant American archetypes representing heroic idealization of rugged individualism and self-reliance include self-made men of industry, yeoman farmers, backwoodsmen, gunslinging plainsmen and even superheroes, their anonymity in deference to the latent potential of the everyman (chapter 7).

As exemplars, heroes also emphasize the nobility of particular principles or callings. They provide a schematic sense of what it means to be something. For example, the saint as exemplary hero embodies what it means to be a good Christian (chapter 4), the cowboy an embodiment of the good plainsman, and the superhero as theatrical exaggeration of the moral mandate of the good citizen (chapter 7). Exemplars represent the ideals that individuals internalize and strive to realize or imitate; they are the inspiration that informs or refines that which we imagine our best selves to be (Sullivan and Venter 2005, esp. 106–107; Schlenker, Weigold and Schlenker 2008, 326–29; Allison and Goethals 2011, 59).

If exemplary heroes speak to the values of the good citizen, as *nation builders* heroes help inform a common cultural identification, a sense of the social solidarity requisite to political stability (see Carlyle 1841, 1; Annus 2000, 121). Often they prevail in justification of the extant regime. As with Aeneas to Augustinian Rome, or King Arthur to early Norman England, or even Princess Diana in the late twentieth century, they are legitimators of political power and authority, clarifying the rules of the game, reinforcing the idea that beyond self-interest and personal preference, the republic stands as something greater than oneself (Grebe 2004). As such, heroic nation builders also represent templates for prevailing social norms and customs; as heuristics for virtuous governance and citizenship. Most prominently, they stand as iconic symbols of a civil religion and the principles by which a people defines itself. Like Spenser's *Faerie Queene*, whose knights embody the discrete virtues constitutive of Protestant England's utopian singularity,[7] nation builders inform a distinctive sense of usness thereby contributing to what modern political scientists call social capital.

Heroic nation builders appear in numerous places in this book. We find, them, albeit indirectly, in the guise of Archaic Greek aristocratic legatees of the Homeric tradition (chapter 1). They are manifest in the mythology (if not always the reality) of the Roman *boni*, trustees of the meta norms and values undergirding the ancient republican constitution of Rome (chapter 3). The self-sufficient common citizen, forged through two spiritual awakenings in America, helped define the nascent America (chapter 6). Chapter 7, meanwhile, represents a case study in heroic nation building, as illustrated by the archetypal common heroes discussed above.

If heroes impact the culture of their times, it is equally the case that heroes—or at least the heroism that attaches to them—are often cultural constructions, heroic not necessarily for what they have done as much as what myth-makers and hagiographers might wish them to have done. Such mythologization need not reflect out and out fabrication. Generally, heroic mythology represents hyperbolic cultural construction. The question is, does this cultural construction, reflecting the ascendent values of the day, permit us to evaluate the quality of these values? Or does it simply suggest that certain values lend themselves more readily to cultural hyperbole? As discussed in the conclusion, the issue of whether or not we live in a postheroic age turns largely on these issues.

What Makes a Hero?

Whatever political role heroes perform, we require an operational definition of what makes someone a hero. This will not be as precise as some might like, but given that we all have our own heroes, there is an unavoidable subjectivity. This book defines heroes in terms of two necessary attributes (capacity and estimability), and one necessary condition (vulnerability). Capacity is technically a gateway, limiting access to any claims to heroism. Understood in terms of greatness or goodness, *capacity* is conceived more restrictively by some than others. An obvious heroic requirement, *estimability* distinguishes heroes from villains. A function of character, deed and ratification, estimability demands just agency. Finally, *vulnerability* is circumstantial. It is what gives context to heroic behavior.

Capacity

Heroic capacity is what makes heroes extraordinary in the literal sense of transcending the ordinary. It speaks to the talents and skills requisite to such transcendence. Most basically, these are acquired through nature, such that some are gifted at birth with natural talents that manifest as extraordinary task-competence. Relatedly, heroic capacity may be the product of supernatural intervention, such as the divine powers and counsel which abet Achilles, King Arthur and Wonder Woman, among others; or the grace that imbues saints with thaumatological powers. Finally, capacity can be volitional, in the sense that one cultivates latent talents through training, character and commitment.

Heroic capacity manifests in two ways: physically or metaphysically. Physically, heroes are notable by extraordinary task-competence (see Klapp 1954, 57). We conceive physical capacity in interpersonal terms, measuring it against the actions of others and affirming it through deviation from the mean. The extent to which one exceeds the ordinary in this physical sense is the degree to which we assign *greatness* to a person. By contrast, we think of metaphysical heroic capacity in terms of *goodness*. (Heroic goodness cannot be exclusively metaphysical, of course. For it to gain heroic purchase it must present on the surface, as action and interaction. Nor does goodness preclude greatness. One can be greatly good.)[8] Insensitive to interpersonal comparison, goodness presents as internal development. Extraordinariness in this context is quite literal, as in transcending the ordinary life of production and reproduction. It is in this transcendence, inherent in realization of the human condition, that we make sense of Roger Rollin's inunction that "[m]ankind endures as animal, but prevails as hero" (1983, 38), and Earnest Becker's that "our main task on this planet, is the heroic" (1973, 1).

Estimability

Heroic estimability connotes a sense of going above and beyond. We can think of estimability in terms of character, achievement and recognition. Character is central to the ideation of heroism. Conducting a modest study of seventy-five college students, Allison and Goethals (2011, 61–62) asked respondents to list the defining traits of heroism. They found that character traits such as modesty, selflessness, altruism, empathy, honesty and reliability are more likely to conform to heroic schemas than are the opposite (see also Harvey, Erdos and Turnbull 2007, 1608; Schlenker, Weigold and Schlenker 2008). In a republican context, heroic character conforms to virtue. Intersubjective—having some sort of positive impact on others—heroic character speaks most readily to social obligation. Such intersubjectivity might be relatively modest, as in the case of serving as exemplar encouraging emulation by others. Or it may be more magnanimous, as with Socrates' claim in the *Meno*, that good men "will be beneficent when they give us correct guidance in our affairs" (Plato *Meno*, 96e; see also Blau 1977; Cmiel 1990, 24; McWilliams 2011; Jayawickreme and Di Stefano 2012).

Heroic achievement is extraordinary contribution to the public good. People tend to appraise estimable action from the standpoint of deviation from what they themselves would be able or willing to do in like circumstances (Markovitz 2012, 297; also Olsthoorn 2005; Blomberg, Hess and Raviv 2009). Pragmatically, heroic achievement attaches most readily to social utility. Successful endeavor is not a requirement for heroic estimability; but it does aid in the cause. The conquering hero tends to present as more heroic than the valiant but vanquished. Typically a supplement to heroic character, achievement can also serve to cover a shortfall. Indeed, so long as no significant moral principles are breached, people seem willing to substitute achievement for character (Shaffer 1987, 26; Becker and Eagly 2004, 164). Achilles more than compensates for questionable character by presenting as the best of the Achaeans. Even as he was booed in ballparks across America, the unlikable alleged drug-cheat Barry Bonds remained heroic to most fans of the San Francisco Giants for his extraordinary accomplishments at the plate.

Finally, heroic recognition is assent to a hero's heroic qualities. It is determined by audience—ratifiers of those worthy of esteem—and measured in terms of breadth (general renown) and depth (posterity). Where audience is broad and deep, the hero assumes cultural relevance. She can be said to be a *singular* hero. Heroic singularity speaks to the spirit of an age; it is what entices us to call the age "heroic."[9] More nuanced is where heroic recognition lacks breadth or depth. We can consider such heroes *unsung*, although some might enjoy their proverbial fifteen minutes of broad recognition. Unsung heroes lack the cultural importance of singular heroes, but not the relevance. The direct impact of heroism upon institutions or individual lives is insensitive to singularity. Neighborhood heroes such as parish priests, favorite high school coaches or community activists can be recognized as having heroic impact on small subsets of the population. Their heroism is recognized neither broadly nor (necessarily) deeply; but is critical nonetheless in helping to mold good citizens. Heroes, then, are heroes, even when forgotten or unsung.[10]

Vulnerability

Moving beyond heroic attributes, a requisite *condition* for heroism is resistance, some countervailing force that challenges heroic capacity and hones estimability. Absent vulnerability there is no heroism. Without it heroes would be redundant or unrelatable. The hero who rescues a child from a burning automobile would merely be a courteous bystander were the car not ablaze. As a rule, the greater the ordeal faced by a hero, the greater her heroism. Without the passion, for example, Jesus' message—however noble—loses much of its heroic and inspirational quality. Absent the vulnerability of the heel by which he was held when dipped in the River Styx, Achilles, invulnerable, would not have been so heroic a figure. Even in modern times, our comic superheroes require vulnerability to keep them heroic. Superman is susceptible to kryptonite. The Green Lantern's superpowers are nullified by the color yellow. Wonder Woman is vulnerable to bladed weapons. And Spiderman's radioactive blood (strangely, this is a positive thing) cannot protect him against teenage angst and self-doubt (see Alison and Goethals 2011, ch. 4).

Vulnerability supplies didactic relevance. Audiences can admire invulnerable greatness, but they cannot relate to it. While Achilles is less awe-inspiring, he is also more heroic than the gods, whose immortality renders them incapable of the extraordinary courage that informs Homeric estimability. Suffering from the frailties and temptations that bedevil all humanity, what sets heroes apart is their ability to overcome their imperfections. Oedipus's arrogant assertion of the worldly ahead of the spiritual, for example, leads him into a cycle of self-destruction that makes possible his heroic transcendence by the time of his death at Colonus. The sexual temptation afforded by Phaedria nearly overwhelms Sir Guyon's temperance in the *Faerie Queene*, which only heightens the triumph of his destruction of the bower of bliss. Cervantes's Don Quixote must transcend his foolish pride before he can be considered truly heroic. Byron's Manfred is compelled to do battle with the monster within before finding release from his Faustian pact. In Virginia Woolf's *To the Lighthouse*, Lily Briscoe transcends her self-doubt to find liberation and fulfillment in her life as an artist. In this same vein, superheroines like Captain Marvel have sought to ameliorate the imposter syndrome that has contributed to the cultural disempowerment of women.

Vulnerability is often portrayed in terms of a quest, what Joseph Campbell (1973) calls the nuclear unit of the monomyth. As with all quests, there is point of departure and return. Whatever heroic capacities the hero may (or may not) have demonstrated at the start of her journey, and whatever her reward at journey's end, the heroic element of the quest lies the intervening struggle distinguishing the heroic from the prosaic. His martial heroism notwithstanding, Odysseus is best known for the expedition to which he lends his name. Independent of the prize associated with the Golden Fleece, it is his tribulations along that way that provide Jason with the authority to assert his claim to kingship. Only Galahad is successful in discovering the mystery of God's grace, but each of the Arthurian knights is heroic in his quest for the Holy Grail. Christian's heroism in the *Pilgrim's Progress* lies not in his arrival in the Celestial City, but in the trials of faith he encounters in his pilgrimage. In Helen Oyeyemi's *Mr. Fox*, Mary Foxe—the eponymous author's fictional muse—engages in a voyage of transformation, challenging Fox to transcend his dysfunctional relationship with women, both fictional and real.

What Are the Types of Republican Hero?

I will use the term "republican hero" in two ways. Most immediately, I identify four heuristic categories of republican heroism. At the conclusion of the book, I distinguish these discrete types of republican heroism from what we will call "complete republican heroism." In the discussion of capacity above, we identified two heroic currencies: (physical) greatness and (metaphysical) goodness. Treating these as binary values yields four categories. Let us introduce them as epic heroes (great not good), magnanimous heroes (great and good), Romantic heroes (neither great nor good), and common heroes (good not great). These hero types do not map to particular heroic functions in the sense of acquiring total proprietorship of the role of defender, steward, redeemer, exemplar, or nation builder, although some heroic functions attach more readily to one hero type than to others. Their greater significance is that they tend to reflect the cultural preferences of particular ages, with the great hero types more prominent prior to the Enlightenment and the not-great generally acquiring heroic purchase only in the modern age.[11]

Epic Heroes

Prototypical, epic heroes are what most of us think of when heroes come to mind. They are extraordinary men and women who appear larger than life, their physical greatness, or excellence, setting them apart from the ordinariness of the masses. We can think of this distinction between great and ordinary in two ways: in kind or in degree. Where excellence differs in *kind*, epic heroes transcend the natural limits that bind ordinary mortals; they possess supernatural capabilities (Di Cesare 1982, 59). Such heroes enjoy superiority over their environments. (Achilles's or Wonder Woman's virtual invulnerability in battle is a good example, as is King Arthur's wielding of Excalibur, the prophecy of the Norse Valkyries, or Superman's ability to fly.) Hesiod conceives such hero-men as the product of union between mortals and gods.[12] In ancient times these heroes were worshipped as *daemons* whose posthumous existence was such that long-dead heroes could affect the fortunes of the living. Where the excellence of heroes differs in *degree*, the result is a slightly more expansive understanding of epic heroism. Excellence in degree need not render heroes larger than life or supernatural; it merely makes them extraordinary in the physical sense. Excellence in degree is the operational definition of epic heroism employed in this book.

Epic heroes possess the defining quality of heroic greatness—extraordinary task-competence, estimability through acquisition of sociometric recognition, and transcendence of vulnerability through individual assertion (Borgatta, Bales, and Couch 1954, 756–57). The principal problem is that the heuristic—represented by the Homeric hero discussed in the next chapter—is not a great fit with republican heroism. Self-assertive, epic heroes facially lack the metaphysical competence requisite to republican virtue. Addressing this problem requires three qualifications. First, although many scholars, cited in chapter 1, have made the case for a theory of social obligation in Homer, the argument here is that such social concern is at best secondary to Homeric heroes. Thus, while important as exemplars of the schematic ideal of the Archaic Age aristocrat, and (indirect) nation builders, Homeric heroes are not republican heroes per se.

Second, subsequent epic heroes have tended to deviate from the heuristic by importing the just agency requisite to republican heroism. There have been three principal mechanisms. The first is to assign to heroes coincidental qualities of goodness and greatness. Such heroes are great independent of their goodness. While they need not be great in their goodness, they must be just agents—satisfying the personal, social, and cosmic obligations requisite to republican virtue. The second mechanism is goodness of cause, such that even if goodness does not demonstrably attach to the hero herself, the cause for which she employs her talent supplies estimability. The third mechanism is that estimability through goodness of cause is often supplemented by aspirational goodness. In this sense, the epic hero is a secondary hero, not perfected in her virtue, but guided in the quest for transcendence by an already perfected primary hero (Bond 2011). In Lucan's *Pharsalia*, for example, Cato the Younger is held up as the apotheotic pinnacle of human virtue, while Pompey represents the secondary hero, sympathetic but weak (Bond 2011, 3–17). Similarly, in Greek tragedy, the gods often assume the role of primary hero, all-too-mortal humans assuming the secondary role, albeit often with less felicitous outcomes than underscore the myriad Christian epics. In the Vulgate Cycle, Lancelot and Galahad fulfill the role of secondary and primary hero, respectively, while in Spenser's *Faerie Queene*, Prince Arthur assumes the role of primary hero in the other knights' epic pursuit of perfection.

The third qualification is that even if heuristic epic heroes lack the just agency requisite to republican heroism, they are an important part of the narrative. Homeric heroes represent the backdrop against which republican heroism emerged. Exemplary manifestations of Socrates's thymotic element of the soul, self-assertive Homeric warriors excelled at the manly virtues of warfare, horsemanship, and athletics. For the Greeks of the Archaic period, they represented an aristocratic ideal, a schematic sense of the qualities requisite to leadership. Even if not nation builders themselves, early epic heroes influenced the institutional structure of emergent republics through the appropriation of their legacy by the Archaic Greek aristocracy. Like Virgil's Aeneas, they also stood as symbols of nationhood, their epic qualities celebrated in proxy for the greatness of their nations. Later epic heroes were Christian martyrs of the late Roman Empire. They were defenders of the faith, takers of the Cross during the high Middle Ages. As chivalric knights, they were both defenders and stewards, their obligation to liege lords foundational to the vassalage of the feudal order.

Magnanimous Heroes

Magnanimous heroes exceed others in the metaphysical capacity requisite to realization of the human condition. In ancient and medieval times, their primacy was predicated upon possession of the elusive moral competence exogenous to common men and women. Magnanimity is a social resource, harvested, refined, and disseminated by heroic social, religious, and political leaders. More than coincidentally great and good, magnanimous heroes are *greatly* good, exceeding others in the perfection of virtue and hence sufficiency to live a good human life. Unlike the self-absorption of the more timocratic Homeric hero, magnanimity demands extension of concern beyond the self and toward the welfare of others. Percy Shelley captures the point nicely, maintaining that to be greatly good, one "must imagine intensely and comprehensively; he must put himself in the place of another and of many others; the pains and pleasures of his species must become his own" (1891, 14).

To be heroic, and not just magnanimous, one must be estimable. To this end, magnanimous heroes—already perfected in their virtue—aid others in fulfillment of the higher purpose for which humanity exists (Grampp 1951, 137), relieving ordinary men and women of "the delirium of the animal spirits" (Emerson *Great Men*, 634). Defined by their extraordinary knowledge of the first principles of justice, they axiomatically fulfill the cosmic obligations requisite to republican just agency.

Magnanimity finds resistance in the relentless forces of nature. Magnanimous heroes swim against the tide of human nature, tending as it does towards gratification of the appetites. Thus, heroic magnanimity is grounded in what Carlyle characterizes as "heartfelt prostrate admiration, burning, boundless, for a noblest godlike Form of Man" (1841, 18). In a Christian context, magnanimous heroes must contend with the immediacy of the natural order in exhortation of others to privilege the greater fulfillment extant in the order of grace.[13] In such great goodness lies the efficacy of saints and divines, to say nothing of the greatest hero of them all (whose name the florid Carlyle darest not speak).

Exceeding others in the perfection of their virtues, magnanimous heroes tend to present as stewards, redeemers, and exemplars. Prototypical are the Socratic philosopher king, Aristotle's great-souled man, and Cicero's virtuous office holders. The philosopher king is steward of the civic architecture, mandating a socially efficient division of labor. Analogous to the reasoning element of the balanced and harmonious soul, Socrates's philosopher king is the law giver, exhorting others to goodness in conformity with the first principles of justice through fidelity to the aptitudes with which nature has endowed them. Such goodness manifests, says Sidney of Tasso's Rinaldo, in one who "doth not only teach and move to a truth, but teaches and moves to the most high and excellent truth; who makes magnanimity and justice shine through all misty fearfulness and foggy desires" (1890, 30). Cicero's virtuous magistrates, collectively the *boni*, are keepers of the *mos maiorum*—the ancient customs and mores of the Roman Republic.

The heroic role of the Roman *boni* was also redemptive, rescuing Rome from the manifold perils and crises endemic to a young republic in transition to a great imperial power. It was a failure of such heroic redemption that Cicero laments in the dying days of the Late Republic. The failure of heroic redemption also manifests in Greek tragedy—specifically the tragic consequences of insufficient or belated magnanimity. Of course, heroic redemption is not always fruitless. We find redemptive magnanimity in Christian divines aiding and exhorting others in their spiritual pilgrimage; or Catherine the Great imposing the ideals of the Enlightenment upon Russia.

While heroic magnanimity is typically not aspirational, it *is* inspirational. The exemplary qualities of the Christ figure, for example, plays out not only in the martyrdom of saints, but also in any number of Christological figures in the arts. The Sir Galahad of the Vulgate Cycle and Edmund Spenser's Prince Arthur are but two manifestations mentioned later in the book. Aquinas finds qualified magnanimity in those who uplift the spirit of Christians, counteracting the pusillanimity attendant to postlapsarian despair and inspiring the scholastic Christian humanism characteristic of the early Renaissance (esp. 1947, II–II, Q. 110, Art. 2, ad. 3, Q. 129, Art. 6, Q. 133, Art. 2, ad. 4, Q.162, Art. 1, ad. 3). In a republican context, magnanimous heroes help provide the motive for goodness, to inspire citizens not only to transcendence of the ordinary lives, but also to be good stewards of the republic.

Manifestly, the modern age is not the heyday of the magnanimous hero. And it is the decline of magnanimity, both religious and secular, that critics of modernity respond to most intensely. Certainly, the waning influence of spirituality in many developed nations, including the staunchest Roman Catholic ones, speaks to the secular egalitarianism and moral elasticity—the *ordinariness*—that some decry as characteristic of the modern age. We can, however, be too hasty in relegating magnanimous heroism to the deep, dark past. Magnanimity remains relevant in the exemplary and redemptive senses. Winston Churchill's prudent and charismatic leadership both exhorted and exemplified a defiant national attitude, transforming Britain's darkest hour into its finest one. What many on the left see as John F. Kennedy's recasting of America as the new enlightened Camelot speaks to his magnanimous redemptive heroism; while what those on the right see as Ronald Reagan's moral reawakening in defense of America's core values could be cast in a similar light. Straddling the line between magnanimous and Romantic heroism, iconic and affective symbols of new social movements, including Simone de Beauvoir, Cesar Chavez, Betty Friedan, Martin Luther King, Nelson Mandela, Rigoberta Menchu,

Harvey Milk, Rosa Parks, and Violetta Zúñiga, led to significant social redemption locally or globally.

Romantic Heroes

Romantic heroes are less obviously heroic than their epic or magnanimous counterparts. In fact, the characterization of the Romantic hero as neither good nor great seems to imply that they are at best antiheroic, and at worst amoral mediocrities disqualified from the jump to any claim to heroic recognition. As such, some qualifications are needed. The first is that applied to Romantic heroes, "not good" does not mean that they are unjust agents, failing to live a transcendent life. Rather, instead of conformity to an objectively good life, the transcendent Romantic life is *authentic*, lived in fidelity to nature—personal, human, and ambient. Facially this supplies a good deal of latitude, as in "it is my nature to be unjust." While there is a degree of moral latitude implicit in fidelity to one's own nature, there exists a concomitant imperative to conform to the moral parameters imposed by the order of nature itself. In addition to commitment to one's own nature, then, authenticity demands fidelity to the laws of *ambient* nature, as well as the primitive nobility that Rousseau finds at the core of *human* nature.

The second qualification is that while Romantic heroism does not demand greatness, neither does it preclude it. Many Romantic heroes were great artists, and like Byron not timid in proclamation of their own genius. To the extent that they were able to export the relevant sentiment to others, they were great in the same way as the magnanimous hero; in their case, provoking sublime emotions that might otherwise have lain dormant, awakening the imperative to take possession of one's own conduct of life. Like nature itself, great art serves as the affective inspiration for an authentic life. However, the locus of heroism is the courage and self-confidence to privilege one's innate moral agency ahead of social convention, and in consequence serving as aesthetic inspiration to others to do the same.

All this is by way of saying that Romantic heroic capacity is not terribly restrictive. It merely demands liberation from the internal constraints that fetter self-mastery (e.g., Berlin 1958). (A good example is the personal development of Jo March in Louisa May Alcott's *Little Women*.) But while all humans have the innate capacity to live authentic lives (and to aid others in their own authentic pursuits), not all employ it. Not all want to. Some are content to be beasts of burden, mindlessly herded by their "betters." Some fashion themselves with pretense and insincerity. Some defy the natural affective core of nobility that compels humans to be concerned with the welfare of others. Romantic heroes are distinctive in their willingness to dispense with hypocrisy, to rise above the herd, to remain true to the inner selves who best guide their lives, and to disregard the opprobrium of the sheep and cattle—Nietzschean last men who have internalized anesthetized conformity to a rote and habituated life, hollow men who have had the life beaten out of them.

Estimability is the most significant obstacle to the marriage of Romanticism and heroism. Romanticism easily devolves into what Keats calls the "egotistical sublime," a fascination with self-obligation that precludes the social and cosmic obligations requisite to just agency. Certainly, the self lies at the heart of Romantic ontology, on full display in Byron's *Manfred* and Goethe's *Sorrows of Young Werther*, for example. However, as I argue in chapter 5, latent in Romanticism is a theory of social (Mary Shelley's *Frankenstein*; Byron's *Prometheus*) and cosmic obligation (Percy Shelley's *Defence of Poetry*; more subtly Byron's *Childe Harold's Pilgrimage*). Indeed, underlying the egotistical sublime is reimagination of a better world in which affect tempers cognition in fulfillment of social obligation and conformity with cosmic design.

Vulnerability is not an issue for Romantic heroes. The imperative to swim against the tide all but defines them. From fighting to get in touch with their own affective cores, to battling the hegemony of the extant moral paradigm Romantic heroism is a study in overcoming resistance. It is this resistance, staking a position outside of social norms, that threatens to defame their heroism. Rebels against extant mores, their audience tends to be narrow, their impact indirect, and their cultural relevance typically manifest only in the long run.

Critical to Romantic heroic function is service as exemplar, a life lived in exhortation of the courage to assert one's claim to autonomy, equality, and human dignity. As with the new moral philosophy of the Enlightenment, early Romanticism insisted upon the dignity that attaches to all individuals. Romantics waged cultural war upon status, hierarchy, and the putative magnanimity that served, above all, to keep those of humble station in their social place. In this sense, Romantic heroes also serve as social redeemers, self-consciously defying conventions extant only to uphold the status of the few against the claims of the many. Prototypical Romantic redeemers are the Satan of *Paradise Lost* and Byron's Prometheus, champions of the humanist challenge to Christian hegemony. Indeed, as with Rousseau's Savoyard Vicar, Romantic redeemers have sought liberation from the moral tutelage of the putatively magnanimous in celebration of the moral endogeneity born of heart, conscience, or some other expression of innate moral agency.

Finally, Romantic heroes are nation builders. The Romantic patriotism espoused explicitly by the likes of Walt Whitman, and less overtly by Norman Rockwell or Willa Cather's Alexandra Bergson, for example, served as a symbol of America's cultural individualist sense of self. The logic applies equally to subnational communities. As discussed in chapter 5, contemporary Romanticism is politically impactful in reinforcing a sense of usness among subnational cultural communities (what Putnam calls "bonding social capital"). The symbolism attendant to the quest for greater racial, gender, and ethnic equality has provoked a communal sense of self—shared social identities—within historically marginalized groups. Indeed, if early Romantics were instrumental in propagation of the norm of individual equality, modern Romantic heroes exist in quest of equality for essentialist cultural communities.

Common Heroes

Like Romantic heroes with whom they share a great deal of affinity, common heroes are not defined by greatness. They are endowed with no extraordinary physical or metaphysical capacities. Moral agents (self-sufficient in their just agency), common heroes abet others in living transcendent lives. Common heroes enjoy an innate, *intuitive*, grasp of the first principles of morality, they are endogenously good, capable of self-direction in conduct of a good human life. If they are more than good citizens, common heroes are less than magnanimous ones. They are as estimable, but less singular, than magnanimous heroes. Their real-world manifestation is often as "hometown heroes," speaking to particular audiences. While some are more celebrated than others, common heroes often present as exemplars—parents, favorite high-school teachers, priests, or community leaders, who go out of their way to hone and refine their charges' latent moral competence.

As stewards and defenders, common republican heroes provide the functions once thought the exclusive preserve of magnanimous or epic heroes. As steward, the common hero underwrites civic function. Rising to the occasion, she is neighborhood activist or interest-group leader. She is the face in the crowd who steps forward to do what has to be done, in conviction that if she does not, who will? As defender, the common hero is the bravest or most committed of the hoplite, George Orwell's rough man standing ready in the night in service of his fellows.

Given their lack of singularity, there is a fairly modest cultural role for real-world common heroes. Instead, the common hero's cultural presence tends toward the archetypal. As defenders, we find such archetypes as protectors of the sylvan frontier of the nineteenth century, backwoodsmen lionized and mythologized in the likes of (the real-world) Daniel Boone and James Fennimore Cooper's Leatherstocking, and glorified in song as the "Hunters of Kentucky." As the frontier moved forward, the perils of the primitive West expanded, the criminal element joining the harsh environment as threats to pioneers and homesteaders. Riding to their defense came gunslinging cowboys and, later, in the urban context of the twentieth and twenty-first centuries, hard-boiled detectives and ordinary citizens-cum-superheroes, going above and beyond in exercising their innate capacities in the cause of justice.

Common heroic archetypes have stood as cultural embodiments of America's defining creed. In civilizing the primitivism of the Old West, backwoodsmen and cowboys also stood as nation builders, not only in the cultural sense of forging a common sense of usness, but quite literally as well. Beyond this, one of the unique qualities of the American republic is that unlike more historically ethnically and linguistically homogenous nations, Americans have tended to define themselves through creed. As such, for the American common hero, nation building extends into cultural reinforcement of the imperative to uphold the American creed. As we shall see in chapter 7, the hard-boiled detective and the superhero contribute to nation building through exemplification of the idealized common citizen in her capacity as defender and steward of the republic.

Common heroes share some of the same vulnerabilities as Romantic heroes, not least the struggle to trust their own sense of self in the face of social opposition. They came to the forefront of popular consciousness in the context of American transcendentalism. Preaching the imperative to search within oneself to find the moral cues requisite to a good and fulfilling life, the likes of Ralph Waldo Emerson urge their readers to exercise self-reliance in their actions, their convictions, and their moral judgments. Emerson speaks to the imperative to recognize and affirm one's own accomplishments in seeking the esteem of the only audience that matters—the one residing within. Where individuals employ intuitive moral agency, they conduct their lives not by rote or conformity to social conventions or learned moral precepts or the decrees of their betters. Nor will their moral competence be dependent upon law or gospel. Rather, they will navigate life as directed by what Emerson calls the over-soul, that internal divinity naturally resident, if not universally accessed. When Brecht has Galileo proclaim, "Unhappy the land in need of heroes," he means very much what Emerson means. It is personally and socially suboptimal to rely on the greatness of others as a substitute for the goodness in oneself.

What Have Others Said?

The relationship between political theory and heroism—to say nothing of republicanism and heroism—has not received a great deal of scholarly treatment. Much of the literature on heroism comes from cognate fields such as anthropology, classics, history, literature, psychology, and sociology, often touching on politics obliquely and often focused on specific periods or places. Still, there has been some excellent politically relevant scholarship on heroism. The touchstone for any broad and systematic discussion of heroes is Joseph Campbell's (1973) exploration of the cross-cultural heroic monomyth which, in proxy for the recursive cycle of history favored by ancient republicans (see Pocock 1975), serves as metaphor for birth, maturation, quest for meaning, and journey's end. In Campbell, we find the basis for much of what is discussed in this book—the symbolic and mimetic value of heroic icons, enlightenment, personal development, human efficacy, and reward.

At pains to show the broad applicability of the monomyth, Campbell provides the foundation of a more elastic conception of heroism than Carlyle's (1841) epoch-defining great man, who persists at the forefront of the historical conception of heroes. Contributing to conceptual evolution, Northrup Frye (1957) was among the first to propose a systematic heroic typology, distinguishing heroes in terms of kind, degree, and environment. His classification of heroes as mythic, romantic, high mimetic, low mimetic, and ironic helps provide the foundation (albeit with significant definitional distinctions) for the typology employed here. Another excellent contribution to the typological progression of heroism is Gregory Kendrick's *Heroic Ideal* (2010). As with this book, Kendrick examines the evolution of the heroic ideal, from the apotheotic Homeric warrior, through the heroic martyrdom of early Christian saints, to soldiers of the *Miles Christi*, to Romantic rebels, adventurers, and explorers, and even antiheroes. Kendrick's interests are broader than those explored here, his primary interest the spirit of the ages he explores rather than the implications for a particular form of government.

More politically focused is Dominic Stefanson's *Man as Hero* (2004), which traces the institutional and cultural impact of the heroic ideal through Homer, Plato, and Rousseau—each of whom serves as prototype for one of the four hero types discussed in this book. Also important to the development of the heroic typology I employ is Orrin Klapp's "Heroes, Villains and Fools as Agents of Social Control" (1954). Highlighting the tension between what we are calling magnanimous and Romantic heroes, Klapp suggests that social organization is informed by the qualities of three social archetypes: those who exceed others in embodiment of consensually derived social values; those who exceed others in their volitional and self-serving defiance of social norms and customs; and those who provoke skeptical challenges to value consensus. Such distinct social functions provide a contextual imitative framework, helping to inform a schematic sense of the things we value and duties we undertake. In the same vein, in *Heroes: What They Do and Why We Need Them*, Scott T. Allison and George R. Goethals (2011) suggest that (in contrast to villains) heroes instill a positive bias of expectations and an ideational construction of the building blocks of civil organization, including good citizenship, good leadership, and appropriate social conduct.

Extant scholarship also exists for the four heuristic hero types discussed above. Not surprisingly, epic heroism is afforded the most attention. Carla Antonaccio's *Archaeology of Ancestors* (1995) and Walter Donlan's *The Aristocratic Ideal* (1999) examine the sociological and political influence of Homeric heroes on the emergent *poleis* of the Greek Archaic Age. M. I. Finley's *World of Odysseus* (1954), Jasper Griffin's *Homer on Life and Death* (2003), and Dean Miller's *Epic Hero* (2002) explore the primary heroic motive of Homeric warriors—the quest for immortality through posterity. The prevailing assumption of much of the literature on epic heroism is that self-assertion and physical excellence dwarf metaphysical competence as heroic qualities. However, an interesting body of scholarship seeks to bridge the gap between the heroic qualities of greatness and goodness. In *Plato and the Hero*, Angela Dobbs (2000) makes the case for Socrates's insistence upon the ethical importance of the *thymos* (the part of the soul that craves recognition and affirmation) in her creative reconciliation of Homeric courage with virtue ethics. Similarly, Patrick Cain and Mary Nichols's "Aristotle's Nod to Homer" speaks to the poet's influence upon the philosopher, particularly the latter's agonal conception of friendship (2013). Peter Ahrensdorf (2014) goes further, finding in Homer a metaphysical conception of heroism that eclipses even the physical greatness of the warrior.

If courage and honor are the watchwords of epic heroism, sagacious virtue (and later saintliness) lays the foundation of heroic magnanimity. For some, as with Robert Eisner's (1982) "Socrates as Hero," heroic magnanimity is an analogue to epic heroism. Using Socrates as exemplar, Eisner claims the magnanimous hero is a product of the same heroic lineage (in Socrates's case, from Daedalus) as Homeric heroes, faces the same vulnerabilities and privations, engages in analogous personal battle with a dread foe (the Sophists), and as with the spear of Achilles, brandishes his own preferred weapon, in Socrates's case the dialectic (see also Segal 1978).

Such coupling of greatness with goodness comes with a built-in dynamic that sets the bar progressively higher. Moving from the Platonic to the Neoplatonic ultimately elevates heroic magnanimity from the purview of philosophy to that of divinity. In Brian Hook and R. R. Reno's *Heroism and the Christian Life* (2000), for example, the authors explore the natural progression in the Gospel of Matthew from Homer to Virgil to Jesus, from the epic to the magnanimous to the messianic. While Hook and Reno note that Matthew is careful to locate the divine and messianic within the human frame of reference, Christopher Bond (2011) is more insistent upon the inherent problem of relatability that attaches to supernatural heroic qualities. In *Spenser, Milton and the Redemption of the Epic Hero*, Bond implies that the great epic poets of the Renaissance sought conscious reintroduction of humanism through heroic duality, in which relatable and imperfect secondary heroes are guided in their quests for human fulfillment by the apotheotic magnanimity of already perfected primary ones.

Epic and magnanimous heroism are bound by their common reliance upon greatness. Removing greatness from the equation risks contribution to what Miller (2002, 2) describes as the "progressive degradation" of heroism. This challenge is faced by Romantic and common heroes alike. The idea of Romantic heroism is particularly problematic in that Romantic heroes' attachment to morality is more tenuous. Even so, an important literature does exist on Romantic heroism. The obvious starting point is Peter Thorslev's (1962) *Byronic Hero*, which traces the lineage of the

Romantic hero from eighteenth-century prototypes, whom he identifies as the child of nature, the hero of sensibility, the gloomy egoist, and the gothic villain. By the nineteenth-century heyday of English Romanticism, each had contributed to Byron's noble outlaw, whose disenchantment with the prevailing social order causes him to operate outside its values, albeit in conformity to an idiomatic sense of moral conduct (also Wolf and Zuckerman 2012).

To this framework of Romantic heroism attaches Lionel Trilling's *Sincerity and Authenticity* (1972), providing greater context to the Romantic hero's conception of a transcendent life. Indeed, as Paul Cantor points out in "The Politics of the Epic" (2007), the Romantic poets redefined heroism, liberating it from reliance upon the trappings of greatness in favor of the sublime and aesthetic (also De Bruyn 1987). Equally important, despite the author's general criticism of modernity, is Charles Taylor's *Ethics of Authenticity*, which rightfully paints authenticity as something distinct from the soft relativism that Romanticism might facially appear to promote (1991).

Sharing numerous qualities with Romantic heroism, common heroism draws from some of the same literature, not least that of American transcendentalists such as Ralph Waldo Emerson and Theodore Parker. The literature on common heroism emphasizes the potential for heroic ubiquity. In addressing the hegemony of the great man theory of history, Carl Friedrich's "Belief in the Common Man" (1940) rejects the premise that common men and women are so much clay, their consciousness malleable by singular figures, their transcendence contingent upon heroic magnanimity. Decoupling character from intellect, Friedrich finds the innate tools for human fulfillment in commonsense moral reasoning (also Noll 1985). If such reasoning is fallible—and Friedrich has no hesitancy is claiming it to be—it is specious to assign to common men and women sole proprietorship of that particular failing.

A larger problem is the assignation of *heroism*—as opposed to mere moral competence—to physically and metaphysically prosaic men and women. Unlike the programmatic heroism of traditional heroes, common heroes are more likely to present in specific contexts or heroic moments (Emerson *Over-Soul*, 188). The unevenness of common heroism has led to the presentation of common heroes as archetypes, often so exaggerated in their goodness as that they are not intended as mimetic figures so much as mnemonic ones, exhorting individuals to draw upon their innate capacities for moral agency. In this way, common heroism takes us full circle, with—as Grant Morrison suggests in *Supergods* (2011)—anonymous (read everyman) superheroes speaking to every individual's latent heroic potential.

Do Heroes Still Matter?

Less optimistically, there is a prevailing sense on the part of critics of modernity that the hero is no longer the figure she once was. She has been tarnished, obscured, or otherwise marginalized by social values that no longer celebrate greatness in cause, principle, or person. Equally, goodness has been debased, subsumed by self-absorption and a diminution of intellectual and theological curiosity. As a consequence, heroes and heroic values find themselves progressively marginalized or discredited (see, for example, Warren 1972; Bellah 1975; McGinnis 1976; Bennett 1977; 1992; Giddens 1991; Glendon 1991; Sikorski 1993; Bork 1997; Blomberg, Hess and Raviv 2009; Graebner 2013; and Del Noce 2014). We may not have reached the point of *Idiocracy*, as portrayed in the dystopian film paying homage to evolutionary stupidity and indolence, but we have settled willfully into a postheroic existence of mediocrity. We are no longer great, critics of modernity aver; we are no longer good; and we no longer seem to care.

In amelioration, the heroism manifest in Friedrich Nietzsche's overman, for example, represents a means to rescue humanity from the meaninglessness of an existence in which God has lost relevance, and no one has emerged to replace him. Nietzsche's complaint is that humanity's failure to transcend the suffocating moral imperative informing the Socratic and Christian paradigms has left it to wallow in mediocrity. Rather than the heroism of the first men of Hegelian history, asserting their wills over others in mastery of their environments, the modern age is the realm of last men—anodyne, insipid, and convinced they have invented happiness. The great tragedy is that excellence does not exceed man's grasp; it exceeds his ambition. Rather than striving for greatness, he settles for goodness, the lamentation not that he fails to realize the human condition, but that he is *content* with it. The failure to recognize the pathological qualities of goodness threatens to seal the nihilistic fate of Nietzsche's last men, robbed of ambition, creativity, and curiosity. Blind to the peril, the ultimate end of last men is to realize a world in which there is no suffering in pursuit of higher ideals, where happiness has been perfected, and in which there is nothing left to fear. Last men might pity the animal for its lack of existential horizon, but they are oblivious to the fact that they suffer from the same affliction, clinging to life and thinking only of their own happiness and comfort (Nietzsche 1955, 200–201; 1956b, I. 14; 1997, 5).

In disentangling himself from the encumbrances of theology, philosophy, and social convention (1955, II. 39), Nietzsche's idealized transcendent overman must be heroic. He must have the strength to defy what it is that others value and speciously elevate to the status of an objective moral truth. He must liberate himself from the slavery manifest in convention. "Thou Shalt" exalts the dragon of submission; "I Will" is the spirit that resides in the dragon-slayer (1966, I.1). Yet the human moral instinct is not towards such transcendence. It is to insulate oneself in the herd, persisting in obedient sociability, waiting for others to command lest one offend against the moral order (1955, 199). For Nietzsche, the lamentable state of the Europe of his day was directly attributable to its rejection of heroes, the great transcendent figures whose efficacy was sacrificed at the altar of pusillanimity and mediocrity. God, it seems, had died in vain. There were no overmen.

In a more nuanced way, Charles Taylor also focuses on a sense of lost moral bearing. He too casts the anodyne values of the modern age—bourgeois and cloistered—as but a specious advancement of human happiness. His specific lament is the affirmation of the ordinary life, in which the lack of true human fulfillment goes unnoticed, promoting a flat-earth moral horizon offering little promise of improving men's prospects for finding fulfillment. Much of the blame lies in the misguided insistence of liberal rationalists that humans are self-sufficient in assenting to their best lives. Rationalists assume away any sort of distinction between the ordinary life and the good life on the tautological reasoning that the life chosen by rational agents is ipso facto that person's best life. Human beings will choose to live distinctively human lives by virtue of the fact that they are, after all, *human*. But for Taylor, these rationally chosen lives are not good lives. They are self-indulgent celebrations of unfulfilling values. Affirmers of the ordinary life reject the ethos of nobility in which greatness manifests in virtue and honor. Instead, they favor the analgesic equality of Nietzsche's last man (see also Becker 1973, 2).

Unlike Nietzsche, however, Taylor does not yearn for an age in which great men are celebrated for their greatness. But he does lament the modernist's intemperate humanism, which champions the terrene above the spiritual, the order of nature ahead of the order of grace. Indeed, the modernist tendency to assert the primacy of man as self-sufficient in the pursuit of human fulfillment has consigned the spiritual order to the background of social consciousness. To the extent that God remains relevant, we have transformed what once were intrinsic values (love of God) into purely instrumental concerns (how can God aid in the quest for happiness?). By placing himself at the pinnacle of that which is meaningful, modern man rejects the premise that there are principles greater than himself. The result is a void that begs the existential question: If there are no principles worth dying for, what exactly is worth living for? (Taylor 1989, 242–43; 2003, 3–6).

Owing no small debt to the liberalism, Deism, rationalism, and Romanticism of the early modern age, the modernist perspective is that God's true and universal gift is the construction of a natural order through which an individual derives clues to her own moral well-being. Implicit is rejection of the foundational principle that man's prerogative is to serve God. Indeed, the logic goes that in perfecting the natural order, God exists chiefly for the general good of man (Taylor 1989, 266–72, 278–79). This elevation of the natural ahead of the spiritual undergirds affirmation of the ordinary life. After all, what could be more *natural* than production and reproduction? It is not a huge leap from this position—that nature is at once the source of the good *and* the ordinary—to the suggestion that the distinction between them is more semantic than meaningful. God has made humans acquisitive and self-interested. Individuals, Taylor therefore takes Locke to mean, "should accept with humility the nature God has given them" (1989, 242). Subsequently, affirmers of the ordinary life have somehow marked human evolution through the swapping-out of revelation for reason, gospel for law, and piety for rationalism. There is a startlingly vacuous quality to such embourgeoisement. Taylor does not mirror Nietzsche's contempt for the common person; but he shares Nietzsche's concern about (last) men who exile greatness to the cause of happiness. The chief casualty is just condition.

Taylor's is more than an elegant come-to-Jesus. He is not a theocrat, a medievalist nemesis of humanism. He does not even seem to object to the modern focus on the natural order, to the scientific inquiry it provokes, the natural liberty it demands, or the appeal to the reason and natural affect that governs it. Instead, his argument is best understood in terms of the intemperance of the modern age, of the pathological hegemony of the natural order. Subtextually, his point is that there is a cost to the loss of heroes and heroism. In alienating ourselves from that greater than ourselves, we banish not only greatness, but also justice. We obviate the cosmic purpose essential to human fulfillment. We eschew the balance requisite to the good life in affirmation of the ordinary one. We try to top up Socrates's jar that can never be filled. Taylor objects to the solipsism of a life without heroes, to the cloistered celebration of autonomy (1989, esp. 2003). In a republican sense, the modern world sacrifices virtue—the obligation to God, society, and ultimately self—as the price of affirming the ordinary life.

It is not just the passing of greatness and great goodness that critics have identified as pathologies of the modern age. Writing before Taylor (in 1961), Daniel Boorstin starts from the implicit premise that Taylor's critique of modern society is, if anything, too generous. Taylor, at least, credits modern humans with a willingness to extract from nature a theory of the good. By contrast, Boorstin holds that modern societies are less concerned with understanding the natural order than with manufacturing a synthetic one, a world of doctored perception, a cocoon of fantasy as insubstantial as the sense of fulfillment it instills. Fashioned in no small part by advertising executives, public image consultations, and what today we would call influencers, the synthetic order is indulgent, conflating aspirations and expectations, expunging the dull moments, rough edges, and hard choices that characterize real-world existence.

The result is a sort of heavily processed world that bears some resemblance to reality in the way that Cheez Whiz bears some resemblance to cheese. In this All-New-and-Improved Cave, reputation trumps character and perception triumphs over reality. Far more than substance, what matters is image, "the kind of ideal that becomes real only when it becomes public" (Boorstin 1987, 189). Not surprisingly, the result is unhappiness. "Never have a people been more masters of their environment," says Boorstin. "Yet never have a people felt more deceived and disappointed" (1987, 4). Blessed with wealth, literacy, technology and philosophy, we use the manifold resources at our disposal to create a "thicket of unreality that stands between us and the facts of life" (1987, 3).

The watchword of the new order is freedom through indolence and fantasy. In liberating themselves from Nietzschean struggle, new last men tailor their existence to create experience without investment, enjoyment without effort. Be it news, travel, art, or education, the objective is to extract the essence of an experience without having to fight one's way through the tedium of actually *experiencing* it. "Have you seen *Omnibook*?" Boorstin has one friend ask another. "It takes five or six books and boils them down. That way you can read them all in one evening."

Friend: "I wouldn't like it. Seems to me it would just spoil the movie for you" (1987, 118).

New last men seek liberation from the natural order not through the spiritual or supernatural, but through the fantastical pseudoreality that shapes modern morals, modern aspirations, and modern heroes. If Taylor's lament is that the Enlightenment represents the start of a shift from a cosmic theory of ethics to a natural (or *micro*cosmic) one, Boorstin's is that we have moved from the rigid moral objectivism of the natural order to the malleable relativism of the synthetic one. This is liberating. Objective moral principles represent a claim upon us—an imperative to conform to obligations at the expense of gratification. A synthetic verisimilitude, by contrast, is something over which *we* have a claim. We can shape it to reflect that which pleases us. We can circumvent ethical imperatives, dedicating such efforts as we wish to invest into perfecting a much more convenient set of values (1987, 198, 212–13).

As with all heroes, those of the synthetic world both reflect and stimulate aspirations. Incarnations of core social values, they transcend the ordinary life. Transcendence, however, no longer means what it once did. In the synthetic order, transcendence takes the form of the *fabulous* life, the one that fulfills extravagant aspirations. The archetype is not the Socratic philosopher, the pious regenerate, or even the rationalist man of reason. It is not even the authentic Romantic. Rather, it is the celebrity, famous for beauty, wealth, or, in a self-perpetuating cycle of fatuity, fame itself. The celebrity hero is the embodiment of the glamour, wealth, and adulation that many of his worshippers imagine for themselves. His most committed admirers do not contemplate deeper cosmic or spiritual meaning. Instead, they hang on the hero's every tweet and Facebook posting. Entrepreneurs sell magazines, gain internet clicks, or increase television ratings by providing insights into the hero's private life. What our celebrity hero is *really* like—disheartening ordinariness notwithstanding—remains a source of localized obsession even by people old enough to earn a living (Ferris 2001; Nagel 2001, 141–43; McCutheon, Lange and Houran 2002). Celebrity heroes—updated additions include the wealthy socialite, reality television star, YouTube personality, and Instagram influencer—fuel the fantasy. The paucity of discernable greatness or goodness is no deterrent to emulation. In fact, it probably helps. In a Trumpian age, it might fairly be asked, if someone like *that* can be fabulous, why not me?

Attendant to the death of heroism is the birth of antiheroism. Generally nihilistic, at its most pernicious antiheroism is about nullification of transcendence, powerlessness, or the inefficacy of Elliot's (1971) hollow men and Nietzsche's last men. Modern antiheroes are darker than Boorstin's celebrities. Their ambivalence towards moral and cultural values bespeaks a deeply pathological social or spiritual crisis. Embodying a sort of cosmic anomie, antiheroes do not nullify heroism in the same way as villains do. (The antihero is not merely a useful foil against which the hero's virtues can be contrasted. He is not Moriarty to Conan Doyle's Holmes.) Instead, he speaks aesthetically to the tragedy of modernity. He is Huxley's John the Savage, alienated and defeated by a brave new world; or Woolf's shell-shocked war hero Septimus Smith, symbol of the Lost Generation; or Camus' Mersault, desensitized, detached, and ultimately doomed. The antihero reflects a dystopian introspection of the damaged everyman elevated to the status of unenthusiastic protagonist. She symbolizes modernity, nihilism, and apocalypse, which form concentric rings around man's helplessness and depravity.

The antihero is tinged with no hint of greatness. She is fraught with the awesome power of silent forces alien to her experience. Buffeted by modernity she confronts Kafkaesque authority, dehumanizing technological innovation, or debilitating warfare. (The war wound that renders Jake Barnes impotent in Hemingway's *The Sun Also Rises*, for example, makes the metaphor plain enough.) The antithesis of the magnanimous hero, the fruit of her wisdom is not greater fulfillment. Indeed, her knowledge often is the source of her misery, the nihilistic *Waste Land* isolating her from any great cosmic or historical sense of place (Eliot 1971, 37–50). Amplifying the torment is disenchantment born of raised expectations followed by dawning realization that human progress is merely an illusion—less eschatological progression than endless cycle of misery, hope, expectations, and despair. The antihero delivers an antidote to the specious optimism that heroism seduces but never consummates, a dose of dystopian realism to offset spiritual and humanist promises left undelivered (Bradbury 1993, 144–48).

Nihilistic angst rarely works out well for the antihero's psychological well-being. But it need not be inherently negative. Antiheroism has a potentially transformative quality, rendering one antiheroic in the context of the extant social paradigm, but hero of an emergent one. A product of the cultural downswing, the antihero often exists as harbinger of the upstroke, portent of the diagnostic and catalyst for the prescriptive. She may well be, to turn the equation on its head, the hero out of step with an unheroic world (Neimneh 2013, 79–84), a tragic and reluctant redeemer, restorer of the homeostatic balance foundational to republican justice. We shall see this quality a couple of times over the course of the book—in the Romantic whose alienation ultimately informs the egalitarianism and self-reliance of the good republican citizen, and in the comic superhero embodying the latent efficacy of the faceless common man.

Taken altogether, critics suggest that Western societies have gone from seeking meaning in the cosmic and spiritual orders, to seeking meaning in the natural order, to seeking meaning in the dominion of fantasy and illusion, to not finding any meaning at all. They have gone from aristocracy (in the sense of government of the best) to democracy (in the sense of government of equals) to within hailing distance of *Idiocracy* (in the sense of governance through addled self-absorption) to tyranny (in the sense of being powerless to combat unseen forces). Societies continue to bestow heroic status upon their fellows, critics claim, but the effect is vacuous. Modern heroism is restricted to theaters with little if any impact on human fulfillment. Spirituality is reduced to a wholly private affair, to the point that in some quarters even declaring one's spiritual beliefs is intolerably provocative. Morality is marginalized as unacceptably judgmental. Reality is negotiable, and humanist optimism is a fanciful relic of earlier times.

Chapter 1

The Epic Hero and the Roots of Republican Governance

Heroism became historically and politically relevant in the context of the epic heroism examined in this chapter. Strictly speaking, epic heroes are protagonists in long narrative poems invoking a muse in elevated and elegant presentation. Epic poetry is an exercise in the proclamation of fame, speaking to larger-than-life heroes imbued with, or aided by, supernatural powers (Speier 1935, 77; Tillyard 1966, 1). Representing the temper of their times, epics typically take place against the backdrop of explicit teleology (Feeney 1986, 137; Robertston 2008, 143). Focusing upon a singular individual or small group of individuals, they represent "spontaneous and anonymous homage paid by people to the greatness of their heroes," typically in consideration of physical virility or proclamation of epiphany (Lagorio 1970, 31; also Tillyard 1966, 12–13; Di Cesare 1982, 59; Risden 1998, 192). Grounded in historical truth or allegory, hagiography or legend, epic poetry inspires, elevates, and edifies thru hyperbolic idealization of the human condition (Lagorio 1970, 31). Masking hyperbole is the environment in which the epic hero operates: often a bygone age refracted through the lens of history that makes epic heroes figures to be emulated but not matched in the generations that succeed them. It need be noted right up front that the definition of epic heroism employed in this book is much looser, representing a fairly elastic extraction from the literary device from which it derives. Here, physical greatness is the defining quality, such that the book locates epic heroism in extraordinary deed and is insensitive to baroque presentation.

The prototypical epic hero is the Homeric warrior upon whom much of this chapter focuses. Painting with broad brushstrokes, the telos driving Homer's heroes is mostly personal, as in Achilles's pursuit of honor at Troy, or Odysseus's long journey of return. Later epics tended towards a more social or spiritual teleology (as in Aeneas's glorification of Rome, the perfection of virtue in the allegorical exploits of Spenser's English Protestant knights, the quest for the Holy Grail, Roland's glorification of Christ, or Christian's peregrination to salvation in *The Pilgrim's Progress*). In all these cases—personal, social, and spiritual—supernaturalism tends to affirm and justify heroic deed and purpose, the mysterious designs of deities cloaking the occasionally morally questionable elements of even heroic mortal behavior. In a less literary context, the Homeric hero's greatest relevance is that he informed the aristocratic ideal of pre-classical Greece (see below), the legacy of which is foundation to the republican balance that pits the interests and virtues of the great against those of the many. Thus, in a very real sense, the early epic hero's political legacy stimulates the emergence of republican institutions and the justice—of balance, condition, and agency—represented by republican values.

This chapter has two principal objectives. First, it establishes Homeric heroes as embodiment of the self-assertive, timocratic warrior-defender, relatively encumbered by the trappings of metaphysics. In this context, it explores the cultural influence—as (indirect) nation builders—of Homeric heroes on the emergence of republicanism. Inspirational and aspirational role models, Homeric warriors were heroic exemplars of the Archaic Greek aristocracy. At the same time, however, their appropriation of government provoked oppositional resistance to aristocratic dominance. Such *stasis*, or class conflict, in turn stimulated the more expansive theory of justice espoused by Solon, as well as the institutional balance, so constitutive of republics. Second, I examine the progression of the epic hero from pre-republican cultural stimulus, into one whose physical greatness is channeled more directly into social cause. Post-Homeric epic heroes are far more metaphysically sensitive, their greatness tied to goodness either through the justness of their cause or the coincidence of greatness and goodness in a singular individual.

The Epic Hero and the Birth of the Republic

The oldest surviving epic tells the tale of Gilgamesh, King of Uruk, whose quest is to uncover the mystery of human mortality. Over the course of the poem, Gilgamesh acquires the wisdom that permits his transformation from savagery (the narrative begins with the portrayal of Gilgamesh as a despotic king) to civilization (and the protagonist's evolution into a wise and just ruler) (Pruyser and Luke 1982). Anticipating later mythological and spiritual cross-fertilization, elements of the Gilgamesh epic underpin the Homeric and Hesiodic poetry that emerged from the shadows of Greece's Dark Ages (Gresseth 1975).

Such poetry spoke to the power of the gods, the mortality of man, his place in the cosmos, and the role of justice in the social order. The heroes of early epics are often flawed by contemporary moral standards. But, as with the Gilgamesh tale, they were foundational to the social mores of a time and place in transition from despotism to *civilitas*. Indeed, epic mythology forged a sense of historical continuity for Archaic Age Greeks, the mists from which Homeric exploits emerged, reflecting a time lost to history. This dark period between the loss of scribal capacity at the end of the Mycenaean Age and its rediscovery in the eighth century BC meant that Greeks' understanding of history came down to them through poetry and other means of oral transmission. If there was a sense that such myths were not literal historical truth, the general understanding as conveyed by Herodotus was that beneath embellishment and artistic license lay a core of historical veracity (McCauley 1993, 75–76).

Epic heroes of Archaic Greece were venerated and even worshipped as the mythical founders of Greek tribal clans, and later of emergent city-states (*poleis*) (Mitchell 2013, 55–58). Their lives were lived in inspiration for lesser individuals. Upon their deaths they were woven into folklore and legend, sanctified by myth, and empowered to affect the fates of mortals who still walked the earth (Kearns 1989; Currie 2005, 54). Epic heroes were towering figures—great warriors, great kings, and great civic benefactors (the last if not necessarily in life, then in daemonic posterity) whose intercession cities relied upon for their prosperity and security. They were not immortal, supernatural in their powers, or perfect in anthropomorphic physiology. But they came close on all three dimensions. The greatest were often the product of the union of mortal and god, which from birth marked them for excellence. They informed the cultural and social identity of Archaic Greece, announcing the importance of greatness to the well-constructed social order. Existing at the farthest boundaries of human achievement, they recreated, however imperfectly, the greatness that permeated the preceding Mycenean and Dark Ages.

Quintessentially heroic though they were, Homeric warriors present in hindsight as imperfect heroes in an imperfect environment in pursuit of an imperfect objective—the immortality that could not be theirs except by allegory in fame. They could be slightly off-putting. Achilles's intemperance, for example, bespeaks a certain weakness of character. He tends towards weepiness (to his mother, no less) when frustrated by Agamemnon's failure to accord him his due (1924, bk. I, 348–92). Enraged at the forfeiture of his concubine, he spends most of the first three-fourths of the poem more or less pouting in his tent, deaf to calls upon his loyalty by his colleagues in arms and episodically threatening to leave the Achaeans in the lurch altogether. Indirectly, his prolonged sulk results in Patroclus's death. Yet such weakness of character does nothing to tarnish his legacy, informed as it is upon his excellence in battle. In the climactic battle at Troy, he defeats Hector man-to-man, contemptuously dragging the body for all to see, thereby announcing his unimpeached status as the best of the Achaean warriors.

Homeric heroes were moved by the culturally ascendant prizes of immediate honor and eternal posterity. The former affirmed the hero's greatness, representing entitlement to deference from those of humbler accomplishment and serving notice of the hero's prerogative to lead. The greater prize was posterity, immortality born of perpetual legacy. It was literally to die for. With no prospects for an afterlife and hence no thoughts for the fate of the mortal soul, legacies were the only prospect for immortality in a time in which "ancestors" existed barely beyond the age of living memory. The greatest posterity came at a price—early death in battle (Griffin 1983, 90–92; Stefanson 2004, 26–27; Mitchell 2013, 31–32). Among the great advantages of such a death, though, was escaping dilution of one's greatest achievements and youthful beauty through insidious erosion born of age and enfeeblement.

So it was that death and immortality in Homer are symbiotic, informing the complicated relationship that mortals have with the gods. The principal difference between heroes and gods turns on heroic vulnerability. While the gods enjoy infinite power, their literal immortality precludes heroic ratification. Indeed, Homer highlights the gods' secondary status by treating them as often capricious, hedonistic, scheming, and petty.[1] Incapable of risking death, theirs presents as an inferior immortality, paling in comparison to the eternal glory of heroic posterity (Nietzsche 1908, 114; 1956a, 3; 2006, preface; Griffin 1983, 88–93; Schein 1984, 53, 55, 95–96; Acampora 2002b, 27–28; Stefanson 2004, 28; Clark 2004).

Masters of themselves, Homeric heroes are beholden to no external limitations. They embody the Athenians' injunction to the Melians that the "strong do what they can and the weak suffer what they must" (Thucydides 2006, bk. V.89).² As with Callicles's great man, Homeric heroes tend to consider the accoutrements of metaphysics to be little more than tools with which the weak seek to constrain the strong (although see Ahrensdorf 2014, esp. ch. 1). Sociologically, then, Homeric heroes exist principally for themselves and to a lesser extent for their families (a *much* lesser extent given Agamemnon's sacrifice of his daughter prior to the Trojan campaign). Their heroism is socially tangential. Certainly, there is an understated sense of a greater good. Indeed, unlike the epic heroes portrayed in Roman, medieval, and Renaissance narratives, intersubjective concerns—undertaken for the welfare of others—are often actual impediments to the quest for immortality. Analogous to worldliness in the teleological quest of the Christian soul, such concerns are a necessary evil at best. Civic benefits that attach to heroes' actions, therefore, tend toward happy externality or calculated means to consolidation of authority (Finley 1954, 124–25; Acampora 2002a, 2; Stefanson 2004, 4, 10).

Seen in this light, Achilles's self-absorption is part of his solipsistic greatness. At least prior to the death of Patroclus, he makes it abundantly clear that having been dishonored, he is unwilling to lift a finger in the Achaean cause. No compensatory gifts can make up for the initial loss of honor. Hector is no less self-absorbed. Yes, he agrees with Andromache, he is likely to be destroyed by Achilles. It is true that contributing to Andromache's misery is the inevitability of her enslavement. But he cannot possibly abandon his quest for honor on account of such lesser concerns (Homer 1924, bk. VI, 400–466). Later, he once again puts his desire not to be shamed ahead of a sense of familial and civic duty. He alone stands outside the gates of Troy waiting to do battle with Achilles, while Priam pleads with him not to engage in a contest he cannot win, and instead to save the men and women of Troy. His later loss of nerve notwithstanding, however, Hector cannot retreat. It was his own failure as a military leader that brought about Troy's impending ruin, and he dares not risk the reproach of lesser men for leading the city into its predicament. Better for him, Hector thinks to himself, "to meet Achilles man to man and slay him, and so get me home, or myself perish gloriously before the city" (bk. XXII, 109–10).

NATION BUILDING: THE NEW REPUBLIC

Manifestly, the influence of Homeric warriors colored the mores of early Western civilization. Indeed, warriors from both sides at Troy (considering Aeneas's status as founding hero of Rome) were for centuries held up as idealizations of civic perfection. The status of Homeric heroes in pre-Socratic Greece was almost biblical. Despite their understated social concern, their qualities served as template for the predominant aristocratic values of reemergent civilization. Self-consumed as they were great, their virtues generally prevailed as discrete excellences adorned by self-assertion, egoism, and physical greatness.[3] Informing a timocratic culture, they were by no means *republican* heroes. But they were catalysts for the emergence of republicanism, even as they themselves evinced little appreciation for the cosmic justice undergirding the values of the good republic.

In order to appreciate the relationship between the Homeric hero and the nascent republic, some sociological context is necessary. As late as the ninth century BC, Snodgrass finds that Dark Ages Greece featured very few nucleated settlements, and those that existed were scarcely more than villages (1980, 18). The looseness of the social structure meant that legitimation of chieftains' authority was utilitarian. Unlike more structured civil societies, in which power is grounded in formal-legal authority, chieftains relied upon greatness and social benefaction in perpetuation of their status. Under conditions of such clientelistic—*big man*—politics, authority was linked to factors such as wealth; personal status; charisma (the ability to attract and command a following); coercive capacity (inherent in military organization and leadership); and most importantly, the means to distribute spoils (Runciman 1982, 358–62). In advertisement of their aptitudes, chieftains engaged in ostentatious displays of status, speaking to past glory and the prospect for more of the same through new wars and plunder. Their houses typically were large feasting halls that served the dual purposes of feting their loyal followers and announcing the economic advantages of their leadership (Finley 1954, esp. 128–33; Donlan 1982, 140; Whitley 1991, 349–51; Anderson 2005, 183–84; Currie 2005; Irwin 2005, 244; Kendrick 2010, 14; Mitchell 2013, 36, 52–55).

The subsequent Archaic Age was somewhat of a renaissance, a reemergence into the light from the ages of darkness.[4] Demographically, the Archaic period is noteworthy for significant repopulation of the Greek peninsula, ameliorating the population loss that had attended the fall of Mycenaean civilization (Snodgrass 1980, 23). Socially, population growth contributed to the reorganization of political authority coincident with the rise of the *polis*. The new age represented an evolution from the monarchical rule of tribal chieftains, toward the shared rule of aristocracy. Repopulation also stimulated changing agricultural patterns, which favored stable arable farming over the widely prevalent (and more nomadic) system of animal husbandry (Snodgrass 1980, ch. 1). The resultant increase in landholding combined with the paucity of arable land on the Greek peninsula and Aegean Islands ultimately led to synoecism, once-discrete village settlements radiating towards one another as nuclear units of the emergent city-states (Finley 1970, ch. 8, esp. 95–99; Bryant 1996, ch. 3, esp. 44–45; Donlan 1999, 37–39, 50–51).

THE HERO AND THE NOBLEMAN

Politically, the Homeric hero represented a schematic ideal for the Hellenic aristocracy of the Archaic Age. With the emergence of city-states, and accounting for variance among the different *poleis* across time and place, power tended to be vested in more formalized institutions than it had in the Dark Ages. This modernizing structure featured role specialization in government, centralization of authority, authority of office, and evolution of authority beyond mere tribal or kinship ties (Runciman 1982, 351; Anderson 2005, 177–78). Somewhat less formally, we can envision a good deal of jockeying for supremacy amongst the *aristoi*, each looking to assert himself as the single best among his peers, but generally being forced to settle (by the collective weight of those peers) for equal best instead. This is not to say that big man politics was banished from the *polis* altogether. But only occasionally was any one man big *enough* to acquire despotic control (Greenhalgh 1972, 190–92).

The political sociology of the new city-states seems to have been heralded by, and modeled after, the cooperative tribalism of the *basileis* assembled at Troy. Prominent was a competitive egalitarianism within the ranks of the chieftains, and strict stratification between noble leaders and commoners. As would be the case with Archaic Age assemblies, the Council was open to all. However, it was the prerogative of chieftains to speak to relevant issues. Common soldiers were expected to limit themselves to ratification of the positions adopted by their leaders or, where there was disagreement, throw their support behind one set of elites or another (Finley 1954, 81–84; Ehrenberg 1972, 10–15; Adkins 1982, 296–97; Schofield 1986, 9; Donlan 1999, ch. 1; Raaflaub 1999, esp. 139; Bryant 1996, 18–21; Raaflaub and Wallace 2007, esp. 28–30; Barker 2009, 40–66; Owens 2010, 36–38; Wallace 2015, 4).

If the Achaean Council is anything to go by, such hierarchy as existed among Archaic Age *aristoi* was nominal. As with the Achaean Council, Archaic Age assemblies served as an adversarial forum for noble elites.

Aristoi were expected to be, as Peleus admonishes Achilles, speakers of words and doers of deeds. Nobles engaged in verbal jousting with rivals as a means of consolidating and enhancing their authority, demonstrating good judgment and the attendant capacity to command men in battle. This dialectic of word and deed would persist throughout ancient times, later elevating rhetorical skills almost to the level of military skills and (in Rome at least) hereditary nobility. The assembly was not the only alternative to the battlefield as a proving ground for Archaic *aristoi*. Mirroring the games accompanying Patroclus's funeral, the Pan-Hellenic games begun in the Archaic Age were to become an important part of how nobles defined themselves. In *The Iliad*, athletics represent more than an amusing diversion to the serious business of war. Rather, they are a way for heroes to settle or reinforce a subtle hierarchy of recognition that others are expected to affirm. In both war and athletic competition, the driving force is the *thymos*, and in both cases (for Homer at least) any honor won is personal and not communal.

Whatever the institutional accuracy of the Homeric epics, a fundamental theme is that heroism is a noble endeavor, the prerogative of the *aristoi*. It represents a bright line of class distinction, emphasized through discrepancies (empirical or presumptive) in status, wealth, courage, nobility, and aesthetics. Greek heroes generally were extraordinary in their physical beauty, a virtue that distinguished them from lesser mortals and emphasized their godlike qualities (Hobbs 2000, 156–57). In making the point, Homer contrasts the magnificence of great warriors with the physiological deficiencies of the lame, bandy-legged, round-shouldered, warped-headed, balding Thersites (Homer 1924, bk. II, 217–20. Similarly, when Achilles gives full vent to his feelings, he calls Agamemnon a drunkard with the face of a dog and the heart of a deer, thereby nailing the trifecta of Homeric ignobility—poor judgement, common homeliness, and cowardice (1924, bk. II, 224–25; see also Tyrtaeus 2008, fr. 10).

The most telling distinction between nobleman and commoner, though, was lineage. Through creative genealogy, Archaic Age aristocrats reenforced their status by establishing—or at least proclaiming—direct ancestral ties to long-dead heroes. Indeed, there was no better way to glorify and legitimate a class of men whose veins coursed with the putatively heroic blood that ordinary men could not claim for their own (Anderson 2005, 183–84; Irwin 2006, 244; Mitchell 2013, 45–46). Asserting a monopoly on noble heredity, the aristocracy reenforced exclusivity through an insular socialization process designed to bring latent greatness to the fore. Befitting their noble status and consistent with their heroic mandate, aristocrats kept up the ostensible family tradition, styling themselves as civic benefactors through public spending, through military and civil leadership, or, more dramatically, through colonial founding and value consolidation by way of enlightened lawgiving (Mitchell 2013, 55–60).

Evidence of aristocratic appropriation of the heroic ideal is plentiful. Throughout the Archaic Age, the decorative motif of the fine pottery affordable to the *aristoi* was dominated by Homeric heroes, or equally by well-dressed aristocrats engaged in martial, athletic, and equestrian pursuits. Funerary practices of the early eighth century were patterned after Patroclus's funeral in *The Iliad*. Animal sacrifices and burial offerings of panoply spoke to the larger-than-life legacy that Archaic noblemen sought to leave to posterity. That the heroic ideal appropriated by the aristocracy reflected a world that no longer existed did nothing to limit its appeal. In fact, the distinction between past and present was a useful metaphor, mirroring an equally awesome contemporaneous gulf between aristocrat and commoner (Adkins 1960, esp. 35; Finley 1970, 100; Ehrenberg 1972, 18–19; Coldstream 1976; Donlan 1999, 52–53; Bryant 1996, 80–81; Hobbs 2000, ch. 5).

In addition to legitimating aristocratic dominance, long-dead heroes also aided in the cultural consolidation of the *poleis*. In numerous cities, heroes were celebrated as discrete civic icons, imbuing new states with the venerable greatness of the heroes of old. Heroes were, quite literally, icons of a civil religion, worshipped alongside the gods as civic deities. Equally, they informed a cultural sense of social solidarity, a unifying usness that bound newly united tribes in common cause in the face of ambient social dislocation. In daemonic form, heroes joined the gods in civic benefaction. Such deification manifested most prominently in the heroic tomb cults prevalent during the Archaic period. The genesis was the often-chance discovery of an ancient crypt, evidencing—and given the properties of Homeric heroes, try proving otherwise—the final resting places of local heroes from another age. Tomb cults reflected a form of historical revisionism that ascribed civic motives to the "heroes" whose skeletal remains were worshipped. Through tomb cults, heroism came to be seen as more than egoistic self-assertion, extending instead to the communal protection afforded by civic benefaction (see Hobbs 2000, 150; also Finley 1970, 99–100; Ehrenberg 1972, 14–15; Snodgrass 1980, 36–38; Runciman 1982, 368; Kearns 1989, ch. 2; Alcock 1991, 453–54; Hubbard 1992, 81; Antonaccio 1994, 390; De Polignac 1995, 129–44; Walker 1995, ch. 1; Bryant 1996, 43; Hobbs 2000, 150; Cole 2004, chs. 1–2; Kendrick 2010, ch. 1).

Stasis and the Emergence of Republican Institutions

Despite the cultural importance of the Homeric ideal, the Archaic Age witnessed important challenges to aristocratic authority. Most significant was the periodic *stasis*—violent conflict between noblemen and progressively empowered commoners—that afflicted most city-states. The causes were many. Aristocratic insularity predictably bred corruption. Particularly provocative was the acceptance of bribes for the adjudication of civil matters, an issue that hit particularly close to home for Hesiod (see chapter 2). Equally destabilizing was the disaffection of subsidence farmers, landless farm workers, and debt-servants, whose problems (as would be the case in Late Republican Rome) were exacerbated by the propensity of aristocrats to assume ever-greater shares of the land at the expense of political stability (Linforth 1919, ch. 3; Finley 1970, 99–103; Ehrenberg 1972, ch. 1; Bryant 1996, 66–79; Donlan 1999, 38–40; Raaflaub and Wallace 2007, 35; Wallace 2007, 50; Owens 2010, ch. 4).

Further provoking civil unrest was discord within the aristocracy itself, exacerbated by vestigial clan and tribal loyalties. As noted, aristocratic governance was a corporate exercise among self-assertive individuals, many with ambitions that reflected a sense of their own natural superiority. The result was no more than a semistable equilibrium rife with potential for factionalization. In and of themselves, factions were not suboptimal, constituting internal impediments to excessive ambition. In times of instability, however, they represented natural fault lines ripe for exploitation; the big man politics subsumed by Archaic civil order not altogether dead (Greenlagh 1972, 192–93; Foxhall 1997, 119; Anderson 2005, 179–80; Mitchell 2013, ch. 1).

Among the greatest threats posed by aristocratic factionalism and excessive social stratification came from singular individuals able to wrest sole power for themselves. Potential *tyrannoi* always lurked, exploiting the disaffection of commoners and positioning themselves as putative champions of the common interest (Anderson 2005, 190–203; see also Irwin 2005, 244). If there was any benefit to them, tyrants held out the promise of greater social balance. However, it need hardly be said that justice and tyranny rarely traverse a common path for long. Singular individuals tend to chafe at constraint, lions being hard to keep on their leashes. More fruitful was for commoners to eschew tyrants in favor of collective uprisings in challenge to aristocratic dominance. Implicit was a clash of legitimacies between freemen (whose prerogative was to remain unenslaved) and *aristoi* (who sought to insulate civil order from the indignity of mob rule). If noblemen couched elite privilege in the venerable legacy of physical greatness, commoners asserted metaphysical principles mandating that no one group be privileged in construction of the law or enforcement of its effects (Morris 1996, 20; see also Aristotle *Pol.*, 1321a; 2001f, 1317b–18a; Snodgrass 1965; Finley 1970, 99–108; Morris 1996; Bryant 1996, 46–57; Raaflaub 1999; Donlan 1999, ch. 2; Owens 2010, chs. 3–4; although see Rawlings 2013, 18–20).

Out of these contested legitimacies arose the fundaments of Solonian republicanism. As supreme lawgiver of Athens, Solon may have been the first statesman to recognize justice as a *common* good and not merely an interpersonal one. Poetically, he saw injustice as a contagion pervading society as thoroughly as plague or famine or, to switch metaphors, stormy intrusion upon his calm sea. Politically, the common peace was undermined by unjust agency, the intemperance of self-assertive, self-serving individuals, who by their rapacious quest for wealth and status bestirred commensurate immoderation on the part of those who resisted them (Solon 2008, fr. 9). His prescription was institutional, reasoning that the designs of unjust men could be mitigated by a well-constructed order. The result would be to privilege the common peace ahead of particular interests, while demystifying the (heroic) mythology contorted to serve those interests. Indeed, for Solon, the common peace represents a public thing (res publica), a foundational principal that would come to inform conceptions of the good *polis* from antiquity to the present day. Grounded in the imperative for just balance, Solon's humanism sought rational solutions for the *stasis* afflicting unjust societies (Vlastos 1946, 69; Solon 2008, fr. W4). Throwing in his lot with neither commoner nor aristocrat, Solon took his stand "with strong shield covering both sides, allowing neither unjust dominance" (2008, fr. W5; also fr. W36, W37).

Solon's appears to be the first magnanimous stance by a leader against the cultural hegemony of epic heroism. Few afforded the role of supreme lawgiver were eager to burden themselves with preservation of the common peace if it came at the cost of personal enrichment and power (see Murray 2001, ch. 9, esp. 143–45). So prevalent was the truism that, somewhat perversely to modern ears, Solon feels compelled to defend his actions in defiance of the prevailing timocratic ethos of his day. "I know many people say 'Solon is a stupid fellow, not a man who thinks ahead: God has given him a fortune, but he hasn't taken it. There he had the prey encircled, but he didn't close the net—lost his nerve, no doubt about it, and his common sense as well" (Solon fr. W33). Solon's stand against the Homeric aristocratic ideal left a lasting legacy. His republicanism rescued Athens during a time of intense class conflict. Philosophically, Solon's rational humanism announced the affirmative obligation republicans call "virtue"—obliging good people to craft civil peace out of ambient chaos. It is from the Solonian ruins that classical philosophy and republican politics were resurrected. In seeking to temper the self-assertion of the epic hero with countervailing metaphysics, Solon opened the door for the transformative paradigm proclaimed by the great voices of classical Greece, not least Socrates, Plato, and Aristotle in the pages of philosophy; and Aeschylus, Euripides, and Sophocles on the stages of Attica. In the process was born heroic magnanimity, of which Solon was the practical archetype.

The Changing Epic Hero

Technically, Archaic epic heroes shared with their Homeric counterparts a lack of goodness, at least in the sense that unlike the magnanimous and common heroes discussed in later chapters, their heroism existed independently of, and sometimes remained resistant to, moral perfection. Yet increasingly, the estimability of epic heroes turned on their commitment to republican virtue. As noted in the previous chapter, there were three principal mechanisms by which estimability attached to post-Homeric epic heroes. One was goodness of the cause for which heroes' epic talents were brought to bear. The second was the coincidence of heroes' greatness and the goodness of their character. The third was to assign to the epic hero aspirational goodness.

Over the course of the Archaic Age, the goodness of cause attendant to the nascent republics fundamentally affected epic heroism. Decreasingly informed by Homeric emphasis on the personal and patronymic, later epic heroes adopted a more social persona, obliging them to temper the narrow ends of honor and posterity—glorification of the self for the sake of the self—with the imperative for good republican citizenship.[5] Such goodness of cause underlies the claim to heroism, for example, of Apollonius's Jason. Indeed, Jason represents a new sort of epic hero. That it is he whom the more traditional heroes of the *Argo* choose to lead the expedition represents significant movement away from the purely timocratic character of the epic hero. It constitutes a shift from one whose considerations are all about himself to one whose quest is for something larger than himself (Apollonius 1912, bk. I, 335 ff). Even the ambiguous nature of the Golden Fleece speaks to the new heroic imperative. What the object is or what it represents beyond a source of collective or communal or social action is immaterial. The point is that the welfare of the whole takes precedence over the physical greatness of the individual (see Clauss 1993).

Goodness of cause affected the nature of honor as well, as war became a progressively less fruitful avenue of singular heroic pursuit. The transition was gradual. Herodotus reports of the Battle of Plataia, for example, that individual Greek soldiers were still honored for their bravery on the field of battle (Herodotus 1952, bk. IX, 71–75). But equally, the new era of warfare demanded less of the extraordinary warrior and more that of the hoplite possessed of the composure and temperance requisite to holding his position in the phalanx. Indeed, Plutarch reports that when the late-Archaic general Miltiades, whose military strategy had helped the Athenians win the Battle of Marathon, demanded that he be honored with a crown of laurels, the Dekeleian Sophanes retorted, "When you have fought and conquered the barbarians alone, you may ask to be honoured alone . . ." (Plutarch 1899, *Kimon*, s. 8; Wallace 2007, 78). Equally indicative of the changing military ethos of the late Archaic Age was the case of Aristodemus, who in the opinion of Herodotus was the best of the Hellenic warriors at Thermopylae. He was not honored, however, insofar as his desire to be slain as atonement for being the sole survivor spoke to the weakness of his character. Aristodemus's experience illustrates the contrast between the culture of Homeric Greece and that of the late Archaic period. For the Homeric warrior, deeds were all that mattered. By the early fifth century, though, motives had overshadowed actions—at least in this instance—as the basis for honor earned in battle (Tyrtaeus 2008, fr. W12; Callinus 2008, fr. W1; Manicas 1982, 675; Bryant 1996, 90–91).

Goodness of cause was also foundational to medieval epics, a common theme being combat pitting the hero of the natural and civilized world against the supernatural evil represented by dragons, goblins, and other monsters. In the Anglo-Saxon epic *Beowulf*, for example, the eponymous hero protects the seat of the Danish king from the swamp-dwelling Grendel. His epic death in battle by a dragon breathing fire once again occurs in estimable social cause, this time defending Geats. The obverse of this nature-versus-evil-magic theme was reflected in Christian epics, featuring heroes serving God through the (supernatural) assistance of his grace. Examples include the martyrdom of Roland or Tasso's Godfrey decimating Saracens in deliverance of Jerusalem. Indeed, through such goodness of cause, Christian heroes are absolved of blame for barbarous practice, acquiring heroic currency solely through the nature of their quest.

By contrast, the coincidence of goodness of character and physical greatness speaks to a different means of metaphysical intrusion into the epic ideal. The Romans, for example, expected their greatest citizens to exhibit both physical and metaphysical virtuosity. While a creation of the early imperial era, Rome's putative founding hero, Aeneas, typifies such heroic completeness. Self-consciously distinct from the Homeric hero, Aeneas is gifted with all the manly virtues (*virilis virtus*) of the Homeric hero. However, in contrast to his Achaean counterparts, he is equally committed to the imperative for justice. In the High Middle Ages, chivalric romance literature also spoke to the imperative for good character coincident to physical excellence. As we shall see in chapter 4, the moral and social virtue of the knight errant is as important as his deeds; his self-assertive virility qualified by the submission and self-restraint attendant to courtly love.

Finally, there is greatness coupled with aspirational goodness. Character-based Christian epics of the Late Middle Ages and Renaissance thus tended to employ the aforementioned mechanism of heroic duality, highlighting the imperfection of the aspirant (physical) hero against the metaphysical perfection of the more Christological hero. Examples of such apotheotic heroes include Beatrice for Dante, Galahad for Malory, Arthur for Spenser, the various manifestations of the church for Bunyan, or Christ Himself for the chivalric soldiers of God. These epiphanous figures temper the worldly greatness of the epic hero with the superior spiritual goodness requisite to heroic estimability in the wake of Homer (Risden 1998, esp. 195).

By the end of the eighteenth century, the metaphysical had begun to eclipse the physical as the basis of heroism, as neoclassicism gave way to Gothic emphasis on greater realism and less heroic adulation (Tillyard 1966, 13, 528–31). Wordsworth's *Recluse*, for example, indulges in the self-centeredness that Romanticism shares with epic heroism, but not the self-assertive greatness or supernatural qualities more typically associated with long narrative poetry. Indeed, to the extent that Romantics embraced epic poetry, it was more dedicated to their core interests—which is to say introspection, aesthetic stimulation through nature, and Promethean social defiance—than classical values or celebration of heroic deeds (Byron 1891, cant. III; also Cantor 2007, 393–96).⁶ Adding to the growing marginalization of narrative epic poetry was the emergence of other forms of literary expression, not least the modern novel (Wilkie 1965, 23–24).⁷

Conclusion

Epic heroes are unambiguously heroic. Prototypically, they were epitomized by patronymic Homeric warriors aided by, even imbued with, supernatural capacity. Homeric warriors' greatness was physical, their virtues—generally limited to a handful of discrete active excellences—largely untutored. They asserted themselves primarily in pursuit of private goals and private gain. Unencumbered by excessive intersubjective social obligations, other goods—social, economic, political and military—were subordinated to self-glorification. They took as their due the usufructs of honor; the wealth, power, and deference commanded by their status. Yet for all this, they did not lack estimability in their times. Skillful and courageous in leadership and martial excellence, they were recognized as the apotheotic perfection of humanity at the close of the Greek Dark Ages and well into the Archaic one. Indeed, for the Archaic Greeks, such heroes were exemplary, defining the mythology of a protorepublican age. Pitted against warriors of equal mettle, more vulnerable in their mortality than the gods, their heroism was at least somewhat relatable. Their vulnerability was measured in terms of the resistance they encountered in their agonal exploits, their legacies burnished by three discrete variables "whom [they] fought, how [they] fought, and how [they] fared" (Finley 1954, 127). The political impact of Homeric heroes was both institutional and cultural, their nation building legacy important, if indirect. Indeed, republican values emerged as much in *response* to Homeric self-assertion as by dint of it.

Over the course of the preclassical period, the Homeric prototype gradually relinquished its social hegemony, as emergent *poleis* began to impose ethical imperatives upon heroic estimability. Culturally, the mythological status of Homeric heroes remained intact. Exemplary figures, they were held up as incarnation of self-assertive greatness by noblemen styling themselves great and self-assertive. But as quintessential big men whose power radiated outward from individuated stature, *aristoi* came up against the countervailing populism of commoners (and their ostensible tyrannical champions), who asserted an egalitarian claim to just social and political arrangements. Out of the conflict arose the prototypical republican institutional structure demanded by Solonian cosmic justice, antithetical interests balanced against one another in the name of the common peace. In such fashion did Solon inspire, albeit impermanently at first, the republican model of government at Athens. Far from the clientelistic tribalism in which the Homeric hero had thrived, the Solonian state became a public thing, a res publica, tempering the self-assertiveness of noble appropriators of the heroic prerogative. It was this model, albeit supplemented with the virtue ethics of the classical period explored in the next chapter, that would lead to the flowering of Western civilization in Greece and Rome, the republic standing as the embodiment of cosmic justice: its institutions in just balance and just condition, its values dedicated to just agency.

With the gradual development of ancient republicanism, then, vestigial Homeric heroism became increasingly anachronistic. Like Pindar's Heracles appropriating the oxen of Geryon in Callicles's telling, the Homeric hero had justified the great man's claim to privilege through his singular strength in contrast to the weakness of the many (Plato *Gorg.* 484b). But such righteousness of just deserts was out of step with the far more metaphysically nuanced conception of justice in the classical period. There was little sense of balance in the timocratic intemperance of the Homeric hero and little sense of virtue—at least not as understood as obligation to realize the human condition through just agency. There was scant consideration of just condition. Homeric heroes pleased or displeased the gods, who themselves were motivated by the same adversarial and self-interested objectives as mortals.

Classical republicanism was forged from the clash of the physical and the metaphysical, the blunting of greatness with goodness. As theories of justice evolved, epic heroes were obliged to accommodate a new form of estimability, couched in terms of goodness. To gain heroic purchase, in other words, post-Homeric epic heroes have had to be coincidentally good and great or, failing that, at least teleologically or aspirationally good. This metaphysical imperative was fundamental to an emergent form of republican heroism, heroism as *great goodness*, or magnanimity. If magnanimous heroes did not share the iconic quality of epic heroism, it is reasonable to assert that they at least as great an impact on republicanism. Certainly, they are the basis of transvaluative conceptions of nobility and aristocracy. Apotheosized, they are foundational to Christianity. It is to them that we turn next.

Chapter 2

Justice, Magnanimity, and the Republic

If Homeric heroes epitomize courage, magnanimous heroes' defining virtue is justice. They are great in that they exceed the ordinary, not (necessarily) in their physical excellence but in their metaphysical singularity. They are good in the dual sense of *knowing* the good and *acting* in accordance with the good. They are less classically heroic than epic heroes. However, they meet the heroic criteria employed here: they are extraordinary in the metaphysical sense, both in terms of exceeding the ordinary and transcending the ordinary life. Perfected in their virtues, they are estimable in the conduct of life. Similarly, through compulsion or exhortation, power or authority, their brief is to provide the social conditions requisite to transcendence, in either a secular (*eudaemonic*) or spiritual (salvational) sense. In this mandate they meet resistance from ignorant and insistent masses and from sophistic rivals, palliative and self-concerned in their rhetoric or worldliness.

Heroic magnanimity has taken many forms. Prototypically, magnanimous heroes are philosophers, qualified through contemplative perfection to guide others in realization of the human condition. Eponymically, the magnanimous hero is Aristotle's great-souled (magnanimous) man, the personification of complete virtue. Theologically, the magnanimous are saints, godheads, or deities. Rhetorically, the magnanimous hero is the speaker of words—the *homo rhetoricus*, never resorting to arms where eloquence serves the cause equally well (Cmiel 1990, 24). Culturally, magnanimous heroes persist as didactic exemplars—inimitable, perhaps, but, like the Christ figure, sources of inspiration, amelioratives of despair. Politically, magnanimous heroes are embodied equally by kings or parliaments of greatly good individuals—a literal aristocracy, government by the best and brightest. Their impact largely institutional, they exist primarily as stewards of the republic. Yet they are perhaps more memorable and recognizable—as with Solon in the previous chapter—as redemptive heroes, champions of virtue in the face of insidious corruption.

Picking up where the previous chapter left off, this one continues to trace the antecedents of ancient republicanism. It begins with a deeper exploration of the metaphysical roots of cosmic justice, focusing to a greater degree on the just agency and just condition that, married to Solonian just balance, brought about the flowering of the republicanism of the classical age. The story begins with Hesiod's insistence that humanity's prerogative is to live in accordance with the imperatives of justice defined and enforced by the gods. Lamenting the depraved condition of his times, Hesiod mourns the injustice and avarice of putatively great men. His pessimism, though, is offset by an underlying message of redemptive hope—that volitional assent to justice is the means to a more fulfilling human existence.

Hesiod's insistence upon the imperative for justice sets up the next section of the chapter, which focuses on heroic magnanimity as a cognitive construct. This section examines the foundational Socratic and Aristotelian republican prescriptions by which the principles of justice are harnessed to social benefit. Socrates and Aristotle both articulate ideal-typical magnanimous heroes. The distinction is interesting insofar as they differ on the estimability (in terms of social utility) of magnanimous leaders; Socrates more comfortable with the idea of *heroic* magnanimity, Aristotle more cognizant of the potentially hazardous consequences of it to the good republic.

The third part of the chapter explores what we might think of as aesthetic magnanimity, viewed through the lens of tragedy, in which rather than exemplifying heroic magnanimity, protagonists suffer from the want thereof. Locating justice in the counterfactual, it is the dearth of requisite magnanimity that dooms the tragic protagonist of the Greek stage to misfortune or death. Equally important to this final portion of the chapter, playwrights such as Aeschylus, Euripides, and Sophocles emphasize the inevitability of conflict between divine and positive law. Setting up the discussion in subsequent chapters on the relationship between the orders of grace and nature, tragedians tend to locate justice in the balance between conformity to the laws of the gods on the one hand and the laws of mortals on the other. The chapter concludes by suggesting that magnanimous heroism is ambiguously optimal for the good republic but sets up the case made later in the book that magnanimity divorced from political authority is far more promising.

Hesiod and the Cosmic Principles of Republican Justice

The magnanimous heroes of classical Greece were shaped by centuries of theological and scientific inquiry into the nature of justice. Even more than Solon, it is Hesiod who stands as the preeminent pre-Socratic student of republican justice. Central to Hesiod's mission is to determine humanity's cosmic place. He assigns meaningful division between the theater of the gods and the theater of mortals. Articulating the prevailing cosmic division of labor, Hesiod identifies leisure as the privilege of the gods, and toil and struggle as the lot of humanity. Failure to conform is the basis of unjust agency, such that ambitious individuals seeking to evade their cosmic responsibilities in order to indulge in the prerogatives of the gods court divine disfavor. In consequence, anticipating the thrust of Plato's *Republic*, Hesiod insists that greater reward attaches to just condition (as cosmic harmony), goodness, and moral character than to greatness and the self-assertive pursuit of personal ends.

While the contours of Hesiod's cosmic moral order are established in the *Theogeny*, it is the *Works and Days* that introduces Western civilization to the idea of humanity's fall and circumscribed prospects for redemption. The aetiological context is the creation by the gods of five discrete ages, or *races*, of humans. The first, a golden race that preceded Zeus, lived like gods, with none of the prosaic concerns of ordinary men and women. The golden age represented a point of departure from which the sorry condition of mortals descended (Hesiod 2006b, 110–12). People of the golden race did not experience the misery of human existence, their lives unmarred by toil or "wretched old age." When these mortals died, it was peacefully in their sleep, their souls sent forth as emissaries of the gods to be guardians and benefactors of humanity (113–25). With the passing of the golden race, a second—ignoble and infantilized—race of silver followed. Those of silver were addled, reckless and impious. Nurtured by their mothers for one hundred years, silver-men were incapable of self-governance. Their mature lives—short and miserable—were passed in toil, and upon their deaths their souls were condemned to the eternal blackness of Hades (Hesiod 2006b, 127–42). The succeeding bronze race was characterized by violence and brutality. Consumed by war, bronze-men were governed by their passions. Rather than infantilization, men of bronze were done in by their appetites and capacity for violence, and "by one another's arms they were subdued and overthrown" (143–56).

The Hesiodic ages are reflective of earlier Indian and Persian mythology which speak of the ages of humanity in terms of progressive moral decay (West 1978, 174–76). In the *Mahabharata*, for example, the Krita Yuga (equivalent to the Hesiodic Golden Age), was a time when humans lived in harmonious and virtuous accord with one another. Daily needs were met through cognitive rather than physical processes. With each successive epoch, however, virtue diminished by a quarter. By the Dvapara Yuga, passions had overtaken intellect in the conduct of human relations. In the final age, the Kali Yuga, people led lives of conflict and misery (Fontenrose 1974, 2–3).

Hesiod follows a similar script in describing his own morally dysfunctional iron age, which consigns individuals largely to toil and misery. However, unlike the *Mahabharata*, Hesiod's is not a linear history of moral disintegration. Between the ages of bronze and iron there existed a liminal race. The result of sexual union between mortals and gods, the penultimate age was populated by a righteous "race of heroes, god-like men" (2006b, 159; also Clay 2003, 92–93). What is righteous about the heroic race Hesiod does not make all that clear. Certainly hero-men practiced the violence that Hesiod sees as antithetical to justice. On the other hand, the gods appear to have tempered that violence, directing it to better purpose than the mayhem unleashed by the men of bronze. The critical distinction appears to be found in Strife—specifically, the teleological discrepancy inherent in what Hesiod conceives as *malignant* and *healthy* Strife. Malignant Strife is mere self-assertion, detached from justice and fostering "wicked war, battle, and heartless plunder" (2006b, 14). Healthy Strife, by contrast represents *aethlos*, obstacles to be transcended in the name of justice and prosperity (2006b, 11–34). As would Augustine later, Hesiod appears to draw moral distinction between just and unjust conflict, emphasizing the distinction in terms of the happy fate awaiting heroic just warriors, who retire eternally upon the Isles of the Blest—that bountiful Shangri-La of the remotest part of the earth which Zeus reserves for them alone (see Fontenrose 1974, 9).

Passingly interesting as it is, we are left to wonder about Hesiod's motive for the awkward insertion of the heroic age into his otherwise metallic typology. No doubt the prevailing cultural preference for epic heroism played some part in its inclusion. But there appears to be a deeper motive as well. In an erstwhile narrative of moral declension, the inclusion of hero-men suggests the prospect for at least partial human redemption. It is clear from the Prometheus myth—in which the theft of fire deprived humans of their Edenic existence—that the primordial happiness enjoyed by the golden men is beyond recovery (Hesiod 2006b, 40–89). However, accepting the constraints imposed by humanity's fall from grace, Hesiod appears to hold that *qualified* human happiness is possible through just agency, even if he is not sanguine about the prospects for his race of iron. ("I wish I were not among this last, fifth race of men," he declares, "But either dead already or had afterwards been born" [2006b, 174–75].)

Supporting this partial redemption hypothesis is that among the metallic races, iron men appear to be uniquely free from predeterminism. Hesiod implies they enjoy the power to *choose* between the justice of the happy ages (golden and heroic) or the intemperance and wanton violence of the unhappy ones (silver and bronze) (Vernant 1960; Querbach 1985; although see West 1978, 173; Clay 2003, ch. 4). Equally unique is the evolutionary transition from the age of heroes to the age of iron. Each of the first four races was created anew—new races did not emerge until the earth had covered up the old. The iron race, however, is an unfortunate derivative of the heroic one; Hesiod bemoaning that his race is *now* iron suggests transformation from a previous condition rather than the construction of a new condition altogether (2006b, 176). Pathology has progressed, the implication seems to be, but the prognosis is not yet certain.

Hesiodic man is rescued from ambient despair by the power of human agency. His is a flickering message of hope for an age afflicted with evil. Volitional, justice authors binary outcomes. Where iron men choose less-than-human lives (infantilized or governed by passions), they will be assigned the chthonic fate of silver and bronze men. Where they live heroic lives, which is to say lives elevated by adherence to the principles of justice, they will retain a form of terrestrial immortality (the men of gold as earthly daemons and the heroic at the Isles of the Blest). Seen in this light, the *Works and Days* is a pagan exhortation to come to Jesus. One's salvational prospects turn on just agency, living her life in accordance with the balance and order (spelled out in the *Theogeny*) pleasing to the gods. Far from a burden to be added to the litany of human woe, Hesiod characterizes justice as an invitation to fulfillment.

While not as culturally celebrated as Homer, Hesiod enjoys a lasting influence upon ancient Greek ethics and aesthetics. In both his poetry and statesmanship, Solon, for example, amplifies Hesiod's implicit humanism. The tragedians continue the theme of humanity's complicated relationship with the gods. And the Socratic philosophers craft Hesiodic justice into the social imperative for heroic magnanimity in realization of just condition. Like Socrates (and as we will later see, Christian theologians from Augustine to Jonathan Edwards) Hesiod explicitly links the prospects of the soul to the fortunes of the ambient civic structure.

> [T]hose who give to strangers and natives what is due,
> Who keep the paths of justice straight, whatever may ensue,
> For them the city flourishes—its people thrive therefore;
> Peace that nurtures children reigns throughout the land, and war
> With all its woes is not ordained by Zeus who sees afar,
> Nor ever with straight-judging men is Famine present, nor
> Disaster, but they feast upon the fruits of what they till.
> Earth bears them a rich livelihood: the oak upon the hill
> Bears acorns in its branches, in its trunk bears honey bees,
> And wooly sheep are laden with the weight of heavy fleece,
> And women bring forth children who are like their fathers; so,
> Continually prospering, on ships they do not go—(225–37).

By contrast, the fate of the unjust city is far less enticing.

> Just retribution is assigned by Zeus who sees afar.
> Often a single evil man, reckless finagler,
> Makes an entire city suffer through his iniquities;
> From heaven the son of Kronos sends great woe to such as these:
> Famine and plague together, so that people get sick and die,
> Babies no longer born to women, households diminish—by
> The shrewdness of Olympian Zeus, who also yet again
> May choose to destroy the citadel or the army of such men,
> Or vengeance the son of Kronos may wreak on their ships upon the sea.
> Kings, you had better yourselves observe this justice carefully;
> For near among men there are deathless ones, yes deathless ones nearby,
> And they watch such men as with crooked judgments, judgments that cheat and lie . . . (Hesiod 2006b, 238–50).

Heroic Magnanimity

If Hesiod lays the groundwork for republican metaphysics, Socrates is the first to identify, however obliquely, the magnanimous hero. While he did not use the term himself, Socratic magnanimous heroes—philosopher kings—are the quintessential stewards of the good republic. Their principal function is to steer the ship of state, their philosophy employed instrumentally to the more prosaic end of politics. In contrast to Solonian and (as we will discuss) Aristotelian republicanism, the Socratic republic thrives not so much on adversarial countervailing institutional balance as an architectonic balance, assigning each individual an optimally efficient place in the great social chain of being.

The Socratic Hero

Socratic heroes' souls are governed by reason, nourished by wisdom, and moved by the love of knowledge. Unlike the masses over whom they should rightly preside, magnanimous heroes are perfected in the virtues that govern both (the last principles of) prudent action and (the first principles of) moral knowledge.[1] Great in their minds, they are good (or just) in their souls, which is to say, their souls are balanced and in cosmic harmony. Such just balance and just condition are not easily achieved. The Socratic soul is akin to a sheath enjoining three distinct entities—a multiheaded beast, a lion, and a human—within. Where the beast or the lion (the acquisitive and thymotic elements of the soul, respectively) enjoy free reign, injustice prevails. The beast and the lion starve and enfeeble the human (the reasoning element of the soul) before turning upon one another in contestation for mastery of the host. Deprived of the balance and harmony afforded by the dominance of reason, the dissatisfied host lurches from pillar to post seeking relief from the insatiability of misplaced values (Plato *Rep.*, 386a–92b; *Gorg.*, 493b–c, 573c–74a, 576c). Individuals governed by their acquisitive or thymotic appetites are possessed of tyrannical souls; they have no use for knowledge of the first principles of justice. They seek gratification only of their basest desires. Rutting about, "with eyes ever bent upon the earth and heads bowed down over their tables they feast like cattle, grazing and copulating, ever greedy for more of these delights, and in their greed kicking and butting one another with horns and hoofs of iron they slay one another in sateless avidity, because they are vainly striving to satisfy with things that are not real, the unreal and incontinent part of their souls" (Plato *Rep.*, 586a–b). It is only when the human within the sheath prevails—where the intellect governs the appetites—that each part will know and keep to its own place, such that when one rules the internal savages, she will be said to live humanly, even divinely.

What is true of the soul, for Socrates, is true of the state. Whether constructed to the pursuit of power by the oligarch, licentiousness or material indulgence by the democrat, honor by the timocrat, or any combination thereof, the city ungoverned by foundational philosophical principles is a republic at war with itself. A city governed by oligarchy is one in which the rich despise the poor and vice versa. One ruled by democracy suffers from the moral fallacies of the sophist. And just as Homer's timocratic warrior does not find fulfillment through his mad love for himself, nor does the city he governs find peace and stability.

In contrast to such suboptimal forms of governance is government by philosophers, vehicles for translation of cosmic principles into law—that magnanimous gift through which transcendent law-givers compel the transcendence of lesser individuals as well (Plato *Rep.*, 590d). The magnanimous philosopher is heroic. She is "the One behind the Many." Morally wise leader of the ignorant masses, perfected in all the virtues, she truly is Peleus's speaker of words and doer of deeds (Segal 1978, 321). She is greatly good—extraordinary in her wisdom, her knowledge of first moral principles, the wellspring from which all unified virtues flow. She knows the good, acts according to the good, and knows *why* the good is good.

To Socrates, magnanimous heroes contrast favorably with epic ones, the latter's heroism qualified by their inability to recognize that discrete excellences cannot, in themselves, be categorically good.[2] At best, epic heroes evince only spurious symptoms of virtue itself. Indeed, failing to understand the intellective substructure of true virtue, they confuse it with superior task-competence. They cannot appreciate the metaphysical truth that knowledge, not action, is the true hallmark of virtue. Illustrative is physical courage, the discrete excellence most venerated by Homeric heroes. Socrates concurs that courage is a virtue. But only as it really is, not as it might *appear* to be. What presents as courage in battle could well be something different, as in the reckless and single-minded pursuit of honor. Such a quest is inconsistent with the true nature—the Form—of courage, accessed through the intellect and only then put to practical purpose. Distinguishing discrete excellences from virtue itself, then, is Socrates's contention that all component virtues flow from a common intellective source. Consequently, the perfection of any single virtue is but a symptom of perfection of *all* the virtues. This unification of virtue constitutes the defining capacity of Socrates's magnanimous heroes and, by extension, the laws of the Socratic republic (Plato *Meno*, 87c–89a; see also Aristotle *NE*, 1144b, 10; *MM*, 24–30; *EE*, 1248b, 25–31).

If there is a metaphysical analog to the Homeric hero, it is the sophist, forebearer of the modern gaslighter. Both aspire to govern; neither is suited to the task. The one presumes a claim upon the deference of the masses, the other a claim upon their ignorance. The one relies on misplaced values; the other actively seeks to distort values. While the perils attendant to the timocrat are obvious, the sophist's mischief might be more pernicious. The timocrat appeals to noble sentiments; the sophist is a professional flatterer and teller of fables, claiming the capacities of the philosopher, while demonstrating only the talents of those best suited to leave the process of governing to others (Plato *Rep.*, 558b–c; *Gorg.*, 464b–66a; see also the position of the Eleatic Stranger in the *Statesmen*, 303c). Sophistry is the calling card not of the philosopher king, but of the populist democrat. It indulges what Socrates sees as the fantasy of a mystical sort of collective magnanimity, an alchemical belief that the aggregated virtues of the masses are somehow a substitute for the singular great goodness of the heroically magnanimous. A good example of such magical thinking is Pericles's *epitaphios* to the dead of the Peloponnesian War, which locates heroism not just in the exploits of dead warriors, but in the civic virtues of Athens itself (Thucydides 1998, II. 39–43; Pearson 1943, 407; Bosworth 2000, 12, 15; Colaiaco 2001, 76, 98). As an amused Socrates tells the eponymous character in the *Menexenus*,

> I . . . become enchanted by [laudations of corporate excellence], and all in a moment I imagine myself to have become a greater and nobler and finer man than I was before. And if, as often happens, there are any foreigners who accompany me to the speech, I become suddenly conscious of having a sort of triumph over them, and they seem to experience a corresponding feeling of admiration at me, and at the greatness of the city, which appears to them, when they are under the influence of the speaker, more wonderful than ever. This consciousness of dignity lasts me more than three days, and not until the fourth or fifth day do I come to my senses and know where I am; in the meantime I have been living in the Islands of the Blest. (235)

Socrates can joke, but he sees good governance as serious business. To his mind, the problem with Athenian democracy, and indeed all democracy, is that it privileges process over outcome, input over output, freedom over justice. Given the diverse quality of democratic participants, the prospects for laws reflective of just cosmic principles are pretty bleak. By contrast, in the best republic, the operative principles of government and law are informed by the apotheotic wisdom of one bound only to the "divine ruler within himself." Obviously, it would be ideal if each person had such capacity for divine wisdom. But ideals should not be confused with expectations. For Socrates, the wisdom to unlock the Forms exceeds the capacity of most people. And the only alternative to that which cannot be cultivated within is for it to be imposed from the outside. For this reason, just as the master governs the household in the best interest of each, so too should the most magnanimous govern the state (Plato *Rep.*, 590c–d; this is also the Athenian Stranger's position in the *Laws* [689e]).

The magnanimous philosopher is a statesman, but like Socrates himself, she is no politician. Her qualification to govern owes nothing to political acumen, to the disingenuous ability to tell the masses what they wish to hear. She is qualified because she is perfected in her knowledge of the objective—and hence noncontestable—properties of goodness. By logical extension, justice is not to be found in restricting the authority of singularly good individuals any more than it is to be found in promoting the self-assertion of strong ones or the collective will of many. The Solonian solution of balancing weak against strong and the Homeric ideal of heroic self-assertions are pathological deviations—corruptions informed by an appeal to self-interest—from the true Form of justice (Saxonhouse 2012, 43). Justice suffers from too many hands in the construction of laws. It does not lie in the evolutionary give-and-take that informs mixed or democratic politics. Rather, the Eleatic Stranger tells Young Socrates, it is imposed and justified by a singular philosopher whose laws exceed those of the evolutionary model both in coherence and applicability to circumstance (Plato *States.*, 293b–96a, 300a–e, 305e). Far from being dependent on the good will of the governed, the Socratic magnanimous hero is liberated by disinterest in the prevailing order, free to act as needed in the preservation of the social good.

What is true for stewardship of stable regimes is even more critical in cases where society has lost its way, as in Athens during the plague that followed hard on the heels of Pericles's panegyric to Athenian virtue.[3]

Wayward societies cry out for redemption, to be rescued not merely from symptomatic crisis, but from the underlying pathology born of "heroic" sophistry or self-assertion. Under such circumstances, the magnanimous redemptive hero can brook no compromise in reimposing anew the principles of cosmic justice. She must operate under no democratic illusions. She needs to be clear in her mind that philosophical redemption is, as Walzer puts it, "an authoritarian business" (1981, 381).

In imposing her virtue as law, the magnanimous hero is at her most estimable. She is the singular embodiment of the apotheotic soul's guardian. Steward of the good society, she imposes the first principles of justice, providing nourishing virtue to otherwise famished souls. Her wisdom is her benefaction, an exhortation to tame the bestial impulse that thrives in darkness and shadow. It is she that casts the light, guiding souls still corporeally bound toward it and permitting ethereal souls to escape the blackness of Hades and the everlasting chthonic slumber that awaits the ignorant and unjust (Plato *Rep.*, 386–91, 540b–c; *Phae.*, 63b–69e; see also Segal 1978, 320–22, 329; Walzer 1981, 380; Eisner 1982, 107–9; Stefanson 2004, 101–2).

ARISTOTLE AND JUSTICE

Far more than Socrates, Aristotle is willing to compromise philosophical singularity in the name of political practicality. As with Socrates, he sees the republic and its laws as the means to such an end. And he acknowledges the differential metaphysical capacity among citizens. However, he differs in a number of ways—most pertinently, in his understanding of a good life realized through the completeness—as opposed to Socratic unification—of virtue; his conception of the relationship between ethics and politics; and his (less heroic) mandate for the magnanimous, or great-souled, man. (The scholarly literature is divided as to the extent to which Aristotelian magnanimity is a political or philosophical good [e.g., Gauthier 1951; Jaffa 1952; Hardie 1978; Hanley 2002]. As discussed below, I interpret him to hold both as central to heroic magnanimity [see also Arnhart 1983].)

Aristotle's point of departure from Socrates begins with his understanding of the virtue requisite to the *eudaemonic* life. Rather than conceiving virtue as product of a common intellective wellspring, Aristotle understands it in terms of realization of a complete end, which he characterizes as self-sufficient, or wanting for no greater quantity or supplement. Fulfilled, in other words, the *eudaemonic* life does not crave *greater* fulfillment (Aristotle *NE*, 1172b, 30–35, 1176b, 6–10). Equally, a complete end is intrinsically good and noncontingent. It is prized for itself, only for itself, and not for any other purpose. Finally, a complete end represents humanity's ultimate purpose. All other ends, even if themselves intrinsically valued, are means to this end (*NE*, 1097a, 26–30, 1097b, 7–21; *MM*, 1183b, 38–1184a, 14).

What sort of life leads to such a complete end? Socrates manifestly favors the apotheotic life of philosophical contemplation. Aristotle is less adamant and in some sense more ambiguous. He begins by laying out the Pythagorean candidates for the best sort of life: the life of material and corporeal gratification; the practical life of active virtue (virtue in deed); and the life of philosophical contemplation (virtue in wisdom) (*NE*, 1095b, 15–16). As with Socrates, he dismisses the first as the basest and least desirable life. The life of pleasure is the ordinary life, governed by the appetites; it is beneath the dignity of humanity, informing instead what Aristotle calls a "life for grazing animals" (*NE*, 1095a, 21).

Aristotle's second life is the life of practical goodness, or good character; it is one in which the agent habitually makes appropriate life choices; one where she not only chooses well, but *wishes* to choose well. It is a life in which goodness has evolved from duty to habit, in which the natural quest for gratification and pleasure has succumbed to goodness as second nature. One does not acquire goodness passively—through fortune or sudden conversion, seized by good character in the way that the Calvinist saint, for example, is seized by the saving grace of God. But neither is it acquired through mere force of will. One cannot spontaneously will herself to a life of active virtue any more than a person might suddenly will herself to good health. Rather, like health born of programmatic exercise and healthy nutrition, one acquires goodness through regimen. It presents as conditioned reflexivity, the moral muscle memory that subdues irrational impulses (Aristotle *NE*, 1099a, 13–21, 1103a, 19–26, 1114a, 12–22; *MM* 1186a, 4–5, 1187a, 7–19; *EE*, 1220a, 11–12, 1220b, 1–4; Sullivan 1974, 34; Korsgaard 1986).

Cosmically, Aristotle's second life is just; it promotes just agency and just condition. Consistent with Solonian balance, one is said to choose well when her actions are temperate, when they find the mean between excess and deficiency of a particular quality, as informed by the circumstances in which that quality is operative. The active virtues are not learned by rote. Rather, deduced from moral precepts, they reflect the judgment of the good citizen, her actions appropriate to ambient conditions. The good citizen benefits herself and her society by being good. The obverse is equally true. A good republic serves its own ends when it teaches its citizens to live their best and most fulfilling lives. The good citizen and the good republic, then, feed off one another in an iterative process of virtuous recursivity. There is a sense in Aristotle that goodness is more foundational to the republic than greatness. Goodness precludes the principal-agent problem attendant to greatness, in that good people are more likely to choose temperate policies requisite to peace and justice and less apt to gratify their own egoistic desires at the expense of the general good (*NE*, esp. bk. 10, ch. 6; *MM*, bk. I, chs. 8–9; *EE*, bk. II, ch. 3, esp. 1220b, 25–1221a, 12).

Aristotle's third life is the philosophical life of contemplative virtue. It is the best life of the three, which we can cast in a strictly ordinal sense as choosing poorly (the life of animals), choosing well (the life of humans), and enlightenment (the life of gods) (*NE*, 1099b, 33–1100a, 5, 1178b, 25–26; see also Cicero *DO*, bk. I, 14). There are good reasons to privilege the philosophical life, it being the most self-sufficient life, the least vulnerable to misfortune. Evil fate can influence what one does and feels, but knowledge and understanding remain unbowed in the face of misfortune (Arnhart 1983, 265–66). Equally, the contemplative life is the best life in that it is the most harmonious with divine principles that inform the universe. It is the life led by the gods and most suited to the gods (*NE*, 1177b, 34–1178a, 1, 1178b, 10–25). Indeed, Aristotle proclaims, "We ought not to follow the makers of proverbs and 'Think human since you are human,' or 'Think mortal since you are mortal.' Rather, as far as we can we ought to be pro-immortal, and go to all lengths to live a life in accord with our supreme element" (Aristotle *NE*, 1177b, 34–1178a, 1). In proclaiming the superiority of the contemplative life, Aristotle leaves readers of the *Ethics* a bit bemused. After spending the majority of his ethical treatises exhorting the life of active virtue, his conclusion that the contemplative is the best of the three Pythagorean lives is disconcerting. One is left to wonder if Aristotle imparts the *intellectualist* position that the philosophical and *eudaemonic* life are one and the same. Or if he means instead that the contemplative life is the best *part* of a *eudaemonic* life. I tend toward the latter, *inclusivist* reading, which emphasizes just balance between the imperatives of the second and third lives.

The intellectualist is correct to note that Aristotle exhorts us to be "pro-immortal," not to think human just because we are human. But in contemplation of universals, Aristotle does not ask us to transcend our humanity, to eschew the uniquely human function (*ergon*) that assigns to humanity its specific cosmic teleology. Aristotle says of mortals, which he would not say of gods, that too much contemplation comes at the expense of the good, that it is possible to pursue to the philosophical life to excess. Human beings are not gods and thus cannot be expected to live like them (*NE*, 1153a, 20; Adkins 1978, 300). In *On the Parts of Animals*, he insists,

> The scanty conceptions to which we can attain of celestial things give us, from their excellence, more pleasure than all our knowledge of the world in which we live; just as a half glimpse of persons we love is more delightful than a leisurely view of other things, whatever their number and dimensions. On the other hand, in certitude and in completeness our knowledge of terrestrial things has the advantage. Moreover, their greater nearness and affinity to us balances somewhat the loftier interest of the heavenly things that are the objects of the higher philosophy. (644b, 31–645a, 4)

Perhaps the strongest argument for inclusivism is that it is the only reading consistent with Aristotle's understanding of completeness.[4] For example, the claim that study makes us happy and more study makes us happier (*NE* 1178b, 29–31) makes sense only from the inclusivist perspective. If we were to read it as evidence of the completeness of the contemplative life, Aristotle runs afoul of his own injunction that a complete end is self-sufficient, wanting for no greater supplement. A complete end axiomatically cannot be enhanced by ever-greater pursuit of the element that makes it the best. Similarly, there is instrumental quality to the life of contemplation, which makes it inconsistent with Aristotle's definition of a complete end. Aristotle suggests that since the gods affect the fortunes of human beings, and since they find the contemplative life most pleasing, they are more likely to favor human beings who engage in philosophical contemplation.[5] But of course, if winning the favor of the gods is the objective, the contemplative life cannot be a *purely* intrinsic end, disqualifying it as a complete end. Finally, the logic of Aristotelian inclusivism solves the intellectualist paradox.

Aristotle's Great-Souled Man and Heroic Magnanimity

Heroically, Aristotle's theory of completeness informs the distinction between his great-souled man and Socrates's philosopher king. If the best individuals are those who perfect both the active and contemplative virtues, who live Aristotle's second and third lives conjunctively, we need to evaluate their heroism and their place in stewardship of the republican social order. To this end, we can think of heroic magnanimity in two ways: as the *singular* magnanimity of the Socratic philosopher and the Aristotelian great-souled man, or as the *class-based* magnanimity supplied by an aristocracy of virtue. Aristotle is far less sanguine about heroic magnanimity of a singular individual than is Socrates. However, he is in accord that the perfection of virtue is, at its core, an intellective exercise.

Like Socrates, Aristotle begins with the soul. He holds that the reasoning element is dichotomous, consisting of a practical, deductive element and a contemplative, inductive element (*NE*, 1139a, 6–10, 1139b, 25–34). The former he calls "right reason" or "prudence" governing the choices we make in our practical, active, day-to-day lives. The latter is wisdom, the knowledge and understanding of first principles. To live the very best, or ideal, life, virtue demands more than prudential knowledge of *how* to be good.[6] It requires knowing goodness itself (knowing the *Form* of goodness, if Aristotle were inclined to couch first principles in such language, which he is not).[7] To illustrate the distinction, when one knows the appropriate course of action in a given circumstance, she is none the *wiser* for her prudence. Her position is akin to knowing what sort of medicine to take in alleviation of her symptoms, while remaining ignorant of the underlying cause of the complaint (*NE*, 1138b, 29–33). She is a good knower of precepts. But she lacks understanding of the originative and immutable principles from which precepts themselves are deduced (*NE*, 1139a, 7–9; see also 1141a, 16–22, 1142a, 25–29, 1151a, 17–19).

Aristotle's great-souled man is singular. Superior to all others in every respect, his conjunctive virtues adorn him like a crown (*EE*, 1233a, 16–26). Given such perfection, one might expect Aristotle to be a little more excited about the great-souled man, more of a champion for his heroism and his place in the well-constituted republic. Yet Aristotle does not share Socrates's enthusiasm for the singularly magnanimous man. At best, the great-souled man is awkwardly heroic. At worst, reliance upon him can upset the social balance in a way that, as we will see in our discussion of Rome in the next chapter, produces the antithesis of a just moral order. Indeed, it is with Aristotle that we get the first important glimpse into the idea that excessive dependence upon singular heroes is unhealthy, that the land in need of such heroes might well be unhappier than the land that has none.

Aristotle's ambivalence is revealed by the unbecoming portrait he paints of the great-souled man. Worthy as he is, the great-souled individual does not bestir himself save for the worthiest of causes. He is a civic benefactor, but only because it is proper for superior individuals to have others in their debt. He takes the time to seek to impress those whose esteem he values; but he does not waste his time seeking to impress ordinary people, since to do so would be vulgar. He is brutally frank with his opinions, the strength of his convictions leaving him indifferent to the opinions of others (*NE*, 1124a, 20–1125a, 16). Recognizing his own extraordinary worth, he expects others to honor it. He is not vain, but only in the technical, it's-not-bragging-if-it's-true, sense that his self-esteem is in keeping with his singular virtue. Expecting to be affirmed in his greatness, he insists that honor be worthy of his stature. To that end, despising the honor of those unworthy, he will assent only to be honored by the very best people. Even so, his pleasure will be tempered with realization that they really cannot bestow any honor *truly* worthy of his peerless virtue (*NE*, 1123a, 35–1124a, 20).

From this sniffy portrait, Aristotle seems to conclude that the great-souled man must govern; he cannot, after all, be expected to follow the laws of inferior men. But is he a good leader? Unlike the philosopher king in the Socratic republic, the great-souled man fits uneasily into the ideal Aristotelian order. In part, this is because Aristotle tends far more willingly towards Solonian balance between the great and the many, than towards Socrates' inevitably authoritarian philosopher king. Indeed, insofar as his singularity threatens balance, the great-souled man threatens (cosmic) justice. Standing in displeasing proportion to others, the analogy is a portrait in which a subject's hands, exquisitely painted, are too large for the rest of the body (Aristotle *Pol.*, 1284b, 3–19). Given the great-souled man's antipathy to cosmic balance, the only alternatives republics face in his presence are to ostracize him or else make him a permanent king (*Pol.*, 1284b, 32–34).

Another nagging question that seems to prevent Aristotle's wholehearted endorsement of the great-souled man turns on whether or not his heroic qualities present as anything other than a heuristic. Rooted as he is in practicality, Aristotle cannot get past the asymptotic quality attendant to singularly great goodness. Indeed, while the great-souled man is peerlessly virtuous, he is still, after all, human. His perfection does not impute infallibility, disinterest in his material condition, or immunity to the trappings of power and prestige. Yet in order to be truly great souled, he would have to, in effect, transcend the pettiness that distinguishes mortals from gods (Howland 2002, 46). Does he? We have already noted that Aristotle characterizes the great-souled man as assenting only to such honors as he feels are worthy of his greatness. Left unmentioned in the *Nicomachean Ethics*, though, is the opposite circumstance, in which he *fails* to receive the honors he feels are due him. Were he truly great souled, we would expect him to accept such a lack of honor with equanimity. He would, like Socrates's just individual suffering material or physical duress, draw his fulfillment solely from knowledge of the goodness of his actions. He would not feel anger or resentment from a failure to be honored by those incapable of recognizing his superiority to them.

Aristotle does make oblique reference to the issue of insufficient honor in the *Posterior Analytics* when he characterizes Achilles, Ajax, and Alcibiades as great-souled men (97b, 15–21). None responds terribly well when his honor is insufficiently affirmed. Achilles contributes to Patroclus's death with his prolonged alienation at Agamemnon's insult. In the same vein, having been denied the honor of Achilles's armor, Sophocles's Ajax melts down completely, ultimately killing himself—but only after a murderous frenzy in which he takes out a sizable platoon of barnyard animals. Alcibiades was undoubtedly a great general, but Plutarch paints a portrait of him as a man whose jealousy for honor drove him to petty and duplicitous actions, culminating in his defection to Sparta during the Peloponnesian War (Plutarch 1952, *Alcib*; Howland 2002, 33–36).

This is not a mere quibble. True magnanimity and asymptotic magnanimity are as different from one another as the good king is to the bad tyrant. Absolutist leaders unable to transcend their personal interests are unlikely to govern in the public interest. For a good king to be superior to a balanced collection of roughly equal noblemen and commoners, disinterest must attach to singularity. Truly heroic magnanimity, for example, would preclude a good king from assigning a hereditary line of succession on the grounds that the greatness of the father represents no immunization against the ordinariness of the son. Yet Aristotle finds it far-fetched that any king could summon *this* degree of magnanimity (*Pol*, 1286b, 23–28). More problematically, where the erstwhile good king's magnanimity is not complete, he himself is liable to be a social danger. Should he feel underappreciated or feel that his position is in any way threatened, the protector of the people's interests becomes a potential antagonist to those very interests. As with the epic hero, the underappreciated great-souled man might very well present as a lion off the leash.

Aesthetics and Magnanimity

Socrates and Aristotle present very different views of the utility of magnanimous heroes to the good republic. Both perspectives will emerge again in this book. Before leaving the discussion of republican metaphysics and magnanimity in classical Greece, however, there is one more dimension of heroic magnanimity that assumes importance. Thus far we have presented the foundation of magnanimity as cognitive, grounded in philosophical ethics. But Socrates and Aristotle concede that goodness is not an exclusively cognitive proposition. Complementing judgment and sagacity, then, is aesthetics. How one is taught to *feel* about justice and injustice is also critical to the internalization of goodness. At the very least, an affective internalization of goodness reinforces cognitive understanding. More profoundly—although admittedly this is more the insistence of the modern Romantic than the ancient tragedian—affective virtue provides a check upon cognitive virtue, provoking inquiry into the nature of justice when the two fail to accord.

Greek tragedy provoked receptivity to didactic tutelage, the locus of tragedy being the absence of heroic magnanimity. Rather than conditioning thought and deed, tragedians employed the sublime emotions of empathy and sympathy to exhort their audiences towards the moral precepts requisite to human fulfillment. The subtext is that where justice is present, it protects weak and strong alike; where it is absent, all are made to suffer. As such, the tragedian portrayal of heroic magnanimity is quite different than its philosophical counterpart. On the stage, heroic relevance resided in the breach—its absence the difference between a good or tragic outcome (Aristotle, *Poet.*, 1448b, 24–1449a, 7, 1452a, 2–6, 1452b, 32–34, 1453a, 5–7; Berlin 1999, 10; Frye 1957, 33).

Aesthetic magnanimity reflects the republican imperatives of just balance, just agency, and just condition. Undergirding the work of classical Greece's great tragedians are a number of themes of interest. One is that the appeal to affect suggests that justice is imparted not merely through imposition of law, but through cultural absorption. Another is the imperative for virtuous balance between the laws of the gods and the laws of mortals. A third is that Greek tragedy represents more evidence of the classical paradigm shift away from the unjust timocracy of the Homeric hero and towards the metaphysical justice implicit in a well-ordered civil society. Finally, tragedy is important to the task at hand in that it sets the stage for two themes explored in later chapters—the basis of Romantic aesthetic heroism and the implicit Christian divide as to the relative importance of the spiritual and natural orders.

Hecuba

A good example of the cultural heroic paradigm shift reflected in Greek tragedy is Euripides' *Hecuba*. Early in the play, Achilles's ghost appears, requesting that the victorious Greeks honor him by sacrificing the daughter of the Trojan Queen. Odysseus, who is in Hecuba's debt for saving his life, is forced to choose: save the child or yield to the duty he perceives to his fellow warriors. Couching cowardice in grandiloquence, Odysseus explains that he cannot subordinate his social duty to a personal obligation. Achilles fought and died for the Achaean cause, and for that he deserves to be honored. It is, after all, poor policy indeed if great warriors cannot count on being honored upon their deaths (1938, 218–331). Of course, since heroic death can be honored in any number of ways that does not involve the slaughter of children, Odysseus's excuse is fatuous. In response, Hecuba rejects the distinction between private and public obligation. There is justice, and there is injustice, cosmic conditions independent of social context. Host is obligated to guest; strong are obligated to weak (as Hecuba had demonstrated in her mercy towards Odysseus); conquerors are obliged to vanquished. Positive laws serve the cause of justice, but justice cannot survive the laws of man when out of harmony with the laws of the gods.

Later, Hecuba makes another unsuccessful plea for justice to another insubstantial timocratic man. To escape the fall of Troy, Priam and Hecuba had entrusted their young son's care to the Thracian king Polymestor. Young Polydorus had with him considerable Trojan gold, for which Polymestor killed him and cast his corpse into the sea. In appealing for retribution, Hecuba speaks to Agamemnon's prerogative as a good man, his duty to "help the right, and to punish evil-doers wherever found" (1938, 844–46). Her appeal is to justice, for her son, for herself, for the gods, and for all humanity. It is to a justice that cannot be parsed or selectively practiced. Indeed, if this foundational principle of justice "is to be set at nothing, and they are to escape punishment who murder guests or dare to plunder the temples of gods, then all fairness in human matters is at an end" (798–805). Like Odysseus, however, Agamemnon takes refuge in a specious hierarchy of obligations, demurring that it would not sit well with the army if Agamemnon were to kill the Thracian king for the sake of his concubine's mother (850–63).

Victimized by injustice—by the decoupling of terrestrial law from cosmic law, and moral obligation from civic—Hecuba now is forced to counter injustice with injustice by taking matters into her own hands. Having lost two children with no prospect for retributive justice, the audience cannot help but sympathize with Hecuba's lust for vengeance. Euripides's moral message, however, cannot be left at the suggestion that vengeance is a substitute for justice, that justice attaches equally well to the balance of vice and the balance of virtue. Hecuba takes her revenge by depriving Polymestor of his sight. She also kills his two young sons. For the audience, this last is a step too far. Sympathizing with her outrage, the audience cannot condone the beastly killing of innocents. And so in the end, having acted like an animal, Hecuba literally is transformed into one, drawing her last breath not as a human being but as a dog, as the beast she has become (Corey and Eubanks 2003, 244–45; although see Mossman 1995, esp. 188–89).

OEDIPUS

Sophocles's *Oedipus* trilogy reinforces Euripides's imperative to balance the laws of gods and mortals. Sophocles employs the metaphor of sight as manifestation of justice. The tragedy of the *Antigone*, for example, is that Creon and Antigone are both too blind to the moral imperative upon which the other insists. Like Hecuba, Antigone is the more sympathetic character. Faced with Creon's unjust decree that her brother Polyneices, as an enemy of Thebes, be left unburied, Antigone couches her defiant and unrepentant response in an appeal to a higher authority. "Not for fear of any man's pride," she proclaims, "was I about to owe a penalty to the gods.... And if my present actions are foolish in your sight, it may be that it is a fool who accuses me of folly" (458–60). The audience's sympathy for Antigone is guided by the Chorus, which, although slow to admit that there exists a greater authority than terrestrial law, eventually comes to take her side. Certainly, Creon's misery at the end of the play—he loses his son and his wife—stands as testimony to the hubris of asserting the supremacy of the laws of man over those of the gods. "The great words of arrogant men," the Chorus tells us, "have to make repayment with great blows, and in old age teach wisdom" (1891, 1347 ff).

In privileging his own monarchical hubris over the law of the gods, Creon is manifestly a knave. But does his villainy justify Antigone's impudence in her provocative defiance of his authority? Antigone's dogmatic attachment to godly principles scarcely leads to greater happiness. She is entombed and subsequently hangs herself, unrepentant to the end. Accusing Antigone of injustice seems strong. But that seems to have been Sophocles's intent. He could have selected a different end for her. Indeed, if she had been in the right, Haemon presumably would have succeeded in his mission to rescue her. But Sophocles does not want his audience to go away with the simplistic message that justice constitutes dogmatic adherence to cosmic principles any more than he wants us to feel it to be found in blind deference to worldly principles.

In a similar vein, in the *Oedipus Rex*, Oedipus shares Creon's hubris in privileging the worldly over the spiritual. Self-sufficient in his worldly reason, he disdains those reliant upon divine principles—imparted, as he sees it, by the chirping and twittering of oracles. It was he, after all, who had solved the riddle of the Sphinx "through my wit alone, untaught by birds" (1887, 395 ff). It is his temporal self-sufficiency—that which permits him to see so clearly—which informs his angry confrontation with the blind seer Teiresias. When Oedipus provokes the reluctant Teiresias into revealing that the killer of his father, Laius, was none other than Oedipus himself, Oedipus refuses to believe it. He admonishes the blind man for his audacious proclamation and equally impudent defense that in the truth of what he sees there is strength. "You do not have that strength, since you are maimed in your ears, in your wit, and in your eyes .... Night, endless night has you in her keeping, so that you can never hurt me, or any man that sees the light of the sun" (Sophocles 1887, 370–75). The irony goes deeper than the fact that endless night soon was to have Oedipus in her keeping as well. It is Oedipus's inability to see things as they really are—that his wife and mother are one and the same and that he is a patricide—that leads to the tragic self-mutilation of the eyes that failed him.

Oedipus's banishment from Thebes ultimately highlights Athens' status as the pinnacle of Greek justice. Hostage neither to the whims of the gods, nor the folly of mortals, Athens represents the temperate mean in which justice resides. By the *Oedipus at Colonus*, Oedipus has fallen to depths that matched the great heights of his days as king. He has passed his days blind and penniless, infamous for murder and incest, sustained only by the love of his daughters Antigone and Ismene. Yet through his ordeal he has purged the guilt that persisted after his self-mutilation. Blind, he has come to see that he was not to blame for defending himself against his father or his unwitting relationship with his mother, and that he is thus deserving of forgiveness. Of course, while the Furies may have forgiven Oedipus, Thebes will not relent in its condemnation of his unintentional moral trespass.

Once again, Creon's injustice is highlighted by his inability to align himself with cosmic principles of justice. In contrast to Creon, the Athenian king Theseus offers Oedipus sanctuary in Athens. And despite Oedipus' wretched condition, Theseus also rescues the blind beggar's daughters (whom Creon had kidnapped to entice Oedipus back to Thebes) from Creon's evil designs. Indeed, just as Creon is the incarnation of Theban perfidy, Theseus represents the majesty of Athenian justice. In refusing Oedipus forgiveness, Creon implies that he knows better than the gods. Theseus, on the other hand, grants worldly forgiveness in accordance with the moral laws of the deities.

Eumenides

The superiority of such balanced Athenian justice is also a dominant theme in Aeschylus's *Eumenides* (1926c). After the Trojan War, the returning Agamemnon is murdered by Clytemnestra. Orestes is faced with the decision of slaying his mother or leaving his father's murder unavenged. In avenging Agamemnon, he is hounded by the Furies, who threaten to wreak havoc upon Athens for his acquittal in the Aerogapus. Calming the crones, Athena invites them to see past their reflexive justice-as-vengeance in favor of an evolved sense of justice that balances emotion and reason, evaluating the justness of an act in its proper moral context. In the case of avenging Orestes's matricide, reason dictates that when irreconcilable moral obligations conflict, culpability cannot attach to the decision to satisfy one moral obligation over an equally compelling one. It is only when the Furies come to terms with this core principle of Athenian justice that reason comes to temper their emotive fury. Indeed, with the acceptance of this transcendent form of justice comes their own transcendence—from chthonic crones to benevolent Eumenides (Fuller 1915, 477–79).

The emotive power of Greek tragedy serves the dual purpose of imparting the first principles of justice as an alternative to the coercive power of law, while simultaneously proclaiming the imperative of good citizens to comply with just law. Subtextually, tragedy decouples justice from strength, removing it from the anarchical martial theater of the epic hero operating under the rules and whims of the gods and situating it within a civil order governed by just laws. Equally, it conceives justice as a Solonian, communal, good, thereby contrasting it with the Homeric hero's conception of justice as a private matter between those of sufficient strength to ensure justice for themselves and those whose weakness precludes it.

Conclusion

The predominance of the epic model of heroism during the archaic and classical periods of ancient Greece overshadowed heroic great goodness. Yet it was during these critical centuries that our enduring understanding of republican justice emerged. Indeed, the refinement of justice—marrying the Hesiodic principle that justice demands conformity to cosmic imperatives to the Solonian humanist one that justice is a social construction—gave rise to the metaphysical dimension of republicanism that emerged in classical Athens. Even today, it is all but impossible to parse conceptions of goodness, such as those inherent to Christianity, the Enlightenment and contemporary politics of social identity, from the foundational ideas discussed in this chapter. Whether such metaphysical perfection was formal and cognitive (as in the unified virtue of Socrates, or the more conjunctive virtue of Aristotle) or counterfactual and affective (as in the didacticism of the tragedians), in classical Athens metaphysics elevated magnanimity from the quaint to the heroic.

For Socrates, the extraordinary metaphysical capacity for transcendence, estimability in virtue, and vulnerability in social marginalization makes the philosopher the quintessential magnanimous hero and steward of the good republic. If Socrates shies away from the word "hero" as too evocative of the timocrat, he is not shy about describing his own experiences and social benefaction in conformity to the heroic criteria established here. The harmony and balance of the Socratic hero's gold-tinged soul represents a template for social architectonics. Socratic magnanimity therefore speaks to the imperative for a strict and cogent division of labor between those suited to govern and those suited to *be* governed. Far more than Aristotle, Socrates celebrates the singularity of the magnanimous hero, assigning to her the mandate of providing the laws and encouraging the optimal social architecture. By contrast, Aristotle's magnanimous man is far more ambiguously heroic, his magnanimity discussed here in anticipation of the exploration of Rome in the next chapter. More Solonian in his institutionalism, Aristotle is skeptical of the means by which the balance and harmony of the magnanimous soul translates into the balance and harmony of the good society. His form of Solonian balance presents as a governing division of labor, in which the prudence of the masses tempers the excesses of a parliament of greatly good individuals.

If the philosophers of classical Athens spoke to ethical magnanimity, the arts inculcated justice through aesthetic didacticism. Rather than promoting a particular archetype of magnanimous hero, tragedian playwrights couched tragedy in the nullification of magnanimity. Their focus, then, is not so much on heroes as antiheroes—protagonists tragic for the want of heroic magnanimity. In their own ways, Euripides, Sophocles, and Aeschylus use their protagonists as exemplars to proclaim the imperative for Solonian balance; not within the Socratic soul or Aristotelian institutions of government, but between the orders spiritual and temporal. In this way, at least, they anticipated a central issue pertaining to the Christian magnanimity discussed in chapter 4.

Chapter 3

Rome and the Limits of Heroic Magnanimity
The Great, the Greatly Good, and the Not So Good

Republican Rome lay at the nexus of epic and magnanimous heroism. Roman republicans understood heroism in terms of the coincidence of physical greatness and metaphysical goodness, epic and magnanimous heroism as flip sides of the same coin. Both were equally important to the process of good republican government. As it pertained to physical heroism, a robust masculinity informed the Roman ideal (esp. McDonnell 2006). Physical virtue was conceived in terms of the manly virtues (*virilis virtus*) of courage, martial prowess, horsemanship, athletic ability, leadership, and other manifestations of virility. At the same time, Roman heroism demanded great goodness and selfless public service on the part of Rome's very best citizens. The twin attributes of greatness and great goodness were essential to Romans' cultural sense of themselves as a people. Good government thus demanded the husbandry of heroic individuals—as defenders, stewards, redeemers, exemplars, and nation builders—and therefore afforded only the very best the privilege of public service (Cunningham 1980, 10). Metaphysically, Roman justice was hard-headed and pragmatic. If it retained the Socratic assumption of unified virtues, it inverted the relative importance of the private and public. The Socratic philosophers had begun from the premise that social goodness is a positive externality of personal development, the good state serving the transcendent soul. Cicero and other Roman philosophers tend toward the opposite perspective—that while virtue brings with it private benefits, it is an inherently public good (Cicero *DO*, bk. I, 19, 51, 57–58, 62, 70–73, 85, 153, 157; bk. III, 25; 2006, 137–139; *Rep.*, bk. I, 3, 7–12, 33; bk. III, 6, 12).

Having demonstrated great martial or administrative capacity, Rome's most heroic citizens were charged with leading and defending the republican empire in service to the common weal. Esteemed to the point of apotheosis, they were stewards of the ancient customs and mores (*mos maiorum*) that constituted the Roman Constitution. In Socratic unification, their bravery bespoke sagacity, metaphysical greatness the presumptive extension of their courage. Such singular individuals were akin to gods among men, selfless saviors bringing the fruits of their talents to bear in such fashion that from its inception the republic took "its character from that of its foremost men. Whatever changes have taken place in the conduct of its leaders have been reproduced in the lives of the people" (Cicero *Laws*, bk. III, 31; see also *Rep.*, bk. I, 43–64, esp. 55; 2006, 98–99; *DO*, bk. I, 70–72).[1]

Yet the republican heroes of the Roman Republic ultimately fought a losing battle, vulnerable to the asymptotic magnanimity of which Aristotle implicitly warns. Indeed, during the Late Republic, many of Rome's very best men became its very worst. In this sense, the current chapter represents a critique of civic humanism, of investment in the enlightened statesmen of whom Madison warns. It views Rome through the perspective of such proponents of personal—as opposed to institutional—perfection as Polybius, Sallust, Livy, and, most prominently, Cicero. It begins with a discussion of Ciceronian republicanism and the conviction that goodness attaches naturally to virtuous individuals. It emphasizes the Roman Republic's unique institutional dynamics that, uncodified, were designed to create what amounted to a market for heroism. The discussion next turns to Rome's tragic failure of heroic magnanimity and the problems posed when greatness diverges from goodness. The weakness of Rome's institutions not only failed to facilitate the civic humanism so integral to Cicero's good republic, but it exacerbated Rome's cultural disposition towards corrupted magnanimity. Taking the form of big man politics, corrupted magnanimity was at the heart of the clientelistic corruption of the Roman state. The chapter thus speaks to a larger argument that undergirds the book: the potential for any republican hero type to become corrupted and hence politically dysfunctional.

Cicero and Roman Civic Humanism

Consul, new man, philosopher, and foremost apostle of Socratic magnanimity in the Late Republic, Cicero captures the ingenuous optimism of the civic humanist—the conviction that the perfection of virtuous leaders trumps the crafting of better rules to constrain them. He retains a commitment to heroic statesmanship even in the face of the corruption that ultimately brought the republic down. His is a utopian view of the symbioses of greatness and goodness, grounded in the conviction that justice ultimately prevails over evil. Clinging to his belief in the efficacy of heroes great and good with the tenacity of a Sophoclean protagonist, he meets the same sort of tragic ending. His perspective is informed by his prominence in public life in the period between the two civil wars of the first century BC. Driven by the conviction that Rome was only as great as the goodness of its best men, his disillusionment over the distemper of his age is tinged with the optimism born of Rome's long and happy history of serendipitous production of heroes in times of need. Alas, for Cicero and Rome, Late Republican Rome—a land without heroes—relied too greatly on the existence of them.

NATURAL GOODNESS

Faith in great and good individuals had long served Rome well. The republic saw times of trouble throughout its history, but none that could best the heroic leaders that reliably emerged to protect and preserve it, to redeem its ills and forge its sense of national self. These magnanimous *boni*, or *optimates*, who had proven themselves physically and metaphysically, distinguished themselves as faithful custodians of the *mos maiorum*. That for four hundred years Rome had produced a succession of such individuals stood as testimony to the iterative power of nobility and the promise of reproductive magnanimity (Cicero *Rep.*, bk. V. pref.). Bulwarks against the depravity of lesser individuals, these servants of Rome embodied virtuous sacrifice for the republic. Heroic exemplars, symbols for emulation, they spoke not only to the moral quality of their own generation, but that of the next as well.

It was a bitter irony, then, that Cicero's times manufactured so little goodness. With a few exclusions—Cicero finds exception in himself, Cato the Younger, and (no doubt out of expediency) Pompey—the greatest men of Cicero's Rome lacked ethical will. Demagogic and self-assertive, they turned against the state in pursuit of narrow and selfish ends. Through the Social War, the First Civil War between Sulla and Marius, the Catiline conspiracy during his own consulship, Pompey's aggressive stance against the Senate in the sixties, Caesar's crossing of the Rubicon, and finally his own execution for opposing Mark Antony, Cicero bore witness to the progressive deterioration of Rome's abiding republican principles. Yet, the obverse of Hesiod lamenting that fate had situated him in his times, almost to the bitter end, Cicero maintains his optimism for heroic redemption of the republic.

Concurring with Socrates that virtue constitutes its own reward, Cicero conceives heroic magnanimity as a robust good. All things equal, he avers, corrupt self-assertion cannot vanquish the just agency, natural and perfected, of the very best citizens (Cicero DO, bk. II, 23–29, bk. III, 26, 31, 47–49, 52–53, 72, 101). He does, of course, allow for unjust individuals. But the condition is deviative and fragile. Like a wall without mortar, the edifice such individuals seek to construct is structurally unsound (Laws, bk. I, 33, 43; DO, bk. II, 9–10, bk. III, 7–31). While unjust individuals may appear great and powerful, their actions are unreasoned. Contending with perpetual vulnerability, they are obliged to rely upon fear as an alternative to the legitimacy that attends just government. Yet when rulers govern by fear, they court the revenge of those who have cause to hate them for their caprice and intemperance. They are obliged to commit extensive resources to the perpetuation of their power, which only intensifies resentment. Contrast this to just governance, whereby magistracies are held by the most magnanimous citizens, acquiring and exercising their just authority through legitimate means. Such heroic leaders enjoy the loyalty and support of their people. Liberated from the imperative to prioritize their own protection from the mobs that despise them, they are rewarded with the honor, reputation, and status that great virtue bestows (Cicero DO, bk. II, 30–43; bk. III, 84–85).

The Market for Heroism

For the magnanimous to govern, however, they must first be identified, a curriculum that represented a considerable component of Roman public life. Identification was a programmatic process in which young men competed with one another in demonstration of the virtue requisite to high office. In theory, there was social profit in such a competitive market for heroic public service. Romans saw the process as a way of identifying young men of substance, optimizing virtue in the same way that an economic market optimizes wealth (Lintott 1999, 65–66; Rosenstein 1990, 4–5).

Unfortunately, the analogy holds only so far. The first significant difference is the assumed conflation of self-interest and public interest. In an economic market it is reasonable to assume such conflation. The logic

Rome and the Limits of Heroic Magnanimity | 81

of the free market demonstrates harmony, as Bernard Mandeville insists, between private vices and public benefit. Self-interest in the single-minded pursuit of wealth yields a temperate balance, an optimal economic equilibrium that emerges from discrete interests operating in competition with one another. By contrast, such single-minded self-centeredness in the market for heroic public service has no such salutary effects. Military commanders, for example, who recklessly risk their men in pursuit of honor, serve their own interests at the expense of the general interest. Liberality on the part of public officials, burnishing their reputations (or fattening their pocketbooks) through excessive public spending, very often leads to less-than-optimal outcomes. Such self-regard erodes the common weal, untempered as it is by the countervailing forces it encounters in an economic market (Rosenstein 1990, 3-4).

A more significant point of distinction between economic markets and the market for heroic public service is that economic markets are bounded by universally accepted rules enforced by a disinterested third party. They mandate a regulatory role for the state as a hedge against market failure or unfair practice. If market principles are to be effectively extended into the political realm, they too must be bounded by common rules and effective enforcement. Certainly, this is possible. The genius of Madisonian constitutional principles, for example, embraces market logic, but demands that competing interests be bounded by generally accepted norms, rules and enforcement mechanisms. By contrast, Rome's market for public service was backstopped by no such regulation. Institutionally, Rome's reliance on the ill-defined *mos maiorum* for its constitutional principles left the rules vulnerable to the interpretation most convenient to the interpreter. The institution best suited to regulation—the Senate—served less as arbiter and more as market participant, as politics in Late Republican Rome became deeply and dangerously factionalized. In the absence of effective regulation, market participants were constrained by little more than the expectation that greatly good individuals would serve the greater good in recognition of their own coincidental long-term interests. Given Rome's history, such expectations were not entirely unreasonable. In the end, though, Rome's ultimate failure speaks eloquently enough to the shortcomings of relying on the magnanimity of heroes while failing to account for what Madison conceives as the defect of better motives.

A third distinction between economic markets and a market for public service is that the former assumes no barriers to entry. Technically, this was true of Rome's market for heroism, but only in the most superficial sense.

In point of fact, market entry was greatly facilitated by noble lineage. The most efficient means was through the *cursus honorum*—the progression of elective magisterial offices that marked one's ascent through the ranks of public life. The portal to this course of honor generally was a military command or promagistracy in the provinces. Both were within the gift of the Senate, Plutarch's council of many kings (1920, *Pyrr.* 19.5). It is hardly surprising, therefore, that a disproportionate share of the appointments went to members of aristocratic families.

(The extent to which the Roman aristocracy represented a closed oligarchy is subject to scholarly debate. Hopkins and Burton [1985, 32] suggest that on examination of consular and praetorian sons in the last two hundred years of the republic, the "senate was wide open to outsiders," concluding that the Roman aristocracy consisted of a hereditary core consisting of a few prominent families [*gentes*] and a much larger periphery of families whose period of political ascendency was comparatively brief [1985, 112]. Pierre Willems's nineteenth-century inquiry supports this minimal oligarchy theory, finding that between 178 and 82 BC, roughly one-quarter of the consuls elected appeared to come from *gentes* that had never before produced one of consular rank [Lintott 1999, 168–70]. On the other hand, consular rank represented only the upper crust of the nobility [Gelzer 1975, 27–40, esp. 32, 38–39; Taylor 1971, ch. 1; although see Mommsen 1895, bk. III, ch. 6; Brunt 1982]. As such, Willems's findings suggest only that *intra-aristocratic* mobility was rather fluid, while saying nothing about the degree of penetration that nonaristocrats made into the aristocracy. Here there appears to have been far less mobility [Syme 1939, 11]. Taylor, for example, notes that Cicero was the only new man to ascend to the consulship between 93 and 48 BC [1971, 3].)

The final distinction between an economic market and Rome's market for heroic public service turns on merit. Merit is the coin of the realm of the dispassionate economic market, in which good decisions are rewarded and poor ones sanctioned. In Rome, virtuous merit counted for something. But for a society so ostensibly committed to manly excellence, actual success in one's endeavors was often surprisingly inconsequential. Neither Senate nor voting public tended to treat failure as a mark against virtue. Indeed, when it came to tangible, electoral rewards for public service, *possession* of a military command or senior administrative posting tended to count for as much as actual success in discharging one's duties. While great victories did bestow honor and could be parlayed into political advantage, military defeats generally had little effect on one's political fortunes. Even in the face of manifest incompetence, senators were slow to relieve noblemen from their commands or remove administrators from office, lest a similar fate attach to their own potential ineptitude or that of their kin (Brunt 1988, 384–85; Rosenstein 1990, ch. 1).

Relative indifference to performance reflected the prevailing elite bias in favor of assumed virtue, as opposed to demonstrated *virtus*.[2] Certainly among the aristocracy, the assumption was that programmatically good character was a greater indicator of virtue—hence more relevant to *dignitas*—than discrete deeds bound to time and place.[3] Rather than the product of the moment, good character was born of education, socialization, refinement, and, typically subsuming all of these, gentle birth. Such character, independent of accomplishment, served foremost to distinguish the aristocracy from members of lower social classes. Unless it could be otherwise demonstrated, the attendant assumption went, the best public servants were those trained from birth for some sort of role in Roman public life.

To those disaffected—and more to the point, populist elites who would capitalize on that disaffection—an aristocracy of (inherited) virtue represented a cynical exercise in limiting access to the spoils of wealth and power. More than a matter of social protocol, the issue of character versus deed lay at the heart of the Late Republic's discord. Setting the tone for the First Civil War, Sallust has Marius proclaim that there is no honor when one's glory is not of her own doing. Indeed, while the splendor of one's ancestors may represent a shining light of posterity, its luminary properties hardly extend to those whose highest achievement is the greatness of their birth. Cicero frames the issue more sharply. To Servius Sulpicius he says, "[Y]our nobility is to be extracted not from the modern conversation of men, but from the antiquity of annals. . . . [Murena] occupies posts and exercises skills to repel the troops of the enemy, you to keep out of the rain" (*Orations, Mur.*, 105).

A Land without Heroes

It was the institutional accoutrements to Rome's tenuous constitutional principles—*dignitas* as much inherited as earned—that represented the greatest pathology of Rome's failed and inefficient market for heroism. Reinforcing class antipathy in Late Republican Rome, Roman institutions alienated commoners grown tired of (and impoverished by) aristocratic insularity. In providing a breeding ground for populist demagoguery and clientelism, the Late Republic's institutions gave rise to an even greater danger—the decoupling of greatness from goodness.

Civic humanists saw it differently, locating pathology not in institutional susceptibility, but on the corruption of moral character. For Cicero and other Roman elites, there existed a recursive relationship between great goodness and social goodness. Cicero claims that since injustice is an unnatural condition, unjust individuals can perpetuate injustice only with the implicit consent of a morally deficient society. Like any distressed organism, weakness invites further decline. Weak societies permit virtue to dissipate and moral standards to become lax. There is a pestilential quality to such ambient moral drift. The permissive condition under which unjust individuals flourish, moral laxity opens the door to demagogues and tyrants. It nurtures narrow interests antithetical to the greater good. It was under such circumstances that the likes of Sulla and Caesar were able to build up armies capable of turning on Rome. Not only did Rome itself lack the resolve to resist them, but Romans proved quite amenable to exchanging their loyalty to the republic for the patronage of great men lacking goodness and temperance. As chickens came home to roost in Rome's miserable final century, Cicero lamented, "We are being punished justly. If we had not tolerated and left unpunished the crimes of many men, such enormous lack of restraint never would have appeared" (*DO*, bk. II, 28).

Cicero is hardly alone in situating Rome's misery in the dissipation of moral virtue. If corruption was indeed endemic, Livy finds the source of infection in the hedonic Eastern cultures of Asia Minor. It was there that during the Galatian War of the early second century BC that Roman soldiers became afflicted under the relaxed command of Gaius (Gnaeus Manlius Vulso). The disease of moral dissolution was carried back to Rome, along with a love of fine furniture and lavish banquets (accompanied by female players of harp and lute!). With the cult of the Bacchanalia and its self-indulgent celebration of the flesh, Rome's moral decline threatened to spread into all corners of public life. Debauchery begat crimes such as bribery and murder, goes this remarkably linear narrative, and it was only through quick action by the consuls and Senate in arranging for the detainment and mass executions of the immoralists that Rome was saved from the prospect of treason and revolution (Livy 1936, XXXIX, 6–8, 15–18).

Sallust attributes a similar cause to moral dissipation. For him, the uncorrupted early Romans produced virtuous young warriors, who took more pleasure in fine armaments and horses than in loose women and frivolity. None had yet been corrupted by greed, and each was satisfied by what he already possessed (1931, *Cat.* 2, 1). Such being the case, most men's aspirations extended no farther than to win the admiration of their fellow soldiers. It is true that some sought general renown, but such pursuit—self-interested to be sure—could only be achieved through demonstration of the greatest virtue. No hardships were too great for these heroic young men great and good, no foes too fearsome. In lockstep war and *virtus* marched Rome towards greatness. In such company there was no place for reckless inclination or cowardly sclerosis. Men did as they were bidden or suffered the consequences (1931, *Cat.* 7, 1–8). Rather than Gaius, it was Sulla, the Marian Sallust bitterly claims, who corrupted the virtuous young men of Rome. It was he that, "in order to secure the loyalty of the army which he led into Asia, had allowed it a luxury and license foreign to the manners of our forefathers; and in the intervals of leisure those charming and voluptuous lands had easily demoralized the warlike spirit of his soldiers" (1931, *Cat.* 11, 5). And it was under his command "that an army of the Roman people first learned to indulge in women and drink; to admire statues, paintings, and chased vases, to steal them from private houses and public places, to pillage shrines, and to desecrate everything, both sacred and profane" (1931 *Cat.* 11, 6).

This contagion theory of moral declension strikes modern ears as theatrically reductionist. But there is more to it than mournful lament for stout-hearted Roman naïfs untainted by worldly appetites. Attendant is poignant recognition that in the context of war, the half-life of virtue is short. As surely as it stimulates military ascendancy, the *kyklos* runs its course. For the victors, triumph produces plunder, plunder creates wealth, and wealth brings with it a corrupting love of luxury and ease (Polybius 2011, bk. VI). Such indolence, Sallust continues, conspires to rob citizens of their moral bearings. With appetite for the finer things, industry yields to sloth, self-restraint to intemperance. Ambition and pursuit of wealth reinforce one another, privileging the particular ahead of the general good (1931, *Cat.* 2, 10). With moral degeneration, the tribulations imposed by virtue, once cheerfully borne, become more burdensome. An insidious corruption advances on civic morals. Greed, inhumanity, and irreligiosity infect duty, justice, and piety. What were once intrinsically valued bonds of friendship become but instrumental associations. Where once there had been chastity, there is instead degeneracy. Whereas in better days individuals had built ostentatious temples to the gods, in times of moral privation, their grand mansions represent only indulgent monuments to themselves (Sallust 1931, *Cat.* 10, 12–13; see also Lucan 1992, bk. I, 158ff).

A Corrupted Republic

If contemporaneous analysts were preoccupied with Rome's moral drift, some failed to account for underlying conditions exacerbated by the establishment of Roman hegemony in the western Mediterranean. As is common with great powers, Rome became a victim of its own success in war. There are at least two reasons for this. First, while military dominance generates great wealth, distribution is typically very uneven. Second, success in war brings peace. Indeed, if there is any virtue to war, it is that it provides an agonal theater for ambitious and self-assertive men who otherwise lack a socially appropriate outlet for demonstration of their *virtus*.[4]

These pathologies of economic inequity and idle hands came to a head beginning in the 120s BC. Until the final war with Carthage, the Roman Republic had been almost perpetually at war. And while the end of the Third Punic War hardly ushered in a period of absolute peace, it represented the point at which armed conflict ceased to be integral to the security of the Roman state. It is likely no coincidence that within a generation of the submission of Carthage, Roman aggression began to turn inward upon itself. In a regime built for foreign war and not domestic peace, peacetime competition for spoils and authority provoked violent social contestation. Sadly for Rome, the only possible mediating body—the Senate—evinced disdain for the abiding magnanimity that had been the foundation of its moral authority. Through deference to a land-hungry aristocracy, senators hitched their wagons not to stewardship of the *mos maiorum*, but to the worldly immediacy of material and political gain. In so doing, that erstwhile repository of heroic virtue abrogated its dispassionate, reasoned mandate to govern in fidelity to the good, thereby bringing the entire republican edifice down around it (Cicero *Rep.*, bk. V, pref.).

The underlying cause of the cascading sequence of events that culminated in the end of the Republic was a familiar threat to republican stability: imbalance manifesting in escalating class antipathy. The flashpoint was the initiative for land reforms undertaken by Tiberius and Gaius Gracchus and the subsequent assassinations of these reforming plebeian tribunes. The Gracchi assassinations sharpened tensions between conservative aristocratic *optimates* on the one hand and populist demagogues like Marius, Sulpicius, Cinna, Lepidus, and Caesar on the other. Extended conflict between *optimates* and *populares* created opportunities for previously unsung individuals to advance their careers in public service. In theory, this loosening of barriers to entry should have been a good thing. In practice, however, the market for public service became as it were, a black market, with individuals not favored by the Senate bypassing formal-legal institutions in aid of crafting their own populist constituencies.

Given this institutional backdoor, it is perhaps not surprising that most of the great populists (Marius an obvious exception) were disaffected aristocrats. Few new men, and fewer heroes, found their way into public life in the wake of the Gracchi assassinations. As had been the case in Greece, populism was a tool of the tyrant rather than the true reformer. The Gracchi assassinations advertised the new reality that plebian sociopolitical prospects were as bleak as their economic ones. Neither side gauged the landscape particularly well. The Gracchi brothers and their supporters overestimated the power and constitutional protection afforded to plebian tribunes. At the same time, *optimates* overestimated the robustness of Rome's formal-legal institutions.

Dobel (1978) characterizes such a lamentable state of affairs as the fruits of a corrupted state, in which a shared pattern of civic virtue and "moral loyalty" has been disrupted (1978, 959). A corrupted republic reflects "a privatization of moral concerns," what Cicero understands as the capitulation of reasoned goodness to unjust self-assertion. A monument to asymptotic magnanimity, a corrupted republic privileges power over justice. Fueling discord is unreasonable inequality of status, wealth, and power—unreasonableness being the point at which citizens no longer remain stakeholders in the regime, the res publica a public thing no more (Dobel 1978, 962).

In an institutionally effective republic, citizen stakeholders will tend to comply with law. In return, they expect lawmakers to demonstrate a general commitment to the common welfare. To mitigate the potential for abuse of power inequalities, citizens retain a significant voice in the administration of public affairs, and such civic participation is facilitated and reinforced by formal legal mechanisms that limit the potential for abuse of power (Dobel 1978, 962–63, 966). By contrast, where inequality is unreasonable, the prospect of class conflict looms. As with the *stasis* of Archaic Greece or the Gracchi crisis in Rome, the implicit republican bargain is an early casualty. Such inequality becomes self-reenforcing. Even elites not motivated by naked greed become obliged to divert their attention from statesmanship towards more single-minded commitment to retention of station. In turn, such abdication of leadership renders inequality even more intractable, and the common good asserts progressively weaker claims on mass loyalty.

At this point, informal and formal legal institutions become rivals for power, and "[v]iolence increasingly becomes the dominant substratum of all relations, and political discourse is reduced to transparent rationalization" (Dobel 1978, 960). Lucan leaves little doubt that such an affliction beset the Roman Republic. "It was an honour great," he writes, "and to be sought by the sword to have more power than the state; the yardstick of legality was violence" (1992, bk. I, 174–76). Controlling a disproportionate share of resources that in healthy and balanced republican societies would be distributed equitably, elites in corrupted republics take advantage of their positions by exchanging putatively public resources for the support of personal political constituencies. Control of the governing process becomes the paramount concern of political actors seeking either to retain and consolidate their positions of power or else to wrest power away from the individual or class of individuals currently in control. The hallmark is a transactional form of politics—clientelism—reminiscent of the more primitive big man politics already discussed. Displacing general loyalty to the res publica, clientelism is born of insular loyalty to particular patrons seeking control of the state.[5] Frustratingly to people like Cicero, even where good citizens are not fooled by such audacious political ambition, in a corrupted republic their choices often come down to aligning with whatever faction represents the lesser evil (Dobel 1978, 965).

That the conditions for clientelism were ripe in the Late Republic is unquestionable. Most pernicious of all was the extension of transactional politics to the military. As with other forms of Roman clientelism, the use of private armies was evolutionary. Patricians abroad had long been accompanied by an entourage of *amici* who volunteered their service as a praetorian cohort. By the Middle Republic, however, it had become the practice of military commanders to craft their entourages into fighting forces. Scipio Aemilianus, for example, employed his entourage in such fashion at Numantia. It was Marius, however, who was first to transform personal loyalty into entire legions of fighting men. Taking advantage of the poverty of displaced plebeians in the Italian hinterlands, he used long-term military employment to rescue them from their plights. Setting aside property requirements for military service, Marius thereby expanded both the size of the army and the dependence of his troops upon him. As such, Marian and post-Marian recruits were more likely to display fealty to their military commanders than to a government that had provided them with little more than poverty and social marginalization. In return for such personal allegiance, it became the practice of military commanders such as Marius and Sulla—even in the face of outright opposition of the Senate—to provide veterans of their campaigns with allotments of land in the provinces upon their retirement from active service. And after Caesar's death, even the Senate employed the tactic to secure the loyalty of Octavius's troops against Mark Antony (Sherwin-White 1956; Brunt 1962, 75–80; Gelzer 1975, 101–3; Taylor 1971, 17, 47; Gruen 1974, 369–77; Roniger 1983, 74–77; Eisenstadt and Roniger 1984, 56–57).

Nowhere was the problem of martial clientelism clearer than in the final chapter of the Republic in need of heroes, which culminated in armed conflict for the second time between *optimas* (Pompey) and *popularis* (Caesar). This was not a principled conflict, a clash of legitimate heroic worldviews. In this consummation of the crisis, neither principal held strong ideological convictions. After Sulla's death, Pompey had supported populist issues, not least the restoration of the tribunate's powers, which Sulla had greatly weakened. In what had become the demagogic strategy du jour, Pompey too had threatened to march on the Roman Senate when that body failed to supply him with sufficient men in his capacity as proconsul in Spain (Taylor 1942, 4–11, 13–14). For his part, Caesar had hardly been a radical populist during the First Civil War. After that conflict, he failed to support Lepidus's rebellion against the Senate and indeed had cultivated sufficiently strong ties among the *optimates* that he was elected to the college of pontiffs in spite of the conservative majority that could have blocked him.

After the triumvirate of 59, Rome became increasingly ungovernable. Rioting accompanied important legislative votes, and election violence was so pronounced that it prevented consular elections. Such dislocation was the fruit of a clientelistic free-for-all, the terms *optimas* and *popularis* having by this point lost all substantive meaning. Nominal *optimates* pandered to the masses, while erstwhile *populares* sought to consolidate alliances within the Senate. For its part, the *mos maiorum* existed as little more than a quaint relic of more heroic times. Amidst the uncertainty, Caesar's tenure as governor of Gaul was almost over. Fearing for his safety as a private citizen, he sought permission for an extension of his governorship.

When told that the Senate was disinclined to grant it, Caesar is said to have touched the hilt of his sword and said, "[B]ut this will give it" (Appian 1899, bk. II, 20–25; Plutarch 1920, *Caes.* 29.6).

Conclusion

The Roman Republic asked the impossible of its heroes. They were to be multifaceted, physically and metaphysically great. They were to be defenders, stewards, and redeemers of the republic; they were to be exemplary role models and nation builders. The fall of the republic was an institutional and cultural failing born of excessive reliance upon heroes. The Romans wanted their heroes strong and manly, imbued with the *virtus* that connoted forcefulness and the ability to defend the state from its enemies. At the same time, their heroes needed to be public spirited in good governance, their virtue a public resource, a patriotic duty to Rome. In the best of times, Rome's heroes were Janus faced, epic, and magnanimous. That the Early and Middle Republics had produced a steady stream of heroes great and greatly good was a mixed blessing. Such heroes led Rome to construction of a great empire. But they also presented the illusion that Roman magnanimity was an infinitely renewable resource capable of curing all ills that might befall the republic, a ready source of social redemption there for the asking. History thus fueled a magical cultural conflation of great men with good, of the heroic multidimensionality of axiomatically flawed individuals. Recognition that the thinking was faulty—that whatever capacities Late Republican Rome's greatest individuals possessed, heroic stewardship and redemption was not among them—came far too late to save the republic. In the worst of times, epic villains routed heroic magnanimity. Sallust feared the worst; Cicero hoped for the best, gambling that a natural sense of justice would win out over the cupidity of the bad apples.

The Roman case illustrates the limitations of heroic magnanimity, born of the fine line extant between magnanimity and asymptotic magnanimity. The distinction not only doomed the republic, but sent republican governance itself into a millennium of hibernation. That Rome was circumstantially unlucky is not the point; the natural fallibility of humanity is. The likes of Livy, Sallust, and Cicero greatly overestimated the efficacy of humanity's natural goodness, Romans' insistent assertion of the natural ascendancy of magnanimous rulers over unjust ones accomplishing little more than drawing attention away from the glaring problem of institutional weakness. Even as the republic failed, Romans gave little thought to the defensive institutional construction favored by later republican diagnosticians as Machiavelli and Madison. If a hero could have saved Rome, she would have been a different kind of hero from the sort glorified by ancient poets and philosophers. Rather than a fighter or a thinker, she would have been an architect, capable of harnessing the self-interest of human beings. She would have recognized that, to borrow from Forrest McDonald's (1985, 71) Machiavellian characterization, the imperative for a good republic was not to create better people, but rather to create better systems of rules.

Chapter 4

The Christian Hero in the Orders of Nature and Grace

The story of Christian heroism is one of duality: duality between classical and modern republicanism, between the orders of nature and grace, and between two perspectives on the proper balance between the two. The first duality is the least conceptually nuanced, and provides the narrative backdrop to this chapter and to the ones that follow. The chapter continues what we have already started—teasing out the relationship between (epic and magnanimous) heroism and classical republicanism. But equally, it is through Christian heroism that we see the earliest manifestations of the more egalitarian heroism that emerges in the wake of the Protestant Reformation in general, and the Puritan and American Revolutions in particular. Christian heroism, then, is the buckle linking classical and modern republicanism. The story is long and hardly linear, inextricably caught as Christian heroes have been between the gravitational pulls of the spiritual and worldly orders.

This brings us to the second duality and the imperative to contextualize the Christian hero in her cosmic place. Early Christian republicanism is Neoplatonic. In the Augustinian (and later Calvinist) traditions, the Christian republic serves as visible proxy for the heavenly kingdom. The philosopher king is recast in divine form, elevated along the Great Chain of Being, now ruling the kingdoms of earth *and* heaven. This had implications for cosmic justice. In light of the natural depravity of postlapsarian man, just condition is realizable only through the soul's salvation. How contingent just condition is upon just agency differs sharply among theologians. The Calvinist extreme—that salvation is realizable only through God's grace, unconditional and irresistible—invites antinomianism and precludes a meaningful theory of republicanism. As such, most Christian republicanism—including that discussed in this chapter—demands a theory of just agency, even if its Arminian tint persists as preparationism, or some other form of camouflage.[1]

The final element of cosmic justice in the Christian republic—balance—informs our third duality. Theories of balance in the Christian republic mirror those of the secular one. Thus, in the Socratic tradition, it will be recalled, balance is realized through the assignation to each element its proper place in the social order. By contrast, the Aristotelian tradition relies not on optimal social efficiency, but rather on the tension between two extremes in realization of the virtuous mean. These different perspectives on balance informs the differential value that Socrates and Aristotle place on heroic magnanimity. Mirroring the distinction, Augustinian and Calvinist Christian republicanism embraced cosmic architectonics and the primacy of the spiritual order. Thomist scholasticism, the chivalric code, and American Protestant evangelism, on the other hand, insisted upon a more Aristotelian—and more humanist—form of Christian republicanism, in which just condition was as important to the order of nature as the order of grace.

The duality that drives this chapter means that Christian heroism covers a good deal of territory. In addition to the broad range of heroic function discussed momentarily, Christianity is relevant to each of the four hero types discussed in the book. Most obviously, and most pertinent to this chapter, Christian heroes present as both epic and magnanimous. In epic form, terrestrial Christian heroes are characterized by physical greatness engaged in goodness of cause. They present as the martyrs enduring, through God's grace, the torments inflicted for their faith; as prolific noblemen taking the Cross in defense of Jerusalem; or as chivalrous knights errant, as deferential to their ladies as they are submissive to God. As magnanimous heroes, Christian heroes are saintly figures reconciled with God, either in death, or—as with Protestant saints—as living beings destined for salvation. Invisible, like dead heroes of Archaic Greece, they provide posthumous benefaction in aid of the faithful. In visible form, saints exhort others to God, assisting pilgrims in spiritual odyssey; they also insist upon construction of the millennial earthly kingdom in preparation for the day. It is through Christian heroism, moreover, that we see harbingers of the Romantic and common heroism discussed in the chapters to follow.

This chapter explores a number of heroic archetypes. Receiving the greatest attention are *soldiers of Christ*, ideally (if not always in practice) heirs to martyred saints as defenders of the faith, taking the Cross in defense of visible institutions. *Chivalric knights* took on a broader range of heroic functions, emerging not just as defenders of the faith, but (through the idealized convention of courtly love) as heroic stewards, incarnate symbols of the vassalage to liege lord so foundational to the feudal order. *English country gentlemen* are social redeemers in the balanced, Aristotelian tradition and exemplars of the self-sufficiency so integral to Romantic and common heroism. By contrast, *Puritan saint-presumptives* are also social redeemers in quest, however unsuccessful, of the millennialist Christian republic in England.

Finally, in terms of chronology, this chapter begins in the early medieval period, moving quickly through the Crusades. Beginning with the age of chivalry and culminating in Renaissance insistence upon well-roundedness, the chapter abdicates its linear narrative, focusing on the duality of the two cosmic orders. We end with the temporary alliance of Puritan laity (country gentlemen) and divines in the tumult of seventeenth-century England, which sets the stage for the emergence of the modern republicanism crafted during the Age of Enlightenment.

The Medieval Christian Hero

Historically, the Christian hero existed in a Neoplatonic hierarchy of magnanimity, in which any extant human virtue is dwarfed by the infinitely greater goodness of God. Implicit is the early Christian imperative to subordinate the (terrene) order of nature to the (spiritual) order of grace. Displacing the Socratic philosopher in the natural order was the visible church, guiding its flock in earthly pilgrimage to fulfillment through salvation. In this endeavor it was supported by temporal heroes imbued by God with the virtues requisite to the godly mission of salvation. As with pagan chronicles like *The Odyssey* or *Argonautica*, the Christian narrative is one of exile and return, of postlapsarian alienation from God followed by the soul's restoration to a state of grace.

We Have Here No Lasting City

For Augustine, the great pathology of pagan civilization was the Siren song of the temporal—attractive in its immediacy, the spiritual diminished by distance. That such a skewed perspective is natural to postlapsarian man is of little comfort to the peripatetic soul, aimless in its journey, and destined for damnation absent the navigational aid of God's grace. Maintaining Socrates's city-soul metaphor, Augustine sees the sack of Rome as the fruit of pagan worldliness. Named for Romulus, who slew his own brother in quest for domination, Rome stands as testament to the ungodliness of temporal reward prized above the soul's salvation, of the brutality of war preferred to the tranquility of peace, of the pridefulness of Cain privileged over the piety of Abel (Barron 2007, 48–50). By placing its faith in the physical virtue of heroic mortals, the turbulent pagan city stands in stark contrast to the serenity of the ecclesiastical city in fidelity to the one true God—a God of creation, not dominion.

Metaphysically, the pagan hero is equally flawed. Having no true conception of God, pagan philosophers misperceive just condition, conflating fulfillment of natural man with fulfillment of the soul. Among the sages of antiquity, Socrates's philosopher—her eye on the soul's apotheotic destiny—is on the right track at least. Certainly, she is less culpable than Aristotle's *eudaemonic* man, guilty as he is of misplaced audience, finding specious completeness in his own virtue. It can be of little wonder, therefore, that to early Christians, such a restrictive moral horizon was insufficient to the survival of the pagan city (Tertullian 1899, chs. XXIX–XXX, L; Benko 1984, ch. 2; Williams 1951; Rahner 1992, ch. 1, esp. 10–12; Cornish 2010, 134).

Getting to the root of the matter, for Augustinians, the great pathology of the pagan philosophers was failure to recognize that true virtue is unified in piety, not sagacity. It embraces compassion and forgiveness and love and humility through submission to the gracious magnanimity that is the sole prerogative of God (Barron 2007, 50). Yet tension between piety and sagacity (or at least between humility and humanism) survives to permeate the Christian narrative. The terrestrial and spiritual orders represent the kingdoms over which God exercises sovereignty. The secrets of the natural order, the source of terrestrial goodness, lend themselves to empirical discovery. In this realm, governed by the visible institutions of church and state, human ingenuity is sufficient to mastery of nature. Such mastery extends to the capacity to carve a sacred civil space out of the profanity of wilderness. By contrast, the spiritual order of grace is invulnerable to the dominion of man. Its secrets remain unknowable, save for those which God has chosen to reveal through scriptural or personal revelation. The individual is a citizen of the natural order, but a subject of the spiritual one, in which her station is informed by submissive obedience.

Foundational as it is to his *City of God*, Augustine understands the distinction between nature and grace as but a postlapsarian artifact of history (*CG*, XIV, 11). Where once the two kingdoms of God were indistinct, all that remains of such Edenic unity is imprinted on the mind. It is experienced in fragmentary flashes, like a memory dancing on the edge of consciousness. Such flashes, unsatisfactory though they are, excite within us a need to know and hold on to God (*Trin.*, bk. XIV, chs. 4, 6; also esp. bk. XII, ch. 3.3, ch. 14.23; *CG*, bk. XIX, 13). Through such *ratio superior*, human nature is imbued with a deep-seated desire to transcend the order of nature and return to a state of grace, to break the bonds of sin that alienate her from God (Te Selle 1965, 239–45).

From this perspective, terrestrial heroism is to be found not in the magnanimity of (cosmically small) individuals or the (putative) greatness inherent in extraordinary self-assertion. Rather it is reflected in the extraordinary humility of martyrs willing to give themselves up for persecution in the name of Christian piety (*CG*, bk. X, 21–22, bk. XIV.9, 13).[2] Even here, what appears heroic to humans is but a mirror to the great goodness of God. Indeed, estimability lies less in the character of martyrs themselves than the divine grace that gives them their strength. So it is that Augustine exhorts Christians: "Value your martyrs. Praise them; love, honor, and tell others about them. But worship [only] the martyrs' God" (quoted in Kaufman 1994, 2–3).

In the *City of God*, Augustine's two heuristic cities represent the binary distinction between the order of grace and the order of nature in which the destiny of the soul is sealed. One city is populated by those who love and will to live for themselves, the other by those who do so for God. One serves the ephemeral body, the other the eternal soul. One glories in the darkness, the other in the light (St. Augustine *CG*, bk. XI.1, 4, 33, bk. XII.19, bk. XIV, 1, 4, 6, 9). In places, Augustine seems to imply that the city of man is Rome, and the city of God, Jerusalem. Yet he also makes clear that the Christianized city cannot be the city of God, for there is no eternal Christianized city. Even the best terrene order exists only in nourishment of the soul, before it too is destroyed at the last judgment. Instead, the Christianized city, like the Church, stands merely as a visible proxy for the glory not yet visible. Like the visible Church, the Christianized city brings citizens together in fortification for the trials of their souls on the long road to salvation (bk. XIX, 13).

Church and state in the Christianized city exist as the locus of peace, the tranquility of things in undisturbed order, the concord of citizens living in "harmonious enjoyment of God, and of one another in God" (*CG*, bk. XIX, 13). The preeminent guarantor of peace is God. Indeed, so magnanimous is God that his protection extends to all virtuous temporal civilizations, Christian and pagan alike. Among the latter, Rome was a prime beneficiary. The great tragedy was that the Romans themselves could not appreciate it. What Romans understood to be the product of good fortune and mortal heroes was in reality the machination of the great goodness of God (bk. V). More ironically still, the martial greatness of Rome's heroes worked against the peaceful serenity inspired by God. Once again, there can be little puzzlement over its ultimate demise.

Augustine's peace is Solon's calm sea. Yet Augustine cannot accept peace as a wholly passive good, as though God's magnanimity were sufficient to thwart all worldly hostility. Instead, given that visible institutions exist in an environment of worldly and violent humans, peace often mandates that the Christianized city prepare itself for war. Violence threatens the pacifism of Christian witness. But equally, the Christianized city cannot cower as if to will the world to leave it be, as though it were the sea awaiting passage of the storm (St. Augustine *Faust.*, bk. XXII, 74). When born of corrupt or prideful motives, such as the glorification of humans, war is a great evil. When undertaken in obedience to God, however, it allies itself with justice (*Faust.*, bk. XXII, 74–75, 78). Such just war is therefore an affirmative obligation, a mandate to hold fast against the insidious incursion of worldliness, a refusal to submit to hostile intent on the part of the ungodly (St. Augustine *GC*, bk. XX, 9). Just war provides the basis of worldly intrusion into Christian spiritualism. It is an imperfect means to an imperfect end—the defense of visible Christian institutions, however impermanent they may be.

THE TAKING OF THE CROSS

The most important manifestation of such godly warfare was the Crusades. In design at least, the Crusades united the Latin and Byzantine Churches in the common cause of expelling Saracen occupiers of the Holy Lands. Belying the tidy Augustinian distinction between just and unjust war, however, were less godly motives, not least those of reforming popes maneuvering to ensure Roman control of a reunified Church. The Crusades also diverted tension between Church and laity over the issue of investiture, redirecting the aspirations of lay nobility to a godlier end—or anyway, one that posed far less risk to the material interests of the Church in Rome (Calabrese 1999, 8–9; Morris 2001, ch. 5; Teschke 2003, 105; Tyerman 2006, chs. 1–2; Latham 2011, 230–31, 234–38). For takers of the Cross, motivation was no less intricate. The Crusades helped reconcile two dialectical imperatives of medieval heroic nobility: demonstration of physical virtues and accordance with Christian ones. The former typically risked the spilling of blood, a sin demanding penance. Yet for those who sinned in liberation of the Church of God in Jerusalem, went Pope Urban's carefully crafted call to arms, pilgrimage would stand in place of penance for all confessed sins.

Even considering Urban's injunction that crusaders be motivated solely by devotion, such Manichean justification failed to alleviate all churchmen's concerns about the sanctity of violence in the name of God. Difficult to ignore was the thuggish brutality practiced by bands of knightly marauders, more piratical than pious, whose primary interests in taking the Cross involved plunder under the protective camouflage of good Christian cause (Kaeuper 2009, 11–17). And while it may have been Gregory VII's assertion that sin was an inevitable consequence of just warfare, others pursued more high-minded means of reconciling crusading and Christianity (Kaeuper 2009, 13). Some clerics sought to constrain martial exuberance by playing upon the ubiquitous medieval fear of posthumous fate, extracting premiums in piety for what Eamon Duffy calls "post-mortem fire insurance" (quoted in Kaeuper 2009, 18). But takers of the Cross often tended towards piety on their own terms, convincing themselves that acquisition of wealth, honor, and other worldly benefits enjoyed inoculation from sin so long as such bounty was but a happy externality of the pursuit of spiritual justice (Kaeuper 2009, 20).

A more systematic and efficacious tack was imposition of a general code of chivalric conduct. This sort of professional reorientation was a central mandate of religious orders such as the Knights Templar, Teutonic Knights, and Knights Hospitalier. Engaged in a simultaneous battle of flesh and spirit, religious orders reinforced the injunction that pillage and plunder dimmed one's prospects for salvation. Instead, exemplars of a programmatic personal and professional commitment to Christ, the Templars' Primitive Rule admonished those "who have until now lead the lives of secular knights, in which Jesus Christ was not the cause, but which you embraced for human favor only, to follow those whom God has chosen from the mass of perdition and whom he has ordered through his gracious mercy to defend the Holy Church, and that you hasten to join them forever" (Upton-Ward 2008, clause 1; see also Kaeuper 2009, 23–25; Latham 2011, 239). As a professional code of Christian ethics, chivalry played a crucial role in elevating the status of the knight from ambitious thug to incarnate link between the worldly and spiritual orders. It carved out a space for him as heroic defender of the spiritual order and heroic steward of the terrestrial one. The nexus of the two cosmic orders was celebrated through the investiture ritual detailed in the anonymous twelfth-century *Ordination of Knighthood*. The process began with the prospective knight being immersed as representation of the baptismal cleansing of sin, bathed in kindness, honesty, and good will. The candidate was then laid upon a bed, the symbolic bed of paradise promising eternal reward for chivalric knighthood. Next, he was clad in a scarlet gown, symbolizing the blood he would willingly shed in service to God and Church. His shoes were black in reference to death, lest he became too prideful. A virginal white belt was a reminder to keep his flesh and thoughts pure, to practice abstinence, respect, and deference to women. Gilt spurs spoke to rapid and decisive service to God, while also harkening to the equine roots of the chevalier. A double-edged sword was to be used to smite God's enemies and defend the weak, one side of the blade symbolizing loyalty, and the other justice of cause.[3] Finally, a white coif upon the head signified that come judgment day, the knight would be satisfied by the purity of his actions and freedom from guilt (Anonymous 1893, 131–38).

Duality, Romance, and Love

Resplendent as the ceremonial allegory might be, as an epoch-defining cultural phenomenon, the code of chivalry needed a little help. So it was that the enduring legacy of the chivalrous knight was burnished through romance tales, glorifying chivalric knights possessed of both the *virilis virtus* and the reflected magnanimity of God. To keep this romance literature light and interesting, God does not appear as an imperious, white-bearded figure. Rather, he presents as purity incarnate, a feminine muse for the submissive deference attendant both to piety and to courtly love. Romance tales typically center on the exploits of a knight errant, whose epic *bona fides* are established in all the usual ways—physical trials imposed by evil supernatural phenomena, hostile knights, and generally unfavorable ambient circumstances. The knight's physical virtues are employed not in glorification of the self, but rather in service of vassal loyalty to liege lord and devotional obligation to lady love.

The knight's lady is no easy conquest. An enchantress, she is a chatelaine of higher social standing than himself. The love story is neither sordid nor straightforward, complicated by the lady's unavailability due to her (often loveless) marriage, sometimes to the knight's liege lord himself. The secret romance typically progresses slowly, with manifold obstacles thrown in its path to heighten both challenge and anticipation. (The knight's loyalty to lady demands, among other things, that he keep secret their illicit love. The knight forced to betray the secret risks sacrificing the love—even the life in cases where despair turns fatal—of his lady.) Ultimately, knight and lady find themselves on the cusp of realizing their love before the imperative for chastity and the prohibition against adultery preclude consummation.

The purely emotional portrayal of courtly love is fundamental to maintenance of appropriate social boundaries. Particularly where the chatelaine is the wife of his liege lord, the knight preserves his temporal oath of loyalty, the repository of the lord's honor being the body of his wife.[4] It also speaks to the cosmic justice implicit in the chivalric code. Hearkening to Greek tragedy, the most noble aspect of courtly love turns on how the knight responds when his commitments to lady and lord come into conflict. Where the knight is unequal to resolution of his conflicted loyalties, the result is typically some form of catastrophe (Markman 1957, 577–79).[5] The chivalric code, then, is cosmically just, establishing the unparsable virtue attendant to just agency, just condition, and just balance.

The spiritual allegory is hard to miss. Like the grace of God, the love of lady is ambiguously attainable. The obstacles to illicit love are emblematic of the spiritual pilgrim's travails in maintenance of his faith. The failure to consummate love is an analog to the inability to commune with God in humanity's fallen condition. Feats by heroic knights in the name of love are analogous to hagiographers' stories of saintly miracles in the name of faith. And the knight's transformation by love into a new man mirrors baptismal rebirth (Russell 1965, 40–43).

The chivalry of Christian heroes as portrayed in the late Middle Ages and Renaissance also reflected the ascendant humanism of the day. It spoke to a more balanced perspective on the two cosmic realms, suggesting the prospect for (qualified) fulfillment within the natural order. Such balance often found voice through the venerable distinction between primary and secondary heroes discussed earlier. The secondary hero, usually epic, tended toward perfection in the terrestrial virtues. The primary hero, by contrast, was Christological and hence more complete in her virtue. Primary and secondary heroes spoke respectively to salvation and aspiration; the secondary hero's deficiencies revealed only through contrast to the primary hero's greater virtue. Prototypical was the legend of the Holy Grail. Arthurian legend presents Lancelot as the greatest knight in the land. Still, he cannot measure up to the more apotheotic Galahad, successful in the quest to penetrate the mystery of the Eucharist. Edmund Spenser's *Faerie Queene* (1903) presents a similar form of Christian dualism. Spenser's manifold heroes are allegorical representations of the secular moral virtues, each represented by a particular knight. None is sufficient in her or himself in the perfection of that virtue. Instead it is the epiphanous Prince Arthur—reflecting the power of God's grace—who must rescue the virtues from the temptations that might otherwise spoil them (Woodhouse 1949; although see Berger 1957).

This reconceptualization of republican equilibrium—from one predicated upon balance between social classes to one based on the simultaneous relevance of the two cosmic orders—would have important spiritual and secular ramifications. First, such contentious duality contributed to social and political unrest in the form of the revolutions—Puritan and American—that bracketed the Enlightenment. In both cases, humanist Christian republicanism won out over the more stratified Neoplatonic form. Second, the increased relevance of duality between the cosmic orders coincided with the marginalization of *terrestrial* magnanimous heroism, as the distinction between the moral capacity of sage and commoner met greater skepticism. Indeed, the new moral philosophy of the Enlightenment and the moral aesthetics of emergent Romanticism, both of which emphasized innate human moral capacity, contributed to the egalitarian republicanism of the modern age. Both are anticipated, albeit somewhat faintly, by the country gentleman.

A Gentleman and a Saint

As the chivalrous knight faded from the forefront of cultural consciousness, two new players, both of whom could lay claim to the knight's heroic legacy, came to promote contested visions of the new republic. The first was the Whiggish country gentleman. An oppositional figure, the country gentleman became the first standard-bearer for the humanist Christian heroism of the transitional seventeenth century. Puritan in sympathy if not millennialist cause, resistant to High Church Anglicanism and Royal absolutism, the country gentleman stood for the republic as commonwealth—the modifier "country" reflecting his broad national loyalty more than his rural antecedents. His spiritual inclinations in harmony with his natural ones, his primary focus was upon redemption of the temporal order. His mandate was to harvest the reason, common sense, and moral affect of humanity in the construction of the good republic. His impact, quite literally, was revolutionary.

The oppositionism of the country gentleman was the driving force behind the parliamentary resistance that sparked the English Civil War. Philosophically pastoral and unpretentious, the gentlemanly ideal was a refined, well-rounded, and self-sufficient virility. In this narrow sense at least, the country gentleman anticipated the immanent naturalist Romanticism of Wordsworth, Coleridge, or Keats by a couple of centuries (Burgum 1941, 481). Indeed, as with the Romantic, his traditional pastoral values came up against ambient embourgeoisement, the insidious urbanization that had begun to intrude upon Elizabethan England. Seconded to the city, he evolved as *bon bourgeoisie* as much as country squire. His ultimate triumphs were the Glorious Revolution—and the assertion of commonwealth principles ahead of a narrow conception of the good that served the few at the expense of the many—as well as the American Revolution almost a century later.

The second relevant figure was the Puritan saint. Privileging the order of grace, her millennialist mandate was construction of a more theocratic Christianized republic—a New Jerusalem in the Neoplatonic mold, standing fast against the forces of Satan until the day of final judgment. As a soldier of Christ, the saint envisioned a republic disdainful of equality and balance. In it, the regenerate would serve as a new aristocracy, guardians of the covenant of works through which the elect society fulfills its fealty to God. Moral surveillance by this aristocracy of the elect would be more vigilant than in its secular republican counterpart, the personal and collective stakes for moral probity being higher. There would be little room for individual autonomy and little need for it; the gracious magnanimity of the saints being far more efficacious than any claim to moral sufficiency on the part of ordinary individuals, reprobate and depraved.

THE COUNTRY GENTLEMAN

The country gentleman, or patriot, was a transitional figure. Aligned with the visible saint in opposition to the Thorough Alliance of king and High Church, he reflected the Renaissance ideal of completeness.[6] He assumes relevance in two fundamentally important ways. The first, as just alluded to, was institutional—the evolution of classical republicanism to the more modern egalitarian liberal republicanism of the modern age. It is through him that Real Whig humanism came to temper (in the British case subsume) the Puritan influence on modern republics on both sides of the Atlantic. The second was contribution to cultural legitimation of the new hero types (Romantic and common) attendant to the transition from classical to modern republicanism.

By strict sociological definition, the country gentleman often was not a gentleman at all. Technically, "gentleman" was a formal rank within the lesser nobility (gentry) which also included esquires and knights. A cut below the peerage and above the yeomanry, gentry were distinctive as a landed class by the fact that their rank brought with it no hereditary title. By the late Elizabethan period, however, the formal definition of gentleman had retreated, a casualty of common parlance and social fluidity. The latter was born of economic diversification, which increasingly obliged the gentleman to move beyond his rural roots. This was particularly so with "second" sons of noblemen, for whom the passing of the chivalric age gradually mandated a greater urban presence, knights errant reborn as professionals, civil servants, or even wealthy merchants. In acquiring a profession through education, many urban gentlemen were not even of gentle birth, a newness that exacerbated the anomie of their station in a modernizing economy holding fast to vestigial social institutions. Awkwardly situated between the venerable and the vulgar, the new country gentleman was burdened by a vexing and pervasive (social) ambiguity—not unlike the salvational ambiguity of the Puritan saint-presumptive—often finding himself relegated to outsider status during the social upheavals of the seventeenth century (Walzer 1969, 247; Cmiel 1990, 37).[7]

As the sociological definition of a gentleman proved unequal to changing times, status as a gentleman increasingly became contingent upon decorum—a social ideal for the best citizens of the post-Elizabethan age. Thus observed Sir John Ferne, "A Gentleman or a Nobleman is he (for I do wittingly confound these voices) which is knowne, and through the heroycall vertues of his life, talked of in eueryman's mouth" (1586, I. 4). Expressed through eloquence, art, learning, and comportment, decorum bespoke estimability in the conduct of life. Chivalry recast as civility, it was an outward projection of inner virtue expressed through the gentleman's lifestyle and proclaimed by his public reputation (Cmiel 1990, 26; Corfield 1992, 42; Bryson 1995, 136; Carter 2000, 57, 124).

Somewhat counterintuitively, given its detachment from the manly arts of warfare, a sort of cultural masculinity pervaded decorum, rescuing it from effeminacy through the stoical way of life now deemed culturally superior to episodic excited demonstrations of manliness (Carter 2000, ch. 4). Decorum's highest station was completeness. Just as valor had characterized the hero of the chivalric age, completeness was the measure of a Renaissance gentleman, constituting the exemplar of a heroic ideal and establishing "a new centre for the values which for centuries had coalesced around the office of knighthood" (Peterson 1992, 77; see also Tawney 1941, 6; Corfield 1992, 43–44; Carter 2000, 74–76). The centrality of completeness as an aspirational good in seventeenth-century England was announced by the proliferation of guidebooks providing instruction in the gentlemanly conduct of life (Belok 1968; Carroll 1981, 468). The complete gentleman was distinguished through virtuous perfection, a magnanimous bearing in clear demonstration that he was "of finer clay than the rest of mankind" (Ustick 1932, 154; see also Ashley 1965, 111–13; Lindholm 2013, 365).

Thus, advises Obadiah Walker in *Of Education*, "Being a gentleman . . . let him consider that he is above the tongues of evil men: That he is engaged in nobler and sublimer designs and actions than other persons; he must steer by higher Stars, and aim at somewhat more Heroical" (1673, 52). The gentleman, Walker continues in this Aristotelian vein, is quick to forgive insults, sees no need to flaunt his status over inferiors, and stands ready with his general benevolence. He exercises more forbearance than the law demands and contributes more than it obliges. Stoic in his fortitude, "[h]e *fears* nothing, he *despiseth* nothing, he *admires* nothing" (1673, 54–55; emphasis in original). Neoclassical in his worldview and defiantly self-sufficient, the country gentleman dispassionately resisted trespass, by man or ill-fortune, upon his dignity (Ustick 1932, 149). Self-sufficiency compensated for deficiency of social status, while distinguishing him from the common herd. Thus, proclaims Peacham, the gentleman's sense of self "hangeth not upon the ayery esteeme of vulgar opinion, but indeed is of it selfe essential and absolute. Beside, Nobility being inherent and Naturall, can have (as the Diamond) the lustre but onley from it selfe: Honors and Titles externally conferred, are but attendant upon desert, and are but as apparell, and the Drapery to a beautiful body" (1634, 3; see also Braithwaite 1641, Dedicatory).

The country gentleman distanced himself from the puffery and corrupted indolence of the effete aristocrat. His dignity demanded he not leave his bidding to others. He rejected the nobleman's aversion to calloused hands and rugged toil. Unburdened by disdain for physical labor, he was more apt to equate it to godliness than vulgarity. He subscribed to the injunction of the Duchess of Newcastle: "Every man should, like a Bee, bring Hony to the Hive, and not, like the effeminat Drone, suck out the sweet, and idely live upon the Heroick labour of others" (quoted in Ustick 1932, 157).

If this did not quite make the country gentleman an egalitarian, it signaled his sympathy towards bootstrapping self-improvement and social mobility. Braithwaite thus posits in the *English Gentleman*, that the patriot's heroic mandate was grounded in the self-worth and moral rectitude attendant to industry. His prerogative was not "to idle out the time in the marketplace, such as those who make their life a repose or cessation from all labour, studies or vertuous intendments. Of which sorte those are, (and too many of those there are) who advanced to great fortunes by their provident Ancestors" (1641, 223). Instead, theirs was an aristocracy of merit, a magnanimous font of emulation, an exhortation to virtuous moral agency. "O Gentlemen, you whose hopes are promising, your more excellent endowments assuring, and your selves as patternes unto others appearing, know that this Perfection whereof we now intreat, is not acquired by idling or sensuall delighting of your selves in carnall pleasures, which darken and eclypse the glory or lustre of the soule, but in laboring to mortifie the desires of the flesh, which is ever levying and levelling her forces against the spirit!" (Braithwaite 1641, 223).

More outlander than tufthunter, the country gentleman also distinguished himself stylistically from the fawning and foppery of the courtier. Indeed, descended from the chivalric tradition as he may have been, the country gentleman did not inherit the cavalier's prerogative to announce his station through external contrivances of dress (Lieber 1864, 38). His decorum demanded neither observation of trivial protocols, nor obsequious purchase of favor (Lieber 1864, 39–40; see also Kelso 1925, 370–71; Ashley 1965, 111–15; Peterson 1992, 78–79). He shared the courtier's repugnance for vulgarity but evinced no reflexive abhorrence of the vulgar classes from whence he himself may well have come. He stood in opposition to absolute monarchical authority, and theologically from the symbiotic episcopalianism of the Anglican High Church and royal court. His politics tended toward republicanism, and in this sense, he drew strength from considerable opposition to an unpopular king.[8]

Prosaic in his ambitions, the country gentleman was committed to the solemnity of his obligations and disciplined in the perfection of his virtue. Rejecting what he saw as the loose sexual mores and political intrigue of the urbane courtier, he championed the public before the private, the pious over the libertine, the virtuous above the unctuous, the disciplined before the frivolous, and the godly instead of the glory seeker (Neale 1958, esp. 84; Trevor-Roper 1959, 82–83; Walzer 1969, 234, 241–47; Zagorin 1970, 33–39, 42–53, 106–18; Christianson 1977, 577–78; Stone 1980, 27, 32; Peck 1981; Morrill 1984, 157–58; Carlton 1995, 166–68). To his mind, the courtier sold his virtue for thirty pieces of silver—or, at the very least, the impure enticement of kingly favor (Knowles 2001, 627). Indeed, from the country perspective, if favoring pageantry and patronage did no credit to the courtier's character, it did even greater harm to his soul. To this point, Edward Panton decries the propensity of young men to embrace court ahead of country, to reject godliness in favor of slick talkers who "deride and flout at what belongs to God's honor" (quoted in Ustick 1932, 160).

Country gentlemen understood the favor bestowed upon them, upon all individuals, to come not from king, but from the gracious benevolence of God. Their decorous self-sufficiency was a rebuke to king, stodgy titled rentier, urban fop, and high churchman alike. Embracing an oppositional Protestantism, in country gentlemen we see more than a little resemblance to Calvinist fatalism—in which natural depravity is reflected in the ubiquity of political and social injustice, and for which programmatic Christ-like constancy is the only temporal ameliorative (see Higgins 1947, 26–27). It is therefore not surprising that oppositional country gentlemen found themselves in sympathy with Puritanical opponents of the Anglican High Church. Indeed, while many country gentlemen were Anglican in name, they were broadly Calvinist in faith. Most were laity, united in opposition to prevailing religious intolerance, socially and religiously awakened by a revivalist spirit calling out for a new social paradigm, even if the contours of that paradigm, like a ship in the fog, were shrouded and indistinct.

The Puritan Saint and the Life and Death of the Godly Republic

In covenant with God, proxies for the saints of the invisible church, English Puritan saints sought reconstruction of monarchy into Christ's millennial kingdom foretold in Revelation. They aspired to such social redemption through marriage of Reformed theology to republican polity. A spiritual aristocracy bound in grace—or at least full membership in the visible church—their divine mandate was to prepare souls in hopeful anticipation of divine reconciliation. In a more tactile sense, much like the virtuous philosopher, their brief was to inculcate civic virtue (reborn as godliness) in purification of the holy commonwealth. As such, stewardship of the Christian republic was the scripturally mandated prerogative of the visible saints (Winship 2012, 199–200).[9]

Originating as an intramural movement to purify the English Church, by the 1630s, a loosely defined Puritanism had begun to feed on social disaffection, spreading its tentacles beyond the spiritual space and into the secular (McLoughlin 1980, 25). If the movement was not particularly theologically or socially cogent, this was partly because no one—friend or foe—knew precisely who a Puritan was supposed to be or what she was supposed to do. Henry Parker, for example, suggests that all but "Papists, Prelates, and Courtiers" might rightly be called a Puritan (1641, 10–11). The Duke of Rutland demands a precise definition of Puritanism "so that those who deserve the name may be punished, and others not calumniated" (quoted in Hill 1964, 19).

Joseph Mead, with slightly more nuance, suggests that Puritans were of three orders. The *ecclesiastical*, "who was at first the onely Puritan," were moved by the singular quest to reform the Church of England (quoted in Shipps 1976, 196). Allied in liturgical opposition to the *Book of Common Prayer* and hostility toward episcopalian prelacy and adiaphora, some ecclesiastical Puritans were outright Separatists. Most, however, remained conforming members of the Church of England, perhaps because to separate would sever the link between Puritans and their lay patrons among the gentry, whose own opposition typically would not carry them quite that far (Hill 1964, 13–20; Zagorin 1970, 158–59; Greaves 1985, 454). From these could be distinguished *moral* Puritans. Lay and clerical, moral Puritans were less pious and more zealous, bequeathing the pejorative connotation from which Puritanism suffered even in its own time (Shipps 1976, 196). Finally, among the laity were to be found *political* Puritans, including the country gentlemen, who privileged limiting the absolutist prerogatives of the sovereign and protecting the autonomy of Parliament and people, even ahead of reforming the Church of England.

The oppositional alliance between ecclesiastical and political Puritan advanced organically. Hobbes finds the root of revivalist symbiosis to be the great universities—the "core of rebellion" as his Speaker A would have it—in which young gentlemen were most susceptible to the influence of charismatic radicals, capable of penetrating at least some of the stoicism and reserve into which their young auditors had been socialized (Seaver

1970, 182; see also Shipps 1976, 197–202; Morrill 1984, 160–61). In more popular fashion, Puritan revivalism was spread from the pulpit, in defiance of directives of both church and state. Common was the somewhat disingenuous practice of lectureships. In several boroughs, lecturers—many of whom were Puritan clergy unable to secure benefice—were hired by local patrons, congregations, or even town corporations that owned advowsons. Technically, these lecturers answered to the episcopal hierarchy of the established Church. Practically, their purpose was nothing short of theological usurpation underwritten by a proselytizing laity opposed to liturgical orthodoxy (Hill 1964, ch. 3). Such lectureships proved effective. Shipp reports a "high correlation" between presence in a borough of a Puritan minister and parliamentary support for the Puritan cause (1976, 203). Indeed, Seaver goes so far as to conclude that by "the spring of 1640 the Puritan lecturers and preachers had become the straw that broke the back of Church and State" ushering in the Puritan Revolution and, at least in the short-term, reformation of the English church (1970, 66–67).

The idealized Puritan commonwealth was godly, its Church populated not by false prophets and faithless hypocrites, but by evangelists—saints and missionaries dedicated to exhortation and guidance to souls in spiritual odyssey. It would prepare the soul to fight the good fight, illuminating the Holy Way by which, like Bunyan's Christian, the spiritual pilgrim would find her way back to God. More ambitiously, the Puritan Christian republic would be a chialistic proclamation of the ascendency of God's Church, a thousand years of peace accompanying its triumph over Satan and his minions, the rebirth of the righteous, and conversion of the multitudes in anticipation of the final judgment. The republic would stand to "put all men into a course of *Order* and *uniformity* in Gods [sic] way" (Cornelius Burges quoted in Zakai 1991, 410; emphasis in original). To this end, Puritan divines admonished the Puritan Long Parliament to undertake immediate reformation of English civil society. Thomas Case, a member of the Westminster Assembly, implored the House of Commons in 1641, for example, that "[r]eformation must be universal . . . Reform all places, all persons and callings. Reform the benches of judgement, the inferior magistrates . . . Reform the universities, reform the cities, reform the counties, reform inferior schools of learning. Reform the Sabbath, reform the ordinances, the worship of God . . . You have more work to do than I can speak . . . Every plant which my heavenly Father hath not planted shall be rooted up" (quoted in Stone 1996, 52–53; see also Miller

1941, esp. 37–44; 1943, 253; Hill 1964, 489–90; von Rohr 1965, 196–200; Clouse 1969, 197; McGiffert 1982, 480–81, 496–97; Hughey 1984, 115; Gardner 1988, 97; Zakai 1991, 415–19; Noll 2002, 38–39).

Yet such a sweeping agenda, by no means uncommon in the context of spiritual awakenings (McLoughlin 1980, 22–23), bespoke a restrictive theological and political vision too rigid to succeed. The revolutionary process is a multistage affair, such that it is one thing to awaken the revivalist spirit that gets the ball rolling in the first instance. It is quite another to construct a coherent social paradigm out of the wreckage (for more see Wallace's [1956] five stages of revitalization). It is therefore not unusual that the revolutionary social alliance fails to survive the revolution itself. So it was for the brief communion of Puritan saints and country gentlemen, many by the time of the Protectorate more radical in their Whiggery than their commitment to the Christianized republic.

The Failed Holy Commonwealth

The great failure of the Puritan republic was that it sought to ape the institutions of republican governance but not the process that sustains it. As exhorters of religious freedom in aid of godly reform, the visible saints of the English Civil War had envisioned themselves as incarnate symbols of the millennial commonwealth on the cusp of realization. As governors in this same cause, however, prerevolutionary latitudarianism evaporated in the headier air of religious ascendency. The fatal flaw was an ingenuous optimism in the expectation of requisite conformity in a context where every aggrieved party, special interest, and region seemingly had its own axe to grind and its own sectarian medium through which to grind it. It was the failure to recognize that it was not spiritual indivisibility that had united oppositional forces, but rather the desire to get out from under a centralized and oppressive alliance of court and church. For much of the splintering revolutionary alliance, civil war had not been waged merely for the privilege of swapping out one form of theologically endorsed tyranny for another.

Central was a fundamental conflict over the relationship between the order of nature and the order of grace. Real Whig heirs to the country tradition could not bring themselves to see humanity as the saints saw it: faithless and graceless, enticed by the false covenant of immediate fulfillment, deceived in worldly hubris by a promise of salvation that could never be delivered. Whiggish republicans insisted upon the freedom of individuals to determine for themselves the good terrestrial life as each understood it to be. Indeed, the country gentlemen's implicit ideal of self-sufficiency increasingly evolved into the Enlightenment assumption that moral agency attached naturally to all of humanity. The principal casualty was the legitimacy of a magnanimous aristocracy of saints charged with constraining the natural depravity of reprobates in covenantal obligation to God.

Equally problematic was that Puritan republicanism represented a contradiction in terms. The Puritan script functionally demoted citizens to subjects, relieving them of stewardship over the res publica—the progressive evolution and perfection of law, a mandate to which already-perfected gospel cannot lend itself. Left unrecognized by the saints was the great political advantage of civic participation in governance—a process that helps legitimate the state and mitigate substantive disagreement over core principles. With Puritan gospel noncontestable (Puritans put the Laudian church to shame in their rigidity) the Puritan republic was forced to choose between theological purity and political legitimacy.

Finally, the Puritan cause was not helped by a very limited cultural assent to Puritan heroism. Whatever their heroic impact, dour puritanical divines were feeble cultural substitutes for medieval knights, resplendent and chivalrous. Equally, there was no real-world heroic figure—Oliver Cromwell falling well short of the mark—to represent the incarnate values of the Puritan Revolution.[10] To the extent that anything like a postrevolutionary Puritan hero existed, she disengaged from the fray, retreating into eremitical resignation from the worldly mess the revolution had wrought. A politically disillusioned Bunyan, for example, portrays the Puritan hero of the late seventeenth century as all but lacking in any meaningful earthly virtues beyond her ability to keep to the Holy Way. Of course (mirroring the difficulties of the Puritan republic in general), any sort of efficacious humanism would have badly missed the point. Christian's ultimate transcendence in *The Pilgrim's Progress* owes itself entirely to the deepening of his faith, his triumph a reflection of the effectiveness of visible godly institutions and God's great capacity for mercy. Unlike tales of Christian epic, Bunyan's does not seek to glorify the Christian life. Rather, his is a frank portrayal of the Christian's struggle, in which salvation represents man's one true objective in his otherwise cursed worldly exile. That *this* was the stuff of heroism helps explain its inefficacy. Faithful's execution at the Vanity Fair, after all, might have spoken to the depraved humanism of Bunyan's times, but it was hardly a clarion call to flagging spirit.

Inevitably, the cold winds of erastianism were soon upon the necks of Puritan reformers, and the era of ecclesiastical Puritan ascendency concluded almost as soon as it had begun (Brauer 1950; Mosse 1960, esp. 437; Bloch 1985, 9–10; Zaret 1989). When the dust finally settled, the true victors were the oppositional country gentlemen who, in the guise of Real Whigs advocating political, religious, and ultimately economic liberty, consolidated their victory with the Glorious Revolution. The order of nature took back whatever had been ceded to the order of grace. The newest new radicals of the dawning Age of Reason espoused far greater balance between the cosmic orders, getting "their ideas from this world and their courage from another" (George 1968, 85). Retrospectively, the Puritan Revolution was Puritan only in its genesis. The ascendance of new values, proclaimed by the Bill of Rights and safeguarded through parliamentary supremacy, paved the way for the rise of classical liberalism, latitudarianism, and the commercialism that contributed to the changing character of eighteenth-century republicanism.

There was even an undercurrent, rarely spoken aloud, of the civic equality that was to manifest far later. In the short term, however, seventeenth-century English Whiggery retained an abiding gentility, a reluctance to abandon altogether the symbolic nobility attendant to a class of great men. It still would take more-committed oppositionists—European Idealists and Romantics, gritty evangelical egalitarians, and American transcendentalists—to turn the cultural tide against the classical republican shibboleth that great men were necessary for good societies. In the process, the Christian hero would once again have to reinvent herself, to reestablish the scholastic balance between the orders of nature and grace that the Reformed theology had so forcefully sought to skew. In the process, as we will see in the context of America, the locus of heroism would shift to a Christianized humanism proclaiming above all the immanence of the common man.

Conclusion

The idea of heroic Christianity is qualified by the relationship between the orders of nature and grace. The most immediate qualification turns on capacity, insofar as the greatest challenge faced by Christian heroes was, like a candle to the sun, the luminous presence of God. Their epic heroism owed its greatness to the endowments of God, their magnanimity a faint refraction of the divine being more greatly good than anything that could be conjured on this plane of existence. A related qualification applies to recognition, which to the eyes of many theologians constitutes a zero-sum game, recognition of Christian heroes' worldly accomplishments detracting from the glory that rightly attaches to God.

As pertains to republican values, the Christian *telos* was transcendence of the self—and all its attendant smallness, hubris, and self-absorption—from terrestrial purgatory. Christian heroes were magnanimous to the extent that they could assist others in their transcendence. For Christian Neoplatonists, however, Christian magnanimity was a contradiction in terms, a pridefulness unseemly in the depraved condition of postlapsarian man. Even in the more balanced Christian humanist tradition, Christian heroes fit awkwardly (as illustrated by the frequent employment of heroic dualism or some other mechanism designed to show worldly greatness in its proper cosmic context). Indeed, the Christian heroic prerogative was to be in the world, but only partly (and often reluctantly) of it. Christians' actions and desires therefore could not be means to the worldly ends that had motivated the pagans. And so they never led to wholly satisfactory worldly resolution. The martyr was slain; the knight errant's longings went unfulfilled; the Calvinist saint-presumptive's status remained ambiguous; the pilgrim was obliged to turn her back on her worldly affections, including friends and family; even the millennial republic would meet its end when the trumpet sounded—and that assuming the holy commonwealth could ever really come to be. Whatever Christian heroes' greatness, it was always accompanied by a countervailing enfeeblement that could be remedied only by the mystic and supernatural. The martyr endured her torment, the knight perfected his virtue, the saint found piety, the pilgrim stayed on the Holy Way, and the republic was chosen, all through the ultimate magnanimity of the only unambiguous hero, God himself.

This facial nullification of Christian humanism was not determinative, however. Nor did it preclude a qualified Christian heroism, estimable in cause and consequence. Institutionally, the heroic archetypes discussed in this chapter affected the course of history in a number of ways—from the Crusades, to the legitimation of the medieval feudal order through the ideal of courtly love, to inspiring defining revolutions in both England and America. Culturally, they served as exemplars, aspirational and inspirational role models symbolizing the incarnate values—most notably chivalry and self-sufficiency—that helped define the politics of their ages. The archetypes were fundamental, albeit often in vastly different ways, in reconciling the imperatives of the spiritual order with that of the wordly. In their own ways they guided the transition from a medieval social order to one hospitable to modern (liberal) republican government. Even the failed efforts of the Puritan saints bore fruit in the New World, indirectly influencing the emergence and development of the American republic.

Christian heroes' uncomfortable liminality between the orders of nature and grace also speaks to the evolution of republicanism. Such liminality hearkened to the emergent country gentlemen's inelegant social insertion between noblemen and commoners, helping to fuel their oppositional alienation. In the broadest sense—and papering over political and religious differences within each camp—it helped bind country gentlemen and visible saints together in spiritual and political revolution. The alliance between these political and ecclesiastical Puritans ultimately proved incompatible. The Christian republic, governed by gospel and subservient to grace, was too narrow in doctrine and constituency. Theologically intolerant, the Puritan holy commonwealth existed for barely a decade. (In America, the Puritan canopy, as Mark Noll (2002, ch. 3) calls it, also collapsed under the weight of its own orthodoxy.) As an exercise in attracting adherents, the Puritan republic was a hard sell.

The Real Whig republicanism of the country gentleman fared better. More tolerant, it was also more accommodating of the dialectic between the orders of nature and grace. Indeed, particularly in America, the balanced republicanism of the Real Whigs was better situated to reconcile Christian and republican principles in the dawning Age of Reason. In the United States, Christian republicanism found the Aristotelian sweet spot between spiritual excess (Puritanism) and deficiency (Deism). Two Great Awakenings over a period of less than a century ultimately would come to accommodate Protestant orthodoxy to the liberty, tolerance, and (nascent) egalitarianism first envisioned by the English country gentleman.

At the same time, the defiant oppositionism that initially sparked attraction between country gentleman and saint was reborn in more radicalized fashion among the Romantics. Radical heirs to the country tradition, Romantics imbibed their spiritualism from the sublime goodness of nature. Informed by such bounty of aesthetic goodness, Romanticism celebrated the efficacy of moral affect over revelation, self-esteem over external affirmation, and moral agency over moral dependency. Romantics envisioned a hero who, objectively speaking, was neither good nor great. Sometimes antiheroic and imperfect in her virtue, from the late eighteenth century onwards she emerged (along with the common hero discussed later) as an integral element of modern republican heroism.

Chapter 5

Romanticism

The Egotistical Sublime and Moral Agency

If Christianity accommodates heroism somewhat inelegantly, the same can be said of Romanticism. As with their Christian counterparts, Romantic heroes speak to the evolution of republicanism. Even more than Christian heroes, they constitute an important element of the *liberal* republicanism characteristic of the modern age, with a particular emphasis on the equality that attaches to it. Rather than grace, at the heart of Romanticism is nature. Hearkening to the self-sufficiency, naturalism, and oppositionism of the country gentlemen, nineteenth-century Romantics embraced a revolutionary spirit, encouraging individuals of humbler status to cast off the subservience that had long defined their social prerogative. Coming of age in sibling rivalry with Enlightenment philosophy, Romanticism shared the new moral philosophy's emphasis on humanity's natural capacities, even if Romantics rejected the primacy of cognition as driver of moral agency. Both evinced an attendant hostility to authority derived from anything other than personal assent, and both conceived transcendence as a product of innate human capacity.

The Romantic is the least facially heroic of the four hero types explored in this book, and a large part of this chapter is dedicated to showing that Romanticism contains a theory of republican heroism. As a first step, we need to establish the basis of Romantic heroism writ large. Defined by neither goodness nor greatness, Romantic heroes present as rebellious iconoclasts, often appearing more *anti*heroic than heroic. They need not be good—at least in the ethical sense of conformity to an objective moral code—but they must be estimable. Social beings, they are at the same time nonconformists. They answer to a subjective, experiential, and natural sense of justice. They are transcendent only when they become wholly self-aware, governed by allegiant fidelity to an authentic sense of self. In their better moments, they accommodate themselves to republican virtue, envisioning a more just society and a cosmically inspired, if individually tailored, sense of the transcendent life. In their weaker ones, they are dysfunctionally atomistic—like Balzac's Louis Lambert or Melville's Bartleby, tragic outcasts in the world beyond themselves.

As with goodness, extant greatness is not requisite to Romantics' heroic capacity. Rather, Romantic heroism is exemplary in the employment of justice through natural affect in the conduct of life and in the cause of social redemption. And while some Romantic heroes *are* great—we will look at the Romantic poets in this sense—they need not be. Romantic estimability is realized through courage of conviction, doing what one feels to be right even in the face of the hostile social conventions, legal jeopardy, and even physical violence. That Romantic heroes swim against the tide, embracing social defiance rather than bowing to conformity, speaks to the vulnerability attendant to heroism. Indeed, Romantic heroes are axiomatically oppositional, heroism acquiring purchase in aid of social reform rather than defense or maintenance of the status quo.

Romantics appropriate the country gentleman's self-containment, some to the point of solipsism. The argument here, however, is that Romantic heroes appeal to the natural human compulsion to share common feelings. Nested within the essence of humanity, then, Romantic heroes conceive a communal individualism—a symbiotic need for autonomy and security, for freedom and a sense of belonging, for deeply personal feelings and an outlet for their expression. Against this communal individualism stands the Enlightenment legacy of atomistic embourgeoisement so distasteful to Romantics. Alienating the individual from nature, bourgeois society exudes the stench of ostentation—puffery noxiously perfumed by civility and politeness. It radiates hypocrisy and insincerity, privileging speciously great individuals, encouraging aspirant social climbers, and rewarding those who, like courtiers of old, stand ready and willing to lick the right set of boots. In contrast to the new moral philosophy of the Enlightenment—privileging rationalism, atomism, and virtue as transactional obligation—Romanticism favors the natural human inclination towards affective union.

At the heart of the Romantic worldview is nature conceived three ways—personal, human, and ambient. To Romantics, nature informs something greater than humanity. Its spiritual principles—accessible through neither revelation nor grace—are imbibed through the senses, processed in the imagination, and regulated by the conscience. Early Romantics embraced such principles, aspiring to the glory of a vaguely defined afterlife in which, like the Socratic soul liberated from corporeal encumbrance, individuals would find their true reward. Often antagonistic towards organized religion, Romantic antipathy did not extend to the divine spirit itself—even if the biblical God (or more accurately his human creators and accessories) employed religion as a tool of hierarchy and tyranny. Instead, early Romantic gods were exhorters of liberty. They encouraged the autonomous self, provoking that insolent heroic quality that urged one to eschew the stultifying postfeudal bourgeois existence in which she languished.

The heroic Romantic self is as the cosmic architects of nature intended it to be, untainted by the servility and avarice acquired in the society of insincere individuals. Ever vulnerable to human frailties, the heroic Romantic self nonetheless retains the dignity of fidelity *to* itself. Morally self-sufficient, the Romantic hero is invulnerable to flattery, pretense, or social affirmation, living her best life when that life is self-directed. Only in such authenticity lies true transcendence. In contrast to Socratic goodness, authenticity represents a natural condition requiring no ethical reconstruction. It does not need to be coaxed by coercive means on the authority of greater individuals. Rather, it resides latent within humans' natural affective core. It informs a custom-tailored moral code resistant to, at least skeptical of, the ethical ontology so foundational to Socratic philosophy.

If nature is muse, art is expression of Romantic authenticity. The ultimate presentation of ego, sociability, and spirituality, art bridges the gap between individual and community. It celebrates the liberty requisite to authenticity. Its defiant composers, insists Emerson, "are free and they make free" (*Poet*, 283). Aesthetically, artists exhort their audiences with the same tenacity as the philosophers or evangelists, but without the same threat of moral censure or damnation. Their didacticism is an appeal, not a decree. Like tragedians of old, artists move their auditors solely through affective sublimity. Deeply personal in its construction, it draws artist and auditor into aesthetic communion (Emerson *Art*, 247–51). It constitutes the egoistic bedrock of a shared sense of self, a community of taste expressed as culture, a *Volksgeist*, a distinctive sense of usness in spirited proclamation of what it means to be *people like us*.

This chapter explores the republicanism of Romantic heroism in quest of social justice. Politically, Romanticism represents an egalitarian quest for human dignity, celebrating the essential humanity of the commoner as an antidote to the coercive power of the great (Burgum 1941, 482). One of the two modern hero types discussed in this book, Romantic heroes stand shoulder to shoulder with the common hero, distinct only in their oppositionism and their unwillingness to move beyond an affective sense of the good in favor of a positive one. Focusing primarily on the nineteenth-century heyday of Romanticism, the chapter has two principal aims. The first is to demonstrate the primacy of nature, egoism, and self-mastery in construction of the authentic self. Rescuing Romanticism from antiheroic self-absorption, the second part of the chapter emphasizes the Romantic hero's republican virtue, particularly as it pertains to the cosmic and social obligation that might appear to be lacking. It is in this context that the last part of the chapter highlights more contemporary Romanticism as the basis of a pluralistic sense of social identification requisite to social equality. Indeed, beginning in the middle of the twentieth century, this expression of shared affective bonds has informed a renewed sense of social belonging in demonstration of the Romantic hero's continued relevance to the preservation of republican virtue.

The Nature of the Romantic Hero

The transformative eighteenth century from which Romanticism emerged represented a significant challenge to the supremacy of extant institutions that couched spirituality and sagacity in mystification, while demanding reflexive obedience to church or state. The growing importance of science and rationalism aided in discovery of solutions to problems that previously had found their sole resolution in faith. Far from the Calvinist premise of natural man depraved and helpless in his postlapsarian state, the prevailing assumption was that individual agents were sufficient in themselves in quest of the good life, or salvation, or whatever transcendent state they deemed most appropriate for themselves. Platonic dualism between mortal body and eternal soul, so central to classical philosophy and Christian theology, gave way to the more natural dichotomy of heart and mind, foretelling the impudent intrusion of nature upon hegemonic grace. Or in Becker's more elegant phrasing, the Heavenly City came to rest upon "earthly foundations . . . the business of justification transferred from divine to human hands" (1932, 49; see also Schneewind 1998, 4; Middleton 2005, 437).

It was sometime around the middle of the eighteenth century that the person of sentiment started to distinguish herself from the person of reason, driven to transcend the ordinary life by an aesthetic sense of the propriety of her actions in allegiance to her natural self (Becker 1932, 41). Prototypically Romantic heroes emerged as the obverse of the magnanimous: authentic rather than good; naturally rather than habitually virtuous; affectively equal rather than cognitively superior; authentically rather than objectively moral. Guided by their feelings, then as now, Romantic heroes manifested as defiant rebels, wresting their freedom from the tyranny of God and man. They were Faustian, Promethean, or even Satanic noble outlaws. No longer passive subjects, they molted into efficacious man, sufficiently comfortable in their own skin to reject the petty social morals they understood to attach—parasitic and ultimately destructive—to prevailing social, theological, and political paradigms.

Like frontiersmen of the American West blazing the trail for the homesteader, Romantic heroes' defiance represents a portal to a new world. Casting themselves as purifiers or redeemers, they are destroyers of old paradigms, contentious social outsiders figuratively declaring war upon the worst excesses of social privilege. They stand against the vestigial constraints that rob individuals of that immature wonder and inquiry, not yet hostage to "the blasphemy of laws" (Byron 1899, cant. III, LXIV). They reject "the puny boundaries" that maturity and wisdom and moral conformity entice us to perceive (Wordsworth 1979, bk. II, 1–30, 219; see also Goethe 1902, 12–13, 35; Thorslev 1962, 17; Cantor 2007, 395–96). They seek refuge from the strictures of social existence—"Here, where men sit and hear each other groan" (Keats 2007, III); and where the "virtue in most request is conformity" (Emerson *Self-Reliance*, 35).

Like Nietzsche's overman, Romantic heroes are self-propelled wheels, eschewing social bondage in the name of human purpose grander than "making a parade in the eyes of others" (Rousseau *Sav.*, 70).[1] Egoistic to be sure, theirs is a quest for the dignity realized through ontological understanding and mastery of the self (e.g., Goethe 1902, 32–33, 111). Declares Werther, "I examine my own being, and find there a world" (Goethe 1902, 10). And Wordsworth: "A Traveler I am; And all my Tale is of myself" (1979, bk. III, 196–97). And Byron: "[T]hy solitude Is as an anchorite's, were it but holy" (1817, III.i, 53–54). Or Emerson, "No law can be sacred to me but that of my nature" (*Self-Reliance*, 36).

Romantic heroes revel in their autonomy. They condemn the tyranny born of submission to a deadened, rigid confessional or bourgeois life that obstinately blocks the path to fulfillment of the human condition by alienating the individual from her true nature. They are autonomous moral agents defining morality on their own terms. In liberating themselves from moral positivism, they announce their unwillingness to settle for such crumbs and table scraps of residual liberty as might be spared by the prevailing moral order. Instead, they begin with the freedom to explore the nature of the self and from there acquire the moral precepts that serve as the basis of a cultural order born of shared aesthetic values. They are perfectly comfortable operating outside the commands of gospel or positive law if guided by a higher moral power—namely, that sentient impulse bespeaking the authenticity of their being.

THE POWER OF NATURE

The majesty of the spiritual order had inspired seventeenth-century man to awe and wonder. It compelled him into goodness against what were thought to be his natural and depraved inclinations. By contrast, the eighteenth- and nineteenth-century individual stood in awe and wonder of her own nature. Her Edenic quest was no longer reconciliation with God, but rather with her essential and idiosyncratic self—the natural core of nobility and curiosity of which organized religion and civilization seemed bound and determined to deprive her. The vastness of nature permitted idealization of something greater than her self, but without the self-effacement of orthodox Christianity. It represented the untouched, uncivilized, and unsullied; its purity the purity of the individual unburdened by the oppressive taint of history.

Inherent in the purity of nature is humanity's untapped potential. A sensuous appeal to the mind, nature opens it to new ideas constructed from the imagination, elevating it beyond the limits imposed by reason's theocratic or bourgeois governors. Says Baillie in his eighteenth-century treatise on the sublime, "Vast objects occasion vast sensations, and vast sensations give the mind a higher idea of her own powers" (1996, 89). To lose oneself in nature is to explore possibilities closed off by the practical imperatives inherent in the society of others. Its sublimity is akin to magnanimity, but only in the Thomist sense of rescuing the soul from the despair of pusillanimity (Schiller 1884c, 139; Barnouw 1980, 499). Indeed, it is in this sense that Victor Frankenstein turns to nature in his grief after the murder of his brother and the execution of Justine. "These sublime and magnificent scenes," he proclaims, "elevated me from all littleness of feeling . . . [and] filled me with a sublime ecstasy, that gave wings to the soul" (Shelley 1888, 132–33).

Nature is also a metaphor for social estrangement and alienation. It represents a retreat into the self as a means of escaping the evils of the external world, of minimizing one's vulnerable surface (Berlin 1999, 37; also Kravitt 1992, 93). It is author of guiding emotion, of "some inner light . . . for which it is worth both living and dying" (Berlin 1999, 8). Goethe's Werther is the quintessence: a martyr to love, a crusader against the numbing conformity and rationalism of his times, a man more willing to die to uphold the laws of the heart than live under the tyranny of reason. Werther speaks to the vacuity of urban civility. He disdains the horrifyingly anesthetized bourgeois aesthetic that Rousseau characterizes as the "art of pleasing"—a bastardized mimetic taking on the pall of ritualized social convention. Such "servile and deceptive conformity" represents a form of enslavement in its own right, alienating individuals from the affections that characterize humanity in its natural condition (Rousseau *DAS*, 132, *DOI*, 171–72, 185–200). Tied together in recursive pathology, far from perfecting humanity, bourgeois ethics and rationalism dilute compassion, subordinating that noble primordial sentiment to the sovereignty of vanity and cupidity (*DOI*, 199, 218).

The Romantic antithesis of nature is not grace. It is hypocrisy. Just as the ethics of the Enlightenment were a reaction against external imposition of moral knowledge by greatly good individuals, Romantic aesthetics of the early modern age were a reaction against the posturing and pretension of great hypocrites. Among other sources, insincerity was a bequest of the Renaissance arts—on the stage and in the parlor—of theatrics and contrivance, masquerade balls and "honest dissimulation," where the capacity for deception represented a virtue in itself. Studied contrivance had been a means of navigating the intrigue and patronage of increasingly complex court life. Attendant self-fashioning made one's identity malleable, its presentation to the world its own form of artistry that rendered the self "a cultural artifact, a historical and ideological illusion generated by the economic, social, religious, and political upheavals of the Renaissance" (Martin 1997, 1315, also 1314; Greenblatt 2005, preface, 2).

In amelioration, the early-Romantic prescription was sincerity, honest self-presentation to the point of highlighting unflattering distinction between the self as it really was, and the self others might have wanted it to be. Byron's Manfred, for example, consumed by incestuous love and remorse, is in no mood to craft a favorable self-impression. One might readily assent to the contempt he has for himself yet cannot help but admire his insistence to exist (even if only in death) on his own terms. Even more defiantly, in his *Confessions*, Rousseau invites his reader to "lament for my unworthiness, and blush for my imperfections." Rather than indulge in condemnation, though, he challenges the reader to reflect upon his own life, to "reveal, with the same frankness, the secrets of his heart . . . and say, if he dare, *I was better than that man*" (Rousseau *Conf.*, 2, emphasis in original; also Trilling 1972, 58). It is only through this type of self-scrutiny that the early Romantic could assure herself of the authenticity of her values and beliefs—of the soundness of her own principles, which anyway was the only moral conviction worth a damn. It was to communicate such personal sincerity that the painter elevated herself to the status of muse, the author indulged in autobiography, and the poet turned her spirituality inward. Each impressed upon the audience the imprimatur of legitimacy, the sense that the artist could not "be false to any man because he has been true to himself" (Trilling 1972, 15–16, 23–25; Shklar 1979, 4–5).

Heroic fidelity to sincere conviction brings with it with little expectation of social recognition. Far from being honored for their authenticity, Romantic heroes are as likely to endure pity, ridicule, or the contempt that the self-satisfied herd reserves for the gadfly. Contingent upon neither grace nor social ratification, dependent not upon character or capacity, Romantic heroes are extraordinary in their self-acceptance, their unwillingness to permit others' reception of their actions to militate against their sense of self-worth. Their authenticity insulates them, an antidote to the indignities imposed by the world beyond the self (Goethe 1902, 40, 70; Berger 1970, 342). Their sole reward is the dignity of living a transcendent life, a life they craft for themselves according to no other expectations than their own. For Taylor, such authenticity announces, "a certain way of being human that is *my* way. I am called upon to live my life in this way, and not in imitation of anyone else's. . . . [T]his gives a new importance to being true to myself. If I am not, I miss the point of my life, I miss what being human is for *me*" (1991, 28–29, emphasis original). So it is that Romantic heroes have little taste for positive morality. What magnanimous heroes call perfection of virtue, Romantic heroes see as nothing more than a metaphysic that one person or group of people has been strong enough to impose on another and that the mass of humanity has been feeble enough to assume. Like Prometheus defying an arbitrary God, the Romantic disdains putatively great individuals speciously elevated above their fellows by duplicitous social contrivances designed to do nothing more than dignify those who lack dignity, to insulate the "parlor soldiers" who shun the "rugged battle of fate, where strength is born" (Emerson *Self-Reliance*, 55).

ART: DEPRAVED AND PROFOUND

The vacuity of hypocrisy is the subtext of Diderot's (1964) *Rameau's Nephew*, in which the iconoclastic eponymous character seeks to show the socially conventional narrator that the true seat of dignity is not *dignitas*. Rather, it is the inner man, liberated from the web of specious civility woven by individuals honored but insubstantial (Berlin 1999, 51). The Philosophe makes little effort to conceal his distaste for the ridiculous Rameau, who cheerily owns up to being a wastrel and a fool. Prior to an unfortunate lapse in judgment that led to his loss of patronage at the home of the pompous nobleman Bertin, he had earned his livelihood through the fool's prerogatives of toadying, pimping, and buffoonery. He now finds himself in dire straits. Ever the man of reason, the Philosophe suggests that Rameau go back to his patron, apologize, and beg for a return to his station. Rameau concedes that while that would indeed be the prudent course of action, it would constitute too great an imposition upon his dignity. His *dignity*? Dumbfounded, the Philosophe questions the fool's capacity for *in*dignity, pointing out there seems to be no level to which the shameless Rameau will not stoop. For his part, Rameau finds this amusing, "I almost think you are making fun of me, Master Philosopher. . . . I am Bertin's fool and that of many others—yours possibly at this minute: or maybe you are mine" (Diderot 1964, 34, 50).

Indeed, who is ridiculing whom? It is Rameau who is sufficiently comfortable in his own skin to play the fool, fleecing real fools while laughing at them to their faces. Why should he not? The haughty and self-satisfied veneer of Parisian high society, after all, masks a morally rotten foundation. Were this not the case, Rameau reasons, his own degeneracy would not be tolerated behind closed doors, far less subsidized (Diderot 1964, 55–56). If his contempt goes unrecognized by those too vain and hypocritical to see him for the rapacious scoundrel he really is, well their stupidity hardly represents trespass upon *his* dignity (77). The thought is unsettling to the Philosophe, who while hardly racing to embrace the sentiment, cannot reject it out of hand. "There was in what he said much that one thinks to oneself, and acts on, but that one never says. This was in fact the chief difference between my man and the rest of us. He admitted his vices, which are also ours: he was no hypocrite. Neither more nor less detestable than other men, he was franker than they, more logical, and thus more profound in his depravity" (74).

Depraved and profound is not a bad way of describing the literary Romantic heroes of the early nineteenth century—"mad, bad and dangerous to know" as Byron was characterized by Lady Caroline Lamb. Early Romantic heroes were more than willing to glory in their depravity, rescued from inestimability only by fidelity to an idiomatic code of justice (Thorslev 1962, 66). Of course, heroic estimability demands that the profound outweigh the depraved. The latter, after all, is not an end in itself, but rather a device to highlight the perversity of bourgeois society, its attendant injustice and the hypocrisy fettering noble sentiment. Early Romantic depravity—often expressed through Gothic horror, atheism, sadism, or incest—thus carried with it shock value, condemnation of the somnolent existence of Nietzsche's last men celebrating a nihilistic society, bowing and scraping to a God cruel and indifferent to their fortunes. Such divine antipathy makes iconic such Romantic defiers of God as Milton's Satan and Prometheus, both of whom announce man's potential for impious apotheosis. Both appeal to "the volition to arrogate to the individual and finite mind those attributes traditionally reserved for God alone: self-sufficiency, creativity, and ultimate freedom" (Thorslev 1963, 251; 1962, 108).

Satan inspires those strong enough to transcend submission. He represents the strong standing in proud distinction from the common herdsmen, from those of submissive wills "weak enough to be restrained" (Blake 1906, 9). Blake thereby portrays Milton's Satan as a champion of liberty, waging war against the twin oppressions of society and theodicy. "Prisons are built with stones of law," he declares in one of his "Proverbs of Hell," "brothels with the bricks of religion" (1906, 15). More than Satan, though, it is the other divine antagonist and source of fire whose voice the Romantic appropriates. Promethean defiance reflects the glorification of self-mastery as an alternative to deference. It assents to nothing that militates against the proper assignation of faith, which is to say faith in human potential (Grene 1940, 27; Thorslev 1962, esp. 117). Hence Byron's ode to Prometheus:

> Thy Godlike crime was to be kind . . .
> And strengthen Man with his own mind . . .
> Thou art a symbol and a sign
> To Mortals of their fate and force;
> Like thee Man is in part divine,
> A troubled stream from a pure source. (1909, 1022)

Promethean, one is her own ruler, liberated not merely from that which constrains externally, but also from the internal constraints that inhibit self-confidence, self-awareness, and self-esteem. The imperative for such self-mastery obliges the Romantic hero to dig deep within to break the bonds of inhibition and to do so as faithfully as she defies such external authority as might restrict her freedom unreasonably.

In keeping with the profound depravity of Romanticism, the ultimate form of Romantic self-mastery is death. Suicide is Werther's definitive means of realizing Lotte's admonition to conquer himself. Byron's Manfred ("Man Freed," e.g., McVeigh 1982, 604) finds self-mastery in defying the demon who has come to take him to hell. ("I . . . was my own destroyer, and will be My own hereafter") (1817, III. iv, 160–61). In this same vein, Byron's *Prometheus* concludes:

> And Man in portions can foresee
> His own funereal destiny;
> His wretchedness, and his resistance,
> And his sad unallied existence:
> To which his Spirit may oppose
> Itself—and equal to all woes,
> And a firm will, and a deep sense,
> Which even in torture can descry
> Its own concenter'd recompense,
> Triumphant where it dares defy,
> And making Death a Victory. (1909)

More practically, self-mastery constitutes asserting control over one's existence, living according to her own convictions. It is the sword of self-assertion raised against the tyrannical caprice of spiritual and worldly authority. Self-mastery permits one to align herself in cosmic harmony with nature, ambient and internal, in living a transcendent life governed by the dignity of fidelity to herself.

As to heroic identification, the Romantic hero is both the artist who channels the Promethean muse *and* the erstwhile hobbit-auditor who imbibes the Promethean spirit—principled defiance of mindless conformity.[2] She is the common (if sadly, atypical) citizen with the courage to steer her own ship through the inevitably hostile waters of convention. She stands apart from the disenfranchised masses, those legally or volitionally precluded from exercising their God-given freedom. The antithesis of the philosophic sage, she eschews ethical conformity to an objective moral good in favor of aesthetic obligation to the authentic conduct of life. The former speaks to order, place, and hierarchy in accordance with the universal properties of ethics and reason. The latter breaks the mold, the Romantic hero celebrating the freedom, equality, and the free-spirited autonomy catalyzed by aesthetics and affect.

There is more to this than affective self-centeredness. Percy Shelley suggests that egalitarian aesthetics succeed where magnanimous ethics fail (1891, esp. 14). Art gives voice to virtue in a way that the innate senses can capture, the imagination can interpret, but which rationalism and science cannot adequately express (Beattie 1783, 621). For all their efforts, greatly good individuals have been unsuccessful in constructing a unified theory of virtue ethics in the same way as it is possible to construct such a theory in mathematics and science. Indeed, because morality is kaleidoscopic, not geometric, it constitutes a giant jigsaw puzzle that, whatever the capability of supernatural beings, is beyond even the greatest human's ability to assemble with any sort of cognitive precision (Berlin 1999, 23; see also Rousseau *Sav.*, 17–18).

Even more than this expressive advantage, Shelley rejects the independence of ethics from aesthetics, reason being operative, he agrees with Hume, only on the evidence of the senses (1915, 3). Consequentially, there is a latent cost—tragically manifest in the French Revolution as discussed below—in the specious assertion of the primacy of reason over affect. Such cognitive ascendancy does, it is true, facilitate mastery over one's environment. But the cost of mastering the external is borne by the internal, by marginalization of the passionate core, the affective powertrain driving a self-directed life and with it, progressive social transformation.

In asserting control over nature, *homo economicus* depresses the creative element of the self. Worse, she subjugates others through rigid division of society into wealthy and impoverished, citizen and subject, autonomous and dependent (1891, 35–38).

The Romantic hero's mandate is to undo the process by reversing the priorities. Only by mastering the internal can a new external can be imagined. Just as an edifice cannot be constructed before it is conceived, meaningful social vision begins in the imagination and is legitimated in the senses before it can be exported into the world (e.g., Emerson *Poet*, 284). If the magnanimous hero is the variously authoritarian philosopher king or divine, the Romantic hero is the Promethean free citizen rebelling against specious authority. Guided by an inner light, hers is a redemptive moral affect imposing its will on reason and faith, rather than the other way around. Trusting to nature ahead of self-interest, it is affect—rather than gospel or secular authority—that guides her. It is affect that admonishes her, with guilt and remorse, when she fails to abide by its imperatives (Rousseau *Sav.*, 14).

The Egotistical Sublime and Republican Justice

For classical republicans, there is something deeply troubling about all of this. From a traditionally republican perspective, the subjectively driven Romantic hero flirts with recklessness in her curiosity and carelessness in her amenity. She is her own source of moral nourishment, her own governor, and even her own hero. She bears, to borrow from Emerson, the standard of antinomianism (1983b, 196). Classical republican teleology, of course, explicitly rejects an individually defined good, dismissing it as mere gratification through pleasure, self-indulgence repackaged and sold as something grander. Indeed, there is something of Keats's "egotistical sublime" in the imperative for Romantic self-mastery (An 2011, 105). At the very least, having the courage of one's convictions often means self-consciously situating herself beyond the social pale (De Bruyn 1987, 213; Berlin 1999, 9). In the Byronic extreme, the Romantic wears her intemperance like a badge of honor, ceding reason to passion, and, it would seem, civic sense to sense of self. Apotheotic in her social detachment, she stands aloof from the conforming—the faithful and the deferential. (To the Chamois Hunter's counsel of Christian patience, Manfred spits:

"Patience and patience! Hence—that word was made For brutes of burthen not for birds of prey; Preach it to mortals of a dust like thine,—I am not of thine order" [Byron 1817, II.i., 38-43].)

Yet egotistical, spiritually unconventional, culturally relativistic, and hedonistic she may appear, in point of fact, the Romantic hero does not present in opposition to republicanism. As the discussion of Mary Shelley and Friedrich Schiller (below) suggests, the egotistical sublime does not define Romanticism. Rather, it is at best a single element of it, at worst a bastardization. Unquestionably, Romanticism represents an obligation to the self. That is the very point of it. Heroic, however, it satisfies the other elements of republican virtue as well: obligation to God and obligation to civil society. Indeed, these other component obligations supply the estimability—and highlight the vulnerabilities—requisite to heroism.

Obligation to God

Considering the pride of place afforded Satan and Prometheus in the Romantic pantheon, obligation to God is the tougher nut to crack. Certainly, this is so, if we take "God" to be the biblical God as commonly interpreted in eighteenth- and early nineteenth-century European Christianity. Sovereign of heaven and earth, this biblical God demanded that humanity affirm the supremacy of grace over nature, piety over imagination, deference over defiance, and humility over humanism. This was a God to whom most Romantics could owe no servitude.

Yet Romantic doctrinal opposition must not be confused with cosmic or spiritual antipathy. Their defiance is not directed toward the creator of nature and all its wonders. In the *Necessity of Atheism*, for example, Percy Shelley's dismissal of Christian belief does not apply to the "pervading spirit coeternal with the universe" (1915, 1). Even Romantic aversion to the biblical God reflects a human failing rather than a spiritual one. The autocracy of God is an artifact of mortal confederates purporting to do his bidding—"madmen who have made men mad" says Byron in *Childe Harold's Pilgrimage* (1891, cant. III, 43; see also Blessington 1850, 379). This doctrinal God supplies nothing that God the architect of nature has not already bestowed. Indeed, of privileging revelation and faith ahead of a natural and affective comprehension of divine obligation, Rousseau's Savoyard Vicar asks, "What purity of morals, what system of faith useful to man, or honorable to his Creator, can I deduce from any positive doctrines, that I cannot deduce equally as well from a good use of my natural faculties? Let anyone show me what can be added, either for the glory of God, the good of society, or my own advantage, to the obligations we are laid under by nature" (*Sav.*, 75).

Critically, the issue at hand, then, is not one of divine *being*. It is one of epistemology. It is a matter of belief in an anthropomorphic God constructed upon nothing more than the application of unverifiable principles. Shelley reserves his faith for the natural spirit he can experience; one who speaks to him through aesthetics and not revelation. After all, he insists, spiritual belief must conform to the procedural imperative of all beliefs: a sense of conformity between an idea and one's assent *to* that idea. This sense typically demands investigation of the obstacles that stand in the way of conformity. The mind takes on this investigative role. But *belief* itself is not born of the cognitive (investigative) process. Cognition is critical to the process of acquiring belief, but it plays a secondary role. It is but an agent to the principal, an aid to the affect that initiates the process and announces the sense of conformity at its conclusion (Shelley 1915, 2–3; see also Rousseau *Sav.*, 20–24). Belief cannot exist where reason is the principal. Were it so, belief would be volitional. And if reason is not the principal, Shelley claims, "belief" through reasoned understanding of the biblical God can be supported by nothing more than the empirical effects of creation.

Beyond this, conclusions pertaining to the essence, prerogatives, or will of the creator are but arbitrary injunctions drawn from the scantiest of ideational evidence. The epistemological leap from *conceiving* of the biblical God to *belief* in his existence is simply too great. We may hypothesize about the creative force. We can respect the revelationary experience of others. We might express fervent desire to know and be reconciled with God. But we cannot truly *believe* in the biblical God insofar as we (those to whom God has not personally revealed himself) are deprived of the sensory conformity that is the underlying source of belief. Of course, Shelley notes, none of this has not stopped theologians from making God speak and have him say what they want to hear (also Rousseau *Sav.*, 76). It has not prevented the weaving of a theological tapestry of prohibition extending all the way to imposition of criminality upon disbelief (Shelley 1915, 5). Indeed, says Rousseau, "We had much rather determine at random, and believe the thing that is not, than to confess that none of us is capable of seeing the thing that is" (*Sav.*, 18).

What one *is* capable of perceiving, Fichte (2010) suggests, is the idealization of that which she herself constructs. So conceived, divinity can be understood as an inner godliness or spirit that accompanies self-consciousness (as in Hegel 1966); it can manifest as part of man's natural affective moral core (as in Rousseau *DOI*). It bespeaks a sensual capacity that guides one towards, and erects no inherent barrier to, agapic love. It attaches to a god of permission rather than restriction, endowing moral comprehension imbibed through different hearts, processed through different minds, filtered through different consciences, and foundational to the authenticity of nonconforming individuals. Divinity is experienced from the inside out, tutelage from an internal instructor more trustworthy than the deceptive devices employed by imperfect purveyors of faith (Rousseau *Sav.*, 19).

Such inner godliness does not wholly alienate Romanticism from tenets of Christianity. It is not incompatible with the imprinted godliness of Augustine's *ratio superior*, or scholastic *synderesis*—a natural impulse toward the good, "a habit containing the precepts of the natural law" (Aquinas 1947, I–II, Q. 94, Art. 1, ad. 2, I–II, Art. 2). Neither does it preclude the pietism that retains faith in Christ while rejecting the dogmatism of objective spiritual truths (Massey 1978, esp. 112). In any case, that which philosophers and divines encourage through contemplative sagacity and piety, the Savoyard Vicar suggests, each of us already possesses in the conscience, that metaknowledge of divine instinct, the "infallible judge of good and evil, who makest man resemble the Deity. In thee consist the excellence of our nature and the morality of our actions. Without thee I perceive nothing in myself that should elevate me above the brutes, except the melancholy privilege of wandering from error to error by the assistance of an ill-regulated understanding and undisciplined reason" (Rousseau 1889, 64–65).

If conscience is deific regulator of the passions, Shelley identifies the imagination as the godhead, the voice of divine exhortation, author of that which "no man foretold" (Emerson *Poet*, 265; see also 278–79). The imagination internalizes godliness through the sublimity of ambient natural beauty and distills it through art. In the process, the imagination serves no less a purpose than a personal interpretation of the word of God. Far from the frivolity dismissed by many wedded to the idea of cognitive moral hegemony, art is more than mere aesthetic adornment to a transcendent life constructed upon the bedrock of philosophy or theology. Nor is art the harbinger of hedonism that civic humanists of the Late Roman Republic blithely dismissed. Instead, art—poetry in particular—lies at the very heart of authentic moral being, composing, as it were, scripture for the senses. Distinct from the Knower or the Doer, says Emerson, the poet is the Sayer, "sent into the world to the end of expression" (*Poet*,

265). She is the high priest of the imagination, drawing "into a certain propinquity with the beautiful and the true that partial apprehension of the agencies of the invisible world which is called religion" (Shelley 1915, 14; see also Whitman 1860b, chant 1, 20–24). There attaches to her art something mystical and eternal, "beyond and above consciousness," that stirs within the auditor a heroic progression from admiration to emulation to actualization (Shelley 1915, 11–12; Emerson *Poet*, 281). More than a petition to reason or belief, poetry is the realm of the hierophant (O'Neill 2011, 34), a sensual appeal to the first principles of the divinity of imagination (Shelley 1891, 34–35). Poetry is, says Shelley, "planetary music for mortal ears" (13).

Romantic rejection of the supremacy of grace therefore represents no inherent trespass upon the divinity of the order of nature or the obligation that attaches to it. More forcefully, there is no transcendent Romantic life without something akin to what we call God. Absent the cosmic ripple forming concentric circles from the divine creator, there could be no moral order. There could be no just condition to which the just agent could attune herself. Instead, she would have to construct her own private order, her disposition not within the radius of God's center, but a Nietzschean center unto itself. To believe such a thing is to embrace the self-centered prerogative of the wicked, whereby all other individuals are orbital to her sun. "If there be no God," says the Savoyard Vicar, "the good man is a mere fool" (Rousseau *Sav.*, 67). Even Promethean proclamation of efficacious humanism in no way diminishes a God unbound by the limitations imposed upon him by humanity itself.

Romanticism, then, is not atheism. The Romantic's acceptance of God as creative cosmic force informing humanity's obligation to higher purpose is neither ambivalent nor begrudging. Just days before his sudden and untimely demise, Shelley insisted that "the destiny of man can scarcely be so degraded that he was born only to die" (Letter of June 29, 1822 quoted in O'Neill 2011, 35). Childe Harold anticipates a time "when, at length, the mind shall be all free, / From what it hates in this degraded form" (Byron 1891, cant. III, 74). Manfred's proclamation upon his impending death that he would be his own hereafter lacks climactic profundity in the context of his meager corporeal hereafter (Byron 1817, III, iv, 160–61). In *Tintern Abbey*, Wordsworth speaks to death in terms of "that blessed mood, / In which the burthen of the mystery, / In which the heavy and the weary weight, / Of all this unintelligible world, / Is lightened . . ." (1798, 203). The Savoyard Vicar longs for "that moment when I shall shake off this incumbrance of body and be myself, without inconsistency or participation with matter, and shall depend upon myself only to be happy" (1889, 71). And Romantic fascination with Milton speaks to a human condition alienated from God, but teleologically desperate for reconciliation; the fact of the fall bespeaking the existence of paradise itself. That the egoistic Romantic fulfills her obligation to God as an externality to self-obligation certainly alienates her from the Christian orthodoxy of eighteenth- and nineteenth-century Europe; but it occasions no inherent estrangement from the unparsable obligations attendant to republican virtue and heroic estimability.

Obligation to Society

More than merely accommodating it, Romantic heroism insists upon social obligation. Among sympathetic critics of Romanticism's worst excesses—Mary Shelley, for example—there is little sense that the development of the authentic self could develop equally in a state of nature as in a civil society. Nature might be a source of sublime inspiration; it may provide cues as to authentic moral agency; it may be divine in its own right. But it is not a substitute for the community, the interchange of sympathies as Frankenstein's monster would have it, aroused by civil society. Such intersubjectivity is interpreted by Herder as culture, a community united in aesthetic taste, the expression of a shared and discrete social identity (*Volksgeist*) (1784, esp. bks. XIV–XV). Grounded in affect, this spirit of a people bonds at a much deeper level than the reasoned transactionalism of the contractarian. It bespeaks a broader set of obligations, not just to the rights of others, but to the values that inform the community—what it means *in the heart* to be people like us.

An inherent danger of the Romantic impulse toward the egotistical sublime is failure to recognize that affective exploration of the self cannot be an end in itself. It may be true, as Emerson suggests, that isolation must be antecedent to true society. But it is no alternative. The Romantic lacking social obligation is akin to the hoarder of gold who cannot bear to part with her bounty. To cast the passions inward to the exclusion of meaningful outward affection is to deprive the heart of the buoyant sentiments that attach to human tenderness and sympathy. The possessor of such a cadaverous soul, Rousseau insists, is "void of sensibility; he is already dead" (*Sav.*, 57). Neither is the fact of social obligation an end in itself. Rather, Romantic social obligation implies an affective union in aid of human dignity. As the French Revolution, so fresh in the mind, suggested, such union cannot be born of cold rationalism. Pitting the tyrannical rationalism of the elite against the affective savagery of the outcast, the legacy of Revolution lay in recognition that civil society demands more than a rational ordering of reciprocal obligations (e.g., Schiller 1884a, letter V, 44, letter VI).

This line of thinking undergirds Mary Shelley's *Frankenstein*. Foundational to the novel's didactic premise is the three books the monster discovers in an abandoned portmanteau. The first reflects the fundamental importance of natural affect to the self's essential humanity (*The Sorrows of Young Werther*). It represents a cautionary tale against the hegemony of reason and scientism. The second book speaks to the excesses of the first, to the imperative of a balanced order, to a republican ideal in which just and temperate individuals are contrasted with the wicked and intemperate. Plutarch's *Lives* thus mimics the dialectic of civil rationalism and primordial affect, reminding the reader that while reason threatens to make people tyrants, passion can turn them into savages.[3]

It is the third book (*Paradise Lost*), though, that speaks directly to the condition of the monster. It is a lament for the marginalization, alienation, and disaffection attendant to the outcast in a rationally ordered bourgeois society—analogue to Milton's cold and uncaring God (Shelley 1888, ch. 15). As with Adam, Frankenstein's monster is forsaken by his creator. He is desperate for the Edenic existence that (unlike Adam) he has never known. His lack of experiential knowledge, however, has no effect on his ability to *feel* it, to imagine the heavenly gratification of love and belonging. His fantasies carry him into the lives of the De Lacey family, the love and acceptance they have for one another extended to him as well. Yet beyond the comforting womb of imagination, he is confronted with the shattering realization that the De Laceys are repulsed by his entreaty to enter their world. His illusions awaken to recognition that he will never be permitted to penetrate the society of humans. Cast out as a freak, an alien, a lesser form of life, the monster reflects, "I allowed my thoughts, unchecked by reason, to ramble in the fields of Paradise, and dared to fancy amiable and lovely creatures sympathizing with my feelings and cheering my gloom; their angelic countenances breathed smiles of consolation. But it was all a dream; no Eve soothed my sorrows, nor shared my thoughts; I was alone" (Shelley 1888, 182).

The monster's melancholy inevitably finds outward expression in savagery, rage against society as insular as the French aristocracy, and a creator as insensitive as Prometheus's God. Confronted, Frankenstein finds himself incapable of truly comprehending the monster's entreaties, even when couched in Victor's native tongue of rationalist transactional obligation. ("Do your duty towards me," the monster says, "and I will do mine towards you and the rest of mankind" [1888, 136].) Despite his godlike creation of life—and no doubt due to the soulless properties of science and scientist—Victor cannot see beyond the monster's physical being. He is blinded to the essence of *meaningful* life. On a cognitive level, he can appreciate the monster's desire for a mate. But he cannot grasp the affective sense that a new social identity might nullify the monster's destructive alienation. To the rational mind, two monsters merely equate to twice as much trouble as one. In failing to recognize the monster's need for affirmation, identity, sociability, and belonging, Victor is both creator of the monster and unwitting catalyst for that which makes him monstrous.

Of course, just as not all reason is tyrannical, social defiance need not be monstrous. More constructively, social defiance is expressed through aesthetics as an outlet for affective expression. In this sense, art becomes transformative and dialogical, transcending the solipsistic and reinvigorating communal values from the stultified into the vibrant, the excessively rationalistic into the human, the exclusive into the just. By its nature, Tolstoy explains, art is socially contagious, the means by which one "hands on to others feelings he has lived through" such that "other people are infected by these feelings" (quoted in Knox 1930, 65). Art provokes communion between the individual and others in her time and place who come to view and make sense of the world in the same way. It begets shared aesthetic judgment. It speaks to a cultural sense of how people come to feel about the morality of a thing. It regards what it means to be a social unit, not as the product of geography or dispassionate compact or social status, but rather a collective identity forged by affective bonds rooted in something beyond circumstance or law (Schiller 1884a, letters XI–XV, XXVII; see also 1884c).[4]

Social Identity and the Romantic Roots of Essentialism

A community united in aesthetic taste speaks to a sort of contextual authenticity. Let us think here of authenticity as fidelity to that which is essential to a sense of self, which is to say, to one's identity. Contextual authenticity represents an extension of the *idiomatic*—the elements of the self that make it distinct from all other individuals—to a contextual sense of self expressed aesthetically through shared cultural values. An amorphous thing, Taylor defines this contextual authenticity—henceforth *social identity*—as "who we are, 'where we're coming from.' It is the background against which all our tastes, desires, opinions and aspirations make sense" (1994, 33–34). Wholly affective, it is essential to being and belonging. Authenticity and social identity, then, speak respectively to the personal and the cultural—the nature with which one is born and the shared essentialist values with which she identifies.

A fundamental distinction between authenticity and social identity is that while the former is natural, the latter is a product of agency. That is, it is active rather than passive. It is something one identifies *with*, rather than is identified *by*.[5] It is generally multidimensional and always nonexhaustive. It is not a zero-sum proposition. One might identify equally with her nation, her gender, her race, and her religion, but there is no fixed quantity of identification such that the more one identifies with her Americanness, for example, the less she identifies with her femininity. This is fundamentally relevant insofar as modern republics boast pluralistic social identities. While most will likely share an affinity with the national culture—that which defines what it means to be Nigerian or Dutch or Brazilian—there will be much greater diversity of subnational cultural identification. This has implications for the unity and integrity of the republic.

Social identity, national or subnational, binds individuals aesthetically—culturally—in common cause. It also speaks to a sense of *placefulness*, or an individual's means of social belonging. In pre-Enlightenment times, placefulness almost invariably turned on rigidly defined class roles, contrasting the *dignitas* and implied nobility of the aristocracy to the humbler social expectations of the underclasses (Taylor 1992, 31). It was such placefulness, of course, that informed the balanced institutionalism of the Solonian/Aristotelian republic. It persisted in the feudal structure, and even into the commercial age, materialism succeeding magnanimity as the basis of social prestige. It was in this last context that we first encountered the Romantic hero as redeemer of civil society in proclamation of the equal claim to dignity that each individual possessed by dint of her humanity and capacity for moral agency.

By the second half of the twentieth century, Romantic focus on the equal claim to human dignity had shifted from an emphasis on formal equality of individuals to what we can think of as situational equality— or the imperative that all essentialist subnational cultural communities be equally valued—equally situated—within the good republic.[6] Such situational equality demands a more granular understanding of what it means to be "people like us." If the social obligation inherent in eighteenth-century Romantic republicanism was to create affective bonds of social solidarity, by the twentieth century, it was those very social bonds that came under scrutiny for their cultural insularity. Indeed, from this microcosmic perspective, the usness inherent in the national social identity begins to look more sinister, a reflection not of the cultural values of the republic as a whole so much as those of the *dominant* essentialist cultural communities. Attendant is a latent rebirth of social hierarchy. Rather than the stratified placefulness inherent in an ordered class structure, in other words, the contemporary republic assigns placefulness according to an implicit stratification of essentialist cultures, social belonging becoming more marginal the farther one's social orbit from dominant cultural communities historically trending white, male, and heterosexual (e.g., Taylor 1992; Kymlicka 1995; Young 2011).

It is in this context that we can think of more contemporary Romantic republican heroes as inspirational redemptive champions of essentialist cultural communities. Seeking recognition and affirmation of subaltern essentialist communities, they are oppositional heroes, reimaginers of "normal" mores and customs. Their brief is universal realization of human dignity by ensuring that *usness* not ossify into *sameness*. Their renaissance was the beat cadence, the cinematic expression, and other artistic accoutrements of the mid-twentieth-century counterculture. Their social defiance was manifest in the iconoclastic aesthetics of Jack Kerouac or Andy Warhol or Lenny Bruce or Bob Dylan or Janis Joplin or Dennis Hopper. Politically, it lay with the leaders and iconic symbols of new social movements, such as Martin Luther King or Rosa Parks stirring the hearts of white and Black America alike. The nonviolent protests King advocated were their own form of aesthetics, the reactive violence they provoked, their own form of sublime horror.

As with Romantics of an earlier day, it was not just the great and celebrated who represented the Romantic heroism of midcentury America. Equally important were the imbibers and exhorters of the message, moved to mobilize in common cause. Ella Baker, James Chaney, Septima Poinsette Clark, Medgar Evers, Andrew Goodman, Diane Nash, Michael Schwerner, the Little Rock Nine, and countless others too numerous to mention were no less heroic than King, and their collective influence was no less great. In this same vein, the feminist movement had its iconic artists and symbols, such as Judy Chicago, Yoko Ono, Helen Reddy, and Rosie the Riveter, as well as activists such as Gloria Steinem and Germaine Greer. However, the enduring symbol of the mid-twentieth-century feminist movement (apocryphal though it may be) is aesthetic—of liberated women burning their brassieres in Atlantic City as a message of symbolic liberation from the indignity of a tradition that valued women primarily for their capacity to please men. The true heroes of the movement, moreover, were the anonymous women enduring ridicule and ritual humiliation as pioneers into traditionally male strongholds such as the boardroom, the precinct house, the bench, and the legislative chamber.

Conclusion

Romantic heroism acquires political currency as a vehicle for redemptive social change and universalization of human dignity. Artists, orators, or auditors, Promethean in their defiance of the intolerant fettered rationalist and narrowly bourgeois values that dull the senses and deny people the completeness of a truly transcendent life, Romantic heroes exhort their fellow citizens through affective excitation. They speak to human dignity through natural just agency, cues to moral action located in the nature—ambient, human, and personal—of divine creation. Fidelity to one's personal nature is authenticity, a transcendent condition constitutive of dignity. Communal and contextualized, authenticity presents as culture, an aesthetic expression of social identity. Most fundamentally, the political message of Romantic heroism is dignity through equality. In attacking the prevailing class structure of post-Enlightenment bourgeois society, early Romanticism reinforced the liberal imperative for formal human equality. Indeed, the endogenous affective capacity for morality delegitimated any claim for differential claim to *dignitas* or social deference. By the middle of the twentieth century, understanding of the nature of the equality requisite to human dignity began to change, from the formal equality of individuals to the situational equality of essentialist cultural communities.

That Romantics face hurdles to the realization of their idealized ends is axiomatic. Romanticism exists in the face of social opposition, and the Romantic heroic narrative generally is tragic. Such heroism is not about glory or posterity. At best, social recognition is belated. Certainly, Romantic heroes do not benefit from the puffery and pageantry enjoyed by many heroes more traditionally defined. Their heroic reward is dignity, not honor; the currency of transcendence, equality, not deference. Heuristically not (necessarily) good, they are *estimable*, sometimes if only on their own terms. In failing to conform to a positive morality, they reject social or divine moral compulsion attendant to magnanimity. Instead, they insist upon an innate human capacity for just agency. Individuals are to be trusted with the liberty gifted to them by the gods and not doled out parsimoniously by a class of individuals somehow deemed singularly capable of determining how others might best contribute to the fortunes of the good republic.

Facially problematic to the reconciliation of Romantic and republican heroism is that Romantics' solipsistic fascination seems to tell against republican virtue. Indeed, what Romantics conceive as authenticity comes perilously close to tautology. Like Werther, their every self-indulgent emotion might seem magically to transform selfish desires into burdens courageously born for the sake of living in accordance with their natures, their self-absorption morally consecrated by the cleansing waters of authenticity. From this perspective, the authentic life is little more than camouflage for hedonic autonomy. It is this charge—that Romanticism sacrifices ethical and social obligation at the altar of the personal—that Romantic heroism must overcome if it is to be reconciled with any meaningful conception of republicanism.

There is little doubt that some early Romantics flew a little close to the sun in their flirtation with solipsistic antiheroism. Accepting the qualification, this chapter has argued that despite their ontological individualism, Romantic heroes are *not* the socially detached selves they sometimes seem at pains to portray. They are not agents free from debt to their past lives, to their communities, or to that cosmic presence greater than themselves. Rather, in battling the despotism of the external, a retreat into the self is but the initial part of the campaign. Romantic heroes first must come to love and accept the internal self, its beauty, and its ugliness, as prerequisite to dignity and self-esteem. It is only by satisfying the obligation to self that they are able to fulfill the other obligations demanded by republican virtue. As such, Romantic heroes have no enmity for the divine spirit or civil society; just the opposite. They seek to redeem corrupted spirituality and sociability. They reject the nullification of humanism implicit in (some) Christian theology, and the vacuity of bourgeois values. Theirs is spirituality without grace, divinity without an anthropomorphic God, and reverence without humility. It is civility absent hypocrisy; exhortation absent compulsion. Their heroism is volitional, a product of the will moved by affect and tempered by the shared aesthetic judgment of relevant communities in pursuit of universal human dignity. In proclaiming the capacity of all individuals to trust their authentic feelings in the conduct of life, Romantic heroes present as warriors for the dignity of authenticity. Theirs is a war against social rigidities, narrow and cloistered, in the name of liberating affective human agency.

Romantic heroes transformed the republicanism of the modern age through promotion of modern values and defiance of anachronistic ones. They inspire individuals, elevating human dignity, attaching it to something more than one's labor and one's place. Along the way, informed by this new paradigm of egalitarian republican citizenship, modern republics have become far more robust than their ancient counterparts. They have avoided the problem that Cicero and other Roman civic humanists lament—the tragic unreliability of great goodness to mediate faction in times of crisis. The Romantic hero's insistence upon autonomy shifts the principal threat to good government from faction to unjustifiable authority. Rebellion at such authority is reflected in the three great revolutions that can, in a Promethean sense, be said to have given mature form to Romantic heroism. Taken together, there is an Aristotelian quality to them. The Puritan Revolution failed because it was insufficiently Promethean. In defying the alliance of the Church of England and king, it represented little more than a changing of the guard, substituting the tyranny of one rigid doctrine for another, the tyranny of a monarchical defender of the faith for the tyranny of a theocratic oligarchy. In promoting the anachronistic institutional arrangement of ancient republicanism, it failed to recognize the latent democratic impulse—the assertion of dignity, equality, and liberty—that had made revolution attractive to so many in the first place. The French Revolution was *too* Promethean insofar as revolutionary fervor proved barbaric, an affective groundswell untempered by reason and therefore unable to accommodate itself to effective republican governance. The American Revolution, however, hit the Promethean sweet spot, reconciling affective liberty with reasoned order, equality with republican governance, and godliness with human dignity.

It is the American Revolution that will interest us in the next chapter, in which Romantic heroism finds egalitarian sympathy with emergent common heroism. As with other heuristic hero types these modern ones blend at the margins, uncelebrated Romantic heroes sharing qualities with their common counterparts. In part, the difference between them is contextual. A Romantic hero during times of social change may be more drawn to common heroism in a more stable environment. Indeed, Romantic and common heroes inspire countervailing virtues, one representing a source of social dynamism, one a source of stability; one blazing the trail for new socio-cultural boundaries, the other consolidating and populating the new frontier; one reimagining an authentically defined good, the other objectifying and institutionalizing that good. The gradual emergence of the common hero in the American context will occupy our attention in chapter 6.

Chapter 6

God, Godliness, and the Birth of the Common Hero

Common heroes are multifaceted. Like Roman *boni*, they manifest in service of all heroic functions. The difference is that they lack the requisite of greatness, that singular quality demanding deference and honor. They are the threads that form the social garment rather than the celebrated designer or craftsman. The grit and not the glamor, their conviction, self-confidence, and sense of social place all contribute to the virtue of the republic as much as—one might well argue more than—the great or greatly good individuals who inform more orthodox conceptions of republican heroism. They are, Friedrich (1940) suggests, the bedrock of democracy. However we conceive them, they speak to the unsung heroic capacity of the everyman that ancients could never have conceived, a quality that permits a far more democratic republicanism than most would ever have sanctioned.

Setting the standard for good citizenship, common heroes are exemplary role models. Prosaically, they are good parents, Little League coaches, teachers, or colleagues, distinctive only in the sense of ongoing above and beyond to exhort others into good citizenship. Archetypally, they have been culturally celebrated as rugged individualists: yeoman farmers, self-made men, backwoodsmen, gunslingers of the Old West, hard-boiled detectives, and, counterintuitively perhaps, superheroes. Politically, their principal brief is stewardship of the good society, including the leadership once reserved for the magnanimous. They are defenders against those who would disturb the common peace. Some, such as early twentieth-century hard-boiled detectives and superheroes, even seek social redemption, although most tend to defer to their Romantic counterparts in that regard. More reasoned, they tend more towards regime consolidation—nation building—than social reimagination.

Though it may be tempting to think so, common heroes exist not as pale, watery replicas of the true heroes of days gone by, artlessly reinforcing the nihilism of a postheroic age. Rather, they are guardians of a new transvaluative paradigm in which freedom, equality, and virtue stand as the core fundaments of human dignity, as nonnegotiable elements of a good republic. Common heroes portray an idealized sense of national character—a republic of self-sufficient citizens. Their heroism embraces Romantic independence from the corruption of the social order, while remaining committed to the moral perfection of that order. It is such volitional heroic individualism tied to social cause that D. H. Lawrence (1964, 20) finds so compelling about classic American literature, in which he finds a theory of freedom as self-mastery—liberation from the internal obstacles (self-doubt most notably) that provoke pusillanimity and the unwillingness to stand up for one's personal, social, and cosmic obligations.

Common heroism is volitional—heroes good because they want to be good, try to be good, fight to be good. Their heroism attaches as much to the struggle as the outcome. "A series of humble efforts," insists Emerson, "is more meritorious than solitary miracles of virtue" (*Ethical Philosophy*, 64). They are resistors of the demons of temptation rather than persons of finer clay or grateful recipients of God's grace. In consequence, such laudation as common heroes receive is as much for their effort as their accomplishments, their imitability rather than their singularity. The great advantage is that their collective moral force is often greater than that of any singular person (Friedrich 1940, 355–58).

Common heroes share many characteristics with their Romantic counterparts. Neither is willing to accept that tyranny or social stratification is a fixed social cost. Inherently egalitarian, jointly they reject magnanimity as little more than specious privilege at the expense of those upon whom fortune has smiled less brightly. Of their heroic potential, says Whitman, "there is no trade or employment but the young man following it may become a hero" (1860a, 343). Theirs is a heroism of what Emerson calls "character," not capacity (Emerson, *Character*). The sometimes-fine line that divides Romantic and common heroes is such that for the former, the heart is the engine that powers the will; the mind simply steers the vessel. By contrast, common heroes are more Kantian, driven by the innate capacity to exercise cognitive judgment, *a posteriori* and *a priori*—empirically and intuitively. For common heroes, in other words, moral competence manifests as an untutored capacity for prudent judgment pertaining to last principles—processed cognitively from that which they desire, feel, and experience—as well as intuitive knowledge of first moral principles.

Common and Romantic heroes also differ on their understanding of a transcendent life. Privileging moral objectivism ahead of authenticity, common heroism is predicated upon the assumption that a transcendent life demands a positive theory of goodness. In this sense, they are more like magnanimous heroes, albeit shorn of their greatness. They differ from greatly good heroes in three principal ways. First, common heroes operate in the world of moral uncertainty rather than absolute truth, a world of moral intuition rather than moral knowledge. They stand in recognition that good government is perforce pluralistic and not monistic, and that if sagacious knowledge of moral principles is the basis of good law, then perfection of just agents through law is a chimera not worthy of pursuit (James 1897, ch. 1). Second, pertinent to good government is not so much the ontology of goodness, as its practical application. Just agency is pragmatic, demanding conformity to rules predicated upon an intuitively derived (as opposed to conclusively known) conception of just balance and just condition. Rather than a flaw, such ambiguity breeds the tolerance attendant to what Rawls (1996) calls reasonable pluralism. Third, just agency is not technical. It is not a product of the specialized knowledge exclusive to the political craftsman or professional statesman. It is attitudinal, in the sense of summoning the will to do right. In consequence, priests and paupers, sages and citizens, poets and philosophers are indistinguishable in their propensity for just agency and realization of just condition.[1]

The capacity for innate just agency predicated upon moral intuition situates the common hero in a liminal position between the sensual authenticity of the poet and the cognitive sagacity of the philosopher (see Kant 1914, ss. 22–24). It connotes a sensational response that attaches to observation, combined with the power of reason to impose an understanding as to wrong and right (e.g., Stewart 1829, s. VI, Art. 2, pars. 197–200). "Object and subject," as Frothingham frames the dialectic, "sterile by themselves, become fruitful in conjunction" (1903, 17). Together sense and reason inform an innate moral competence accommodating a coherent deontology, a native processing of moral judgments into syllogistic moral agency (Holyoak and Powell 2016).

In order to unpack the logic, we must divide common moral competence into two parts. The first is common sense, or deontic moral reasoning informed by experience. The second is a noumenal (what Kant calls *transcendental*) understanding of first moral principles. Wholly pragmatic, common sense exists independently of metaphysical inquiry into first moral principles. It bears the same relationship to sagacity as athleticism does to comprehension of the first principles of biomechanics, or effective communication to ontological understanding of language. It assumes human capacity to construct moral precepts from self-evident truths, and from there to exercise appropriate moral judgment. Analogous to hearing or sight, the *common* sense is a form of comprehension, says James Harris indelicately in the notes to his *Treatise on Happiness*, "common to all, except Lunatics and Idiots" (1744, 287; see also Brownson 1997, 183–85).

Transcendentalism, on the other hand, acquires purchase beyond phenomenological impression. It represents an expansion of moral consciousness through the *a priori* principles Kant associates with pure reason (1914, s. 37; 2002, Ak 4: 408–9, 426). Sensibility is the basis of what Kant calls *a posteriori* judgments, the great limitation of which is that it provides no insurance against unexperienced counterfactuals. (Limited to the phenomenological, for example, one might be tempted to judge that since the only squirrels one has seen are grey, there are no black squirrels [Kant 1998, B 2–8].) Kant contrasts *a posteriori* judgments with judgments born of prognostic—*transcendental*—knowledge extant independent of sensory input. For the American transcendentalists discussed later, such transcendental knowledge reflects a mystical capacity to grasp the supersensual. It is "a faculty of vision to which truths respecting God, Providence, Immortality, Freedom and the Moral Law are palpably disclosed" (Frothingham 1903, 24). In this same faintly Unitarian vein, the seat of transcendentalism is what Emerson calls the over-soul, neither intellect nor affect, but immanent master of both. Its latent presence is ubiquitous and universal such that even in the prosaic interaction of neighbors in the street, "Jove nods to Jove behind each of [them]" (Emerson *Over-Soul*, 197).

In this chapter we will chart the foundations of the American common heroism, from the Scottish and German Enlightenments through the first two American Great Awakenings to the antebellum age of Jacksonian democracy. From such minds as Reid and Stewart, Kant and Emerson, and Edwards and Finney, common heroes imbibed the secular and theological in the name of the just agency requisite to transcendence of the ordinary life. Rugged individualists, they tempered their liberty with virtue, self-interest with moral consciousness, efficacy with piety, individual assertiveness with communal obligation, and equality with respect for, but not blind deference to, authority. The chapter is divided according to the two bases of common moral competence indicated above: common sense and transcendentalism. Rather than focusing on specific heroes, it lays the philosophical and theological groundwork for the discussion of archetypal American common heroes in the next chapter.

Common Sense

Manifesting as both capacity and resource, common sense is the currency of positive liberty, of freedom from the internal constraints (not least ignorance) that long had mandated deference to magnanimous heroes. As capacity, common sense is the source of innate and universal enlightenment (Brownson 1997, 185). The base layer of common heroism, it is a fundament of moral volition, an aptitude that all possess and some employ—individuals variably motivated to engage it in the conduct of their lives (Reid 1785, VI, ch. 2, 522). (Grumbles Emerson, "We are all wise in capacity, though so few in energy" [*Great Men*, 626].) Indeed, it is upon the quality of conduct that we distinguish estimable individuals from blackguards and fools, common heroes from common knaves. In America in particular, the political implications attendant to recognition of common moral sense were profound. Common sense stimulated human efficacy, empowering individuals to think and act freely, opening "whole realms of verifiable knowledge to ordinary men . . . [previously] considered incapable of discerning truth for themselves" (Noll 2002, 233). Of its potency, Brownson enthuses that common sense "furnishes all the ideas we ever have; teaches us all the truths we ever know. As this reason is the same in all men, it gives to all men the same ideas, furnishes them with the same truths, the same beliefs" (1997, 185).

The effect in nascent America was to reconceive the source of moral authority, to reassign moral competence from the exclusive preserve of the sagacious to the prerogative of the masses. This simple truth resonated in an increasingly pragmatic and egalitarian new republic, firmly wedded to the idea that to subjugate common sense to the ostensible nobility of greater people was to assent to tyranny and absolutism (Singer 1986, 246). Inherent was a sense that democracy was not merely a practical means of governing a rebellious people, but the keystone to a better and more just society (Brownson 1997, 186).

As resource, common sense is common knowledge, an ever-expanding storehouse of communal wisdom—born of philosophy, science, art, law, gospel, experience, memory, and other cognitive or affective benefactors—

upon which each may draw in the conduct of her life (Bock 1956, 157; Singer 1986, 227–29). As with all human understanding, common sense is imperfect. Offering no guarantee against faulty moral precepts, it is most aptly understood in Kuhnian terms—as a prevailing paradigm of knowledge. In this sense, it is hostage to coloration by cultural norms and beliefs, kin to the aesthetic community of tastes visited in the previous chapter (Somerville 1986, 239; Singer 1986, 236, 241). And yet even with this qualification, common sense really does not differ in kind (or possibly even in degree) from the philosophical wisdom of sages who, also seeing through a glass darkly, suffer from the same limitations of fallibility and perspective that distance mortals from gods.

If metaphysical principles accessed through common sense risk contamination through cultural distortion, it is equally the case that there exists a core that transcends discrete cultures, an objective canon of ethics we cannot *not* know. These first principles of common sense are self-evident moral truths that defy obfuscation. They nullify relativism as deftly as they penetrate the mystification of magnanimity (Reid 1785, VI, ch. 2. 520–24; Emerson *Over-Soul*, 197–99; Pollack 1882, 264–65; Moore 1993; Budziszewski 1999, 23–25). The residuum is reasonableness, a meeting of the minds in which ethical disagreement is bounded by commonly-known moral principles (Murphy 1965, 17, 70, 83). Common sense, then, represents an appeal to moral judgment that, if less than a complete and cogent system of metaphysics (Emerson *Ethical Philosophy*, 68–69), is considerably more structured than the ancient conception of popular self-government as "a disorderly clutter of opposing judgments that reflect the idiosyncrasies of individuals and the variety of traditions to which they subscribe" (A. I. Melden, quoted in Singer 1986, 251).

THE ROOTS OF COMMON SENSE IN AMERICA:
RELIGION AND REVOLUTION

Given its rooting in natural practicality, it is ironic that common sense found stimulation in America through organized religion. Or perhaps it is not so ironic. The emergent American common hero was a study in dialectics, coupling individual self-determination with an ethical mandate for objective goodness in the conduct of life (e.g., Singer 1986, 238–39). She sought "moral order seen through the medium of an individual nature" (Emerson *Character*, 329). Organized religion worked as well as any other metaphysical framework in provision of that moral order. The marriage of American religion and common sense had its basis in the pervasive mythology of an America grounded in the purity of newness. The genesis was inauspicious. Far from promoting egalitarianism and moral autonomy, John Winthrop's exhortation to his fellow Puritans on the *Arbella* was to construct a new order along the well-trodden path of sociospiritual hierarchy. The civil covenant binding Winthrop's ascendant city mandated a strict and abiding commitment to send all sinners on the path to Christ, to live in service to the Lord, and to construct God's earthly kingdom (Winthrop 1996, 8). Through this covenant of duty, humanity's innate depravity would be constrained by the moral surveillance of visible saints (Tweney 1997, 365).

Implicit was the elect society's corporate responsibility, its terrestrial duties jointly borne. Hanging over a chosen people was the dire consequence of breaking covenant with a God not given to parsing his wrath between sinner and saint.[2] The burden of moral responsibility thus weighed heavily on the elect society. Far from being private concerns, immorality and apostasy were issues of public policy. One whose business failed, therefore, or whose son had indulged in foolish indiscretions, was subject to communal opprobrium for any attendant ripples of communal harm (Rotundo 1993, 2–3). Indeed, it was imperative that the common good "oversway all private respects, by which, not only conscience, but mere civil policy, doth bind us" (Winthrop 1996, 8).

Collective moral responsibility also stimulated intense social introspection among second- and third-generation New England Puritans. Worryingly, the signs of moral decline were everywhere one cared to look for them (Miller 1953, 14–16). The Synod of 1679, for example, despaired of such sins as prideful and worldly airs on the part of the prosperous, the unwillingness of social inferiors to know and keep to their place, the presence of heretics in their midst, foul language, violation of the Sabbath, insufficient parental control of the young, factionalism, dishonesty, the decline of civic virtue, and the panoply of sins wrought by sex and alcohol (Miller 1953, 8–10). Equally menacing was ascendant materialism. The creation of wealth (often through what could only loosely be called vocational calling) promoted an individualist dynamic, distracting folks from their obligations as good citizens and exhorters of their brethren in service of God.

Two distinct responses emerged to such ubiquitous declension. More conservative Old Lights doubled down on strict imposition of moral, civil, and theological order as a means of insulating themselves from ambient ungodliness of the Enlightenment—that "vile peece of Paganism," as it appeared to Cotton Mather (quoted in Noll 2002, 102). Intensified moral oversight, though, was a double-edged sword, provoking a crisis of legitimacy within a Puritan tradition cleaving to a generous view of apostasy and parsimonious one of natural liberty. In response, more progressive New Lights dissented from centralization of authority, gradually (if begrudgingly in some cases) accommodating their theology to the tolerance and reason of the dawning age (Rossel 1970, 908; see also McLoughlin 1980, 69–70; Koch 2009, 5–9, 16–17).

It was in the face of such spiritual dissonance that Americans experienced their First Great Awakening, a fiery arousal of souls perjured in their covenantal obligations to God. Mid-century revivalism, it need hardly be said, scarcely qualified as a rallying cry for liberty, equality, or common moral sense. The theologically progressive evangelism of the Second Great Awakening had yet to mature into a sustainable Christian republican paradigm. Yet it was the First Great Awakening that sowed the synergistic, faintly Arminian seeds of Christian just agency in New England and beyond. It was here that the evangelical exhortations of George Whitefield, Gilbert Tennent, and, most prominently, Jonathan Edwards established themselves as a buckle between the Puritanism of the Old Lights and the pietism of the New.

At once Puritanical and mystical, Edwards in particular distanced himself from the covenantal legalism into which the Old Light had descended; dismissing it as little more than ideational residue—what Miller (1948b) calls a "decaying phantasm"—of overly deterministic shibboleths resonating with the hollow ring of insubstantial piety (Edwards 1948, esp. 135–37). In such spiritual poverty, Edwards says, individuals live by rote, lulled into increasing remoteness from the source of their salvation. To counter this, redemption demands revival from the torpor of remoteness through salvational resuscitation (Edwards 1948, 143–44). Yet the minds of sinners sleep soundly, reluctant to reawaken to godliness. In amelioration, the spiritual light of God finds receptivity through affective penetration of the heart. The revivalism of the early 1840s thus represented a fiery call to piety in much the same way that a surge of adrenaline promotes reaction to physical danger. Herein lay ambiguously volitional hope for sinners, albeit hope tinged with a reminder of the hot and unpleasant future awaiting those whose habitual wickedness stood in the way of salvation by stubbornly refusing the entreaties of an angry God (Carpenter 1931, 629–31; Miller 1941, esp. 37–44; 1948a, 50–52, 69–70; 1948b, 125–28;

Edwards 1734, esp. 13–15, 27–28; 1818, pt. I, sec. IV, pt. III, sec. IV, esp. 210–11; Alexis 1966, 336–39; Guelzo 1995, 408–10; Stewart 1999, 60–69; Noll 2002, 38–39).

In addition to bestirring spiritual consciousness, the First Great Awakening was an injunction for individuals to seize control of their circumstances and influence their destiny. Implicit was political reawakening, stimulating a latent reorientation of Americans' sense of spiritual identity, cultural identity, and self-identity. Indeed, more than transitory expressions of mass sentiment, the nature of awakenings is that they remedy an anomic loss of legitimacy in prevailing secular and spiritual norms, institutions, and leaders. Revivals reflect a paradigmatic shift; an interruption of the social equilibrium; a process in which spiritual and cultural norms are realigned with ambient circumstance; a means by which old rigidities are softened and reformed. What had once been experienced as the guilt of living one's life out of step with the old ways and customs is reborn as ecstasy in discovery that it was the old ways, and not the new, that truly were cross-wise with God's purpose (McLoughlin 1980, 58–59). Revivals thus celebrate a charismatic revival of efficacy—breaking "the crust of custom" (1980, 15), infusing cultural or spiritual self-confidence sufficient to regenerate a social or spiritual order grown stale from dissonance "between norms and experience, old beliefs and new realities" (1980, 10). Like all revivals, awakenings are folk movements, representing the impulse to change the magnanimous guard; or in the most extreme examples, overturn the regime in its entirety (McLoughlin 1980, esp. 2–3, 12–14, 17; also Wallace 1956, 265–71).

So it was that the greatest legacy of the First Great Awakening was more procedural than substantive. Even if they were not motivated by explicitly political ends, evangelical New Lights were not blind to the political effects of stirring the spiritual pot (e.g., Edwards 1840d, pt. II, s. VI, pp. 293–94, pt. III, s. IV, 309). Indeed, in its indictment of the soporific formalism of Old Light Calvinist clerics, it inspired a sense of inquiry into the source of religious and political authority (McLoughlin 1980, esp. 62–66). Edwards believed that among God's manifold purposes in arousing the souls of sinners, after all, had been to fortify the defenses of the godly republic. Such had been a call to banish the tyranny of popery and Satanic impurity (a distinction without a difference to many Protestants of the day) once and forever from the New World's northern shores (Bloch 1985, 58–60). And what better proof of God's postmillennialist intentions could there have been, New Lights mused, than victory in the French and

Indian War? Yet the work was far from complete. If the defeat of France diminished the prospect of papal oppression, it only served to heighten the threat posed by the "popish" alliance of English Church and state, so emblematic of British tyranny (Hatch 1977, 154).

In response was mobilized a heterogeneous Protestant movement politically united in opposition to religious tyranny, to the fallacy that godliness might be parsed from personal liberty. Implicit was rejection of any form of authority by exclusion and default. Whether the culprit was monarchy, religious establishment, or reactionary covenantal theocracy, embryonic revolutionaries insisted upon sharp distinction between the legitimacy of the law and the power of any one group to sanctify it (Bailyn 1967, 247–48; Hatch 1977, 142; Noll 1993, 626). Into this pre-Revolutionary mix were thrown evangelizing Baptists such as Isaac Backus, who underscored the spiritual equality of individuals—an enormously attractive sentiment to rural and urban underclasses who had chafed under the exclusivity of Puritan orthodoxy or Virginian Anglicanism. Scotch-Irish Presbyterians, unflinchingly democratic, had the effect of fueling rising anti-English sentiment (Koch 2009, 9–10). Even staid New England ministers increasingly began to couch their sermons in the language of individual liberty (Hatch 1977, esp. ch. 2; Noll 2002, 75–78). It had been pursuit of such liberty, New Englanders were told with more than a little revisionist license, that had sent the first Bay colonists into the wilderness. That Winthrop's city upon a hill shone not just the light of piety, but civil liberty as well, would have been news to seventeenth-century Puritans laboring under strict New England preparationism. But it conformed to a New Light narrative realigning the normative and experiential into a coherent paradigm for the changing times (Heimert 1966, 96–97; Hatch 1977, 44–51, 156–70; Hughey 1984, 125; Bloch 1985, 60–63).

Equally important was the influence of the Enlightenment. The last four decades of the eighteenth century saw the emergent republican paradigm decouple both religious and political authority from blind faith and tradition. The Revolutionary era, characterized by dawning realization of humanity's religious and political potential, was one in which reflexive acceptance of revelation gave ground to evidentialist apologetics. Sovereignty of king yielded to the volitional efficacy of common individuals. Deference succumbed to the primacy of common sense—the self-evident truth of the natural equality of men. Moral emphasis shifted to favor the epistemologically democratic core of the Scottish Enlightenment—the idea that for all intents and purposes, moral enlightenment is informed by nothing more than one's own reflective sense of the world (Noll 1985, 218–21, 227–32; 2002, 234).[3]

The challenge to the old social order ramified into resistance to anything resembling governance by one's betters. Rather than princes and sages, the repository of American justice was deemed to be morally competent, *sensible* citizens exercising stewardship over a social order of their own construction (Noll 2002, 217–19). Far from the rigidity, helplessness, and human depravity that informed the seventeenth-century Puritan order, the *novus ordo seclorum* took root in the commonsense conviction that governance of body and soul was the exclusive privilege of neither a moral aristocracy nor the selectively saved. This philosophical revolution elevated the status of the self-sufficient upstart. Indeed, the two-fisted individual whose sense of self rested upon nothing grander *than* herself contrasted favorably with her magnanimous counterpart adorned with the mummery, pageantry, and inherited accoutrements of privilege (Hatch 1989, 35–39; Noll 1993, 635–37; 2002, 234–37).

By the late eighteenth century, then, Old World distaste for vulgarity became all but a point of pride in differentiating the new American identity. Certainly, urbane civility failed to keep the nascent common American hero in her place. If anything, commonness abetted heroic ratification, vainglory or presumption having the opposite effect. Far from seeking the spectacle of recognition, the emergent common hero couched her exploits in the camouflage of modesty or anonymity. Hers was a celebration of individualism, inclusiveness, provincialism, and sincere presentation, all of which helped distinguish the idealized American from the sniffy and effete English nobleman. Indeed, while colonial Americans had sought the medial sweet spot between vulgarity and foppish overrefinement, a somewhat coarse antipathy to gentility was the price paid for a frontal attack on imperial sophistication and social deference (Cmiel 1990, 39–41).

The Second Great Awakening

The American Revolution begged the question bedeviling most successful revolutionaries: now what? Certainly, the implicit post-Revolutionary decree for loosely regulated individual liberty was not without its problems. Foremost, a teleology of autonomy came perilously close to assigning the mandate to serve as one's own priest and lawgiver. Largely missing was the venerable republican directive that even Paine sees as foundational to good government—subsidization of the virtue deficit that accrues over time as individuals come to relax their duty and attachment towards one another (1986, 66–68). The cities were a source of moral concern. Footloose men, fresh off the farm or the boat, found themselves confronted by the anomie of strangeness, not much mitigated by the freedom to drink, carouse, and generally get up to no good (Herman 1998, 437–38). Meanwhile, the lifting of restrictions on settlement west of the Appalachians stimulated both westward migration and a decline in spirituality on the part of fast-moving settlers more mobile than their churches (Thomas 1965, 657; Hankins 2004, 3). Finally, in intellectual circles, rationalist Deism threatened to overwhelm the vestigial spirit of mid-eighteenth-century revivalism. As had been the case in the wake of the Puritan Revolution, the practical imperatives of the natural order threatened to overwhelm spiritualism in post-Revolutionary America (Gabriel 1950, 35).

Remedy for each of these problems took the form of revived evangelism, which as early as the 1790s again began to make deep inroads into American consciousness. Unlike the First Great Awakening, which arose in redemptive response to a crisis of spiritual authority, the nascent new awakening reflected the imperative to consolidate the authority of the new order. Attendant was conviction that godliness and social gospel went hand-in-hand (Mathews 1969, 26, 37; Noll 1985, 226). For many (new) New Lights of the early nineteenth century, the market niche afforded by post-Revolutionary social disruption was a gift not to be squandered by blind fidelity to Calvinist rigidity. If successful evangelization favored emphasizing uplifting sentiments like prevenient grace and innate moral agency at the expense of such staples as limited atonement and postlapsarian depravity, the resulting bull market for spiritual reconnection spoke eloquently to its effectiveness (Mathews 1969, 28; Noll 2002, 234; Hankins 2004, 7). Rather than pounding away on humanity's innate moral incapacity, then, evangelists of the Second Great Awakening married natural moral reason to spiritual revelation, appealing to Americans' common sense in determination of conduct requisite both to salvation and the good human life (Noll 1985, 222).

The Second Great Awakening unfolded differentially in the increasingly heterogeneous United States. It can rightly be said to have begun in the South, with revivalist Methodist and Separate Baptist camp meetings more or less continuing—with only brief abatement during the Revolutionary period—from the First Great Awakening to the Second. Southern revivalism was an emotional appeal to personal self-discipline and familial and community obligation, reinforcing a cultural sense of white Christian homogeneity, a communitarian order in which folks were relieved of the necessity of confronting the anomic social disorder and political factionalism so prominent in the North (McLoughlin 1980, 131–32).

Differently awakened were New England liberal Congregationalists (such as Timothy Dwight, Lyman Beecher, and Nathaniel W. Taylor) and mid-Atlantic latitudinarian Anglicans, who sought to soften Calvinist inflexibility through occupation of the middle ground between Deist rationalism and orthodox Christian principles. Theirs was an appeal to the mind. Rejecting humanity's innate depravity, they emphasized the capacity of even the humblest individuals to navigate their temporal journeys by the light of common moral reasoning—a light dimmed not by the taint of original sin, but fueled by learning, spiritual diligence, and self-discipline (Taylor 1849). Indeed, innate human reason was sufficient to alert people to the symbiotic relationship between republican virtue and personal self-interest. Certainly, proponents believed that moral reasoning represented a force more reliable than fire and brimstone, "counting on irrational revival experiences to turn men toward true virtue" (McLoughlin 1980, 72–73).

Borrowing from both southern enthusiasm and staid northern reason was the western tradition that gave rise to Jacksonian democracy. More formally, it was embodied by the likes of New School Presbyterian Charles Grandison Finney, who preached the saving efficacy of free will in fulfillment of obligations to God. To Finney, Calvinist inefficacy was but a volitional failure of the will: a sinner's "cannot" her "will not"; conversion no more miraculous than a willingness to open one's heart to God (McLoughlin 1980, 125). For Finney, the sinner who embraced God also embraced the social gospel, transcending her selfishness for the benevolent desire to help others. Rather than seeking to restrict human behavior through law, Finney couched his appeal in the language of liberty (McLoughlin 1980, 129). Implicit was a sort of Romantic perfectionism (Thomas 1965), stripping away extant impediments to individuals' natural perfectibility, producing an unprecedented relationship between self-government and self-governance, and reinforcing a democratic division of labor in which sovereignty over spiritual beliefs and moral convictions, no less than in politics, was vested firmly in the hearts and minds of the people (e.g., Hatch 1989, 22–27).

Less formally, the western evangelical tradition manifested in adherence to good old common sense. The frontier was populated by roughhewn individuals—unlettered, often subliterate—whose restless spirits, financial setbacks, or enthusiasm for the lure of the wild left them constitutionally unsuited to flourish in the more civilized quarters of the new republic. Such individuals, Timothy Dwight observes, constituted in themselves a crude mixture of boisterous sentimentality, intemperance, and shiftlessness on the one hand, and untutored wisdom, practicality, and sociability on the other. Their sylvan worldview was grounded in a pragmatic individualism loosely couched in a primitive moral order—admittedly guided, often as not, by fists rather than metaphysics. Where the latter did prevail, it took the form of enthusiastic Protestant folk spiritualism, typically expressed through clapping and swaying in accompaniment to white spirituals in ecstatic anticipation of the day. Such "shouts" had the effect of binding worshippers in common cause, the frontier just one more stop for pilgrims in progression to their heavenly destination, their way accessible not through irresistible grace, but volitional capacity to conquer sin (Gabriel 1950, 36–39).

As much as it ultimately may have contributed to regional cultural differences, the heterogeneity of the Second Great Awakening reinforced the pluralist nature of American democracy. Almost as important politically as spiritually, popular revival helped quell Americans' fears that in throwing off the yoke of tyranny and creating a society of equals, they were tumbling into an abyss of moral chaos (Miller 1965, 12; Mathews 1969, 40; Bloch 1985, ch. 4; McWilliams 1987, 455–57; Noll 1993, 624; 2002, ch. 4). In conflating the cause of America with the cause of Christ, evangelists of the Second Great Awakening helped engineer what Noll sees as the load-bearing columns of nationhood (1993, 636; see generally Miyakawa 1964; see also Miller 1965, 12; McLoughlin 1980, 1). Preaching the egalitarian godliness of American self-sufficiency, evangelists spoke to the manifest truth that the good citizen went about armed with conviction that autonomy and godliness were but the same thing by a different name (see McWilliams 1987, 451; Noll 2002, 110–11, 173–75, 193).

A symmetrical elegance emerged. To the state, Paine's predatory necessity was bequeathed the narrow contractarian mandate to defend the natural rights of a people sensitive to any illegitimate intrusion of authority. The countervailing mandate to temper rampant self-interest through moral perfection and promotion of civic virtue fell to evangelical churches. Consequent was a commonsensical appeal to the social gospel, reinforced by united evangelical penetration into such secular concerns as slavery, temperance, education, and prison reform—a "homeopathic strategy of fighting democratic excess with democratic remedies" (Thomas 1965, 657, see also 658; Kett 1977, 72–74; Noll 1985, 226–27; Howe 2007, 186–88, 191–93).[4]

Institutional checks and balances reflected the pessimistic vestiges of eighteenth-century Calvinism—belief in the inherent depravity of humanity and the superiority of dispassionate institutions over self-interested governors (Thomas 1965, 659). Emphasis on evangelical common sense, by contrast, embraced nineteenth-century optimism as to individuals' innate moral competence, rendering them free to pursue their own best lives as dictated by godliness and moral reasoning. Ironically and ingeniously, the coercive powers of the state, heavily regulated through the mechanics of institutional balance, were employed to the end of individual liberty. At the same time, the perfectionism requisite to good republican citizenry was left to agents of moral exhortation exercising no authority beyond an appeal to the will and faith extant in what Finney calls humanity's "natural ability to obey God" (quoted in Noll 1993, 638). Indeed, it was a truth often repeated by American clergy that the greater part of justice resided in the conscience rather than in the laws of man or the wrath of God (Tocqueville 1941, esp. 332–36, Wood 1993, 66; McWilliams 1987, 449–55; Zuckert 2004, 58–65; Howe 2007, 165–66, 172–73, 189).[5]

Nineteenth-century evangelists may not have sung in perfect harmony, but they came together in grounding theology in empiricism rather than chimeric and mystification (Noll 1983, 224–25). As expressed through the Second Great Awakening, evangelical common sense spoke to human capacity for civic virtue through fidelity to self-evident moral principles that encouraged responsible employment of liberty, self-reliance, equality, and intolerance for impediments to such godly ends. The extent to which the good citizen consumed her moral nourishment readily and of her own volition speaks to the light touch of this evangelical social gospel. The subtext was that just agents were responsible for their actions and that tyranny, not self-directed pursuit of human fulfillment, was the true enemy of godliness (Tocqueville 1941, 329–32, 424–25; Hofstadter 1963, 56; Thomas 1965, 658–60; Heimert 1966, 141–42; Mathews 1969, 35; Bloch 1985, 14–15; Hatch 1989, 9–10; Noll 1993, 615–16, 621–22; 2002, 79–83; McWilliams 1987, 448; Mailer 2011, 242–43, 248).

Transcendentalism and Common Heroism

If the evangelical response to nineteenth-century declension took the form of proselytization in the name of common sense, New England transcendentalists—the likes of Bronson Alcott, Orestes Brownson, William Henry Channing, Charles Mayo Ellis, Margaret Fuller, Theodore Parker, George

Ripley, Henry David Thoreau, Walt Whitman, and, preeminently, Ralph Waldo Emerson—sought refinement of moral competence as something above and beyond reasoned processing of sensical impressions. Varyingly Unitarian in their theology and liberal in their politics, transcendentalists located morality in an internalized divine spirit, a noumenal "over-soul" inhabited by human intuition of super-sensible moral truths (Ripley 1836, disc. 3; Emerson *Self-Reliance*, 189–91, 203–4; *Trans.*, 193–195; Ellis 1842, 11; Whitman 1860b, chant 3.23; Parker 1876, ch. 2; Bancroft 1997, 424).[6] Transcendentalists spoke to the apotheosis of humanity in terms of "a pilgrimage from the idolatrous world of creeds and rituals to the temple of the Living God in the soul. It was a putting to silence of tradition and formulas, that the Sacred Oracle might be heard through intuitions of the single-eyed and pure-hearted. Amidst materialists, zealots, and skeptics, the Transcendentalist believed in perpetual inspiration, the miraculous power of will, and a birthright to universal good" (Channing quoted in Goffman and Joy 2005, 167).[7] They shared the Romantic's distaste for the "city dolls" of Emerson's disdain, whose Old World affectations contrasted unfavorably with the bootstrapping efficacy of the more provincial and less refined (*Self-Reliance*, 55–56). At the same time, though, committed to an objective moral good, transcendentalists distanced themselves from the subjectivity of authenticity (Ellis 1842, 36). They conceived good law as something above and apart from shared aesthetic judgment. Absent social commitment to moral objectivism, Ellis reasons, there could be no social progression or cosmic blueprint. And without such a metaphysical foundation, "what is civilization but a change of the ring from the nose to the ear, a flat head or a high one, a coat turban or skin of a wild beast, according to the fashions of men?" (1842, 50).

Transcendentalists evinced no hostility to the evangelists of common moral sense. New England intellectuals shared with their more primitive countrymen an abiding faith in human nature and the moral competence of the individual (Emerson *Heroism*, 177–78).[8] However, they appealed to something above and beyond common sense. If common sense spoke to innate human capacity, transcendentalism announced the very apotheosis of humanity. The one informed the untutored individual's ability to know and obey the will of God, the other portrayed the commoner—at least she who willed herself to rise above the vacuity of the common herd—as the godhead herself (Ellis 1842, 24). "Have you thought there could be but a single Supreme?" Whitman asks. "There can be any number of Supremes" (1860b, chant 1.3; see also 13.3). In the same vein, Emerson admonishes: "See to it that only thyself is here, and art and nature, hope and dread, friends, angels and the Supreme Being shall not be absent from the chamber where thou sittest" (*Heroism*, 182–183).

Transcendentalists sought to awaken torpid individuals to their fullest potential, to divest them of the satisficing moral conformity in which they found respite from the admonition of conscience (Ellis 1842, 28). The objective was to provoke individuals into critical social inquiry and principled response to manifest injustice. "Who are you," Whitman asks again, "that wanted only to be told what you knew before? Who are you, that wanted only a book to join you in your nonsense? Are you, or would you be, better than all that has ever been before? If you would be better than all that has ever been before, come listen to me, and not otherwise" (Whitman 1860b, chant 1. 9–10). Such exhortation was an appeal to unfettered moral consciousness, moral agency grounded in the wherewithal of individuals to trust in their latent immanence just as they trusted in God. It was a command above all else to take counsel of themselves for the good of all (Emerson *Heroism*, 186).

Transcendentalists implored common citizens "to stand for the interests of general justice and humanity" (Emerson *Young American*, 226), to follow "the rule of right between man and man" (Ellis 1842, 19), to "leap from their seats and contend for their lives" (Whitman 1860b, chant 1. 8, 17). They wanted no part of a society weakened by its willingness to compromise principles in the name of efficiency or interest. They lamented the institutions and parties that loomed as wicked obstacles on the road to civil perfection (Emerson *Trans.*, 203–4; Ellis 1842, 102–4; Thomas 1965, 672).

Transcendentalists envisioned a republic not of regenerate saints or philosopher kings, but of common heroes. America's founding principles offered so much hope. Indeed, the problem was not so much one of redemption in the form of reimagining a new order; it was one of consolidating values, of encouraging citizens to accept the full mantle of citizenship. In their fully realized America, the heroic commoner supplanted the fussy nobleman, the selfish knave, and the timid conformist (Emerson *Heroism*, 178; Bancroft 1997, 428). She trusted her own judgment as to the nature of the good, accessible through self-evident truths *and* moral intuition. She therefore condemned social privilege and the specious magnanimity of "the fop, who, by the magic of title" sought to appropriate the rightful dignity and liberty of others (Emerson *Young American*, 229). She embraced her true genius, avoiding the shame of finding in others' brilliance ideas she herself might have already rejected for want of conviction (Emerson *Self-Reliance*, 32). She had proper, which is to say appropriate, respect for authority, recognizing that as a citizen of a free republic, she was not a child to be tutored by those more virtuous or learned than herself. Instead of the philosopher king, her heroic self was the philosopher citizen, accepting responsibility for her conduct and the values of her society. To this end, says Parker, "it is we who are the ancients, and have forgotten more than all our fathers knew. We will take their wisdom joyfully, and thank God for it, but not their authority" (1907, 128).

Yet discouragingly, even in the face of such national promise, there persisted in Jacksonian America a morass of mindless conformity, an abundance of cupidity, and a deficiency of morality. Transcendentalists found in Jacksonian America a great nation in danger of losing its way. In addition to the monstrous evil of slavery, found wanting was education, the plight of organized labor, sympathy, the equality of women, and human flourishing in general (Gabriel 1950, 46; Ronda 2017, 12). In fighting for a nation of Americans as great as America itself, transcendentalists found a society of people whose lives were insolvent, who could not satisfy their own desires, whose ambitions outpaced their efforts (Emerson *Self-Reliance*, 55). America had its full share of self-assertive citizens willing to stand up for their own rights and freedoms. As for the rights of others, however, many of these self-same individuals were only too happy to accommodate their consciences to the safe harbor of unjust laws. Self-reliant in their own cause, they turned pusillanimous in the aid of others, willingly submitting to the archaic frailty of anachronistic moral paradigms, speciously pleading ignorance as to its deficiencies. In this fashion they accommodated slaveholder and chauvinist—parsing the logic that ensured their own pursuit of happiness from that which deprived others of freedom and equality (Ellis 1842, 36).

To put the most generous spin on it, many Jacksonian Americans tended to be too reliant on biblical or historical injunction, too credulous, too readily convinced to conflate unjust common practice with the common good. They were too willing to internalize the conviction that goodness and tradition were indivisible. Their affect betrayed them and their logic deceived them. In fact, so pervasive was such false moral consciousness, that heroic goodness itself—particularly as it pertained to the great evil of the day—presented as a source of shame. A good example of what I am talking about here is the scene in *Huckleberry Finn* when Jim and Huck are on the raft towards Cairo, Illinois.

> Jim said it made him all over trembly and feverish to be so close to freedom. Well, I can tell you it made me all over trembly and feverish, too, to hear him, because I begun to get it through my head that he was most free—and who was to blame for it? Why, *me*. I couldn't get that out of my conscience, no how nor no way. It got to troubling me so I couldn't rest; I couldn't stay still in one place. It hadn't ever come home to me before, what this thing was that I was doing. But now it did; and it stayed with me, and scorched me more and more. I tried to make out to myself that I warn't to blame, because I didn't run Jim off from his rightful owner; but it warn't no use, conscience up and says, every time, "But you knowed he was running for his freedom, and you could a paddled ashore and told somebody." That was so—I couldn't get around that noway. That was where it pinched. Conscience says to me, "What had poor Miss Watson done to you that you could see her nigger go off right under your eyes and never say one single word? What did that poor old woman do to you that you could treat her so mean? Why, she tried to learn you your book, she tried to learn you your manners, she tried to be good to you every way she knowed how. *That's* what she done." (Twain 1885, 80–81)

What Huck disgustedly condemns as weakness for defying moral convention is, of course, just the opposite. In aiding Jim—in going to great lengths to do so—Huck abdicates the "duty" to which custom, reason, and conscience all conspire to direct him, in favor of his superior moral intuition. For transcendentalists, this is precisely the hallmark of the common hero. Far from reflexively acceding to the grandeur of law or custom, she defers to a moral intuition deaf to learned philosophers, sanctimonious divines, and sundry moral sophists. She is guided by her own process of critical judgment—is judged not by the standards of others, but by her own intuitive grasp of the properties and precepts of morality (Emerson *Heroism*, 177; *Self-Reliance*, 53; Ellis 1842, 41–46; Fuller 1997, 370).

Asserting moral intuition against moral convention, the common hero's first priority is to overcome resistance, to counter the minions of conformity, to vilify unjust agency vindicated by nothing more substantial than indolent assent to custom or law (Pollack 1882, 266–68). It is to resist capitulation "to badges and names . . . and dead institutions" (Emerson *Self-Reliance*, 36;

see also Ellis, 1842, 27, 65–66; Whitman 1860b, chant 3.21). It is to exhort her fellow citizens into moral maturity, "to fan the flame of human love and raise the standard of civil virtue" (Emerson *Heroism*, 180; also Ripley 1997, esp. 256–57). Her obligation is to convince those unwilling to be treated as children to move beyond adolescence and comport themselves as mature just agents. Her message is that latent moral capacity is fairly useless. Even merely wanting to be good doesn't cut it in the absence of courage of conviction. Thus, laments Emerson, "Good nature is plentiful, but we want justice, with heart of steel, to fight down the proud. The private mind has access to the totality of goodness and truth, that it may be a balance to a corrupt society; and to stand for the private verdict against popular clamor, is the office of the noble" (*Young American*, 227).

Common heroism encourages maturation from one sentiment: "I am as good as you, so get out of my way," to another: "You are as good as I, and let us help one another" (Parker 1907, 143). It speaks to a sort of moral revivalism in which the end is a universal culture of goodness; the means not Calvinist conversion, but transcendental moral consciousness. It calls not for singular heroism so much as a party of common heroes, questioning and perpetually ameliorating law and social mores through the uncompromising prism of moral perfectionism. It promotes a "huge brotherhood of divine average men," a chorus of uninhibited consciences, singing in harmonious praise of the timeless and divine principles of justice (Thomas 1965, 674–75; also Ellis 1842, 62–65, 97–98, 100; Emerson *Character*, 330; *Great Men*, 617). It locates such common heroes at the vanguard of goodness, breaking down the barriers imposed by conventional fonts of wisdom and justice whose cognitive and affective machinations lag in comparison to heroic intuition.

Redoubtable in her goodness as the Homeric hero is in her courage, the common hero is "of a different dust" only in the sense that she wills herself to be, in a way that anyone *could* be if only she would (Ellis 1842, 24, 29–32, 67–68, 79–85). She mocks those whose abiding interest resides in their own material comfort or ostentation. She derides the solemnity of the righteous seeking to puff themselves up through pious hypocrisy, lambasting the sophists and social conformists whose "every truth is not quite true" (Emerson *Self-Reliance*, 39). She demystifies the veneration that attaches to great names, relocating it to apparently paltry and prosaic individuals who just might prove to be the best there ever had been (Emerson *Heroism*, 178–82; Whitman 1860b, chant 9). She rejects the deification of history and tradition, as though what once had been could or should be somehow greater than that which presently is (Emerson *Self-Reliance*, 48–49). She transcends envy and imitation, embracing the responsibility to till her own moral field. She opens herself to the intuitive revelation that God reserves for those of fortitude and withholds from the weak and timid. She recognizes what the great have always recognized in themselves: that a transcendent life is founded upon nothing more, and nothing less, than awakening to one's own mystical goodness (*Self-Reliance*, 32–33).

The common hero stands up not just to chauvinism, but to self-regard posturing as social concern. Emerson spares no contempt for those who, like Glaucon's wearer of the ring of Gyges, take care to make a spectacle of their virtue and be invisible in their vice. He blasts those whose infantilization of the weak serves no greater end than harvesting the affirmation of others. ("If malice and vice wear the coat of philanthropy, shall that pass?" [*Self-Reliance*, 36].) He chastises those who employ nobility of cause to compensate for meanness of soul. ("Thy love afar is spite at home" [36].) And he evinces disdain for individuals whose virtues are merely pocket change to pay the toll for favoring themselves, first and last (37). The common hero appropriates the virtue of the greatly good sage. But she divests it of insularity, that precious exclusivity that mandates honor and privilege and deference (Emerson *Over-Soul*, 196, 204; Ellis 1842, 34–35; Brownson 1997, 184–85). She has no time for those who assume greatness as ornamentation. (Of the outrageous grifters—the Faux Dauphin and the Duke of Bilgewater—who join Huck and Jim on the raft, Huck says, "What was the use to tell Jim these warn't real kings and dukes? It wouldn't a done no good; and, besides, it was just as I said: you couldn't tell them from the real kind" [Twain 1885, 137].)

Equally, she reacts against the rote conformity of an enfeebled mass. She chastises any who would aid the putatively magnanimous in the nonsensical presumption to know an agent's duty better than the agent herself. Indeed, it is only through the conscription of the weak that the ostensibly great can lay claim to the heroism that more rightly belongs to the common keeper of her own godly counsel. Even more than charlatans, then, transcendentalists' contempt was directed towards those who would not do for themselves. They condemned individuals immobilized by the paralytic pusillanimity of a Prufrock or the dull-witted orthodoxy of those content to let others (which is to say other than God and self) direct the course of their lives (Emerson *Self-Reliance*, 48). "The imbecility of men," summarizes Emerson, "is always inviting the impudence of power" (*Great Men*, 623).

To be sure, the lot of the individual is to know her place. But too many fail to understand what that place is. Most emphatically it is not to "skulk up and down with the air of a charity-boy, a bastard, or an interloper in the world" (*Self-Reliance*, 44). It is to be neither mendicant nor sycophant. It is not to confuse the accomplishments of others with poverty of the self, as though the great somehow appropriate all virtue for themselves and leave nothing for the rest but a collar and a leash.[9] Instead of praising the submissive penitent, Parker celebrates the one who, excommunicated by the church, responds in kind by liberating herself from *its* heresies. He exalts the atom that extracts itself from the compound, that manufactures new matter or encourages new growth in substitution for Emerson's flower of nobility gone to seed (Parker 1907, 131–32; see also Emerson *Manners*, 352; *Self-Reliance*, 45; Ellis 1842, 104).

The transcendentalist common hero fulfills her duty to self, society, and God. In this she is virtuous, but not remarkable or even heroic. Any individual may be habituated. What makes her heroic, sets her apart from the Aristotelian good commoner, is volitional employment of moral independence. It is her intransigence to the legal, social, or metaphysical expectations of others. This is not to say that she has no appreciation of great genius; just that she appreciates genius for what it is—a source of inspiration rather than idolization, a resource to be employed in the development of the self, but ultimately outgrown. Indeed, the great danger is that the magnetic pull of great men robs commoners of their sense of self, transforming what would be a society of equals into what Emerson calls a population of pygmies (*Great Men*, 627).

At the same time, the common hero musters her will, not as an end in itself—not to show, like Zarathustra, that God no longer controls the fate of free citizens—but in fulfillment of the divine mandate. She casts her own light, not in aid of Romantic authenticity, but in the command of justice itself. She absolves herself, not in justification of Manfred's license or Werther's emotive self-indulgence, but in humble submission to her own sense of duty (Emerson *Great Men*, 617). She joins in prayer, not in the "disease of the will" that is the mean pursuit of self-regard, but in the uplifting unity with God that empowers her own moral intuition. She courts the disdain of lesser individuals, not out of spite, but for the love of God, imparting the often-harsh truths that more amenable (and contemptible) individuals are content to obscure with weak platitude (Emerson *Self-Reliance*, 54–57).

If there is a defining quality to the common hero it is comfort in her own skin. Like her ancestral forbearers, the oppositional country gentleman and the Promethean Romantic, she envelops herself in self-mastery (Whitman 1860b, chant 1.42). She is as comfortable abroad as she is at home—in this context as in that—her self-sufficiency portable and cosmopolitan. In Emerson's ever-colorful imagery, she never distances herself from her soul, never seeks to gad about as something other than the self she truly is ("My giant goes with me wherever I go" [*Self-Reliance*, 60]). She is a noble person in disguise, her pageantry and refinement exclusive to herself, her entourage a procession of one. By the same token, she does not seek to absorb her goodness by osmosis, as though by experiencing the world she might assemble the accouterments of virtue. Self-sufficient in the Aristotelian sense of completeness, she differs in that she is self-reliant in her arrival at such *autarkes*. To that transcendent end, Emerson implores his readers to "Insist on yourself; never imitate. Your own gift you can present every moment with the cumulative force of a whole life's cultivation; but of the adopted talent of another you have only an extemporaneous half-possession. . . . Dwell up there in the simple and noble regions of thy life, obey thy heart and thou shalt reproduce the Foreworld again" (*Self-Reliance*, 61).

This sort of autonomy is as important for the good republic as it is for the hero herself. A self-sufficient republic is informed by a sense of itself. It does not imitate tastes and customs. It self-consciously distances itself from the well-worn grooves of the past and is no more defined by foreign custom than the good traveler abroad (Emerson *Self-Reliance*, 60). Released from aristocratic cloister, its principles reside in the safe custody of its citizens. ("When did the Gospel of all truth, that redeems, and blesses, and sanctifies the world, live in the hearts of so many millions?" [Bancroft 1997, 429].) It is coarse and egalitarian, its heroes heroic not through affirmation by a docile class of ritual affirmers, but in incremental manufacture of a collective greatness born of ubiquitous and prosaic goodness. Common heroes differ from more genteel ones in that they are not the "men of fine parts [who] protect themselves by solitude, or by courtesy, or by satire, or by an acid worldly manner, each concealing as best he can, his incapacity for useful association" (Emerson *Nominalist*, 422). Instead, says Whitman to the common hero, "All I love America for, is contained in men and women like you" (1860b, chant 3.31–32, and generally chants 2–3). And Bancroft, "we have made Humanity our lawgiver and our oracle; and, therefore, principles which, in Europe, the wisest receive with distrust, are here the common property of the public mind" (1997, 427).

Conclusion: A Hero New

Facially, the idea of common heroism is a contradiction in terms. It simultaneously anticipates and nullifies greatness. Like Calvinist evangelists seeking to arouse the piety of sinners in order to save themselves from a fate they have no power to change, the proponent of common heroism appears to have taken hold of a contradiction she is unable to release. Common heroism is not a mark of distinction, at least in the way of more traditional hero types. It does not distinguish extraordinary individuals from those less capable. Rather, in concert with Romantic heroism, it speaks to cultivation of universal and innate capabilities. What distinguishes common heroes from ordinary people living ordinary lives is not capacity but volition and conviction, the fortitude to bring their latent heroism to the fore. To the likes of Ralph Waldo Emerson, common heroism speaks to the inclusive immanence of humanity. It connotes a moral aristocracy of the will, exclusive of the ordinary and unwilling—"such men as do not belong to me and to whom I do not belong" (*Self-Reliance*, 37).

There is an inherent anonymity to common heroism. In the main it is depersonalized. Culturally, it tends toward a quality of occupation (farmer, frontiersman, cattle handler). Even where it is personalized, the common hero's distinctiveness is often qualified by her ordinary social status and her lack of social ambition. She cloaks her heroism in the humility of a Daniel Boone or, better yet, in the anonymity of a Lone Ranger or a costumed superhero. She exercises authority rather than power. Leatherstocking remains a frontiersman and not a leader, Ishmael, a sailor on the *Pequod* and not the captain, Uncle Tom, a slave and not one of wealth or standing (Poli 1968, 230). To the common hero, there is nothing less heroic than the putting on of airs. Indeed, of the internal mystical goodness that guides her in the conduct of her life, Emerson says simply, "Great is the soul, and plain" (*Over-Soul*, 209).

The common hero is most obviously a creature of the American republic. The emergent America cried out for a new heroic ideal fit for a new nation on a new continent destined to fulfill its divine mandate to construct a new order for the ages. She spoke not only to capacity, but to cosmic place, revealing the conjunctive power of humanism and godliness. She reflected humanity's innate ability to intuit her way out of the cave and into the light, inspiring a vision that "man can become more and more endowed with divinity; and as he does he becomes more and more God-like in his character and capable of governing himself. Let us go on elevating our people, perfecting our institutions, until democracy shall reach such a point of perfection that we can acclaim with truth that the voice of the people is the voice of God" (Andrew Jackson quoted in McLoughlin 1980, 139). America's common hero was the incarnation of an American civic ideal, embodying muscular individualism and godly moral conviction. Poised to expand her continental empire, America's common hero was—as Lowell says of Lincoln—"a hero new, wise, steadfast in the strength of God and true" (Lowell 1902, st. VI).

In the next chapter, we shall examine the evolutionary personification of this hero new. Indeed, the story of the common hero is the story of liberation from what Americans came to see as illegitimate constraint. The original source of constraint was theocratic, the hegemony of the order of grace marginalizing the natural order. Yet as in Britain, America's Puritan republican ideal was a will-o'-the-wisp, a heuristic unable to serve a Reformed Church in construction of the New Jerusalem. In contrast to the British experience, however, the sparking of the evangelical new light twice reawakened American consciousness to the prospect of the godly republic, to the realization of just balance between the orders of nature and grace. The First Great Awakening opened eyes to new possibilities, ideas that challenged citizens to abandon slothful deference in demonstration of moral efficacy, exercised in aid of worldly and, possibly spiritual, fulfillment. The Second Great Awakening helped usher in an appreciation of the power of common sense moral reasoning, later perfected by transcendental moral intuition. It reconciled Promethean defiance to volitional godly obedience, glorying in the liberty of the individual and the virtue requisite to civil society.

Chapter 7

The American Common Hero

In the previous chapter, we traced the religious roots of common heroism, focusing on the uniquely American marriage of humanism and spirituality—an egalitarian doctrine that claimed "for all men what a more restricted Christian perfectionism extended only to the redeemed" (Thomas 1965, 671). The result was cultivation of dignity, sui generis, not imbibed as the gift of magnanimity, but harnessed as power within, radiating outward. This second chapter on American common heroism concentrates upon heroic archetypes in the defense, stewardship, and even redemption of the American republic. Culturally, these heroic archetypes present as idealized citizens and nation builders, consolidating the values—individualism, self-reliance, autonomy, justice, human dignity, and morality—that have informed not only the American national identity, but the core values of all modern republics. As good citizens, common heroes help bind the nation in a common sense of itself. They contribute to what Giles Gunn describes as a thickening of public culture, whereby civic virtue is husbanded not only through the *substance* of shared beliefs, but also by the *process* of civic discourse. Central to maintenance of the democratic aspect of republicanism, common heroes bring together elements of society that would otherwise have limited means for "rendering differences conversable" (Gunn 1992, 37; Athanasourelis 2012, 6).

That common heroes came into their own in America is not surprising. While the fundaments of evangelical Protestantism were hardly unique to the nascent United States, the purity and potential of the new continent had always conjured visions of man in his prelapsarian state, as a new *American Adam* (Lewis 1955, 5). American common heroism has reflected a coarse primitivism, a sort of muscular masculinity, a sense of national destiny reflecting an egalitarian human capacity in the conduct of life (McLoughlin 1980, 105–6). Early on, it self-consciously distinguished the primitively virtuous American from the posturing genteel European, rugged pioneer from affected burgher, straight-shooting backwoodsman from sophisticate and obfuscator. As iconic representation of the prosaic everyman, archetypal American common heroes refuse to put on airs. Rather than aspire to honor and recognition, their preference is to retreat into anonymity or, failing that, to take extra pains to present themselves as little more than good neighbors.

Finding literary voice in the mid-nineteenth-century American Renaissance and popular voice through the dime novel, common heroism is an expression of just human agency, volitional employment of innate capacity in service to the good. It is an exhortation to good stewardship and a concomitant disavowal of the hoary social conventions sanctifying pusillanimity. It highlights the imperative for self-mastery, liberation from ossified traditions prompting deference, inefficacy, and the irrational need to be beholden to the approval of others. Common heroes stand as reminders that civic fecklessness is fecund soil for the emergence of evil, be it lawlessness or corruption, weakening the republic and leaving it vulnerable to hostile takeover.

This chapter explores the evolution and political functions of the archetypal American common hero. First, it looks at Crevecoeur's idealized yeoman farmer and the self-made New World urban man as role models for good citizen of the emergent American republic. For the nineteenth century, the focus shifts to nation building in consolidation of the new republic and defense of the new frontier. Here we highlight the sylvan adventurer lionized in the legend of Daniel Boone and the novels of James Fennimore Cooper, as well as the self-contained cavalier of the plains. These early American common heroes existed at the nexus of the primitive and the civilized, cultivating their moral conviction through the purity of the one and the intersubjectivity of the other. In the latter part of the chapter, the landscape changes. With the passage of the Old West and the shifting demographics favoring the big city, American common heroes of the twentieth century and beyond metamorphosize into the earthy hard-boiled detective through the unsettled decades of the early century, and later, more optimistically, as the theatrical superhero. These newer archetypes represent heroic defenders, and to a lesser extent redeemers.

They play a didactic role, symbolizing the efficacy of common citizens in just stewardship of the just republic.

The Primitive Common Hero

As noted in the previous chapter, the cultural stimulus for the emergence of American common heroism was the social dislocation culminating in the American Revolution. It was that event that mythologized the efficacy of the heroic underdog. Attendant to the emergence of the new republic was the cultural imperative to create a schematic ideal—in the form of archetypal role models—for just agent (the good citizen) and just condition (an egalitarian republic). The result was not exactly a triumph of vulgarity, more like an assertion of coarse and virtuous provincialism, a celebration of commonness as antidote to the pernicious trappings of specious magnanimity, civil and spiritual.

As with any cultural revolution, complete transformation was not immediate.[1] Thus, for the first couple of decades of the country's existence, an abortive faux-aristocratic elitism pervaded American high culture. Greene, for example, notes that the spirit of American magazines of the era tended toward parallels between the great republics of antiquity and potential for the newly emergent America. The editorial predilection was to an aristocracy of virtue. Published as they were "by gentlemen, for gentlemen and . . . about gentlemen," the not-so-subtle subtext was that while heroes *could* emerge from all classes, providential destiny tended to smile disproportionately upon those of respectable birth and breeding (Greene 1970, 33). Biographic articles were a common theme, the better to mythologize an indigenous class of refined gentlemen capable of exercising the prerogatives of their nobility. Such periodicals had limited circulation, however, and their brief lifespans suggest that enthusiasm for neoclassical noblesse oblige was less than robust, even among the upper crust (Greene 1970, 19–42).

THE NEW MAN . . .

At the popular level, vestigial American elitism was unambiguously on the outs, victim of growing intolerance for the "brave apery of foreign absurdities" (Parker 1907, 130). Representative of the quest to define idealized

American citizenship was Royall Tyler's (2008) comedy of manners *The Contrast*, which opened in April 1787. Distinguishing nascent American integrity from stratified Old World pretension, *The Contrast* portrays two suitors for the hand of Maria Van Rough. The first is the foppish Anglophilic dandy Billy Dimple, slavish devotee of Lord Chesterfield's *Art of Becoming a Man of the World* and personification of the debauched patrician gentleman given to sweet-talking a woman into his bed and himself into her purse. The other is the stoic patriot Colonel Henry Manly, a stolid provincial Revolutionary War veteran. Billy is a bon vivant, ostentatiously au courant in his fashions (although his valet laments his master's habit of rounding his fingernails as unpardonably passé). Manly is bemused by social frivolity, maintaining a square-jawed commitment to duty and Polybian disquiet that luxury and indolence stand poised to corrupt the virtue of his new republic (Tyler 2008, act III, sc. 2).[2]

Given the contrast, the play unfolds with shop-worn predictability. Maria explains to her true love Manly that though she despises Billy for his lack of virtue, she has agreed to give him her hand in order to please her father. After all, in the venerable way of the world, having made his own fortune, the arriviste Mr. Van Rough's aspirations would have turned to marrying his wealth to good name. It is true that Manly is stout of heart while Billy is a supercilious twit, but filial duty takes precedence. And so forth. The payoff comes in the final scene with a cascade of didactic revelations. Billy reveals himself to one and all as the four-flusher the audience already knows him to be. Van Rough, evincing more common sense than his daughter had credited him with, reveals that it was he who had contrived all along to bring Manly and Maria together. Charlotte reveals dawning comprehension that self-presentation and virtue actually *are* divisible. And, just to ensure resonance with even the dullest of Tyler's auditors, Manly reveals: "And I have learned that probity, virtue, honour, though they should not have received the polish of Europe, will secure to an honest American the good graces of his fair countrywomen, and, I hope, the applause of *the public*" (2008, act V, sc. 2, emphasis original).

For present purposes, the relevance of *The Contrast* lies not so much in the dismissal of European gentility as in the characterization of the indigenous American hero. Manly and Van Rough—Tyler's allegory grants subtlety no quarter—represent two sides of the new America's heroic ideal. Manly is most comfortable in his provincialism. Out of place in the big city, his rigid republicanism fails to tint his Puritan roots. Yet his plain-speakin', straight-shootin' manliness is illustrative of the pastoral dimension of the nascent American identity, helping to inform a sense of usness favorably contrasted with the arcane, effeminized, luxury-addled themness of British aristocracy.[3] In Manly, we find echoes of Crevecoeur's Andrew the Hebridean, as well as the faint harbinger of the heroic potential of Daniel Boone, Natty Bumppo, and Huck Finn.

Van Rough, on the other hand, is a prototypical idealization of the urban man whose bourgeois bona fides announce the prevailing virtues of nineteenth-century urban America—freedom, self-assertion, equality, fortitude, common sense and honest dealing. A bit ahead of his still-Jeffersonian times perhaps, Van Rough speaks to the efficacy of the new man, self-made, his economic success standing testimonial to his virtue (Kimmel 1996, 22; Howe 2007, 190). If Manly is moved by moral affect (complains Charlotte, "every sentence is a sentiment"), Van Rough speaks to the power of the reason requisite to successful free enterprise. Conjunctively, the emergent common American hero of the pugnacious nineteenth century conscripted Van Rough's self-sufficiency, Manly's primitive republican virtue, and the guileless egalitarianism that bonds them. This new heroic ideal projected a "just folks" kind of bootstrapping hominess, a more alluring prospect for the American imagination than the urban dandy, the genteel rentier, or the idle heir, each disqualified from heroic validation by failure to conquer the *aethlos* that contextualizes heroism in all its forms.

America's emergent bourgeois culture bespoke its own sort of virtue, a remnant of its Protestant orthodox ancestry, an ethic unifying agonal individualism, communal responsibility, and godly calling. The muscular masculinity of self-made common heroes mandated vigilance against the threat of effeminization, virtue very much a manly quality. It guarded against slipping into the virtue-sapping indolence of overrefinement—as with the gentle aristocrat, leaving others to do her bidding while resting on unmerited laurels. Heroic bootstrappers cultivated decisiveness, hypermasculinity, and the sense of rugged individualism that, like the portrait of Aeneas to Rome, Americans saw in themselves. There was a godly weightlessness to robust American masculinity, the individual a free-floating molecule rather than a brick bound in place by social mortar brittle through weather and decay.

The virtuous qualities of self-made commoners were qualified somewhat by their appetitive quest for wealth. Nineteenth-century Americans faced anomic undercurrents wrought by progressive urbanization, as individuals sought to hold fast to something in the maelstrom of social, economic, theological, and political changes characteristic of that turbulent time. That the commoner found herself in a world of equals in nineteenth-century America was all to the good. But equality also implied the frantic and competitive milieu so destructive to Thoreauvian men's lives of quiet desperation. Conjuring the spirit of Late Republican Rome, greed threatened as an ominous apparition hanging over the new republic.

Helping to allay traditional republican concerns about the corrupting potential of wealth, however, was a growing sense of the market virtue emphasized most prominently by Smith and Montesquieu—that one's prospects for success in a free market were greatly enhanced by a reputation girded with integrity and honest dealing. In a twist on Rome, then, the market for American virtue was quite literally a market, one's material success therein a proxy for her virtue. Embracing the grind of ascendant embourgeoisement, Americans internalized the belief that free competition rewarded the best individuals through employment of the talents God had seen fit to provide (Rotundo 1993, 19). Their mandate was to do well and do good, employing their natural gifts as God would have it and enjoying the fruits of their efforts—recompense of which God would approve as well (Sellers 1991, esp. ch. 7; Carwardine 2002).[4]

The self-made man idealized the commoner reliant upon none but herself and a providential God. Lionized in the pages of Horatio Alger, he never permitted circumstance to intrude upon his virtue. In assuming responsibility for charting his life's course, he took the same leap of faith as the newly independent America itself, facing the same binary prospects of prosperity or ruination, the free market kicking away the prop of the protective guild, leaving the entrepreneur to fend for himself, and devil-take-the-hindmost (Kimmel 1996, 22–25). At the same time, the self-made man of the early republic made his way without descending into the Hobbesian anarchy of morally liberated savages, without regressing into the immature primitivism of governance entirely by one's own self-regard (Rotundo 1993, 21). Relying foremost upon himself, he exercised his liberty without embracing the licentiousness that ancient republicans had convinced themselves would attend to the mob detached from the magnanimous. As cultural icon, he helped prove the robustness of dignity absent *dignitas*, portraying the liberated individual's innate capacity to temper her material ambition with social responsibility.

While the urban common hero was an embodiment of the power of self-sufficiency, it is important to bear in mind the perspective of the times. The self-made man remained as yet largely uncorrupted. In the early American republic he had not yet evolved into the single-minded capitalist, the robber baron whose eye for the main chance was only partially mitigated by the philanthropy employed to soften his image (Greene 1970, 127–33). Yet even with greater historical perspective, there remains in America a sense that an individual capable of achieving economic success is of sufficiently fungible virtue that her talents can be fruitfully employed in public service. Indeed, Americans of the early twenty-first century saw fit to elect a president on little more than the strength of such logic.

. . . And the New Land

The self-made man was not the only archetypal role model for the new American citizen. For those to whom the urban grind held little appeal, a second means of dealing with the turbulence of nineteenth-century American life was an escapist Romantic perfectionism (Thomas 1965) or self-mastery in perfection of the virtue attendant to frontier life. A person may have been powerless to affect the relentless march of nineteenth-century social and technological progress, but nothing could deny her dominion over herself. The first iconic embodiment of such Romantic perfectionism was the yeoman farmer, imbibing her moral competence from proximity to nature and perfecting it through the disciplined habituation demanded by successful cultivation. Her self-mastery radiated outward—from control of her own actions, she assumed influence over her sociopolitical and, possibly, even cosmic circumstances. Self-mastery thus equipped her with the confidence to assert the prerogatives of the good republican citizen: dominion over the private space, stewardship of the public space, and harmony with the spiritual space (Eisinger 1947, 44–45).

Typical was Crevecoeur's Andrew the Hebridean, a didactic source of emulation for the good Jeffersonian citizen of the new republic. A new country gentleman, Andrew's heroism relies upon no literary contrivance. It is born not of some miraculous twist of fate that magically sets an individual seemingly destined for indigence on the road to prosperity and substance. Instead, Andrew's heroism is volitional. He stands for the efficacy of programmatic agrarian virtue, self-discipline, and the vast promise of fulfillment unimaginable in the prevailing inequity of the Old World. Possessing few skills, Andrew comes to America fired only by "manly pride excited by vivid hopes and rising independence" (Crevecoeur 1904, 92). He begins his American experience as a simple laborer, benefiting equally from his own good character and the kindness of Crevecoeur's friends and acquaintances. With time, he acquires land, wealth, and community influence, becoming as generous with his own resources as those who had aided him in his establishment in the Pennsylvania woods.

We find later manifestations of Andrew in nineteenth-century pioneer homesteaders. Willa Cather's Alexandra Bergson, for example, embodies the virtuous self-reliance of a woman challenged no less by patriarchal social convention than the harsh Nebraska environment in which her family homesteaded.[5] Bergson draws her strength from the pastoral values with which she was raised. She is steadfast in her convictions, indomitable in spirit, and open in her sincere dealings with others. She evinces the Romantic qualities that imbued the Old West with its primeval attraction. Equally, as we see with other heroes of the frontier, the fruits of her common heroism are foundational to the taming of the new land as a requisite to the building of a nation. Thus, Cather concludes the novel, "Fortunate country, that is one day to receive hearts like Alexandra's into its bosom, to give them out again in the yellow wheat, in the rustling corn, in the shining eyes of youth" (1913, 309).

Prosaic heroes these landholders may be, common in both ubiquity and station. Unsung and uncelebrated, they lack the heroic singularity of the magnanimous or epic hero or the adventurous spirit of later common heroic archetypes. But their kind makes up the hero deficit in numbers. The magnanimous hero outshines Andrew or Alexandra. But she cannot outshine the combined virtue of a thousand Andrews and Alexandras, which was, after all, only a fraction of the homesteaders who began to cultivate the new land along the western frontier. Equally, when contrasted with the epic hero, often purchasing stature in the coin of death and destruction, the social fruits of the yeoman farmer's heroic self-mastery come cheap at the price.

Facially, the yeoman farmer sets up in cultural opposition to the self-made urban man. The one is temperate and controlled in her ambitions; the other throws caution to the wind. The one is nourished by the pastoral Jeffersonian wellspring of agrarian virtue, the other potentially corrupted by licentious embourgeoisement; the one offers others a gentle hand, the other throws a sharp elbow. One presents as rough and provincial, the other comes, inevitably, to acquire a degree of polish and refinement. Yet, the apparent chasm between rural and urban American common heroism was not as formidable as it first appears. More than just a wistful echo of the Cincinnatian ideal, lionization of the humble Western farmer joined tongue-in-groove with celebration of the self-made man, both keystones in the diffusion of wealth and power. Indeed, underlying the Jeffersonian agenda was the ideal of land distribution, designed to preserve America's

Edenic bounty from being swallowed up by a new aristocracy of rapacious landholders, while encouraging the realistic prospect of material success for broad swaths of American civic stakeholders (Eisinger 1947, 43–44). Like the self-made man, then, the freeholding yeoman farmer constituted a fundamental bulwark against the attendant tyrannical peril of centralized political and economic authority. Her egalitarian smallholding stood her in stark contrast, for example, to the plantation system of the Deep South, in which the old feudal hierarchy was perpetuated along racial and class lines. The yeoman farmer lived a life good in its simplicity. She liberated herself not just from the urban grind, but also from the moral tutelage of more sagacious individuals—what she herself saw as instruction in the pedantry and obfuscation of synthetic urban morality (Boatright 1966, 11–12). She may have tamed the soil, but nature remained her internal guide, nurturing intuitively informed just agency and reinforcing it through natural revelation.

Others sought to extract even more out of nature—either physically or in vicarious imagination. Rather than the drudgery of the farmstead, the more adventurous cast their eyes even farther to the west, to the "sylvan range of . . . fee-simple empires" at the vanguard of the ever-expanding frontier (Flint 1827, 170). The sublime experience of self-reliance and primitivism—of the individual alone in the vastness of nature—resonated with bold and timid alike. Indeed, anyone could identify in her mind with those adventuresome souls who had made the escape from civilization into nature. Anyone could put herself in the moccasins of the leather-stockinged natural bumpkin (Natty Bumppo) who spoke to the efficacy of common sense, freedom, manliness, purification through nature, solitude, mobility, morality, rescue of those in need, personal honor, disdain for recognition, and indifference to the charms of corrupting domesticity and material wealth (Leverenz 1991, 755; Taylor 2004, 513–14; Smith-Rosenberg 2004, 1331).[6]

Even more than the yeoman farmer, the Western frontiersman was the quintessence of the nascent spirit of Americanism. As iconic archetype, he was heroic defender and nation builder. He enjoyed a number of literary advantages over his agrarian forebearer. Rootless in his physical space, he roamed the free range of the imagination. Rather than follow the plow, he led with the rifle. His heroic exploits were personal rather than ambient—he confronted circumstantial hardship with stoic fortitude more sublime than Hesiodic toil with the hard earth. His faith—both literal and (in proxy) to civilized America—was regularly tested. And, even more than the yeoman farmer, his self-reliance epitomized the ethos of rugged individualism. He emerged as something of a Byronic hero for the embryonic republic, in rebellion against anything that smacked of restriction, self-denial, or the timidity of the Nietzschean last man. His cause was "gratification in adventure, through dramatic discovery and through violent struggle with a great antagonist"—the wild animals and wild men inhabiting nature conjuring the repulsive attraction of sublime terror (Slotkin 1998, 68).[7]

For the likes of Frederick Jackson Turner, American identity—the "vital life forces" requisite to transformation of country into nation—was born on the frontier. It was forged along that line of "most rapid and effective Americanization." Each iterative push westward demanded adaptation and reinvigorated a nation radiating ever farther from its European cultural ancestry (1920a, 2–4, 9–10). Demographically, westward expansion fused an increasingly de-Anglicized, composite people united in its desire for autonomy. Economically, it contributed to national self-sufficiency by mitigating America's dependence upon European trade. Geographically, it unleashed an unstoppable flood of emigrants from the old national boundaries, mandating free dispersal of public land. In this broadly distributive sense, there is a clear line of ideological transmission from the agrarian democracy of Jefferson to the frontier democracy of Andrew Jackson (Turner 1920a, 23–29). Turner's frontier philosophy reflected an egalitarian preference for the doer over the speaker, the commoner over the magnanimous, or as Jackson purportedly portrayed himself in his 1828 presidential campaign against John Quincy Adams, one who can fight over one who can write (Kimmel 1996, 34). Of the prevailing ethos in the frontier settlements that followed, Turner references an unnamed representative in 1830, distinguishing the talking politician of the East from her working counterpart to the West. The former is a statesman, rhetorician, and metaphysicist. The latter is a commoner politically regenerated by Western air and Western habits. The one returns home to be fanned gently to sleep by servants. The other "takes off his coat and takes hold of the plow. This gives him bone and muscle, sir, and preserves his republican principles pure and uncontaminated" (1920a, 31).

Despite his self-sufficiency, the manly woodsman could never be completely about himself. Life on the frontier was as much a collective enterprise as an individual one. Personal escape and national purpose were flip sides of the same coin. A predatory hunter the early frontiersman may have been, but he was also a defender, a willing fighter for his small piece of civilization on the frontier. Fulfilling obligations to others required no great metaphysical calculus. His autonomy and intersubjectivity harmonized in republican virtue. His frontier philosophy was summarized in words immortalized more than a century later by Colonel James Howell Howard: "I seen my duty and I done it." His straight-shooting rectitude was memorialized in the iconic "Hunters of Kentucky," evoking the heroic self-sufficiency of an era named for the commanding general of the Battle of New Orleans. Of that battle's final British retreat, the Hunters sang with chivalric derision:

> They found at last 'twas vain to fight, where lead was all
>   their booty,
> And so they wisely took to flight, and left us all our beauty,
> And now if danger e'er annoys, remember what our trade is,
> Just send for us Kentucky boys, and we'll protect your ladies.

The mythology of the frontiersman was heralded in the appendix to John Filson's *Discovery, Settlement and Present State of Kentucke*. Telling of the exploits of Daniel Boone—he too would protect your ladies—Filson paints him as a knight errant for the modern age. Boone anticipated the cowboy—that mounted cavalier of the West, freer than his medieval counterpart, dutiful and independent of social constraint. Ostensibly narrated by Boon [*sic*] himself, the chronicle is replete with tales of the constant harassment of the settlers of Boonesborough and nearby forts by Shawnee Indians. In the most compelling part of the narrative, Boone is taken prisoner, but he forges a rapid bond with his Native captors. Earning their trust, he is adopted by a Shawnee family and assimilates easily into the culture (Filson 1784, 49–51; see also Flint 1856, chs. 8–9). (This is a remarkable vignette, insofar as for most of the tale, Boone is pleased to paint Indians as savages and barbarians. For this brief moment, though, he is at pains to humanize them as well, portraying a Romantic nobility lacking only the perfection afforded by civilization [Slotkin 1998, 67].) At the same time, however, when 450 Shawnee plan to march on Boonesborough, all bets are off. Boone escapes and makes the arduous trip back to civilization ahead of the Indian incursion.

This capture-and-escape narrative was a common one in early American culture, going back at least as far as the taking of Mary Rowlandson during the war with "King Philip." Inherent was a post-Puritan mythology of regeneration through baptismal purification—in this case immersion into the immanent world of nature. Living among the Indians represented a figurative regression into infancy; return a form of rebirth. The ever-present danger was that the captive would remain in her natural condition, losing her faith (her civilized identity)—go native as it were—choosing to remain in her regressed state. It was only by finding her way back to civilization that the personal and social fruits of such harrowing regeneration could be harvested (Slotkin 1998, esp. 63).[8] In the case of Boone's narrative, the social benefits are immediate and persistent. Evincing no ambivalence as to the source of his loyalties, he is instrumental in breaking the brief siege of Boonesborough.

Underlying the Boone legend was a nascent impetus for nation building. Filson, a Kentucky land speculator, had a pecuniary interest in portraying "Kentucke" as the place to be for the restless settler of the late eighteenth century. In the same vein, Daniel Bryan's *Mountain Muse* glorifies Boone in epic form, couching his exploits in terms of heroic regime consolidation, the divine mandate to bring commerce and civilization to the early nineteenth-century frontier, the seraphic beauty of the unspoiled land secondary to the need to tame it. For others, Boone tended more towards the Romantic. He was less a standard bearer for civilization than a refugee from it (Smith 1950, 54–55). His adventures appealed to a psyche threatened by the tyranny of farmstead, industry, technology, social institutions, or government—all offering in some form or other to relieve Americans of the burden of personal autonomy. Surveyor of an unspoiled environment, free of "both the wigwam and the Metropolis" (Slotkin 1998, 68), Boone embodied the nation's own Adamic quest (Taylor 2004, 521–22). In joyous contrast to the plowman or urban cogwheel, he was divested of social gravities and refashioned in natural self-possession. Like heroes of antiquity, he occupied the Isles of the Blest, a realm of freedom right there on the map, a liminal space between the primitive savage of the West and the sallow and emasculated city dweller in the East.

Foundational to the Boone legend was his station as a common man. Through Filson he confesses to the normal circumstantial torments of loneliness and fear, hunger and deprivation. It is his equanimity in facing the hardships of the frontier, rather than any superhuman quality, that informs his heroism. Boone was an ordinary man looking simply to provide for his family and protect his territory, rising to every challenge without complaint or lament. One cannot help but feel for him. Those of an escapist mindset cannot help but want to *be* him, losing themselves in solitary explorations of nature at its most sublime, drawn inexorably westward by the prospect not only of changed circumstance but regeneration of the soul as well. Best of all, there was nothing about him that precluded emulation. His hagiographers epitomize him as the idealized republican citizen, a man beholden to no other, yet to whom it would no more occur to shirk his duties than seek to grow feathers and fly (e.g., Filson 1784, appendix; Bryan 1813; Bogart 1856, 70–85, 96, 140–44, 174, 223–24, 328–29; Peck 1904, 63–64, 108).

HOME ON THE RANGE

The Janus-faced mandate of the early nineteenth-century woodsman—to glorify nature and civilize the land—moved with the frontier, extending to the mountain men, scouts, guides, and buffalo hunters of the West as well. The resultant mythology would become the bedrock of American cultural exceptionalism for the better part of a century. Emerging out of the dime novel Westerns of the latter half of the nineteenth century, the Old Western mystique riffed on the Boone/Leatherstocking theme of peripatetic heroism in defense and construction of the nation. As with other heroic archetypes—warriors, knights, gentry, clergy, farmers, woodsmen, and entrepreneurs—the heroism of most real-life Old Western plainsmen often does not bear close scrutiny. Real-life rangers were hard individuals living nomadic and often lonely existences. Like the gamblers and prostitutes with whom they often associated, many existed at the margins of even the loosely civilized societies of the West. Of course, Old West lore appropriates or exaggerates or constructs out of the whole cloth the exploits of a number of real-life figures, including Calamity Jane Canary, Buffalo Bill Cody, Wyatt Earp, Pearl Hart, Wild Bill Hickok, Bat Masterson, Annie Oakley, Frank Palmer (the original Deadwood Dick), Belle Star, and Buck Taylor. But it is generally the fictional ranger of dime novels, pulp magazines, and B movies from whom was culled the mythology of a semirefined self-sufficient commoner, balancing Byronic defiance and moral perfectionism in the context of patriotic service to country. That these heroic exploits were mostly contrivance, an ideal driven by consumer demand, does nothing to mitigate the importance of the Old West in construction of the new heroic ideal. As with Homeric Greeks, it is not historical truth that interests us so much as the aspirations of the age.

Two predominant themes prevailed. Subtextual to the more primitive is the portrayal of the natural man of the West as ethical kinsman to the noble savage with whom he shared all affinity but national (and racial) loyalty. Writers who adopted this perspective, which had begun to a certain extent with Cooper, and culminated in the twentieth-century novels of Zane Grey, tended to portray Native Americans as victims worthy of emulation (Blake 1995, 214). This first theme perpetuated the literary tradition of Romantic purification through nature. In the context of *Old Hicks the Guide*, for example, Charles Webber idealizes the primitivism of the Old West as liberation from unreasonable restrictions on liberty and conscience. Rather than law, rangers appropriated this sense of autonomy, relying on their affect and intuition in defiance of all "conventional and unnatural requisitions" (1848, 311). Such individuals, says Webber, "do not look back to society except with disgust, but look into the face of God as revealed in his natural world, and into the instincts of their own souls and hearts for what is just and true" (311).

The other theme focused more on nation building in construction of the good republic. It sought just balance between the primitive and civilized, between the freedom and authenticity of the West, and the social refinement of the East. Early heroes in this balanced tradition tended to be primitive hunters or guides, foiling the evil designs of hostile Indians, Mexican banditos, parasitic road agents, and lascivious Mormons. Prototypical was Ann S. Stephens's (1862) roughhewn Kirk Waltermyer—"Nature's Nobleman"—riding the "perarers," in selfless defense of tenderfoots and homesteaders, righting wrongs in embodiment of the tough fiber of a new nation justified in its conquest of the new land (Boatright 1951, 158; Streetby 2002, ch. 8). What Waltermyer lacks in refinement, he makes up for in volitional employment of his innate common sensical and intuitive goodness. In the process, he embodies a pervasive moral code that violators reject at their own risk. Other early dime novelists quickly appropriated the theme of natural nobility, creating heroes who thought nothing of risking their lives for principle and cause, their selfless heroism as reflexive as breathing. Speaking for any number of nature's noblemen, W. J. Hamilton's Big Sam affirms the conviction that putting one's own welfare ahead of that of others is "a ridiculous failing in a prahary man" (1872, 16).

Second-generation dime novelists tempered primitive natural nobility with urban sophistication, the common hero existing between worlds as the perfected individual of both (Smith 1948, 282; Boatright 1966, 17; Butler 1977, 56–57). More refined than the ruffians with whom they were often forced to associate, second-generation gunslingers tended to be clean-shaven, elegantly presented, and shorn of country dialect. Like

Prentiss Ingraham's fictionalized Buck Taylor, they flirted with extravagance; like Gilbert Patten's Wild Bill Hickock, they displayed an undercurrent of menace; like (the mythical) Deadwood Dick, they tended to be smooth with the women-folk and quick with their six-shooters. All, however, found themselves on the side of the good, their methods direct perhaps, but never unjustified (Smith 1950, 100–102; Boatright 1966, 18–19; Butler 1977, 58–59, 62).

These dime-novel heroes in turn paved the way for the most enduring icon of Old Western common heroism. The cowboy was an unlikely beneficiary of heroic posterity. Few contemporary writers, Joseph Badger a notable exception, found the quotidian habits of hired cattle herders sufficiently interesting to enrapture Eastern audiences. More typical of the 1860s and 1870s was the portrayal of cowboys as little more than waddies and ruffians, uncouth in manner and uncivilized in temperament. There was a sniffy quality to literary and public references to the emergent cowboy legend. Laura Winthrop Johnson, for example, finds little to admire in such "rough men with shaggy hair and wild staring eyes, in butternut trousers stuffed into great rough boots." In his first address to Congress, President Chester Arthur was alarmed by "armed desperados known as 'Cowboys,'" committing wanton acts of mayhem and violence in the Arizona Territory (both quoted in Smith 1950, 109–10). Frederick Whittaker, who for a decade had been writing about the dissolute and violent life of the cow herder, has one citizen opine in *Top Notch Tom, the Cowboy Outlaw*, "A caowboy will be a caowboy, anyway ye can fix him, and ye can't no more keep him from goin' on a tear when he gets paid off than ye can get a steer to stop bellerin' when he feels the hot iron at round-up time" (quoted in French 1951, 227).

In point of fact, the cowboy's occupation was incidental, a sort of off-duty vocation for the wandering gunslinger, antagonist of the Old West's rotten element, resplendent in the primitive armor of the plains cavalier, rescuing naïve homesteaders or damsels taken captive by those with hostile and un-American intent (Fishwick 1952, 81). Mythologized, cowboys were otherwise ordinary men, their commonness manifest in an ethics of common sense, a true moral compass, and a straight-forward (if not prominently emphasized) Protestant worldview which informed their sense of justice. Cowboy heroes were temperate in their habits, rarely drinking even in saloons, and avoiding cigarettes (although pipes and cigars were acceptable). They were honest men who resorted to deception only for good cause. And while obliged to counter violence with violence, they wouldn't stab an adversary in the back or shoot from ambush. They exercised the good citizen's prerogative of good and fair judgment. They were quite enlightened for their time (this is especially true of Grey's heroes) in their dealings with racial and religious minorities. Even their physical talents were imitable—born not of supernatural assistance but of countless hours on horseback with six-shooter and long rifle. The cowboy code stood them in sharp contrast with the scoundrels and barbarians who would tarnish the image of their Old Western creed. Mobile, they embodied the freedom of the morally sufficient individual; indomitable, they stood for strict prohibition against murder and cruelty (the latter extending to horses and other beasts). Upstanding, they condemned debauchery and failure to respect the infirm and downtrodden. Above all else chivalric, theirs was a humble deference to women. In short, cowboys responded to the call of duty that any red-blooded American plainsman should instinctively heed (Boatright 1966, 28; Butler 1977, 58; Speck 1981, 270–74; Bosworth 2010, 299).

In exchange for their benefaction, cowboy-heroes insisted upon social detachment, upon freedom from fencing and constraint. They rarely took lasting employment, sought no permanent residence (sleeping indoors was a major concession). They upheld lawfulness but rejected the social conventions and rule-bound conformity that constrained individuals within nineteenth-century civil society.[9] Emersonian individualists to the core, cowboys stood for all that is good in the republican model of governance and against all that is wrong with it. They spoke to the primeval cultural need for good to prevail over evil. In a more superstitious age, they would have slain dragons; in a more spiritual one, they would have vanquished Saracens or heretics (Speck 1981, 272–74). As it was, they were the idealized everyman, fictionalized, sometimes anonymized, and exaggerated not in illustration of the hero's exclusivity, but rather as a symbol of what the common individual could accomplish for herself through the marriage of innate virtuous capacity and a willing spirit.

For the cultural mythmakers most responsible for promoting the cowboy legend, the Romanticism and chivalry of the Old West were not ends in themselves. The subtext was of the Wild West as a transitory existence, a means of hardening one in preparation for a more civilized life. As with the Boone and Leatherstocking legends, ultimately regeneration on the frontier found complete meaning only through reconciliation with civil society. For this reason, like knights errant finally consummating their courtly love, cowboys often wound up marrying and settling down (the fair lady typically of superior refinement), elevated by their virtue to find their proper places in society. This was how it had to be, of course. In doing battle with narrowly interested land speculators who stood against statehood in the territories, or lawless villains who sought to disrupt the telegraph, Pony Express, and other vital symbols of national expansion, their ultimate mandate was to march the Old West into practical obsolescence (Butler 1977, 61–62; Bosworth 2010, 297–98).

Hero and Superhero of the Twentieth Century

The urban analog to the cowboy was the gritty, hard-boiled detective, who came of age in pulp magazines of the 1920s and 1930s, most famously *Black Mask*. Where the cowboy spoke to the purity of nature, the hard-boiled detective made the same point in reverse, emphasizing the rot of urban corruption. Like the Western novel, the hard-boiled genre emphasized the Emersonian mandate of the self-reliant individual, intuitively cognizant of just condition, motivated by just agency. Hard-boiled crime fighters represented the nested individualism—the autonomous individual in the virtuous community—so central to the American Renaissance and its influence on modern republicanism. Contributing also to the cosmic dimension of virtue, notes Susanna Lee in her excellent treatise on the subject, the hard-boiled detective embodies "an outstanding characteristic of Western culture's most treasured modern ideals, or most precious heroic commodities: the secular individual for whom spiritual ideals come naturally, unforced, and constitute durable character attributes" (2016, 7). Standing in sharp contrast to the urbane Sherlock Holmes and other European sleuths were rough-and-tumble private eyes like Carroll John Daly's Race Williams, Dashiell Hammett's Continental Op and Sam Spade, and Raymond Chandler's Philip Marlowe, two-fisted working men riding streetcars instead of horses, but imparting the same imperatives for civic virtue, common sense moral reasoning, and intuitive self-reliance in defense against crime of their more peaceful fellow citizens. There is nothing very special about these heroic defenders. Williams sees his greatest attributes as a good eye, a quick trigger finger, and an ability to get himself out of trouble almost as fast as he gets into it (e.g., Daly 1927, 11). Marlowe is a hard-drinking loner who ekes out a living. The Op doesn't even have a name. Short, fat, and forty, he is unglamorous and, at least by his own admission, possessed of few skills rather than a willingness to stir things up and doggedly run down any clues that might emerge out of the resultant chaos.

Hard-boiled detectives lent themselves poorly to anything that smacked of gentility and refinement. (Hammett usually portrays the "better element" as effete, officious, corrupt, or tyrannical; often all of the above.[10] Williams and Marlowe cheerfully boast that their manners are nothing to brag about.) They had a job to do, and civility simply got in the way. Where literary cowboys embodied Romantic perfectionism, hard-boiled detectives were fatalistic. The former sought to marry natural purity to civil order; the latter took out the garbage as an alternative to letting it rot in the street. The one spoke to the edifice of an idealized republic of virtue; the other was content merely to try to shore up the foundation. The one did her duty and rode into the sunset; the other embraced the Sisyphean task of restoring moral order in the face of perpetual challenges to it. But the underlying imperative to choose justice over injustice survived the transition intact. So did the metaphor of life on the frontier, that line of moral demarcation between civilization and savagery which cleaved American cities and along which detective heroes, like cowboys before them, insinuated themselves between the good homesteader and the predator with evil intent (Svoboda 1983, 557–60).

The proximity of the urban frontier provided its sublime attraction, enticing imaginations to accompany detective heroes as they patrolled the mean streets of San Francisco or Los Angeles in a way that once drew them to the plains and mountains of the Old West. Yet unlike earlier heroes, hard-boiled detectives did not radiate utopian promise. In addition to protection of citizens, theirs was a fight in defense of the republic itself against systemic and dystopian forces of which their human antagonists were just a symptom. Far from perfecting the system, the best Hammett has to offer is the prospect of temporary reclamation of the public space from the corrupt elites—politicians and businessmen—plundering the common weal to feather their own nests. He explores this theme most fully in *Red Harvest*, in which the Op seeks to clean up the mess that is Personville ("Poisonville") after the city boss loses control of his henchman. The Op is tasked with delivering the town from Hobbesian anarchy back to a state of civil order. Like the gunslinging cowboy of old, he is forced to be as violent and ruthless as the rotten element he faces. The difference between the Op and the ruffians he backs down is that (the death of Dinah Brand notwithstanding) there is nothing personal at stake for him. Duty demands that he clean up the mess and not profit from the endeavor. He is an honest tradesman doing an honest job for honest pay. Tomorrow he will get up and do the same thing again somewhere else.

Marlowe is both more utopian and more pessimistic. He is frustrated at the honest citizen's helplessness against the prevailing power structure. Like the recurring metaphors of bad weather and illness, corruption for Chandler is an irresistible force of nature (Fontana 1995, 161). An honest man in a dishonest society, Marlowe's clients are not a whole lot more inspiring than most of the officials he encounters. He is the self-reliant citizen caught in the middle, a common hero amidst the morally rotten, brutal in his honesty, using truth like a scythe to cut through the pretense and hypocrisy surrounding him, protecting deceitful clients while battling the soul-destroying arbitrariness of authorities who resent intrusion into their fiefdoms. The futility of it all has made him cynical. At the same time, Marlowe struggles to prevent ambient corruption from tainting his sense of self. He retains his essential humanity—a metaphysical sense of goodness—the one thing that social corruption and capricious authority cannot take from him. And at his core is the faintest hope that his efforts are not all in vain. Sometimes this manifests, as with Velma in *Farewell My Lovely*, in finding the good in otherwise bad people. Conversely, optimism often turns to disappointment when latent moral qualities fail to manifest in otherwise decent men that Marlowe would like to count among his friends. In *The Long Goodbye*, for example, he says to Terry Lennox,

> You're just that kind of guy. For a long time I couldn't figure you out at all. You had nice ways and nice qualities, but there was something wrong. You had standards and you lived up to them, but they were personal. They had no relation to any kind of ethics or scruples. You were a nice guy because you had a nice nature. But you were just as happy with mugs or hoodlums as with honest men. Provided the hoodlums spoke fairly good English and had fairly acceptable table manners. You're a moral defeatist. I think maybe the war did it and again I think maybe you were born that way. (Chandler 1995b, 872)

Again, the hard-boiled detective reversed the Socratic formula. Rather than the republic (under the sage leadership of magnanimous leaders) imprinting its values on the easily corruptible individual, it was the individual who sought to impose virtue on an easily corruptible society. What made the hard-boiled detective attractive was the unsung valiance of the individual in conflict with the nameless, faceless collective and its attendant menace of power and corruption manifest in the trusts and city machines.[11]

The culmination of Emersonian transcendentalism, the hard-boiled detective was the assertion of the autonomous common individual of common sense, armed with an intuitive sense of goodness, a moral compass, a couple of fists, and a handgun. He might have needed to get his hands dirty from time to time. But the rest of him was clean.[12] Like the cowboy, the hard-boiled detective married the self-containment of the Romantic to the metaphysical imperatives of the philosopher. In his ultimate summation of the genre Chandler declares,

> [D]own these mean streets a man must go who is not himself mean, who is neither tarnished nor afraid. The detective in this kind of story must be such a man. He is the hero; he is everything. He must be a complete man and a common man and yet an unusual man. He must be, to use a rather weathered phrase, a man of honor—by instinct, by inevitability, without thought of it, and certainly without saying it. He must be the best man in his world and a good enough man for any world. (1950, 20)

More than other common heroes, hard-boiled characters not only defended the civil order but longed to redeem it. In this role, they were not terribly successful. Indeed, generally missing from the hard-boiled genre was the uplifting message that, when all is said and done, provides requisite contrast between the republican hero and the dystopian antihero.[13] Further undermining heroic redemption, the hard-boiled character cannot remain totally unaffected by the depravity he encounters. Despite Chandler's portrayal of the heroic detective, Marlowe concludes at the grubby end of *The Big Sleep* that *he* is part of the nastiness now (Lee 2016, 97). The Op, going blood-simple as he calls it, has murder on the mind in *Red Harvest*; so much so that he considers himself among the suspects for Dinah's murder. Indeed, having flirted so long with nihilism, the hard-boiled genre—this is especially clear in the writing of Cornell Woolrich and James M. Cain, for example—ultimately devolved into the darkness that presented cinematically as film noir.

The Superhero

Depression-era progeny of pulp fiction, early comic book superheroes mitigated the darkness of the hard-boiled detective. Theirs was an uplifting heroism. In a world of economic depression, labor unrest, relentless urbanization, and technological innovation implying the redundancy of the working man and woman, early superheroes spoke to the power of human efficacy. However, awesome the technology of the age or the grandeur of the city, the humanoid Superman—to take the example of the pioneering superhero—is more awesome and grander. He is faster than a speeding locomotive (and later, a bullet). He can leap tall buildings in a single bound (and later, fly). Bullets bounce off him. He is the John Henry of the twentieth century, appearing in the nick of time to rescue humanism from its apparent nihilistic destiny (Morrison 2011, 19).

Superheroes present as heroic defenders. Equally prominent is their relevance as heroic stewards—idealized citizens—in perfection of the good republic. Far more than hard-boiled characters, superheroes are role models, their political functions often didactic, highlighting the goodness of the extant moral order by illustrating the evils of deviation from it. Indeed, almost from the start, superheroes have been agents of political socialization, helping shape civic attitudes toward issues ranging from wartime solidarity to less momentous contemporary ones, such as the politics of plastic surgery, performance-enhancing drugs, genetic engineering, cybernetic implants, and the importance of physical activity in the internet age (Di Paolo 2011, 16–17).

With dark European storm clouds on the horizon, early superheroes stood not only in defense of individuals, but also of the republic against hostile Axis forces. They mirrored the sublime power and superiority of the objectively good republic, reflecting the values that bound republican citizens together in virtuous solidarity. Vehicles of propaganda, it is no coincidence that Captain America came onto the scene shortly after the start of the Second World War. Wartime Superman made no bones about his loyalties, taking on both Hitler and Tojo, making it obvious why Superman comics were widely distributed to American soldiers (Jewett and Lawrence 2003, 32).

Reflecting greater diversity than was featured in earlier ages, a number of superheroines, some with greater popularity than others, emerged during the early 1940s, including Fantomah, Lady Luck, Invisible Scarlet

O'Neil, Golden Girl, Black Fury, Wonder Woman, Phantom Lady, and Miss Fury. Relatedly, many established superheroes came to have female equivalents such as Batwoman (and Batgirl), Supergirl and Spider-Woman. These superheroines, moreover, were permitted to evince feminine qualities, the hypermasculinity of earlier common heroes not nearly as foundational to their identities. African American superheroes were slower to emerge, having to wait until the 1960s for the Black Panther and the Falcon. Northstar, the first gay superhero, debuted in 1979 but remained mostly closeted until 1992.

There is a counterintuitive quality to superheroes as common heroic role models. Facially, they are hardly mimetic, presenting more as epic heroes than common ones. Certainly, their superpowers suggest extraordinary physical capacity. My point in assigning them to the camp of common heroism is not to deny their epic qualities, only that the political significance of their epic powers is metaphorical. As imitable incarnations of good republican citizenship, their superpowers are as cartoonish as their outfits. Their mimetic relevance is in incitement of common citizens to recognize and act upon innate human potential. In justifying himself in *Batman Begins*, for example, the eponymous character tells Alfred, "People need dramatic examples to shake them out of apathy, and I can't do that as Bruce Wayne. As a man I'm flesh and blood. I can be ignored. I can be destroyed. But as a symbol, as a symbol I can be incorruptible. I can be everlasting."

Like Emerson's giant, the enormity of superheroes' being is not physical, but metaphysical, their audience ordinary citizens mobilized in dawning recognition of their *own* untapped (super)powers. That many superheroes maintain dual identities further speaks to this idea of common citizens harboring an inner greatness. Unlike more traditional heroes, superheroes are not necessarily molded of a different clay (Superman and Wonder Woman are exceptions). Instead, they are—like Peter Parker bitten by a radioactive spider, or Steve Rogers testing a government serum, or Hal Jordan aided by the green lantern in amplifying the power of his will, or Sue Storm bombarded with the "cosmic radiation" that bestows invisibility, or Bruce Wayne with no superpowers at all—good common citizens transformed (McSweeney 2020, 40). Theirs is the ubiquitous presented as the theatrical, a "spectacular banality," as Beaty calls it (2019). As with secondary heroes of old, it is their everyman qualities that make them more relatable and hence imitable than the masked insect-man in spandex tights. It is in identifying with Parker (or Bruce Wayne, Clark

Kent, Steve Rogers, or Sue Storm), that we also identify with, and come to recognize ourselves in, his or her alter-ego (see Richmond 2012, 116). Morrison posits, with a touch of hyperbole perhaps, that this is why Superman wears the S on his chest, flying his own personal ensign, presaging "a future when we'd all wear our own proud emblems of revealed, recognized greatness" (2011, 28).

Standing in proxy for apotheotic human potential, superheroes are a graphic representation of the Emersonian over-soul, guided by moral intuition, even to the extent of defiance of positive law. They represent the amplification of our qualities, fanciful and realistic. They also speak to communal aspirations, a unifying monomyth, as Campbell (1973) calls it, that ties singular heroes to time and place. Captain America, to take a ready example, exists not only in celebration of American usness, but also to frame social expectations (Dittmer 2005, 697; McSweeney 2020, 114–15). Upon injecting him with his secret serum, government scientist Professor Reinstein proclaims, "We shall call you Captain America, son! Because, like you, America shall gain the strength and the will to safeguard our shores" (quoted in Jewett and Lawrence 2003, 33). As Americanism incarnate, Captain America speaks to the qualities of its citizens—to be self-reliant within appropriate moral boundaries.[14]

Like the hard-boiled detective, the superheroes' midcentury glory days were brief. With the restoration of peace, the new technology of television, and a general sense of lurid grubbiness that attached to the comic book industry as a whole (Hajdu 2008), superheroes suffered cultural decline in the late 1950s and 1960s. In part, they had to compete with the revival of their iconic forebearers, particularly the popularity of cinematic Westerns that, beginning with John Ford's classic *Stage Coach* (1939), elevated the Western from the ranks of the B movie, and paved the way for a host of Ford, Clint Eastwood, Henry Hathaway, Anthony Mann, and Sam Peckinpaugh classics.[15] The trend was bolstered by the elevation of the Lone Ranger from radio to the small screen, as well as by long-running television hits such as *Gunsmoke* and *Bonanza*.

The reincarnation of hard-boiled detectives into more refined and less dystopian standard-bearers for civil order and individual efficacy also cut into superheroes' cultural significance. Television, even more accessible than ten-cent comic books, promoted alternative and more realistic heroes inspired by smooth operators such as James Bond. The new breed of 1960s justice seeker accepted broader avocation than the shop-worn PI, ranging from attorneys (*Perry Mason, For the People, The Bold Ones*) to secret agents (*Danger Man*, *Mission Impossible*, *I Spy*) to police officers (*Dragnet*, *Hawaii Five-O*, *The Mod Squad*) and even private citizens (*The Saint*). Equally, superheroes faced competition from new types of heroes for whom justice was not central to the mission. Recasting the science-fiction genre, the space age focused on exploration, making heroes of real-life Apollo astronauts, as well as characters from such television hits as *Space Patrol*, *Lost in Space*, and *Star Trek*.

Yet there is a remarkable robustness to the superhero genre, its appeal extending beyond children to the extent that it has recaptured its iconic status in recent decades. That superheroes went into cultural eclipse during the 1950s and 1960s perhaps says more about the failure of cinematic technology to capture their exploits than about their cultural relevance.[16] The mid-1970s witnessed a partial rebirth of the superhero. *Shazam* (featuring Captain Marvel) ran for three seasons on network TV, outpacing *Isis* and *The Amazing Spider-Man*. More successful were *Wonder Woman* (1975–1979) and *The Incredible Hulk* (1977–1982). However, it was 1978's *Superman* movie that stimulated a superhero renaissance that has surpassed the glory days in terms of both duration and, perhaps, cultural import (e.g., McSweeney 2020). Indeed, according to *Box Office Mojo*, as of February 2022, thirty-three superhero movies had grossed more than a quarter-billion dollars, with seven topping a half-billion dollars.[17]

Conclusion

Low cultural proxies for high cultural values, American common heroes are an idealization of *the People*. They represent that amorphous quantity constitutive of legitimate sovereignty, not so much descended from God as risen up from the public source of the public thing—the res publica. Indeed, like God, *the People* are the "source of law and bestower of meaning. They are first cause, prime mover, beginning and end" (Curtis 2016, 13). Common heroes are defenders, stewards, and even redeemers of the republic; culturally, they serve as nation builders and exemplars of good citizenship. As defenders, they protect against crime and other forms of hostile intent. As redeemers, they are curative of corrupted magnanimity, tyranny made grandiose through the specious garb of sagacity or piety, the insincere profession of peace, order, and good government by those who view power as but a means to private reward. As stewards, their impact is harder to gauge, except to say, as Fukuyama (1992) has pointed out, the values and institutions of modern republics tend to persist. Good citizenship, even if not always heroic, seems to have guided America in the absence of heroic magnanimity. Certainly, as with the US Civil War and in the current political climate, stewardship of the republic in a society of equals has been uneven. But if perfect regime harmony is the standard, then all hero types fail as effective stewards. This is why Madison pointed out at the founding of the republic that a robust institutional structure represents a necessary backstop to a failure of heroic stewardship.

Culturally, common heroes speak to the freedom of the individual, to rugged individualism not just in the sense of pursuing of one's own interest, but nested in the imperative to preserve the moral order—the good republic—as well. Archetypical, common heroes have helped define the American creed, to build the nation through the sense of commonality that binds disparate peoples into common identity. Simultaneously embodying civilization and natural regeneration, early American common heroes spoke to the ambiguous mandate of a new nation seeking to define the values of a vast new continent. Untutored, guided by common sense and transcendental moral intuition, they gloried in their autonomy, moral agency, and self-sufficiency. They stood not above their peers, but among them, reflecting their best demonstrated and aspirational qualities. They found equal purchase in the city and on the frontier, evolving into archetypes relevant to time and place. All were charged in some way or other with preservation, in Superman's incantation, of "truth, justice and the American way." Unaided by nobility through heredity, they were self-made individuals compensating for their rough edges with the sort of drive and ambition that early Americans came to see as a symbol of independence—as a point of contrast between the virile young America and effeminized and archaic Old World gentility. As ready to imbibe their goodness from nature as from God, they imparted a personal mandate to exercise one's liberty in the name of the tripartite elements of republican virtue—obligation to self, society, and the objectively good.

Common heroes rarely possess the singularity of more typical hero types. Instead, they represent the incarnation of what it meant to be a good American citizen. They symbolize glorification of the prosaic and unsung. They are not always heroic or programmatic in their goodness. They are not gods among mortals. They are susceptible to the weaknesses and temptations attendant to all of humanity. Common heroes reflect us at our best, the metaphor of the superhero marrying the epic powers of human potential with the more prosaic qualities of quotidian existence.

Indeed, common heroes exist not in glorification of singular individuals, but rather to glorify the potential goodness of humanity in general and the good republic in particular. They emphasize the ubiquitous and volitional qualities that make each of us as good as we choose to be.

Like the other forms of heroism we have discussed in this book, common heroism suffers from the potential for corruptibility, from the space that separates self-interest from the common weal. The transcendentalist movement in particular chastises Jacksonian Americans for not being as good as they should have been; for accepting slavery and second-class status for women and racial minorities and those impoverished through misfortune (though not indolence). The likes of Hammett and Chandler lament the moral defeatism of their time, of individuals surrendering their autonomy to the machines that increasingly marginalized their importance in the workplace while transforming democracy into modern oligarchy. It is to this theme of corruption, not just of common heroes, but of each of the others as well, that the discussion turns to in the final chapter. Ironically, it is this potential for heroic corruption that makes the strongest case for the continued relevance of republican heroism in the twenty-first century.

Conclusion

What Is a Republican Hero?

Lamentation of an age speaks to the ordinariness of lives uninspired by heroes. Ancient commentators from Hesiod, Plato, Sallust, and Cicero through critics of modernity like Nietzsche, Taylor, and Boorstin suggest the fruit of wanton disregard of great or greatly good individuals is mediocrity or moral corruption or perdition. It is an anodyne and self-satisfied existence informed by misplaced values or misplaced appetites. From the perspective of critics of modernity, the watery heroes that do emerge tend toward the vulgar and synthetic, famous for being fabulous and fatuous, sophists and celebrities esteemed for little more than their populism or popularity. That hero worship has come to this, from a world of hero-as-apotheosized-individual to a world in which grown-ups actually care which Hollywood couples are dating, married, or ending their relationship while remaining the best of friends, seems a sad and tragic end.

Looked at differently, however, trivialization of heroes could be considered a mark of transcendent progress, evidence of apotheosis itself. People will always choose a small number of their fellows to idolize, to represent an ideal they themselves are incapable of realizing. The more trivial the criteria for such idolization, it might be reasoned, the more substantial the realms from which people no longer feel themselves to be excluded. For example, if in the past, civilizations made heroes of individuals of great moral sagacity or great piety and insight into the order of grace, perhaps it was because citizens failed to recognize moral wisdom and spirituality in themselves. From this perspective, citizens in modern societies have, like a slow-moving lava field, slowly subsumed the heroic functions that were once the sole prerogatives of the great or greatly good. As with Emerson's giant going wherever *he* goes, modern citizens may have embraced the portability and fungibility of their own heroic capacity, making venerable hero worship quaint and anachronistic; gods, of course, having no real need of other gods—except perhaps for their entertainment.

Neither argument diminishing the modern republican hero is convincing. It is true that evidence of insubstantial heroism abounds in the modern age. But such evidence has *always* existed. Vulgarity and nihilism and hubris and fatuity are not uniquely modern phenomena. When one undertakes to plumb the depths or embrace the vanities of any society, she shouldn't be disappointed when what she finds is none too appetizing. For lamenters of modernity, emphasis upon the nihilism of the modern age appears to smack of immediacy bias (itself a historical constant). The past always looks better than the present when scrubbed clean and left to bask in the soft glow of posterity. Doubtless for this reason, lamenters from Hesiod onward have looked to history to discover exemplars of extraordinary human accomplishment. They have emphasized antiquated values, once ascendant now discounted, and measured declension in the difference. If one looks to Homeric warriors, Christian martyrs, eremitic paragons of Christian piety, chivalric knights, or Old Western gunslingers as the pinnacle of mortal perfection, she is going to be disenchanted with the dissipation of her age.

Nor have mortals become gods. Human nature is a constant. No amount of insistence on its perfectibility makes angels of men. We may have outgrown singular heroes, those to whom we are pleased to defer and submit. Certainly, we cast a skeptical eye towards individuals elevated above their peers for ostensible moral greatness. However, we have not transcended heroism itself. We haven't realized Galileo's utopian humanism—happy in a land without need of heroes. The fact is that republics have always needed heroes. And such heroes have usually existed, albeit in manifold guises. Modern times are not unique for the lack of heroism. Rather and in keeping of the more egalitarian republicanism of the times, what makes the current age distinctive is that rather than indulging singular heroes, heroic virtues are more equitably distributed. Ultimately it is possible to concede that the modern age lacks material for heroic mythology, without suggesting that we lack the heroes and heroism requisite to the good republic.

The Singular Hero and Republican Heroism

Each heuristic hero type discussed in this book may be defined as a republican hero. Each can be shown to uphold republican values. Each contributes to at least some of the core institutional functions—defense, stewardship, and redemption—republican heroes are expected to perform. Culturally, each breeds iconicism, typified by heroes who embody and glorify the attendant qualities of their respective hero types. Most contribute to social solidarity, that cultural sense of usness, requisite to the republic as a *nation* rather than just a country. The hero types vary in the singularity of exemplars, greatness outdistancing goodness or authenticity as a mark of distinction. More singular heroes lend themselves to the hagiography and mythology that colors literary or cinematic heroic didacticism. They stand in sharp and vibrant relief against the dull gray backdrop of ordinariness. Singular heroes thoroughly define their times, so much so that it is not unreasonable to point to the paucity of such heroes in lamentation of nihilistic mediocrity. Equally, there is little doubt that the modern age suffers with respect to singularity of its heroes. The introspective, tragic, and often solipsistic Romantic hero fails to tower over her fellows in the manner of a benevolent enlightened philosopher king or a saintly emissary of God. Even archetypal exaggeration to the point of cartoonish theatricality does not favor the (common) superhero hero over the supernatural greatness of the (epic) Homeric hero. Boorstin's portrait of the modern hero as the fatuous celebrity in quest of the fabulous life is too stark. But it speaks to the relative vacuity of the singular hero of the modern age.

Against this comparative failure of heroic singularity in the modern age, I offer two points in rebuttal. First, heroic singularity generally bespeaks a corresponding unidimensionality, an arbitrary elevation of certain heroic qualities that, even in the case of Socrates's philosopher king, fails to capture and unify all of the heroic virtues requisite to the good republic. Second, the often-overlooked downside to heroic singularity is the social consequences that attach to the corrupted form of the hero type. Such corruption has not gone unnoticed by contemporaneous analysts. Aristotle warns of the potential for the corruption of the magnanimous person who falls just short of the mark, for example. The fall of the Roman Republic attests to the danger of great persons corrupted, lions who slip the leash. Mary Shelley's *Frankenstein* warns of problems attendant to Romantic atomism.

As pertains to unidimensionality, emphasis upon discrete hero types suggests a certain *incompleteness*. Such emphasis takes the excellence of a discrete *part* of the organism as a proxy for the excellence of the whole. Completeness—synthesizing the virtues embodied by epic and magnanimous and Romantic and common heroes—the argument here suggests, affords greater social benefit. The point (albeit not all the relevant virtues) is fairly Aristotelian. Conjunctive and dialectical, complete republican heroism's defining qualities offset one another, tempering excesses and supplementing deficiencies. The problem is that such heroic completeness is difficult to portray in singular figures. The issue thus becomes one of the cultural parsimony so foundational to heroic myth and legend. All things equal, the more singular the hero, the more parsimonious her symbolism. The obverse is also true; generally speaking, completeness suffers from inefficient cultural packaging in that it generally demands broader distribution of the heroic division of labor. Indeed, the social benefits of completeness typically require not so much discrete heroes as corporate *heroism*.

Privileging heroic completeness does not constitute a retrospective apology for our times. It isn't a second-best outcome. Nor does it preclude the existence of singular heroes. In fact, if you squint, you can find heroic completeness in the philosopher king and the superhero. Finding exemplars of complete singular republican heroes, however, is not really the point. Central to rebutting the claim of nihilistic postheroism is the *range of virtues* supplied by republican heroes, rather than the nature of the cultural packaging. The four hero types discussed in this book infuse—either directly or by extant social legacy—a more fulsome range of virtues than any discrete republican hero type. Indeed, the great advantage of heroic completeness is that while more prosaic, it tends to afford greater stability. Like a good stock portfolio, the implicit diversification stands as bulwark against the failure of a single (or singular) security. Completeness implies not investing too heavily in one or few axiomatically flawed individuals who, unless dead and historically sanitized, will be as likely as not to disappoint you in the end.

If the argument for heroic completeness is Aristotelian, so is the case for mitigation of heroic corruption. A significant problem with heroic hagiography is that it tends to overlook the ugly flip side of heroic singularity—that is, the social costs incurred when singularity loses its claim to heroism by virtue of inestimability. An effective way to frame the issue is to borrow from Aristotle's cycle of regimes, such that discrete hero types can be said to exist in both pure and corrupted form. The faddish history of ascendant republican hero types does not import the cycle and predictable nature of Aristotelian regimes. But it is prescriptively similar. As with Aristotle's republic retarding the cycle of pure and corrupted regimes, complete republican heroism inserts itself between heroic purity and corruption by balancing the qualities that attach to each republican hero type.

Central to the heroic completeness I claim for the modern age is heroic *posterity*. By posterity I do not mean remembrance of the extraordinary deeds of individual heroes. Instead, posterity in this context manifests as a social legacy, the derivative social virtues bequeathed by heroes and internalized within the cultural mores woven into their societies. Posterity means that even if a particular hero type loses cultural ascendency, its derivative social virtues persist. More than just countervailing forces, the derivative social virtues discussed below are complementary. They represent a symbiotic web, a unification of the virtues that defines complete republican heroism. To gain a better sense of all this, we need to visit each hero type one final time, with particular attention paid to pure and corrupt forms of the relevant hero type, as well as the social legacy each bequeaths to posterity.

The Epic Hero: A Legacy of Efficacy and Ambition

As a literary device, epic heroism demands a baroque, larger-than-life quality, transcendence of the boundaries that nature imposes upon ordinary men and women. In this book, we have loosened the conceptual definition, assigning epic heroism to physical greatness attached to estimability and vulnerability. The epic hero tends towards self-assertion in pursuit of cause. For early epic (Homeric) heroes, that cause was personal, the quest for honor and immortality through eternal glory. Later, estimability demanded at least some metaphysical competence. In terms of function, epic heroes present most prominently as heroic defenders, role models, and nation builders. In fulfillment of these roles, we have come across them as Homeric tribal warriors, martyred saints possessed through grace and faith of supernatural thaumaturgical powers, and chivalric takers of the Cross.

The Enlightenment witnessed the cultural decline of epic heroism, such that even in the generous way I have defined them here, epic heroes have become increasingly marginal to the politics of modern republics. They tend not to fight wars or defend the visible church against secular or demonic intrusion. Generally speaking, our egalitarian age precludes the political elevation of individuals solely in recognition of their demonstrable greatness in a single area of competence. There are exceptions. Especially during times of crisis, war, or conflict, singular individuals may emerge, their exploits glorified in celebration of the republic's invincible spirit. It is through such physical heroism that George Washington, Andrew Jackson, Ulysses S. Grant, Theodore Roosevelt, and Dwight D. Eisenhower, for example, all parlayed military heroism into the presidency of the United States. More common is for self-assertive individuals to demonstrate their extraordinariness in less overtly political realms. The most obvious direct link to the epic hero of old is through demonstration of athletic ability, heroes speaking to civic or collegiate pride, uniting citizens in common cause.

Beyond this, the political impact of epic heroes is felt most keenly in the derivative social virtues—efficacy and ambition—that constitute their legacy. (We need to be clear that this legacy, like those left by other hero types, is not constitutive of epic heroism itself. One who exercises efficacy or ambition is not an epic hero merely by dint of these virtues.) Efficacy and ambition speak to the importance of active, rather than passive, citizenship. They are physical virtues more than metaphysical ones. They empower and motivate citizens to mobilize in support of particular social values. Presenting as rational self-interest, the virtues promote benign factionalization, enticing citizens into the agonal arena of value-contestation. Politically, this adversarial process manifests as a contest for political persuasion, contestants brandishing slogans rather than swords, the arena the public square and not the battlefield. In holding elected officials accountable, such efficacious civic warriors constitute the ultimate defense against tyranny, ensuring that the res publica indeed remains public.

Efficacy and ambition permit not only the functioning of the pluralist democratic process, but other critical social institutions as well. The partisan dimension of politics, for example, is driven by the same self-assertive, agonal dynamic as democratic pluralism. The free economic market relies upon ambitious and efficacious individuals pitting themselves against equally equipped opponents. As virtues, efficacy and ambition are the basis of a complex system of social checks and balances that, assuming a well-constructed social order, generates good outcomes, not through painstaking cultivation of moral character, but, in the Machiavellian sense—through the infinitely renewable resource of rational self-interest.

Epic Corruption

Corrupted, however, the erstwhile epic hero is a dangerous force. Socrates conceives her as the thymotic lion doing battle with the reasoned man for control of the organs of soul and state. Unbound by law or convention, she represents a study in reckless self-assertion and social disinterest. At her worst, she is a villain, no hero at all. She is Sulla, Henry VIII, or Hitler, source of disastrous foreign or civil conflict in the name of personal power and posterity. Ironically, so thoroughly corrupted, the villain's malevolence actually bestows (admittedly marginal and costly) social benefit, evil highlighting the imperative for heroic goodness and sympathy for moral values. In the same way that Moriarty serves Holmes, or the Joker serves Batman, the evil totalitarian's sole puny grace is that she constitutes an effective foil for republican heroism.

A more nuanced manifestation of the corrupted epic hero is as republican antihero. Unlike the villain, the antihero's epic qualities, while self-serving, are born more of social disinterest than malignant intent. By this definition, Achilles, the most celebrated Homeric hero, also represents a prototypical republican antihero, employing great powers in service of his own private ends, with any advancement of the greater good a mere byproduct of private ambition. The distant echo of such epic antiheroism finds resonance in the timocratic governor or populist manipulator of alienated individuals, the most notorious of whom, Julius Caesar, played no small part in bringing down the Roman Republic. The most recent of whom, Donald Trump, has endowed a legacy of civic irresponsibility.

The social virtues that derive from epic heroism are not immune from corruption either. As with all discrete virtues, efficacy and ambition are spoiled by excess or deficiency. Deficient in efficacy and ambition, citizens are mere subjects, Nietzschean last men vulnerable to the capricious whims of their betters. Such pusillanimous individuals cede the process of governing, eschewing the civic oversight that encourages honesty and trust among leaders, even if it does not guarantee it. They stand for few principles beyond their own comfort, which in any case is an exercise in self-defeat in the face of the tyranny they tempt. By contrast, excessive efficacy and ambition foster disorder: violence and even anarchy. They breed individuals unconstrained by the norms and customs by which good citizens are expected to abide. History records so many examples of individuals corrupted by untempered efficacy and ambition that it might be as common for these qualities to present as vices than as virtues. Indeed, the argument here is that efficacy and ambition, like all social virtues that derive from republican hero types, must be tempered and balanced by countervailing virtues extant as derivative social virtues bequeathed by other hero types.

The Magnanimous Hero: A Legacy of Rectitude and Ingenuity

The magnanimous hero has long represented a metaphysical corrective to the sometimes morally ambivalent epic hero. Greatly good, she was long considered a requisite source of justice, a vehicle for social importation of cosmic first principles. Her stock in trade was sagacity as knowledge of the good. Prototypically, she was the Socratic philosopher king, the Aristotelian great-souled man, the selfless lawgiver leading the unenlightened from the cavernous confines of ignorance and impiety. She later manifested as Neoplatonic divine or mystical saint, interceding for the penitent or instructing reprobate in the mysterious ways of God. She was the king or noble, cloistered in the pageantry that proclaimed her nobility. Perfected in unification of the virtues, the magnanimous hero supplied a society of otherwise ignoble individuals with their moral sustenance, aiding in the transcendence requisite to fulfillment of the human condition be it in the order of nature or the order of grace. The great goodness of the magnanimous hero was, remains, uplifting—an exogenous exhortation to the immortal souls of humans to vanquish the despair and depravity intrinsic to humanity in its natural state.

As with the epic hero, the modern age has somewhat devalued the magnanimous hero, her heroism qualified by the anachronism of greatness. While magnanimity has not lost all currency in the face of egalitarian skepticism, great goodness no longer legitimates a claim to govern. The assumption of innate moral endogeneity has forged a broad chasm between philosophers and kings, civic power well-guarded against the immanent claims of nobles, divines, and princes. On the other hand, the magnanimous hero has not departed the political scene altogether. She remains a source of moral exhortation, even when relinquishing coercive capacity for formal authority.

As contemporary figures, magnanimous heroes continue to fulfill heroic functions. Institutionally, they present mostly obviously as redeemers and defenders. Like Plato's divine pilot navigating away from the abyss of unlikeness, they ameliorate values and policies gone stale or corrupted by misplaced convention. The readiest recent example is Martin Luther King (whom we discussed also in the context of Romantic heroism, heroes not always accommodating themselves to conceptual boundaries). Even without the force of law behind him, no Socratic philosopher king could have been more morally redemptive than King, dragging as he did white America from the cave of racial ignorance.

All this said, it is equally the case that in conforming to a just moral order, republics do not demand the continuous presence of greatly good heroes. As with epic heroism, derivatives of magnanimity persist even in the absence of heroic incarnation. The most important derivative social virtue is a culture of rectitude, which we can think of as the first moral principles of a well-functioning republic. A culture of rectitude serves as a sort of moral constitution, manifesting not as the decree of the law giver, but rather of shared and internalized values. It stands as foundation of social solidarity, speaking to the touchstones of a civil religion, the glue binding people in common cause whatever else might divide them. In addition to shared moral conviction, a culture of rectitude fosters concern for the welfare of others, promoting the reciprocal trust and solidarity that induce citizens to fulfill their obligations to others in the expectation that others will fulfill their own moral obligations. A culture of rectitude, then, implies means to the production of social capital. Finally, a culture of rectitude implies democratic legitimacy, predicated upon reasonableness and tolerance. Again, the moral constitution implied by a culture of rectitude supplies not so much an ontological understanding of the good as a process through which an evolving conception of the good coordinates and synthesizes the disparate convictions of a society of autonomous moral agents. Put differently, rather than articulating a narrow vision of the good, a culture of rectitude speaks to prohibition of the bad, a shared sense of the morally *ultra vires*.

Ingenuity presents as a second social virtue derived from heroic magnanimity. It drives the ontological quest for ever-greater understanding of first principles, even when magnanimous heroes are not there to provide it. Ingenuity is distinct from genius in that it is more pluralistic and democratic. It manifests in contemporary society not so much through interpretation of arcane philosophical or theological principles, but rather through technology and science. Once again, we need to be clear that magnanimity and its derivative virtues are not one and the same. Ingenuity is not great goodness. Instead, it contributes to goodness through technological and scientific enlightenment. It broadens the base of knowledge requisite to a transcendent life, by making knowledge at once more accessible and more practical. Indeed, in its most modern manifestation, ingenuity represents a path out of the cave and into the artificial sunlight radiating from computer monitors and smartphones. In at least one way, moreover, ingenuity can be considered a greater social resource than magnanimity itself, insofar as unlike magnanimity, ingenuity never stakes a claim to legitimation of political authority. There is no scientific or technological correspondent to the philosopher king, no latent legitimation of the imperative to govern. Indeed, says Simpson, "science views political power as an attribute of truth, not truth as an attribute of political power" (1951, 132). Thus, in this narrow sense, at least, while itself not incorruptible, ingenuity is resistant to the forces that corrupt magnanimity.

Ingenuity and a culture of rectitude are symbiotic. I do not mean this merely in the obvious sense that good things come from nifty innovations and transformative science. Rather, symbiosis resides in the metaphysical harmony of a culture of rectitude and ingenuity, reliant on the same logistical imperatives and teleology. Both ingenuity and a culture of rectitude are socially contingent goods, contributing to (and dependent upon) the accumulation of relevant resources—social capital for the one, incremental knowledge for the other. Both are rooted in "joint action and mutual aid," as Simpson conceives the scientific analog to republican virtue (1951, 132). Both build progressively upon the groundwork laid by others. Both are culturally contagious, rectitude and ingenious innovation readily accepted and internalized across society as a whole, giving rise to a common set of customs and beliefs (Simpson 1951). Most importantly of all, ingenuity maps to republican government in that it represents a quest for truth. As Socrates makes clear in defense of heroic magnanimity, truth and goodness are inextricably bound—the closer we get to truth, the closer we get to goodness. Indeed, to the extent that magnanimity and innovation are both ontological categories, they exist to such common purpose (Latour 2002, 256).

Magnanimous Corruption

That corruption militates against magnanimity is hardly a revelation. Even the most magnanimous of all, the great goodness that is God, is corruptible—if only through distorted interpretation of his will or revelation. Corruption of the magnanimous hero takes many forms. The most recognizable is venality, Lord Acton's injunction depressingly applicable across time and space. As Aristotle implies in his ambivalence towards the magnanimous man, narrow self-interest lurks erosive of even the greatest human goodness. A less conscious, if no less pernicious, form of magnanimous heroic corruption is the sense of the infallibility of one's own great goodness. A godlike sense of self is great for self-confidence, but it promotes authoritarianism born of misguided certainty that the magnanimous individual knows best how others should live their lives, the appropriate bases of their moral beliefs, how they should worship, and the limitations that should be imposed upon their freedom. Finally, a third form of magnanimous corruption is the specious contention that magnanimity is somehow hereditary, imbibed through gentle birth and superior socialization. Socrates, of course, sees this as a fatal flaw in his republican ideal. Even if the greatest of greatly good individuals could somehow be identified and trained, he prophesizes, with time meritocracy invariably yields to nepotism and, inevitably, mediocrity. Or as Aristotle sees it, aristocracy inexorably devolves into oligarchy.

Magnanimity's derivative social virtues are corrective to the derivative social virtues of (among others) epic heroes. A culture of rectitude, for example, encourages ambition and efficacy, but only to a point. Ingenuity focuses ambition and efficacy along a socially productive course. Of greater interest at this point, though, is that the virtues that derive from magnanimity are also corruptible. A culture of rectitude is corruptible both ethically and aesthetically. As to the former, like magnanimity, rectitude is corrupted by a misplaced sense of ethical certainty and attendant moral rigidity. It becomes captive to its own experiences and evolutionary trajectory. A corrupted culture of rectitude calls out for redemption as, having lost touch with a true sense of the good, it navigates toward the abyss of unlikeness. Along the way shared moral convictions become strained, dissipating social capital and breeding intolerance and unreasonableness. Corrupted rectitude speaks not to a moral constitution so much as a code of ethics in service to narrow minds and narrow interests. In an earlier day, for example, it provided justification for slavery. The currency of populists and demagogues, a corrupted culture of rectitude promotes an environment in which sophistry and self-concern overwhelm endogenous moral capacity. Indeed, this is a threat that raises its head in twenty-first-century America and puts the primary contention of this book to the test.

Aesthetically corrupted, a culture of rectitude devolves into a culture of chauvinism—cloistered, majoritarian, intolerant, and reactionary.

Among its sins, chauvinism favors a narrow sense of nationhood. It reduces usness to an exclusionary *sameness*—"people like us" defined according to whatever ascriptive characteristics have been nominated as proxies for full social membership. Consequent is what many see as an unjust social division of labor in which it is *normal* for one sort of person to govern, and another to obey; for one class to manage the economy, and one to provide auxiliary support; for one group to oversee the public square, and the other to manage the private space. This division of labor, in other words, is the basis of any number of exclusionary "isms," each of which is antithetical to a culture of rectitude and a just moral order.

Neither is ingenuity incorruptible. It requires no great feat of imagination, for example, to see that in the wrong hands, the scientific and technological innovations republics rely upon for their own defense possess enormous potential for social chaos and mass destruction. Criminals employ science and technology as readily as honest citizens. The Dark Web persists as sanctuary for anonymous pornographers, pimps, pedophiles, and pushers. Also problematic is that while ingenuity promotes equality with one hand, it undermines it with the other. It empowers the masters of information and, by dint of the zero-sum nature of power, disempowers individuals increasingly dependent upon it. The same mass communication that enlightens and liberates citizens also encourages slavish devotion to populists dismissing any limitations on self-serving authority as hoaxes, artifacts of "fake news." Corrupted ingenuity affords the state greater capacity to monitor its citizens, listen to conversations inside their homes, and capture their public behavior on camera. The social effects of this kind of power imbalance are manifest in such dystopian admonitions as Aldous Huxley's *Brave New World*, George Orwell's *Nineteen Eighty-Four*, Ray Bradbury's *Fahrenheit 451*, William Gibson's *Neuromancer*, and Suzanne Collins's *Hunger Games*.

The corruption of both magnanimity and its derivative social virtues reinforces the imperative for the conjunctive completeness of republican heroism. It is to this end that the more popular hero types assume importance, countering the worst excesses of heroic greatness. Among other virtues, Romantic and common heroism help militate against excessive rationalism and avarice, empowerment of the state at the expense of the individual, concentration of social power, rigidity and exclusivity of the moral order, and the unreasonable intolerance that attends to such rigidity and exclusivity. Of course, what is true of the virtues of the great is equally true of the virtues of the common. They are corruptible and therefore most socially beneficial when tempered by the virtues of other types of heroes.

The Romantic Hero: A Legacy of Liberty, Equality, and Identity

The Romantic hero emerged in the second half of the eighteenth century to address the power imbalance privileging the greatly good—the noble and the pious. The specious elevation, as Romantics saw it, of certain flawed individuals above others led to the construction of a social order that increasingly alienated citizens from the spiritual and natural bases of their humanity. *Spiritually*, the evolved order of the Christian world obliged people to privilege revelation over testimony of the senses, faith over epistemology as the basis of belief. *Naturally*, individuals were alienated from the true essence of themselves in the name of civilization, reasoned, hypocritical, and dehumanizing. In amelioration, eschewing pretense and hypocrisy, the emergent Romantic hero strove for authenticity. She rejected the metaphysical hegemony of ethics, tempering it with the authenticity of aesthetics. Her grasp of first principles was not cognitive, but sensual—Shelley's planetary music internalized in the heart, regulated in the conscience, and asserted through the will.

The emergent Romantic hero's mastery of the internal stimulated reimagination of the external. She refused to accept the world as she found it and, in defiance, went in search of a better one newly conceived. Abjuring deference and convention, she rejected social hierarchy root and branch. Hers was a Promethean gift to humanity; *her* fire put to the crumbling edifice of postfeudal hypocrisy and its odious usurper, bourgeois vacuity. She attacked the rigidity of reason with the seductive power of the senses, grounding social mores in shared aesthetic judgment, expressed and appreciated through art. She exhorted humanity to apotheosis; she moved replacement of God as author of grace with God as benefactor of nature. Artist or auditor, the emergent Romantic hero was a redemptive republican stimulant, recharging a paradigm gone stale with a new sense of inclusive citizenship and civic purpose.

The modern Romantic hero has had less propensity to recede into the background than the epic or magnanimous. Countercultural, she continues to provoke the status quo, to bestir her fellows from the lethargy of mindless conformity. Mover of paradigms, changer of her world, she persists in blazing her own trail while celebrating and legitimating the authenticity of others. She is not Nietzsche's over-the-top overman, nor necessarily possessed of Emerson's over-soul. Transcendent, she is moved by a subjectively derived sense of self to live a transcendent human life, true and tailored to her own nature. Analogous to the Socratic gadfly, the Romantic hero's living legacy manifests in the derivative social virtues foundational to authenticity: liberty, equality, and social identity.

Liberty and equality are two sides of the same coin, born of dual requisites of an authentic life. Romantic heroes cannot claim total credit for the legacy of liberty and equality. They do, however, provide affective legitimation, helping to supply the passion that attaches to defense of a moral claim. Liberty is the bedrock of principled defiance of authority, a natural right to moral autonomy that attaches to all humans in aid of living a fully human life. Unlike an ontologically good life, transcendence through authenticity cannot leave the starting gate absent the liberty requisite to its realization. The moral claim to liberty inextricably binds it to equality. Indeed, the existence of one without the other is pathological. Absent equality, liberty relinquishes the moral claim that elevates mere preferences to rights. It is shorn of the duty that attaches to any right—concomitant regard for the equal rights of others. Freedom reduces to a tool of anarchy and license, a Hobbesian means to realization of personal ends, an environment in which others exist primarily as obstacles. Rather than a moral claim to pursue an authentic life, liberty without equality proclaims little more than the means by which the strong oppress the weak. On the flip side, absent the liberty imputed by free employment of the will, human equality achieves no currency. It exists as an abstract concept lacking practical application. Humans endure in perverse existence as moral agents robbed of their agency by the tyrannical claims of others. Only in concert can liberty and equality announce the moral claim of every individual to act in pursuit of her authentic life and to judge for herself the legitimacy of the extant moral order. They represent filters through which citizens assent to political or spiritual authority or, conversely, exercise the prerogative to withdraw that assent.

The third derivative virtue of Romanticism is recognition of social identity. As noted, social identity reflects an affective sense of placefulness, a shared cultural affinity with others of one's type (whatever type that is). Authentic social identity defines what Young styles *social groups* bonded by shared worldviews, cultural mores, and lifestyles (2011, 43). Such a community of authenticity affirms one's sense of whom she feels herself to be, the common cultural values to which she subscribes, the community(ies) with which she identifies most intimately. Ideally, social groups exist on equal footing as subsets—cherished and integral components—of the larger whole, of "people like us." Practically, social groups often meet cultural pushback when authentic social identities fail to conform to traditional social expectations. As a consequence, social groups are forced to fight for recognition and affirmation of their place, to engage in cultural contestation to diversify national identity, to pluralize what it means to be "people like us."

The Romantic tradition draws a sharp distinction between authentic social identities and common interests. Instead of a manifestation of common interests, authentic social identity *informs* common interests. The distinction is captured in Michael Sandel's (1984, 85) assertion that an individual is prior to her ends, the authentic self existing as more than a vehicle for pursuit of rational self-interest. Just as Romantics understand affect to drive cognition, authentic social identity gives rise—is prior—to rationality. Because authentic social identity is part and parcel of whom a person is, justice demands recognition and affirmation of social groups in a way that groups bound only by common preferences cannot claim.

Recognition and affirmation of authentic social identity implies its own form of equality and its own form of liberty. In this context, equality speaks to something more than formal or procedural equality among individuals, more than equal treatment under law. Instead, the requisites of justice are satisfied only when groups are situated equally. As we have discussed, situational equality—where social identity is a perfect nonpredictor of social or economic success—presumes that formal equality is just if, and only if, groups are already equally situated. Where such is not the case, where a legacy of bad laws has privileged some groups over others, insistence upon formal equality serves merely to institutionalize extant inequality. Grounded in situational equality, liberty too takes on a more inclusive cast. It manifests not just as individual autonomy, but also as cultural emancipation, the capacity to break free from social molds and stereotypes, the freedom to recast one's means of belonging to the larger society in a way that feels right to the *belonger* rather than the society to which she belongs.

Romantic Corruption

Inevitably, Romantic heroism and its derivative social virtues are vulnerable to corruption. In waging battle against the tyrannical hegemony of reason, for example, the Romantic hero risks overcorrection. She flirts with the emotive self-indulgence of a Werther. More perniciously, as in Mary Shelley's metaphor, the Romantic hero corrupted is a monster, an affectively driven savage. Like the Revolutionary French mob's antipathy to a rigid regime of reason, such savagery runs amok in incontinent rage. In amelioration, the uncorrupted Romantic hero restricts herself to the just ambience of balance. Again, to rely on Shelley, she is virtuous only when she tempers subjective affect with countervailing reason. To do otherwise is mere solipsism, slavery to the sentiments, a failure of proportionality in which republican virtue is sacrificed to Keats's egotistical sublime.

Equally, Romantic heroism is corrupted by the temptation of misplaced audience. The Romantic devolves into insincerity, public acclaim seducing the erstwhile hero to abandon her authenticity. It is this sort of corruption that motivates Rameau's condemnation of his uncle, who, as far as the nephew is concerned, has sacrificed his artistic genius to the altar of vulgar affirmation. It is such democratization of aesthetics—the appeal to low sentiment—that Boorstin objects to in his portrait of the celebrity hero. Indeed, the prerogative of the celebrity hero is to indulge in flattering self-presentation, to subordinate her authentic self to the one her adoring public favors, and to entice her audience into equally inauthentic (and fatuous) expectations and desires. Obviously, there are costs to this. Celebrated inauthenticity is the means by which sophists and populists manipulate sycophantic apostles. It presents as uncritical conformity to conventions of style and belief, perversely deriding authenticity as apostasy. It is the stuff of deep cultural cleavages, speciously distilling virtue into simplistic values and beliefs; promoting divisive distinction between those it paints as estimables and deplorables.

Equally corruptible are the Romantic hero's derivative social virtues. Like all virtues, these are corrupted in excess. Excessive liberty and equality, for example, manifest respectively as hedonism and nihilism. Bork (1997) refers to such pathologies as radical individualism and radical egalitarianism—symptoms of the modern liberalism that, as he sees it, has set republics upon the road to Gomorrah. As virtues, liberty and equality work in seamless harmony. In excess, they prove unable to coexist. Hedonistic liberty is indulgence in the Aristotelian life of pleasure. It is an atomistic existence in which the liberated individual shrugs off the dead weight of social obligation as gladly as the immortal Socratic soul leaves behind its corporeal shell. Nihilistic egalitarianism is the socially oppressive flip side. It restricts individual liberty in service to mediocrity, an existence in which excellence is decried by the radically egalitarian masses as readily as the union boss calls out the rate buster. Excessive egalitarianism manifests in an aesthetics of ordinariness, a cultural sense that equality trumps excellence, a conviction that individual success is but a trapping of unmerited social privilege.

The same corruptibility attaches to excessive recognition of social identity. Virtuous, affirmation of authentic social identity tempers the rigidity of the extant moral order, militating against *sameness* as the basis of usness. Excessive, however, it breeds insularity. Rather than expanding the scope of meaningful social belonging to the larger national community, excessive protection of social identity has the potential to become an end in itself. Under such conditions, it erodes virtue, sowing the seeds of distrust among groups, undermining the common identity that gives the republic itself its sense of place and purpose. Excessive, communitarian values crowd out individualist ones, such as (individual) liberty and (formal) equality. Indeed, the flip side of cultural emancipation is cultural tyranny, in which the group appropriates individual members' prerogatives to make their own life choices. Often this takes the form of cultural pressure, such as that designed to persuade homemakers that they are selling out the cause of women, or closeted homosexuals "outed" against their will by revealing sexual identities that individuals prefer to keep concealed, or racial groups that shame members who fail to identify sufficiently with the cause with labels such as "Uncle Tom" or "Oreo."

The Common Hero: A Legacy of Reasonableness and Tolerance

Romantic heroism has helped usher in a new, more inclusive, paradigm of justice. Attacking the specious bases of hierarchy and privilege, it locates justice in fidelity to the self. In this task, it is joined by common heroism, reinforcing Romantic insistence upon reliance upon the self and the equality of human beings. While speaking to similar ends, however, Romantic and common heroism protect distinctive values. Indeed, if the derivative social virtues of the Romantic hero nullify corrupted magnanimity, common heroism serves as a corrective to corrupted Romanticism, reasserting the objectivity of ethics in the face of corrupted aesthetics. Proclaiming the efficacy of moral intuition and reason, the common hero guards against the corruption of liberty into license, equality into mediocrity, and social identity into intolerance.

Although not *greatly* good, the common hero has usurped some of the functions that in earlier times fell to magnanimous heroes. Endowed with common sense and transcendental ethical intuition, she is autodidactic in her moral competence. She is not infallible, of course. But fallibility doesn't set her as far apart her from her greatly good counterpart as ancient republicans would have had us believe. The greatly good individual, after all, though perfected in her virtue, retains the imperfection endemic to her humanity. The magnanimous hero is more obviously heroic, singular in her capacity for goodness. Comparatively prosaic, the common hero makes up in volume what she lacks in distinctiveness, her ubiquity her greatest strength. She is the everyman, or at least the embodiment or idealization of every good and transcendent person. Her corporate presence is not a perfect substitute for heroic magnanimity—she is less likely to effect a redemptive paradigmatic shift in social justice, for example. But she relieves the magnanimous hero of the need to manage the quotidian affairs of public life, removing the temptation for magnanimous absolutism and short-circuiting the metaphysical basis of social hierarchy.

The common hero is the most aspirational hero type, the most mimetic. She takes numerous forms in the literature of her nineteenth- and twentieth-century glory years. Indeed, magpie-like, over the years she has appropriated attendant qualities of other hero types, a trait that culminated with the comic superhero. Beyond this, the common hero has effected the guise of the self-made man, the yeoman farmer, the backwoodsman, the pioneering homesteader, the scout, the mountain man, the cowboy, the gunslinger, and the hard-boiled detective. Comfortable in her own skin, she eschews Romantic fascination with the self, evincing concern for the welfare of others as more than merely a by-product of self-exploration. Unsung, she is the selfless public servant: the fire fighter or police officer. She is the church leader, the Little League coach, the good parent. She exists not to win broad acclaim, but to maintain the esteem of herself and those most dear to her.

The common hero remains at the heroic forefront. Her social virtues of reasonableness—or reasoned judgment—and tolerance are less derivative than implicit, her heroic heritage less an inheritance than a living legacy. Reasonableness resides at the heart of common sense, affording cognitive temperance to Romantic affect. It militates against the self-conscious defiance of the Romantic, the prerogative of the agitator, pioneer of new worlds imagined. Instead, reasonableness defaults more readily (though not blindly) to the ethics of the extant moral order. At the same time, assent to order and custom is on the reasonable agent's own authority—on her own reasoned intuition of just moral principles. In consequence, she reserves the right to reject any rules, norms, or form of political authority that violate her sincerely held moral convictions.

Critical to such moral judgment is tolerance. The common hero is not magnanimous. She does not impose moral order on the strength of her own superior ethical capacity. Rather, she concedes her moral fallibility, deferring to judgment rather than adjudication. She is more ready to accept the legitimacy of others' moral convictions when they do not accord with her own (Perry 1968, 383). Tolerance prevails in recognition that conviction and ethical truth are not one and the same. If they were—if magnanimous individuals truly were imbued with complete knowledge of first principles—tolerance would be pernicious, there being no need to tolerate untruth when perfect knowledge is at hand. But since even the most magnanimous mortals see through a glass darkly, their convictions cannot stand as truths. Tolerance, then, implies acceptance that moral autonomy is stipulative, predicated upon first principles that cannot be proven or known unconditionally. Such principles can only be sensed, reasoned, or intuited. For this reason, tolerance insists only upon the reasonableness of another's intuitive grasp of first moral principles (Perry 1968, 384).

The common hero employs her reasonableness and tolerance to good moral ends. She puts her moral convictions out there, not as a decree but as an offering to collective endeavor, to the pursuit of social perfection. She pits her convictions against others', subjecting them to the crucible of scrutiny and judgment in her conduct of life. In fidelity to intuited moral principles, she joins the Romantic in risking condemnation and opprobrium, doing so not in the name of authenticity, but in transcendent realization of a good and fulfilled life. Her exhortations to others tend support the broad framework that is the extant moral order. As to finer details, she tends toward insistence upon deontic *processes* rather than contestable moral principles. She recognizes, in other words, that while all must be bound by a common moral order in quest of a fulfilled life, there are different pathways to that good destination.

In concert, reasonableness and tolerance are foundational to democracy. Standard bearers of moral endogeneity, they speak to republican citizens' capacity to conduct their own political affairs, not merely as ratifiers of great men, but as governors in their own right. Armed with reasonableness and tolerance, common heroes permit modern republics to dispense with the social hierarchy that attaches to greatness, with magnanimous conviction disguised as truth, with the tyranny that attaches to nobleman or theocrat convinced that she alone sees what others fail to see. Reasonableness and tolerance are the civic tools of the citizen checking the power of the philosopher king, blunting theocratic indulgence, demagoguery, and populism.

Common Corruption

As we saw with liberty and equality, reasonableness and tolerance are symbiotic virtues. Corruption resides in the space between them. Where reasonableness abandons tolerance, moral conviction becomes impermeable. Reasonableness shrinks upon itself; impassive and rigid, it breeds dogmatic resistance to dissent (Skitka and Mullen 2002, 36). Such dogmatism shares unfortunate qualities with corrupted magnanimity, although the underlying pathology differs. With corrupted reasonableness, we are talking less of a singular sense of moral superiority than tenacious closed-mindedness—a cultural sclerosis of moral conviction, a numbing sameness stubbornly resistant to evolution. Absent tolerance, reasonableness is reactionary. Doing things a particular way is good because they have always been done that particular way; and because they have always been done that particular way, the experiential legacy imposes its own moral mandate. Consequent is reflexive majoritarianism, an environment in which general agreement and cultural tradition stand as nonnegotiable proxies for goodness. Such mechanical conformity invites social stratification, in which there are conforming (good) members of society, and nonconforming ones.[1] It justifies second-class citizenship for subaltern groups. It clings, to take one example, to assignation of traditional gender roles in perpetuation of a social division of labor that has existed for centuries and that therefore represents some sort of morally justified institution in a just society.

Tolerance liberated from reasonableness fares little better. Corrupted, tolerance becomes infinitely permissive, imputing equal legitimacy to all convictions. It rejects any sort of moral judgment as intolerably intolerant. It assigns equal moral weight to piety and pederasty (assuming, of course, that piety dispenses with impermissible moral judgment). Corrupted tolerance represents an abdication of moral responsibility, a relativistic broadening of the erstwhile moral order. It cultivates an environment in which liberty presents itself as license, elevating desires to rights and demoting moral obligation to the ranks of tyranny or vice. It mandates that all shared values and practices, however barbaric, be deemed equally worthy of affirmation. More than merely erosive of republican virtue, corrupted tolerance sets its sights on the *destruction* of virtue.

Conclusion

It is premature to announce the demise of heroes, even if the greatness associated with the more conventional hero types is a casualty of the modern age. Critics of modernity are on solid ground when they point out that we no longer defer to the singular heroes who defined earlier times. They are, I think, more vulnerable in the implications. It does not hold that with the decline of great heroes has come an attendant decline of the values and aspirations to which great individuals exhorted the rest. Beginning with the Enlightenment, the recognition and liberation of the endogenous capacity for just agency has democratized heroism, rescuing it from the cloistered exclusivity of the great and greatly good, filling out dimensions that had gone unrecognized for centuries. In the process, heroism was not dissipated so much as diffused and made more complete. If such heroic distribution has made singular heroes less readily identifiable, it has made republican heroism itself more robust.

The failure to concentrate heroic resources in one or few heroes offers no guarantee against corruption, of course. The virtues we associate with more egalitarian hero types—Romantic and common—are no less vulnerable to spoilage than those of epic and magnanimous heroes. However, their contribution to the completeness of republican heroism offers the best hedge against injustice through imbalance. Romantic and common heroes join their more singular counterparts in lending derivative virtues to the conjunctive completeness of modern republican heroism. The point is not that everyone is a hero. Nor is it that heroes remain heroic throughout their existence—that is too great a burden for any type of hero to carry. It is that the diffusion of heroic virtues means not only sharing the burden of heroism, but also balancing it, tempering the effects of excess or deficiency in the virtues—countervailing and synthesized—that inform the republicanism of the modern age.

Notes

Introduction

1. I use "justice" here in its cosmic sense discussed in greater detail below.

2. For more on republicanism and its evolution see among others, Fink (1945); Lane (1966); Pocock (1975); Hatch (1977); Appleby (1986); Skinner (1990); Ward (1991); Rodgers (1992); Black (1997); Pangle (1998); Colish (1999); Pettit (2002); Nederman (2003); Cornish (2010); Winship (2012); and Lusztig (2017).

3. Aristotle defines the good citizen as one who holds "indefinite office," such as dicast (juryman) or ecclesiast (assemblyman) (*Pol.* 1275a, 29–34, 1275b, 18–19). She differs from the good man in that her virtue is relative to the constitution of her state; by contrast the virtue of the good man is relative to that which is objectively good (*Pol.* 1276b, 29–35). As such, the province of the good citizen is not wisdom, but merely *true opinion*, or good judgment (1277b, 27–28).

4. Keeley suggests that tribal societies typically lost one half percent of their populations to warfare each year (1997, 93).

5. The majority of the heroes discussed in this book are men. This, of course, is not to discount the heroic importance of women. However, through much of history, the public square has been dominated by men, and much of the heroic hagiography has been directed to them. The gender imbalance is somewhat rectified as we progress, in proximity to more egalitarian times. That said, there are a number of important works that have explored the emergence and progression of heroines as figures of cultural import (in particular see Lyons 1997; also Wiersma 1990; Jones 2013).

6. Says the Stranger, "When [the world] is guided by the pilot, it produces much good and but little evil in the creatures it raises and sustains. When it must travel on without him, things go well enough in the years immediately after he abandons control, but as time goes on and forgetfulness sets it, the ancient condition of discord also begins to assert its sway. . . . Beholding it in its troubles, and anxious for it lest, racked by storms and confusion, it sink and be dissolved

again in the bottomless abyss of unlikeness, he takes control of the helm once more" (Plato *States.*, 273c–73d).

7. Discrete virtues are not the same as the "virtue" I discussed above. Rather, they are component elements of virtue, desirable qualities, competences, and actions that contribute to virtue itself. In addition to the *virilis virtus* recently noted, examples include courage, self-confidence, compassion, and so on. The relative importance of discrete virtues is culturally informed, such that the most pertinent discrete virtues of Homeric heroes are not necessarily the same as those of chivalric knights, Protestant saints, or gunslinging cowboys.

8. By goodness, I mean something more specific than just agency, a distinction that becomes relevant in our discussion of Romanticism. Goodness demands conformity to an ontological good. Just agency relaxes this demand.

9. Of course, there is an artificial quality to such singularity, heroism amplified by mythologization, hagiography, or selective memory. The point is not as cynical as it sounds. I do not mean that ratification of singular heroes is a process of pernicious deceit and manipulation on the part of myth makers. Nor is the point blindingly profound. Were singular heroic recognition not a product of presentation, it is hard to see how heroes could *achieve* singular heroic recognition.

10. This relationship between heroic singularity and unsung heroic estimability assumes relevance in the Conclusion, in assessing whether or not we live in a postheroic age.

11. Because these are heuristic categories, some definitional relaxation is required to make them relevant. As discussed, from the classical period onward, estimability of epic heroes demands a degree of goodness. Heroic magnanimity is less about the coincidence of greatness and goodness as the interaction, such that we speak of magnanimous heroes as greatly good. Finally, while Romantic heroes are categorized as "not good," I do not mean they are unjust. As noted previously, I use "goodness" to employ conformity to an ontological, objective good.

12. Hence, Hesiod's *Catalogue of Heroines*, "Now sing about the race of women, sweet-voiced Olympian muses, daughters of the aegis-bearing Zeus, sing of those who were the best of their time, who loosened their girdles, mingling in union with the gods" (fr. 1, quoted in Lyons 1997, 10).

13. The distinction between the orders of nature and grace reflects a pervasive tension in this book between humanism and Christianity, orthodox Protestantism in particular.

Chapter 1

1. Against this is Zeus's complaint in *The Odyssey* 1 (1919, 34–43) that immortals are but scapegoats for men's folly and that the wickedness of man is

of his own making (Dodds, 1959; 32–33; Lloyd-Jones 1983, 28–29). Similarly, in *The Iliad*, the gods are often praiseworthy—Athena is largely responsible for the clever ideas that pop into Odysseus's head, and it is she who stills Achilles's sword in the face of Agamemnon's insults in *The Iliad* 1 (1924, 188–214).

2. The timocratic Callicles summarizes this worldview perfectly in *Gorgias*. "[A]nyone who is to live aright should suffer his appetites to grow to the greatest extent and not check them, and through courage and intelligence should be competent to minister to them at their greatest and to satisfy every appetite with what it craves . . . Luxury and intemperance and license, when they have sufficient backing, are virtue and happiness, and [justice] is tinsel, the unnatural catchwords of mankind, mere nonsense and of no account" (491e–92c).

3. This should not be read to suggest that Homeric warriors were entirely unidimensional in their objectives. Achilles's return to the battlefield was not in quest of glory so much as vengeance for the death of Patroclus.

4. The luminescence was not overwhelming. Historical understanding of the Archaic period rests on relatively little documentation, not all of it contemporaneous.

5. To this end, interstate athletic competition emerged as a new forum of civic focus, athletic excellence rivaling martial prowess as the heroic theater of relevance to post-Homeric Greece. Most iconic were the Olympic Games, which began in 776 BC; as well as the Pythian, Isthmian, and Nemean Games. These Pan-Hellenic events were sufficiently illustrious to warrant temporary truces among warring cities. The laurels for which athletes competed reflected both individual and corporate glory, such that cities were given to honoring their athletic heroes with statues and other symbols of civic pride (Tyrtaeus 2008, fr. W10–12; Finley 1954, 128–29; Currie 2005, 57–58; Kendrick 2010, ch. 4).

6. "Then farewell to the Warrior's Schemes, farewell," declares Wordsworth, "That other hope, long mine, the hope to fill; The heroic trumpet with the Muse's breath" (1888c, 49).

7. Of course, epic novels do exist, as in Elizabeth Barrett Browning's *Aurora Leigh*, J. R. R. Tolkien's *Lord of the Rings*, and even (despite the unconventional heroism of Leopold Bloom) James Joyce's *Ulysses*. The epic hero, moreover, survives her natural genre. We see this primarily in contemporary athletics, epic heroism once again inculcating civic or collegiate spirit through extraordinary physical capacity. More ambiguously, although I cast superheroes in this book as proxies for common heroism, there is an obvious epic quality to their supernatural powers in pursuit of good cause and in illustration of the completeness of physical and metaphysical virtue. Liberated from long narrative form, the superhero continues to marry physical greatness with the supernatural (or at least the science fictive) in contributing a grounded moral message amidst the chaotic swirl of real-world motives (Risden 1998, 194–95; Shippey 1995, 85–86, 89–91).

Chapter 2

1. Socrates understands first principles as Forms, or ideational constructions of all that we perceive or conceive.

2. The contrast is reinforced by Socrates's myth of the metals, whereby just condition is a product of social division of labor predicated upon the metallic quality of one's soul. In this Hesiodic analogy, the gods fashioned the souls of those with aptitude to reason with gold, while the warrior's soul was mingled with silver (*Rep.* 415a).

3. In Socrates's day, the virtue that Pericles had lauded as the defining characteristic of Athenian heroism dissipated in the face of plague and war. Thucydides tells us, in the context of Corcyra but applicable to all of Greece at the time, that "human nature, which is always ready to transgress the laws, having now trampled them under foot, delighted to show that her passions were ungovernable, that she was stronger than justice and the enemy of everything above her" (1998, III. 84; also Colaico 2001, 89–91). To Socrates, far from the democratization of heroism, Periclean Athens in the grip of crisis would have showed itself to be as weak as the sum of its parts.

4. Again, for Aristotle, an end is complete if it is *noncontingent*, which is to say valued for itself, only for itself and not for the sake of any other end (1999, 1097a, 26–30, 1097b, 7–21, 1915a, 1183b, 38–1184a, 14). It is complete if it is *teleological* such that all other ends, whether intrinsically valued or not, are pursued in the name of this end. And an end is complete if it is *self-sufficient* in that it wants for no greater quantity or supplement (1999, 1172b, 30–35, 1176b, 6–10). *Eudaemonia*, then, is a complete end in that: "(i) you cannot say of *eudaemonia* that you seek it for the sake of something else; you can say of anything else that you seek it for the sake of *eudaemonia*; (ii) you cannot say that you prefer *eudaemonia* plus something extra to *eudaemonia*" (Ackrill 1980, 22).

5. "The person whose activity accords with understanding and who takes care of understanding would seem to be in the best condition, and most loved by the gods. For if the gods pay some attention to human beings, as they seem to, it would be reasonable for them to take pleasure in what is best and most akin to them, namely understanding; and reasonable for them to benefit in return those who most of all like and honor understanding" (*NE*, 1179a, 23–29).

6. Here we need to distinguish between the best life an individual can live (a *eudaemonic* life) and the very best life it would be possible to live (the ideal life). All can live a *eudaemonic* life, but the ideal life demands the conjunctive perfection of the active and contemplative virtues (see Lawrence 1993, esp. 7–14). Only the magnanimous individual can be thought to live the ideal life.

7. Aristotle understands first principles to be first causes, rather than ideational constructs, a distinction that permits him to avoid the logical and

logistical ambiguity of assigning to everything a unique Form (*Poet.*, 990b–991b, 20; see also *Phys.*, bk. I, esp. 184a).

Chapter 3

1. In the *Pharsalia*, for example, Lucan has the narrator proclaim, "[I]f you Romans ever stand upright, your necks freed, you will make Cato a god" (quoted in Bond 2011, 4). In Cicero's *Republic*, Scipio may doubt the literal truth of Romulus's descent from the god of war, but nonetheless proclaims that "the great public servants should be deemed divine by birth as well as in ability" (bk. II, 4). Like the Hesiodic hero on the Isles of the Blest, Scipio is advised by the ghost of his grandfather that "for everyone who has saved and served his country and helped it to grow, a sure place is set aside in heaven where he may enjoy a life of eternal bliss" (Cicero *Rep.*, bk. VI, 13). In his own voice, Cicero tells us that there is no occupation "which brings human excellence closer to divine power than founding new states and preserving those already founded" (*Rep.*, bk. I, 12); that governing and training peoples by good men reflects "an almost incredible and superhuman kind of excellence" (*Rep.* III, 4–5); and that "it is right that Good Sense, Devotion, Moral Excellence and Good Faith should be deified" (*Laws*, bk. II, 27–28).

2. As with its English-language cognate, *virtus* enjoyed a degree of conceptual elasticity in ancient Rome. Generally, it implied the discrete virile qualities of bravery, self-assertiveness and capability, although it was occasionally imbued with metaphysical content as well (albeit more so by civilian statesmen like Cicero than men of action) (Earl 1967, 20–21; Johnson 1975; Gorman 2001, 264–66; McDonnell 2006).

3. *Dignitas* represented a claim upon social deference. Far from the dignity that modern republicanism recognizes in every human being, *dignitas* was more akin to what today we would think of as institutionalized social status.

4. A good example of this logic is the Crusades which, among things, precluded disruptions of the peace in Europe by providing a more felicitous outlet for demonstration of knightly virility.

5. An informal redistributive model, clientelism constitutes an alternative to formal legal institutions as a means of exercising power and authority. A good example of this is the machine politics that afflicted numerous American cities in the first half of the twentieth century. Political machines displaced more legitimate formal legal institutions, effectively rendering such institutions weak or even powerless. It was only with the welfare state that informal power through private wealth redistribution was finally curtailed. An even more recent example of clientelistic politics in the United States is Trumpism. In addition to seeking

to delegitimize the electoral process, Trump recast good citizenship, such that it was no longer predicated upon public concern, but rather transactional loyalty to the person of Donald J. Trump.

Chapter 4

1. The Puritan doctrine of preparation held that while reprobates—those not yet bound in covenantal grace—were incapable of influencing their prospects for (unconditional) saving grace, they could *prepare* their souls for salvation should they become regenerate.

2. In drawing out the distinction between pagan barbarism and Christian humility, Augustine also points to the proto-Christian heroism of the Sabine women (*CG* bk. II, 17, bk. III, 13; see also Tuttle 2021).

3. Lull's *Book of the Order of Chivalry* (1991, ch. 3) is especially insistent upon this point, suggesting that a knight's role is to honor, defend, and spread the faith of the Roman Catholic Church.

4. Not all analysts believe courtly love to be historically meaningful, and some of its conventions do strain credulity (see Robertson 1968). Even so, romance literature taken as a whole helps to define an idealized chivalric tradition.

5. The readiest example comes from Arthurian legend, where Camelot is thrown into civil war due to Lancelot's adulterous relationship with Guinevere.

6. Rather than the Aristotelian completeness discussed in earlier chapters, Renaissance completeness connoted the well-roundedness of capacity and character attendant to the gentleman. There was also a feminine analogue that emerged from the medieval ideal of woman whose extraordinary faith, pastoral virtue, and financial wherewithal were integral to maintenance of the family unit. Typically, such complete medieval women insisted upon marrying for love and possessed the strength of capacity and character to carry on their husband's public responsibilities in the case of his absence or death. (In this sense, Matilda of Flanders might be seen as the prototype for idealized medieval femininity [Connolly 2017, ch. 1].) With the skillful employment of these qualities, Renaissance heroines gradually emerged as social beings in their own right, thereby provoking the faintest stirrings of an evolved feminine heroism born of a distinctive social identity (see Starke 2007, ch. 1). A good example is the rugged individualism of Willa Cather's Alexandra Bergson (discussed in the American context later on) defining femininity on her own terms in defiance of any form of gender subordination.

7. Ambiguity bred insecurity among new gentlemen, their precarious liminal status "much contested and much insisted upon" (Shapin 1994, 46). It provoked the generally unsuccessful quest to establish objective sociological criteria. William Harrison, for example, in his *Description of England* claims, "Who soever studieth the lawes of the realm, who so abidith in the universitie giving his

mind to his book, or who professeth physicke and the liberall sciences, or beside his service in the roome of a capteine of the warres, can live without manuell labour . . . shall . . . be called master which is the title men give to esquires and gentlemen, and reputed for a gentleman ever after" (quoted in Smythe-Palmer 1908, 14). For his part, Peacham is in high dudgeon about the prevailing trend in Europe for every common lackey to insist upon being called "monsieur" or its linguistic equivalent. Symptomatic of the pernicious blurring of social lines was the spoofing of coats of arms, not least the singularly boorish Dutch example of three pigs embracing a dog above the motto *endracht mackt macht* (concord makes might) (1634, 10–16).

    8. There arose manifold points of conflict between court and country, including the centralization of power through the royal prerogative and the prerogative courts, the forced loan of 1626 and later ship-money assessments to inland counties as an alternative to conventional Parliamentary taxation, financial exactions against Catholic recusants even as Charles I was distrusted for his perceived Catholic sympathies, and the general intolerance of the Laudian Church of England. Closely allied with Charles, Laud himself was a polarizing force. He saw liturgical uniformity as requisite to reestablishment of Church stature that had been eroded by "flabby inertia" and too many impositions upon its power and wealth since the beginning of Elizabeth's reign (Stone 1980, 30). Striking the right balance between Reformation Protestantism and the traditional episcopalianism of the established Church demanded a lighter touch than that of the overbearing archbishop. Indeed, it required little imagination to see in Laud a counter-reforming Catholicism that precluded true reformation of the Church of England (Morrill 1984, 163).

    9. The Puritan saints exercised a fairly restrictive view of citizenship in the Christianized republic, the franchise limited to the godly (Winship 2012, 197–200).

    10. Of course, the same might very well have been said about country gentlemen/real Whigs as well. Indeed, heroically speaking, the values of the country gentleman did not find full voice until the Idealism and Romanticism of the following centuries. However, in the requisite quest for hearts and minds—to say nothing of souls—liberty, tolerance, and innate moral competence are a much easier sale than is the nullification of these values.

Chapter 5

    1. Unlike the overman, as we shall see, their will is constrained by moral agency.

    2. "Hobbits are just rustic English people, made small in size because it reflects the generally small reach of their imagination—not the small reach of their courage or latent power" (Humphrey Carpenter, quoted in Risden 1998, 194).

3. Shelley echoes Schiller's contention that the human condition demands harmonization of a person (form) and her condition (sense). The attendant impulses, of form and sense, are not incompatible; but each has the potential to pull the individual in a direction that leads to the excess of one and deficiency of the other. The temperate mean is the product of its own impulse, which Schiller calls the "play impulse," reflecting sensual form, or beauty, that brings the individual into completeness, or harmony with herself (1884a, letters XI–XV).

4. Kant gets at the same thing slightly differently and with greater emphasis on cognition. For him, a *sensus communis* constitutes consensual appreciation of the beauty reflective of sense and form. It is, then, an aesthetic judgment, albeit one contingent upon perfection through universal and cognitively derived moral principles (Kant 1929, s. 29, 132).

5. Critically, social identity does not presume that possession of certain characteristics creates essentialist cultural affinity. Not all women, for example share a gender identity. Some women feel they are defined by their gender, that gender is essential to their identities. Others see themselves as people who happen to be women.

6. More precisely, we can say that situational equality is realized when ascriptive characteristics become a perfect nonpredictor of material, political, or social success.

Chapter 6

1. The idea of common individuals possessing moral self-sufficiency, the moral competence requisite to a transcendent life, is generally a modern construction, albeit not wholly so. We encountered it earlier in Pericles's elegy to the dead of the Peloponnesian War. It is faintly discernable in the utopian Aristotelian ideal of each governing and being governed in her turn. Aristophanes's comedies speak to the potential for popular heroism, the playwright elevating ordinary individuals to the status of protagonist at the expense of the Athenian elite (Zumbrunnen 2004, 2012, ch. 2). Still, the prospect of an egalitarian republic peopled by morally self-sufficient citizens was improbable to most philosophers and theologians prior to the Enlightenment. At best, it was generally thought, the practical judgment of the commoner could be harnessed through tutelage by magnanimous statesmen.

2. "When God gives a special commission, He looks to have it strictly observed in every article. Thus stands the cause between God and us. We are entered into Covenant with Him for this work. We have taken out a Commission. The Lord hath given us leave to draw our own Articles. Now if the Lord shall please to hear us, and bring us in peace to the place we desire, then hath He ratified this Covenant and sealed our Commission, [and] will expect a strict performance of the articles contained in it; but if we shall neglect the observation of

these Articles which are the ends we have propounded, and dissembling with our God, shall fall to embrace this present world and prosecute our carnal intentions, seeking great things for ourselves and our posterity, the Lord will surely break out in wrath against us, and be revenged of such a people, and make us know the price of the breach of such a Covenant" (Winthrop 1996, 9). In this same apocalyptic vein, the destruction wrought by King Philip's War beginning in 1675 was seen as tangible demonstration of God's displeasure (Slotkin 1998, 55–57).

3. Hence Reid's admonition that God "has given to men the faculty of perceiving the right and the wrong in conduct, as far as is necessary to our present state, and of perceiving the dignity of the one, and the demerit of the other" (quoted in Noll 1985, 221).

4. No cause was too obscure, as the National Truss Society for the Relief of the Ruptured Poor would tend to suggest (Howe 2007, 192).

5. A good example was abolitionism. Grounding slavery in sin—a manifest and volitional flouting of the divine will—abolitionists preached repentance, aiming their message not at lawmakers, but at the consciences of moral agents, theirs a message of remonstrance, entreaty, warning, and rebuke (Thomas 1965, 661).

6. While this might present facially as conscience, the over-soul is more akin to the scholastic idea of synderesis. That is, while conscience is a sensual response to a particular act, synderesis represents an intuitive understanding of first moral principles.

7. Quotes Ellis of an unnamed contemporary: "This, then, is the doctrine of Transcendentalism—the substantive, independent existence of the soul of man, the reality of conscience, the religious sense, the inner light, of man's religious affections, his knowledge of right and truth, his sense of duty, the honestem [sic] apart from the utile—his love for beauty and holiness, his religious aspirations— with this it starts as something not dependent on education, custom, command, or anything beyond man himself. These can only add new motives for obedience to that which he feels to be of imperative obligation; but they do not create and cannot contradict the law within him. This cannot be proved by evidence clearer than that which each man has of himself. Habit and education cannot eradicate it. Things may seem painful or inexpedient, but nothing can be just and true which this condemns" (1842, 19–20).

8. Says Ellis, for example, "Christianity is spiritualism applied to life; the cultivation of the divine part of man; the pursuit of goodness, truth, beauty, obedience to right, adherence to duty, not from pleasure, interest present or future, or habit or fear, but because it is the call of nature, which must be obeyed, for which no reason can be given stronger than that it is right, and that God has made it pleasing in our sight" (1842, 74–75; see also 73–78).

9. Whitman: "Is it you then that thought yourself less? Is it you that thought the President greater than you? Or the rich better off than you? or the educated wiser than you?" (1860b, chant 3.9).

Chapter 7

1. Pease (1987) conceives of the process in terms of progressive cultural legitimation, in which symbols of the old order are sanitized and reconstructed in the new. The effect is to relieve the new cultural order of the anomie of strangeness while at the same time moving past the extant pathology of the old order. As an illustration, Washington Irving seeks cultural legitimation for post-Revolutionary America, extracting cultural relevance from the British colonial past, while at the same time distancing the new America from that past. To this end, Irving employs hauntings ("Legend of Sleepy Hollow") and suspension of time ("Rip Van Winkle") (Pease 1987, 14–17). Writers of common heroic fiction have employed other mechanisms. Idealized heroes of the Old West—from Daniel Boone, to Natty Bumppo, to Seth Jones—were agents of cultural legitimation in moving between the worlds of civilized society and natural isolation (Butler 1977, 61–64; Slotkin 1998, esp. 63; Bosworth 2010, 297–98).

2. Tyler employs Manly's sister Charlotte's outrageous social posturing as foil to her brother's common virtue. Complaining of Manly's shortcomings, she laments that he lacks the pallid urbanity of more fashionable men about town (presenting instead a "horrid robustness of constitution, that vulgar corn-fed glow of health, which can only serve to alarm an unmarried lady with apprehension, and prove a melancholy memento to a married one") (Tyler 2008, act II, sc. 1). He is so common as to wear his coat for comfort and has no patience at all for the social niceties attendant to a trip to the theater, which, more than anything else, is an exercise in self-presentation. ("Everything is conducted with such decorum. First we bow round to the company in general, then to each one in particular, then we have so many inquiries after each other's health, and we are so happy to meet each other, and it is so many ages since we last had that pleasure, and if a married lady is in company, we have such a sweet dissertation upon her son Bobby's chin-cough; then the curtain rises, then our sensibility is all awake, and then, by the mere force of apprehension, we torture some harmless expression into a double meaning, which the poor author never dreamt of, and then we have recourse to our fans, and then we blush, and then the gentlemen jog one another, peep under the fan, and make the prettiest remarks; and then we giggle and they simper, and they giggle and we simper, and then the curtain drops, and then for nuts and oranges, and then we bow, and it's pray, Ma'am, take it, and pray, Sir, keep it, and oh! not for the world, Sir; and then the curtain rises again, and then we blush and giggle and simper and bow all over again" [2008, act II, sc. 1].)

3. An evocative metaphor for the day, manliness highlighted the independence of the man against the dependence of the boy; the one having developed the capacity for self-governance, the other not yet having learned to temper his passion with reason (Rotundo 1993, 20–23; Kimmel 1996, 18–20). Manliness was also relevant in a more literal sense. Not only was there no expectation that

a girl mature in the same fashion as a boy, but feminine virility was generally considered an unattractive trait (Rotundo 1993, 22).

4. Going even further, the likes of William Makepeace Thayer saw in the acquisition of wealth the finest qualities of heroism. As a December 1894 piece in *Munsey's* had it, America's most valiant "fight the battles of life where they now must be fought, in the markets of the world, not in the fields or forests, and among whom real progress can be made only by manly and moral qualities. Financial exigencies today try a character not less than did the test of fire in more martial times. He who lives a modern business life with unblemished honor throughout, has had quite as much of the reality of struggle, if less of the romance, as had the soldier in earlier days. They who would be leaders in commerce must be fit to stand anywhere" (quoted in Greene 1970, 158).

5. Cather's manifest intent is to demonstrate that the manly qualities of social dominance and rugged individualism attach as readily to one sex as the other. The word "pioneer" attaches uneasily to Bergson, given that she is a second-generation homesteader. In fact, as inspired by Whitman's poem from which Cather's novel draws its title, Bergson's true pioneering lies in the theater of gender equality (Werden 2002).

6. Natty, also known by the nicknames "Leatherstocking" and the "Deerslayer," is a man of two worlds. White and educated in the Christian tradition, he was socialized into the mores of the Delaware Indians. Even more than Daniel Boone, he embodies the duality of the frontier and the conflicted loyalties and affinities it provokes. As would be subtextual to much of the legend of the Old West, Natty represents the interplay between primitive nobility and invasive civilization.

7. Native Americans in particular were a perpetual source of atavistic fascination, providing context for the frontiersman's exploits, while simultaneously establishing her heroic bona fides. As with nature itself, to nineteenth-century European Americans, Native Americans were unpredictable: sometimes benign, sometimes wild and resistant to civilization (Herman 1998, 432; Smith-Rosenberg 2004, 1328–30).

8. The Puritan allegory of capture and escape was similar, reflecting liberation of the soul from the clutches of Satan (see Downing 1980/81).

9. This distinction, underpinning Owen Wister's *The Virginian* and the backstory of the Lone Ranger, is illustrated in Dashiell Hammett's "Corkscrew," in which the Continental Op has been dispatched to "make ladylike" the lawless quarters of rural Arizona. As temporary sheriff, he offers the Milk River Rider employment as his assistant. "I think you're going to have a hell of a lot of fun," Milk River grinned at me, "so I reckon I'll take that job you was offering. But I ain't going to be no deputy myself. I'll play around with you, but I don't want to tie myself up, so I'll have to enforce no laws I don't like" (Hammett 1972, 271).

10. In a similar vein, Marlowe responds to Carmen's dissolution in *The Big Sleep*. "A pretty, spoiled and not very bright little girl who had gone very, very

wrong and nobody was doing anything about it. To hell with the rich. They made me sick" (1995a, 77).

11. In addition to *Red Harvest*, Hammett returns to this motif in his other work. It features prominently in *The Glass Key*, and "Nightmare Town," and to some extent in "Corkscrew," and "This King Business" as well. Chandler touches upon it in *The Big Sleep*. Daly, less nuanced, explores the theme (as in "City of Blood" and "Tainted Power"); as do, among others, Leslie White in "City of Hell"; Frederick Nebel in the "Crimes of Richmond City" and "Graft"; and Joseph T. Shaw in "Greed, Crime, and Politics."

12. Williams describes himself as a halfway house between cops and criminals, willing to shoot it up, but never to bump off a person who didn't need it. Spade is willing to play footsie with both Gutman and Cairo in quest of the Maltese Falcon but admonishes Brigid not to be *too* sure he is as crooked as his reputation.

13. The closing lines of *The Long Goodbye* speak to Marlowe's ultimate disgust and disaffection. Defeated, feeling (again) alone and foolish he concludes, "[Lennox] turned and walked across the floor and out. I watched the door close. I listened to his steps going away down the imitation marble corridor. After a while they got faint, then they got silent. I kept on listening anyway. What for? Did I want him to stop suddenly and turn and come back and talk me out of the way I felt? Well he didn't. That was the last I saw of him. I never saw him again. I never saw any of them again—except the cops. No way has yet been invented to say goodbye to them" (873–74).

14. Specifically, as an editor wrote in 1970, "Captain America is not a representative of America itself, but of the American ideal—individual freedom, individual responsibility, moral sensitivity, integrity, and a willingness to fight for right" (quoted in Jewett and Lawrence 2003, 6).

15. The chronology is not quite as neat as presented here, which is to say there are outliers. The first Western film, for example, was *The Great Train Robbery* in 1903. The first superhero was the short-lived Hugo Hercules who emerged, and disappeared, in that same year (Coogan 2013, 7).

16. It is true that *Batman*, starring Adam West, enjoyed success as a television series from 1966 through 1968. But the tone was ironic, more spoof than celebration of heroism.

17. To put these numbers in context, only four Westerns had grossed $250 million, led by *Django Unchained* ($449 million). *Box Office Mojo* lists *The Departed* (2006, $132 million) as the highest grossing law enforcement film.

Conclusion

1. A good example is the US House of Representatives' House Un-American Activities Committee.

Works Cited

Acampora, Christa Davis. 2002a. "Contesting Nietzsche." *Journal of Nietzsche Studies* 24: 1–4.

———. 2002b. "Nietzsche Contra Homer, Socrates and Paul." *Journal of Nietzsche Studies* 24: 25–53.

Ackrill, J. L. 1980. "Aristotle on *Eudaimonia*." In Amélie Oksenberg Rorty, ed. *Essays on Aristotle's Ethics*. Berkeley: University of California Press.

Adkins, A. W. H. 1982. "Values, Goals, and Emotions in the *Iliad*." *Classical Philology* 77: 292–326.

———. 1978. "*Theoria* versus *Praxis* in the *Nicomachean Ethics* and the *Republic*." *Classical Philology* 73: 297–313.

———. 1960. *Merit and Responsibility: A Study in Greek Values*. Oxford: Clarendon.

Aeschylus. 1926. *Eumenides*. In Herbert Weir Smyth, trans. and ed. *Aeschylus*. Cambridge: Harvard University Press.

Ahrensdorf, Peter J. 2014. *Homer on the Gods and Human Virtue: Creating the Foundations of Classical Civilization*. New York: Cambridge University Press.

Alcock, Susan E. 1991. "Tomb Cult and the Post-Classical Polis." *American Journal of Archaeology* 95: 447–67.

Alexis, Gerhard T. 1966. "Jonathan Edwards and the Theocratic Ideal." *Church History* 35: 328–43.

Allison, Scott T., and George R. Goethals. 2011. *Heroes: What They Do and Why We Need Them*. Oxford: Oxford University Press.

An, Young-Ok. 2011. "Manfred's New Promethean Agon." In Matthew J. A. Green and Piya Lal-Lapinski, eds. *Byron and the Politics of Freedom and Terror*. New York: Palgrave Macmillan.

Anderson, Greg. 2005. "Before *Turannoi* Were Tyrants: Rethinking a Chapter of Early Greek History." *Classical Antiquity* 24: 173–222.

Annus, Epp. 2000. "National Mythology: Past and Present." *Interlitteraria* 5: 115–30.

Anonymous. 1893. "The Ordination of Knighthood." Trans. Edward Morris. In F. S. Ellis, ed. *The Order of Chivalry: "The Order of Chivalry," "Le Ordene de Chevalerie," and "The Ordination of Knighthood."* Hammersmith: Kelmscott Press.

Antonaccio, Carla M. 1995. *Archaeology of Ancestors: Tomb Cult and Hero Cult in Early Greece*. Lanham: Rowman and Littlefield.

———. 1994. "Contesting the Past: Hero Cult, Tomb Cult, and Epic in Early Greece." *American Journal of Archeology* 98: 389–410.

Apollonius Rhodius. 1912. *Argonautica*. Trans. R. C. Seaton. London: William Heinemann.

Appian. 1899. *The Civil Wars*. Trans. Horace White. London: Macmillan.

Appleby, Joyce. 1986. "Republicanism in Old and New Contexts." *William and Mary Quarterly* 43: 20–34.

Aquinas, Thomas. 1947. *Summa Theologica*. Trans. Brothers of the English Dominican Province. Cincinnati: Benziger Brothers.

Aristotle. 2001a. *Metaphysics*. Trans. W. D. Ross. In Richard McKeon, ed. *The Basic Works of Aristotle*. New York: Modern Library.

———. 2001b. *On the Parts of Animals*. Trans. William Ogle. In Richard McKeon, ed. *The Basic Works of Aristotle*. New York: Modern Library.

———. 2001c. *Physics*. Trans. R. P. Hardie and R. K. Gaye. In Richard McKeon, ed. *The Basic Works of Aristotle*. New York: Modern Library.

———. 2001d. *Poetics*. Trans. Ingram Bywater. In Richard McKeon, ed. *The Basic Works of Aristotle*. New York: Modern Library.

———. 2001e. *Posterior Analytics*. Trans. G. R. G. Mure. In Richard McKeon, ed. *The Basic Works of Aristotle*. New York: Modern Library.

———. 1999. In Terrence Irwin, trans. and ed. *Nicomachean Ethics*. 2nd ed. Indianapolis: Hackett.

———. 1962. *The Politics of Aristotle*. Trans. Ernest Baker. New York: Oxford University Press.

———. 1915a. *Ethica Eudemia*. In W. D. Ross, trans. and ed. *The Works of Aristotle*. Oxford: Clarendon.

———. 1915b. *Magna Moralia*. In W. D. Ross, trans. and ed. *The Works of Aristotle*. Oxford: Clarendon.

Arnhart, Larry. 1983. "Statesmanship as Magnanimity: Classical, Christian & Modern." *Polity* 16: 263–83.

Ashley, Leonard R. N. 1965. "Spenser and the Ideal of the Gentleman." *Bibliothèque d'Humanisme et Renaissance* 27: 108–32.

Avramenko, Richard. 2011. *Courage: The Politics of Life and Limb*. South Bend: University of Notre Dame Press.

Baillie, John. 1996. "John Baillie, *An Essay on the Sublime*." In Andrew Ashfield and Peter De Bolla, eds. *The Sublime: A Reader in Eighteenth-Century Aesthetic Theory*. Cambridge: Cambridge University Press.

Bailyn, Bernard. 1967. *The Ideological Origins of the American Revolution*. Cambridge MA: Belknap.

———. 1962. "Political Experience and Enlightenment Ideas in Eighteenth-Century America." *American Historical Review* 67: 339–51.

Bancroft, George. 1997. "On the Progress of Civilization." In Perry Miller, ed. *The Transcendentalists*. New York: MJF Books.

Barker, Elton T. 2009. *Entering the Agon: Dissent and Authority in Homer, Historiography and Tragedy*. Oxford: Oxford University Press.

Barnes, Douglas F. 1978. "Charisma and Religious Leadership: An Historical Analysis." *Journal for the Scientific Study of Religion* 17: 1–18.

Barnouw, Jeffrey. 1980. "The Morality of the Sublime: Kant and Schiller." *Studies in Romanticism* 19: 497–514.

Barron, Robert. 2007. "Augustine's Questions: Why the Augustinian Theology of God Matters Today." *Logos* 10: 35–54.

Beattie, James. 1783. *Dissertations Moral and Critical: On Memory and Imagination, On Dreaming, The Theory of Language, On Fable and Romance, On the Attachments of Kindred, Illustrations on Sublimity*. London: W. Strahan and T. Cadell.

Beaty, Bart. 2019. "The Spectacular Banality of the Superhero." In Alejo Benedetti, ed. *Men of Steel, Women of Wonder*. Fayetteville: University of Arkansas Press.

Becker, Carl L. 1932. *The Heavenly City of the Eighteenth-Century Philosophers*. New Haven: Yale University Press.

Becker, Earnest. 1973. *The Denial of Death*. New York: Free Press.

Becker, Selwyn W., and Alice H. Eagly. 2004. "The Heroism of Women and Men." *American Psychologist* 59: 163–78.

Bellah, Robert N. 1975. *The Broken Covenant: American Civil Religion in Time of Trial*. New York: Seabury Press.

Belok, Michael V. 1968. "The Courtesy Tradition and Early Schoolbooks." *History of Education Quarterly* 8: 306–18.

Benko, Stephen. 1984. *Pagan Rome and the Early Christians*. Bloomington: Indiana University Press.

Bennett, William J. 1992. *The De-Valuing of America: The Fight for Our Culture and Our Children*. New York: Simon and Schuster.

———. 1977. "Let's Bring Back Heroes." *Reader's Digest*. December.

Berger, Harry. 1957. *The Allegorical Temper: Vision and Reality in Book II of Spenser's Faerie Queene*. New Haven: Yale University Press.

Berger, Peter. 1970. "On the Obsolescence of the Concept of Honor." *European Journal of Sociology* 11: 339–47.

Berlin, Isaiah. 1999. *The Roots of Romanticism*. Princeton: Princeton University Press.

———. 1958. *Two Concepts of Liberty*. Oxford: Clarendon.

Black, Anthony. 1997. "Christianity and Republicanism: From St. Cyprian to Rousseau." *American Political Science Review* 91: 647–56.

Blake, Kevin S. 1995. "Zane Grey and Images of the American West." *Geographical Review* 85: 202–16.

Blake, William. 1906. *The Marriage of Heaven and Hell*. Boston: J. W. Luce.

Blessington, Marguerite Countess of. 1850. *Conversations of Lord Byron with the Countess of Blessington*. London: Colburn.
Bloch, Ruth H. 1985. *Visionary Republic: Millennial Themes in American Thought, 1756–1800*. New York: Cambridge University Press.
Blomberg, S. Brock, Gregory D. Hess, and Yaron Raviv. 2009. "Where Have All the Heroes Gone?" *Public Choice* 41: 509–22.
Boatright, Mody C. 1966. "The Beginnings of Cowboy Fiction." *Southwest Review* 51: 11–28.
———. 1951. "The American Myth Rides the Range: Owen Wister's Man on Horseback." *Southwest Review* 36: 157–63.
Bock, Hellmut. 1956. "Anglo-American Common Sense and German Geist." *American Quarterly* 8: 155–65.
Bogart, W. H. 1856. *Daniel Boone and the Hunters of Kentucky*. New York: Miller, Orton and Mulligan.
Bond, Christopher. 2011. *Spenser, Milton and the Redemption of the Epic Hero*. Newark: University of Delaware Press.
Boorstin, Daniel J. 1987. *The Image: A Guide to Pseudo-Events in America*. New York: Harper and Row.
Borgatta, Edgar F., Robert F. Bales, and Arthur S. Couch. 1954. "Some Findings Relevant to the Great Man Theory of Leadership." *American Sociological Review* 19: 755–59.
Bork, Robert H. 1997. *Slouching Towards Gomorrah: Modern Liberalism and America's Decline*. New York: Reganbooks.
Bosworth, A. B. 2000. "The Historical Context of Thucydides' Funeral Oration." *Journal of Hellenic Studies* 120: 1–16.
Bosworth, David. 2010. "Saving the Appearances: John Ford's Rescripting of the American Mythos." *Georgia Review* 64: 293–319.
Bradbury, Malcolm. 1993. *The Modern British Novel*. London: Penguin.
Braithwaite, Richard. 1641. *The English Gentleman and the English Gentlewoman*. London: John Dawson.
Brauer, Jerald C. 1950. "Puritan Mysticism and the Development of Liberalism." *Church History* 19: 151–70.
Broder, Anne. 2008. "Mahikari in Context: *Kamigakari, Chinkon kishin*, and Psychical Investigation in Ōmoto-lineage Religions." *Japanese Journal of Religious Studies* 35: 331–62.
Brownson, Orestes A. 1997. "Francis Bowen." In Perry Miller, ed. *The Transcendentalists*. New York: MJF Books.
Brunt, P. A. 1988. *The Fall of the Roman Republic and Related Essays*. Oxford: Oxford University Press.
———. 1982. "*Nobilitas* and *Novitas*." *Journal of Roman Studies* 72: 1–17.
———. 1962. "The Army and the Land in the Roman Revolution." *Journal of Roman Studies* 52: 69–86.

Bryan, Daniel. 1813. *The Mountain Muse: Comprising the Adventures of Daniel Boone; and the Power of Virtuous and Refined Beauty*. Harrisonburg: Davidson and Bourne.
Bryant, Joseph M. 1996. *Moral Codes and Social Structure in Ancient Greece: A Sociology of Greek Ethics from Homer to the Epicureans and Stoics*. Albany: State University of New York Press.
Bryson, Anna. 1995. "The Rhetoric of Status: Gesture, Demeanour, and the Status of the Gentleman in Sixteenth- and Seventeenth-Century England." In Lucy Gent and Nigel Llewellyn, eds. *Renaissance Bodies: The Human Figure in English Culture c. 1540–1660*. London: Reaktion.
Budziszewski, J. 1999. *The Revenge of Conscience: Politics and the Fall of Man*. Dallas: Spence.
Bunyan, John. 1840. *The Pilgrim's Progress in Two Parts*. London: L. and G. Seeley.
Burgum, Edwin Berry. 1941. "Romanticism." *The Kenyon Review* 3: 479–90.
Burke, Edmund. 1999. "A Philosophical Inquiry into the Origin of Our Ideas of the Sublime and Beautiful with an Introductory Discourse Concerning Taste." In *The Works of the Right Honourable Edmund Burke in Twelve Volumes*. Vol. 1. London: John C. Nimmo.
Butler, Michael D. 1977. "Sons of Oliver Edwards; or, the Other American Hero." *Western American Literature* 12: 53–66.
Byron, George Gordon. 1909. "Prometheus." In William Stanley Braithwaite, ed. *The Book of Georgian Verse*. London: Grant Richards.
———. 1891. *Childe Harold's Pilgrimage*. London: Cassell.
———. 1817. *Manfred: A Dramatic Poem*. London: John Murray.
Cain, Patrick N., and Mary P. Nichols. 2013. "Aristotle's Nod to Homer." In Ann Ward, ed. *Socrates and Dionysius: Philosophy and Art in Dialogue*. Newcastle: Cambridge Scholars Publishing.
Calabrese, Michael A. 1999. "A Knyght Ther Was." In Laura C. Lambdin and Robert T. Lambdin, eds. *Chaucer's Pilgrims: An Historical Guide to the Pilgrims in the Canterbury Tales*. Westport: Praeger.
Callinus. 2008. "Callinus." In M. L. West, trans. and ed. *Greek Lyric Poetry*. Oxford: Oxford University Press.
Campbell, Joseph. 1973. *The Hero with a Thousand Faces*. Princeton: Princeton University Press.
Cantor, Paul A. 2007. "The Politics of the Epic: Wordsworth, Byron, and the Romantic Redefinition of Heroism." *Review of Politics* 69: 375–401.
Carlton. Charles. 1995. *Charles I: The Personal Monarch*. 2nd ed. London: Routledge.
Carlyle, Thomas. 1841. *On Heroes, Hero-Worship and the Heroic in History*. London: James Fraser.
Carpenter, Frederic I. 1931. "The Radicalism of Jonathan Edwards." *New England Quarterly* 4: 629–44.

Carroll, John. 1981. "The Role of Guilt in the Formation of Modern Society: England 1350–1800." *British Journal of Sociology* 32: 459–503.

Carter, Philip. 2000. *Men and the Emergence of Polite Society, Britain 1660–1800*. London: Routledge.

Carwardine, Richard. 2002. "Charles Sellers' 'Antinomians' and 'Arminians': Methodists and the Market Revolution." In Mark A. Noll, ed. *God and Mammon: Protestants, Money, and the Market, 1790–1860*. Oxford: Oxford University Press.

Cather, Willa Sibert. 1913. *O Pioneers!* Boston: Houghton Mifflin.

Chandler, Raymond. 1995a. *The Big Sleep* in *The Big Sleep, Farewell My Lovely, The Long Goodbye*. New York: Quality Paperback.

———. 1995b. *The Long Goodbye* in *The Big Sleep, Farewell My Lovely, The Long Goodbye*. New York: Quality Paperback.

———. 1950. *The Simple Art of Murder*. New York: Ballantine.

Christianson, Paul. 1977. "The Peers, the People, and Parliamentary Management in the First Six Months of the Long Parliament." *Journal of Modern History* 49: 575–99.

Cicero. 2008a. *The Republic*. In *The Republic and the Laws*. Trans. Niall Rudd. Oxford: Oxford University Press.

———. 2008b. *The Laws*. In *The Republic and the Laws*. Trans. Niall Rudd. Oxford: Oxford University Press.

———. 1974. *De Officiis/On Duties*. Trans. Harry G. Edinger. Indianapolis: Bobbs-Merrill.

———. 1908. *The Letters of Cicero*. Vol. 1. Trans. Evelyn S. Shuckburgh. London: George Bell and Sons.

———. 1900. *The Orations of Marcus Tullius Cicero*. Trans. Charles Duke Yonge. New York: Colonial.

Clark, Philip. 2004. "Kantian Morals and Humean Motives." *Philosophy and Phenomenological Research* 68: 109–26.

Clauss, James J. 1993. *The Best of the Argonauts: The Redefinition of the Epic Hero in Book 1 of Apollonius's Argonautica*. Berkeley: University of California Press.

Clay, Jenny Strauss. 2003. *Hesiod's Cosmos*. Cambridge: Cambridge University Press.

Clouse, Robert G. 1969. "Johann Heinrich Alsted and English Millennialism." *Harvard Theological Review* 62: 189–207.

Cmiel, Kenneth. 1990. *Democratic Eloquence: The Fight over Popular Speech in Nineteenth-Century America*. New York: William Morrow.

Colaiaco, James A. 2001. *Socrates against Athens: Philosophy on Trial*. New York: Routledge.

Coldstream, J. N. 1976. "Hero-Cults in the Age of Homer." *Journal of Hellenic Studies* 96: 8–17.

Cole, Susan Guettel. 2004. *Landscapes, Gender and Ritual Space: The Ancient Greek Experience*. Berkeley: University of California Press.

Colish, Marcia L. 1999. "Republicanism, Religion and Machiavelli's Savanarolan Moment." *Journal of the History of Ideas* 60: 597–617.
Connolly, Sharon Bennett. 2017. *Heroines of the Medieval World*. Gloucestershire: Amberley.
Coogan, Peter. 2013. "Comics Predecessors." In Charles Hatfield, Jeet Heer, and Kent Worcester, eds. *The Superhero Reader*. Jackson: University Press of Mississippi.
Corey, David D., and Cecil L. Eubanks. 2003. "Private and Public Virtue in Euripides' Hecuba." *Interpretation* 30: 223–49.
Corfield, Penny. 1992. "The Democratic History of the English Gentleman." *History Today* 42: 40–47.
Cornish, Paul J. 2010. "Augustine's Contribution to the Republican Tradition." *European Journal of Political Theory* 9: 133–48.
Crevecoeur, J. Hector St. John de. 1904. *Letters from an American Farmer*. New York: Fox Duffield.
Cunningham, Lawrence S. 1980. *The Meaning of Saints*. New York: Harper and Row.
Currie, Bruno. 2005. *Pindar and the Cult of Heroes*. Oxford: Oxford University Press.
Curtis, Neal. 2016. *Sovereignty and Superheroes*. Manchester: University of Manchester Press.
Daly, Carroll John. 1927. *The Snarl of the Beast*. New York: Edward J. Clode.
Davis, Blair. 2017. *Movie Comics: Page to Screen, Screen to Page*. New Brunswick: Rutgers University Press.
De Bruyn, Frans. 1987. "Hooking the Leviathan: The Eclipse of the Heroic and the Emergence of the Sublime in Eighteenth-Century British Literature." *Eighteenth Century* 28: 195–215.
De Polignac, François. 1995. *Cults, Territory, and the Origins of the Greek City State*. Trans. Janet Lloyd. Chicago: University of Chicago Press.
Del Noce, Augusto. 2014. *The Crisis of Modernity*. Trans. Carlo Lancellotti. Montreal: McGill-Queen's University Press.
Di Cesare, M. A. 1982. "'Not Less but More Heroic': The Epic Task and the Renaissance Hero." *Yearbook of English Studies* 12: 58–71.
Di Paolo, Marc. 2011. *War, Politics and Superheroes: Ethics and Propaganda in Comics and Film*. Jefferson: McFarland.
Diderot, Denis. 1964. *Rameau's Nephew and Other Works*. Trans. Jacques Barzun and Ralph H. Bowen. Indianapolis: Bobbs-Merrill.
Dittmer, Jason. 2005. "Captain America's Empire: Reflections on Identity, Popular Culture, and Post-9/11 Geopolitics." *Annals of the Association of American Geographers* 95: 626–43.
Dobel, J. Patrick. 1978. "The Corruption of a State." *American Political Science Review* 72: 958–73.
Dodds, E. R. 1959. *The Greeks and the Irrational*. Berkeley: University of California Press.

Donlan, Walter. 1999. "The Aristocratic Ideal in Ancient Greece." In *The Aristocratic Ideal and Selected Papers*. Chicago: Ares.

———. 1982. "Reciprocities in Homer." *Classical World* 75: 137–75.

Downing, David. 1980/81. "'Streams of Scripture Comfort': Mary Rowlandson's Typological Use of the Bible." *Early American Literature* 15: 252–59.

Earl, Donald. 1967. *The Moral and Political Tradition of Rome*. Ithaca: Cornell University Press.

Edwards, Jonathan. 1948. *Fragment 782* reproduced in Perry Miller, "Jonathan Edwards on the Sense of the Heart." *Harvard Theological Review* 41: 123–45.

———. 1840. "An Humble Attempt to Promote Explicit and Visible Union of God's People in Extraordinary Prayer for the Revival of Religion and the Advancement of Christ's Kingdom on Earth." In Edward Hickman, ed. *The Works of Jonathan Edwards*. Vol. II. London: Ball, Arnold, and Co.

———. 1818. *A Careful and Strict Enquiry into the Modern Prevailing Notions of that Freedom of the Will: Which is Supposed to be Essential to Moral Agency, Virtue and Vice, Reward and Punishment, Praise and Blame*. Edinburgh: Ogle, Allardice and Thomson.

———. 1734. *A Divine and Supernatural Light*. Boston: S. Kneeland and T. Green.

Ehrenberg, Victor. 1972. *The Greek State*. 2nd ed. London: Methuen.

Eisenstadt, S. N. and L. Roniger. 1984. *Patrons, Clients and Friends: Interpersonal Relations and the Structure of Trust in Society*. Cambridge: Cambridge University Press.

Eisinger, Chester E. 1947. "The Freehold Concept in Eighteenth-Century American Letters." *William and Mary Quarterly* 4: 42–59.

Eisner, Robert. 1982. "Socrates as Hero." *Philosophy and Literature* 6: 106–18.

Elliot, T. S. 1971. *The Complete Poems and Plays*. New York: Harcourt Brace Jovanovich.

Ellis, Charles Mayo. 1842. *An Essay on Transcendentalism*. Boston: Crocker and Ruggles.

Emerson, Ralph Waldo. 1983a. "The Transcendentalist." In Joel Porte, ed. *Ralph Waldo Emerson: Essays and Lectures*. New York: Literary Classics of America.

———. 1983b. "The Uses of Great Men." In Joel Porte, ed. *Ralph Waldo Emerson: Essays and Lectures*. New York: Literary Classics of America.

———. 1983c. "The Young American." In Joel Porte, ed. *Ralph Waldo Emerson: Essays and Lectures*. New York: Literary Classics of America.

———. 1951a. "Art." In *Emerson's Essays*. New York: Harper and Row.

———. 1951b. "Character." In *Emerson's Essays*. New York: Harper and Row.

———. 1951c. "Experience." In *Emerson's Essays*. New York: Harper and Row.

———. 1951d. "Heroism." In *Emerson's Essays*. New York: Harper and Row.

———. 1951e. "Manners." In *Emerson's Essays*. New York: Harper and Row.

———. 1951f. "Nominalist and Realist." In *Emerson's Essays*. New York: Harper and Row.

———. 1951g. "Self-Reliance." In *Emerson's Essays*. New York: Harper and Row.
———. 1951h. "The Over-Soul." In *Emerson's Essays*. New York: Harper and Row.
———. 1951i. "The Poet." In *Emerson's Essays*. New York: Harper and Row.
———. 1896. "The Present State of Ethical Philosophy." In *Two Unpublished Essays: The Character of Socrates, The Present State of Ethical Philosophy*. Boston: Lamson, Wolffe & Co.
———. 1892. *Representative Men*. Philadelphia: David McKay.
Engmann, Joyce. 1991. "Cosmic Justice in Anaximander." *Phronesis* 36: 1–25.
Euripides. 1938. *Hecuba*. Trans. E. P. Coleridge. In Whitney J. Oates and Eugene O'Neill, Jr. eds. *Euripides: The Complete Greek Drama*. Vol. 1. New York: Random House.
Feeney, D. C. 1986. "Epic Hero and Epic Fable." *Comparative Literature* 38: 137–58.
Ferne, Sir John. 1586. *The Blazon of Gentrie*. London: John V. Vindet.
Ferris, Kerry O. 2001. "Through a Glass, Darkly: The Dynamics of Fan-Celebrity Encounters." *Symbolic Interaction* 24: 25–47.
Fichte, Johann Gottlieb. 2010. *Attempt at a Critique of all Revelation*. Trans. Garrett Green. Cambridge: Cambridge University Press.
Filson, John. 1784. *Discovery, Settlement and Present State of Kentucke*. Wilmington: James Adams.
Fink, Zera S. 1945. *The Classical Republicans*. Evanston: Northwestern University Press.
Finley, M. I. 1970. *Early Greece: The Bronze and Archaic Ages*. London: Chatto and Windus.
———. 1954. *The World of Odysseus*. New York: Viking.
Fishwick, Marshall. 1969. *The Hero: American Style*. New York: David McKay.
———. 1952. "The Cowboy: America's Contribution to the World's Mythology." *Western Folklore* 11: 77–92.
Flint, Timothy. 1856. *The First White Man of the West*. Cincinnati: H. M. Rulison.
———. 1827. "Review of *America* by a Citizen of the United States." *Western Monthly Review* 1: 9–20. Collected in Timothy Flint, ed. *The Western Monthly Review, Volume 1: May 1827, to April 1828, Inclusive*. Cincinnati: E. H. Flint.
Fontana, Ernest. 1995. "Chivalry and Modernity in Raymond Chandler's *The Big Sleep*." In J. K. Van Dover, ed. *The Critical Response to Raymond Chandler*. Westport: Greenwood.
Fontenrose, Joseph Eddy. 1974. "Work, Justice, and Hesiod's Five Ages." *Classical Philology* 69: 1–16.
Foxhall, Lin. 1997. "A View from the Top: Evaluating the Solonian Property Classes." In Lynette G. Mitchell and P. J. Rhodes, eds. *The Development of the Polis in Archaic Greece*. London: Routledge.
French, Warren. 1951. "The Cowboy in the Dime Novel." *University of Texas Studies in English* 30: 219–34.
Friedrich, Carl J. 1940. "Belief in the Common Man." *American Scholar* 9: 350–60.

Frothingham, Octavius Brooks. 1903. *Transcendentalism in New England, A History.* Boston: American Unitarianism Association.
Frye, Northrup. 1957. "Historical Criticism: Theory of Modes." In *Anatomy of Criticism: Four Essays.* Princeton: Princeton University Press.
Fukuyama, Francis. 1992. *The End of History and the Last Man.* New York: Free Press.
Fuller, Benjamin Apthorp Gould. 1915. "The Conflict of Moral Obligation in the Trilogy of Aeschylus." *Harvard Theological Review* 8: 459–79.
Fuller, Margaret. 1907. "Menzel's View of Goethe." In Perry Miller, ed. *The Transcendentalists.* New York: MJF Books.
Gabriel, Ralph H. 1950. "Evangelical Religion and Popular Romanticism in Early Nineteenth-Century America." *Church History* 19: 34–47.
Gardner, E. Clinton. 1988. "Justice in the Puritan Covenantal Tradition." *Annual of the Society of Christian Ethics* 8: 91–111.
Gauthier, René Antoine. 1951. *Magnanimité: L'idéal de la Grandeur dans la Philosophie Païenne et dans la Théologie Chrétienne.* Paris: J. Vrin.
Gelzer, Matthias. 1975. *The Roman Nobility.* Trans. by Robin Seager. Oxford: Basil Blackwell.
George, C. H. 1968. "Puritanism as History and Historiography." *Past & Present* 41: 77–104.
Giddens, Anthony. 1991. *The Consequences of Modernity.* Stanford: Stanford University Press.
Glendon, Mary Ann. 1991. *Rights Talk: The Impoverishment of Political Discourse.* New York: Free Press.
Goethe, Johann Wolfgang von. 1902. *The Sorrows of Young Werther.* Trans. R. D. Boylan. Boston: Francis A. Niccolls.
Goffman, Ken, and Dan Joy. 2005. *Counterculture through the Ages: From Abraham Lincoln to Acid House.* New York: Villard.
Gorman, Vanessa. 2001. "Lucan's Epic *Aristeia* and the Hero of the *Bellum Civile.*" *Classical Journal* 96: 263–90.
Graebner, William. 2013. "'The Man in the Water': The Politics of the American Hero, 1970–1985." *Historian* 75: 517–43.
Grampp, William D. 1951. "The Moral Hero and the Economic Man." *Ethics* 61: 136–50.
Greaves, Richard L. 1985. "The Puritan-Nonconformist Tradition in England, 1560–1700: Historiographical Reflections." *Albion* 4: 449–86.
Grebe, Sabine. 2004. "Augustus' Divine Authority and Vergil's *Aeneid.*" *Vergilius* 50: 35–62.
Greenblatt, Stephen. 2005. *Renaissance Self-Fashioning: From More to Shakespeare.* Chicago: University of Chicago Press.
Greene, Theodore P. 1970. *America's Heroes: The Changing Models of Success in American Magazines.* New York: Oxford University Press.

Greenhalgh, P. A. L. 1972. "Aristocracy and Its Advocates in Archaic Greece." *Greece & Rome* 19: 190–207.
Grene, David. 1940. "Prometheus Unbound." *Classical Philology* 35: 22–38.
Gresseth, Gerald K. 1975. "The Gilgamesh Epic and Homer." *Classical Journal* 70: 1–18.
Griffin, Jasper. 1983. *Homer on Life and Death.* Oxford: Oxford University Press.
Gruen, Erich S. 2011. *Rethinking the Other in Antiquity.* Princeton: Princeton University Press.
———. 1974. *The Last Generation of the Roman Republic.* Berkeley: University of California Press.
Guelzo, Allen C. 1995. "Calvinist Metaphysics to Republican Theory: Jonathan Edwards and James Dana on Freedom of the Will." *Journal of the History of Ideas* 56: 399–418.
Gunn, Giles. 1992. *Thinking Across the American Grain: Ideology, Intellect, and the New Pragmatism.* Chicago: University of Chicago Press.
Hajdu, David. 2008. *The Ten Cent Plague: The Great Comic-Book Scare and How It Changed America.* New York: Farrar, Straus and Giroux.
Hamilton, W. J. 1872. *Old Avoirdupois; or, Steel Coat, the Apache Terror.* New York: Beadle and Adams.
Hammett, Dashiell. 1992. *The Maltese Falcon.* New York: Vintage.
———. 1989. *Red Harvest.* New York: Vintage.
———. 1972. "Corkscrew." In *The Big Knockover: Selected Stories and Short Novels.* New York: Vintage.
Hankins, Barry. 2004. *The Second Great Awakening and the Transcendentalists.* Westport: Greenwood.
Hanley, Ryan Patrick. 2002. "Aristotle on the Greatness of Greatness of Soul." *History of Political Thought* 23: 1–20.
Hardie, W. F. R. 1978. "'Magnanimity' in Aristotle's *Ethics*." *Phronesis* 23: 63–79.
Harris, James. 1744. *Three Treatises: The First Concerning Art; the Second Concerning Music, Painting, and Poetry; the Third Concerning Happiness.* London: H. Woodfall.
Harvey, J., G. Erdos, and L. Turnbull. 2007. "How Do We Perceive Heroes?" In Terje Aven and Jan Erik Vinnem, eds. *Risk, Reliability and Societal Safety.* Vol. 2. London: Taylor and Francis.
Hatch, Nathan O. 1989. *The Democratization of American Christianity.* New Haven: Yale University Press.
———. 1977. *The Sacred Cause of Liberty: Republican Thought and the Millennium in Revolutionary New England.* New Haven: Yale University Press.
Hegel, G. W. F. 1966. In J. B. Baillie, trans. and ed. *The Phenomenology of Mind.* London: George Allen & Unwin.
Heimert, Alan. 1966. *Religion and the American Mind: From the Great Awakening to the Revolution.* Cambridge: Harvard University Press.

Herder, Johann Gottfried von. 1784. *Outlines of a Philosophy of the History of Man*. Trans. T. Churchill. New York: Bergman.
Herman, Daniel J. 1998. "The Other Daniel Boone: The Nascence of a Middle-Class Hunter Hero, 1784–1860." *Journal of the Early Republic* 18: 429–57.
Herodotus. 1952. *The History*. Trans. George Rawlinson. Chicago: William Benton.
Hesiod. 2006. *Works and Days*. In Catherine M. Schlegel and Henry Weinfield, trans. and ed. *Theogony and Works and Days*. Ann Arbor: University of Michigan Press.
Higgins, Michael. 1947. "The Development of the 'Senecal Man': Chapman's *Bussy D'Ambois* and Some Precursors." *Review of English Studies* 23: 24–33.
———. 1945. "Chapman's 'Senecal Man.' A Study in Jacobean Psychology." *Review of English Studies* 21: 183–91.
———. 1944. "The Convention of the Stoic Hero as Handled by Marston." *Modern Language Review* 39: 338–46.
Hill, Christopher. 1964. *Society and Puritanism in Pre-Revolutionary England*. New York: Shocken.
Hobbs, Angela. 2000. *Plato and the Hero: Courage, Manliness and the Impersonal Good*. Cambridge: Cambridge University Press.
Hofstadter, Richard. 1963. *Anti-Intellectualism in American Life*. New York: Knopf.
Holyoak, Keith J., and Derek Powell. 2016. "Deontological Coherence: A Framework for Common Sense Moral Reasoning." *Psychological Bulletin* 142: 1179–1203.
Homer. 1924. *The Iliad*. Trans. A. T. Murray. Cambridge: Harvard University Press.
———. 1919. *The Odyssey*. Trans. A. T. Murray. Cambridge: Harvard University Press.
Hook, Brian S., and R. R. Reno. 2000. *Heroism and the Christian Life: Reclaiming Excellence*. Louisville: Westminster John Knox.
Hopkins, Keith, and Graham Burton. 1985. "Political Succession in the Late Republic." 249–50. In Keith Hopkins, ed. *Death and Renewal. Vol. 2. Sociological Studies in Roman History*. Cambridge: Cambridge University Press.
Howe, Daniel Walker. 2007. *What Hath God Wrought: The Transformation of America, 1815–1848*. New York: Oxford University Press.
Howland, Jacob. 2002. "Aristotle's Great-Souled Man." *Review of Politics* 64: 27–56.
Hubbard, Thomas K. 1992. "Remaking Myth and Rewriting History: Cult Tradition in Pindar's Ninth Nemean." *Harvard Studies in Classical Philology* 94: 77–111.
Hughey, Michael W. 1984. "The Political Covenant: Protestant Foundations of the American State." *State, Culture, and Society* 1: 113–56.
Hume, David. 1888. *A Treatise of Human Nature*. Oxford: Clarendon.
Irwin, Elizabeth. 2005. *Solon and Early Greek Poetry: The Politics of Exhortation*. Cambridge: Cambridge University Press.
Jaffa, Harry V. 1952. *Thomism and Aristotelianism: A Study of the Commentary by Thomas Aquinas on the Nicomachean Ethics*. Chicago: University of Chicago Press.

James, William. 1897. *The Will to Believe, and Other Essays in Popular Philosophy*. New York: Longmans, Green.
Jayawickreme, Eranda, and Paul Di Stefano. 2012. "How Can We Study Heroism? Integrating Persons, Situations and Communities." *Political Psychology* 33: 165–78.
Jewett, Robert, and John Shelton Lawrence. 2003. *Captain America and the Crusade against Evil: The Dilemma of Zealous Nationalism*. Grand Rapids: William D. Eerdmans.
Johnson, Benton. 1992. "On Founders and Followers: Some Factors in the Development of New Religious Movements." *Sociological Analysis* 53: s1–s13.
Johnson, Penelope D. 1975. "Virtus: Transition from Classical Latin to the 'De Civitate Dei.'" *Augustinian Studies* 6: 117–24.
Jones, Christine A. 2013. "Thoughts on 'Heroinism' in French Fairy Tales." *Marvels & Tales* 27: 15–33.
Kaeuper, Richard W. 2009. *Holy Warriors: The Religious Ideology of Chivalry*. Philadelphia: University of Pennsylvania Press.
Kant, Immanuel. 2002. *Groundwork for the Metaphysics of Morals*. Trans. Allen W. Wood. New Haven: Yale University Press.
———. 1998. *Critique of Pure Reason*. Trans. Paul Guyer and Allen W. Wood. Cambridge: Cambridge University Press.
———. 1996. *The Metaphysics of Morals*. Trans. Mary Gregor. Cambridge: Cambridge University Press.
———. 1929. *Immanuel Kant's Critique of Pure Reason*. Trans. Norman Kemp Smith. London: Macmillan.
———. 1914. *Kant's Critique of Judgment*. 2nd rev. ed. Trans. J. H. Bernard. London: Macmillan.
Kaufman, Peter Iver. 1994. "Augustine, Martyrs, and Misery." *Church History* 63: 1–14.
Kearns, Emily. 1989. *The Heroes of Attica*. London: Institute of Classical Studies.
Keats, John. 2007. "Ode to a Nightingale." In John Barnard, ed. *Selected Poems*. London: Penguin Classics.
Keeley, Lawrence H. 1997. *War Before Civilization: The Myth of the Peaceful Savage*. New York: Oxford University Press.
Kelly, Susan, and R. I. M. Dunbar. 2001. "Who Dares, Wins: Heroism Versus Altruism in Women's Mate Choice." *Human Nature* 12: 89–105.
Kelso, Ruth. 1925. "Sixteenth-Century Definitions of the Gentleman in England." *The Journal of English and Germanic Philology* 24: 370–82.
Kendrick, M. Gregory. 2010. *The Heroic Ideal: Western Archetypes from the Greeks to the Present*. Jefferson: McFarland.
Kett, Joseph F. 1977. *Rites of Passaage: Adolescence in America, 1790 to the Present*. New York: Basic Books.
Kimmel, Michael. 1996. *Manhood in America: A Cultural History*. New York: Free Press.

Klapp, Orrin E. 1954. "Heroes, Villains and Fools, as Agents of Social Control." *American Sociological Review* 19: 56–62.

———. 1949. "The Folk Hero." *Journal of American Folklore* 62: 17–25.

Knowles, Ronald. 2001. "The 'All-Attoning Name': The Word 'Patriot' in Seventeenth-Century England." *Modern Language Review* 96: 624–43.

Knox, Israel. 1930. "Tolstoy's Esthetic Definition of Art." *Journal of Philosophy* 27: 65–70.

Koch, G. Adolf. 2009. *Republican Religion: The American Revolution and the Cult of Reason*. Eugene: Wipf and Stock.

Korsgaard, Christine M. 1986. "Aristotle on Function and Virtue." *History of Philosophy Quarterly* 3: 259–79.

Kravitt, Edward F. 1992. "Romanticism Today." *Musical Quarterly* 76: 93–109.

Kymlicka, Will. 1995. *Multicultural Citizenship: A Liberal Theory of Minority Rights*. Oxford: Clarendon.

Lagorio, Valerie M. 1970. "Pan-Brittonic Hagiography and the Arthurian Grail Cycle." *Traditio* 26: 29–61.

Lane, Frederic C. 1966. "At the Roots of Republicanism." *American Historical Review* 71: 403–20.

Latham, Andrew A. 2011. "Theorizing the Crusades: Identity, Institutions, and Religious War in Medieval Latin Christendom." *International Studies Quarterly* 55: 223–43.

Latour, Bruno. 2002. "Morality and Technology: The Ends of the Means." Trans. Couze Venn. *Theory, Culture and Society* 19: 247–60.

Lawrence, D. H. 1964. *Studies in Classic American Literature*. New York: Viking.

Lawrence, Gavin. 1993. "Aristotle and the Ideal Life." *Philosophical Review* 102: 1–34.

Lee, Susanna. 2016. *Hard-Boiled Crime Fiction and the Decline of Moral Authority*. Columbus: Ohio State University Press.

Leverenz, David. 1991. "The Last Real Man in America: From Natty Bumppo to Batman." *American Literary History* 3: 753–81.

Lewis, John. 2006. *Solon the Thinker*. London: Duckworth.

Lewis, R. W. B. 1955. *The American Adam: Innocence, Tragedy and Tradition in the Nineteenth Century*. Chicago: University of Chicago Press.

Lieber, Francis. 1864. *The Character of the Gentleman*. 3rd ed. Philadelphia: J. B. Lippincott.

Lindholm, Charles. 2013. "The Rise of Expressive Authenticity." *Anthropological Quarterly* 86: 361–95.

Linforth, Ivan Mortimer. 1919. *Solon the Athenian*. Berkeley: University of California Press.

Lintott, Andrew. 1999. *The Constitution of the Roman Republic*. Oxford: Oxford University Press.

———. 1990. "Electoral Bribery in the Roman Republic." *Journal of Roman Studies* 80: 1–16.

Livy, Titus. 1936. *History of Rome*. Trans. Evan T. Sage. London: William Heinemann.

Lloyd-Jones, Hugh. 1983. *The Justice of Zeus*. Rev. ed. Berkeley: University of California Press.

Lowell, James Russell. 1902. *Ode Recited at the Commemoration of the Living and Dead Soldiers of Harvard University, July 21, 1865*. Unknown Binding. Access at https://archive.org/details/oderecitedatharv00lowe/page/2.

Lucan, M. Annaeus. 1992. *Civil War*. Trans. Susan H. Braund. Oxford: Oxford University Press.

Lull, Ramon. 1991. *Book of the Order of Chivalry*. Trans. William Caxton. Huntsville: Sam Houston University Press.

Lusztig, Michael. 2017. *The Culturalist Challenge to Liberal Republicanism*. Montreal: McGill-Queen's University Press.

Lyons, Deborah. 1997. *Gender and Immortality: Heroines in Ancient Greek Myth and Cult*. Princeton: Princeton University Press.

Mailer, Gideon. 2011. "Historiographical Review: Nehemias (Scotus) Americanus: Enlightenment and Religion between Scotland and America." *Historical Journal* 54: 241–64.

Manicas, Peter T. 1982. "War, Stasis, and Greek Political Thought." *Comparative Studies in Society and History* 24: 673–88.

Marcus, John T. 1961. "Transcendence and Charisma." *Western Political Quarterly* 14: 236–41.

Markman, Alan M. 1957. "Sir Gawain and the Green Knight." *PMLA* 72: 574–86.

Markovitz, Julia. 2012. "Saints, Heroes, Sages, and Villains." *Philosophical Studies* 158: 289–311.

Martin, John. 1997. "Inventing Sincerity, Refashioning Prudence: The Discovery of the Individual in Renaissance Europe." *American Historical Review* 102: 1309–42.

Massey, James A. 1978. "The Hegelians, the Pietists, and the Nature of Religion." *Journal of Religion* 58: 108–29.

Mathews, Donald G. 1969. "The Second Great Awakening as an Organizing Process, 1780–1830: An Hypothesis." *American Quarterly* 21: 23–43.

McCauley, Barbara A. 1993. "Hero Cults in 5th Century Greece." PhD diss., University of Iowa.

McCutcheon, Lynn E., Rense Lange, and James Houran. 2002. "Conceptualization and Measurement of Celebrity Worship." *British Journal of Psychology* 93: 67–87.

McDonald, Forrest. 1985. *Novus Ordo Seclorum: The Intellectual Origins of the Constitution*. Lawrence: University Press of Kansas.

McDonnell, Myles. 2006. *Roman Manliness*. Cambridge: Cambridge University Press.

McGiffert, Michael. 1982. "Grace and Works: The Rise and Division of Covenant Divinity in Elizabethan Puritanism." *Harvard Theological Review* 75: 463–502.

McGinnis, Joe. 1976. *Heroes*. New York: Touchstone.
McLoughlin, William G. 1980. *Revivals, Awakenings, and Reform: An Essay on Religion and Social Change in America, 1607–1977*. Chicago: University of Chicago Press.
McSweeney, Terence. 2020. *The Contemporary Superhero Film: Projections of Power and Identity*. New York: Wallflower.
McVeigh, Daniel M. 1982. "Manfred's Curse." *Studies in English Literature: 1500–1900* 22: 601–12.
McWilliams, Wilson Carey. 1987. "Civil Religion in the Age of Reason: Thomas Paine on Liberalism, Redemption, and Revolution." *Social Research* 54: 447–90.
Middleton, Niamh. 2005. "Aquinas, the Enlightenment and Darwin." *New Blackfriars* 86: 437–49.
Miller, Dean A. 2002. *The Epic Hero*. Baltimore: Johns Hopkins University Press.
Miller, Perry. 1965. *The Life of the Mind in America: From the Revolution to the Civil War (Books One through Three)*. New York: Harcourt Brace.
———. 1953. "Errand into the Wilderness." *William and Mary Quarterly* 10: 3–32.
———. 1948a. "Jonathan Edwards' Sociology of the Great Awakening." *New England Quarterly* 21: 50–77.
———. 1948b. "Jonathan Edwards on the Sense of the Heart." *Harvard Theological Review* 41: 123–45.
———. 1943. "'Preparation for Salvation' in Seventeenth-Century New England." *Journal of the History of Ideas* 4: 253–86.
———. 1941. "Declension in a Bible Commonwealth." *Proceedings of the American Antiquarian Society* 51: 37–94.
Mitchell, Lynette. 2013. *The Heroic Rulers of Archaic and Classical Greece*. London: Bloomsbury Academic.
Mommsen, Theodor E. 1895. *The History of Rome*. Vol. 3. Trans. by William P. Dickson. New York: Charles Scribner's Sons.
Moore, G. E. 1993. "A Defence of Common Sense." In Thomas Baldwin, ed. *G. E. Moore: Selected Writings*. New York: Baldwin.
Morley, Neville. 2004. "Decadence as a Theory of History." *New Literary History* 35: 573–85.
Morrill, John. 1984. "The Religious Context of the English Civil War." *Transactions of the Royal Historical Society* 34: 155–78.
Morris, Colin. 2001. *The Papal Monarchy: The Western Church from 1050 to 1250*. Oxford: Clarendon.
Morris, Ian. 1996. "The Strong Principle of Equality and the Archaic Origins of Greek Democracy." In Josiah Ober and Charles Hendrick, eds. *Dēmokratia: A Conversation on Democracies, Ancient and Modern*. Princeton: Princeton University Press.

Morrison, Grant. 2011. *Supergods: What Masked Vigilantes, Miraculous Mutants, and a Sun God from Smallville Can Teach Us about Being Human.* New York: Spiegel & Grau.
Mosse, George L. 1960. "Puritan Radicalism and the Enlightenment." *Church History* 29: 429–34.
Mossman, Judith. 1995. *Wild Justice: A Study of Euripides' Hecuba.* Oxford: Clarendon.
Murphy, Arthur Edward. 1965. *The Theory of Practical Reason.* Ed. A. I. Melden. La Salle: Open Court.
Murray, Oswyn. 2001. *Early Greece.* 2nd ed. Cambridge: Harvard University Press.
Nagel, Robert F. 2001. *The Implosion of American Federalism.* New York: Oxford University Press.
Neale, J. E. 1958. "The Elizabethan Political Scene." In J. E. Neale, ed. *Essays in Elizabethan History.* London: Cape.
Nederman, Cary J. 2003. "Rhetoric, Reason, and Republic: Republicanisms—Ancient, Medieval, and Modern." In James Hankins, ed. *Renaissance Civic Humanism.* Cambridge: Cambridge University Press.
Neimneh, Shadi. 2013. "The Anti-Hero in Modernist Fiction: From Irony to Cultural Renewal." *Mosaic* 46: 75–90.
Nietzsche, Friedrich. 2004. *Ecce Homo.* In *Ecce Homo: How One Becomes What One Is & The Antichrist: A Curse on Christianity.* Trans. Thomas Wayne. New York: Algora.
———. 1997. "Schopenhauer as Educator." In Daniel Breazeale, ed. *Untimely Meditations.* Trans. R. J. Hollingdale. Cambridge: Cambridge University Press.
———. 1974. *The Gay Science: With a Prelude in Rhymes and an Appendix of Songs.* Trans. Walter Kaufmann. New York: Vintage.
———. 1968. *Twilight of the Idols: Or How to Philosophize with a Hammer* in *Nietzsche: Twilight of the Idols and The Antichrist.* Trans. R. J. Hollingdale. London: Penguin.
———. 1966. *Thus Spoke Zarathustra.* Trans. Walter Kaufmann. New York: Penguin.
———. 1956a. *The Birth of Tragedy* in *The Birth of Tragedy and the Genealogy of Morals.* Trans. Francis Golffing. New York: Anchor.
———. 1956b. *The Genealogy of Morals* in *The Birth of Tragedy and the Genealogy of Morals.* Trans. Francis Golffing. New York: Anchor.
———. 1955. *Beyond Good and Evil.* Trans. Marianne Cowan. Chicago: Regnery.
———. 1908. *Human, All too Human: A Book for Free Spirits.* Trans. Alexander Harvey. Chicago: Charles H. Kerr.
Noll, Mark A. 2002. *America's God: From Jonathan Edwards to Abraham Lincoln.* Oxford: Oxford University Press.
———. 1993. "The American Revolution and Protestant Evangelicalism." *Journal of Interdisciplinary History* 23: 615–38.

———. 1985. "Common Sense Traditions and American Evangelical Thought." *American Quarterly* 37: 216–38.

O'Connell, Rev. Father James. 1962. "The Withdrawal of the High God in West African Religion: An Essay in Interpretation." *Man* 62: 67–69.

O'Neill, Michael. 2011. "'A Double-Face of False and True': Poetry and Religion in Shelley." *Literature and Theology* 25: 32–46.

Olsthoorn, Peter. 2005. "Honor as a Motive for Making Sacrifices." *Journal of Military Ethics* 4: 183–97.

Owens, Ron. 2010. *Solon of Athens: Poet, Philosopher, Soldier, Statesman*. Eastbourne: Sussex Academic Press.

Paine, Thomas. 1986. *Common Sense*. Harmondsworth: Penguin.

Pangle, Thomas L. 1988. *The Spirit of Modern Republicanism: The Moral Vision of the American Founders and the Philosophy of Locke*. Chicago: University of Chicago Press.

Parker, Henry. 1641. *A Discourse Concerning Puritans. A Vindication of those, Who Uniustly Suffer by the Mistake, Abuse, and Misapplication of that Name. A Tract Necessary and Usefull for these Times*. London: Bostock.

Parker, Theodore. 1997. "A Sermon of Merchants." In Perry Miller, ed. *The Transcendentalists*. New York: MJF Books.

———. 1907. *The Slave Power: The Full Works of Theodore Parker*. Vol. 11. Boston: American Unitarian Association.

———. 1876. *A Discourse of Matters Pertaining to Religion*. London: Trübner and Co.

Peacham, Henry. 1634. *The Compleat Gentleman: Fashioning Him Absolut, in the Most Necessary and Commendable Qualities Concerning Minde and Body, That May be Required in a Noble Gentleman*. London: Francis Constable.

Pearson, Lionel. 1943. "Three Notes on the Funeral Oration of Pericles." *American Journal of Philology* 64: 399–407.

Pease, Donald. 1987. *Visionary Compacts: American Renaissance Writings in Cultural Context*. Madison: University of Wisconsin Press.

Peck, John Mason. 1904. *Makers of American History: Daniel Boone*. New York: University Society.

Peck, Linda Levy. 1981. "Court Patronage and Government Policy." In Guy Fitch Lytle and Stephen Orgel, eds. *Patronage in the Renaissance*. Princeton: Princeton University Press.

Perry, Thomas D. 1968. "Moral Autonomy and Reasonableness." *Journal of Philosophy* 65: 383–401.

Peterson, Michael Thomas. 1992. "Sir Thomas Malory and the English Gentry: Romance, Society, Identity." PhD diss., McMaster University.

Pettit, Philip. 2002. "Keeping Republicanism Simple: On a Difference with Quentin Skinner." *Political Theory* 30: 339–56.

Plato. 2008. 1992. *Statesman*. Trans. J. B. Skremp. Indianapolis: Hackett.

———. 1982a. *Gorgias*. Trans. W. D. Woodhead. In Edith Hamilton and Huntington Cairns, eds. *Plato: The Collected Dialogues including the Letters*. Princeton: Princeton University Press.

———. 1982b. *Laws*. Trans. A. E. Taylor. In Edith Hamilton and Huntington Cairns, eds. *Plato: The Collected Dialogues including the Letters*. Princeton: Princeton University Press.

———. 1982c. *Protagoras*. Trans. W. K. C. Guthrie. In Edith Hamilton and Huntington Cairns, eds. *Plato: The Collected Dialogues including the Letters*. Princeton: Princeton University Press.

———. 1982d. *Republic*. Trans. Paul Shorey. In Edith Hamilton and Huntington Cairns, eds. *Plato: The Collected Dialogues including the Letters*. Princeton: Princeton University Press.

———. 1982e. *Symposium*. Trans. Michael Joyce. In Edith Hamilton and Huntington Cairns, eds. *Plato: The Collected Dialogues including the Letters*. Princeton: Princeton University Press.

———. 1982f. *Timaeus*. Trans. Benjamin Jowett. In Edith Hamilton and Huntington Cairns, eds. *Plato: The Collected Dialogues including the Letters*. Princeton: Princeton University Press.

———. 1981a. *Apology*. In G. M.A. Grube, trans. and ed. *Plato: Five Dialogues*. Indianapolis: Hackett.

———. 1981b. *Euthyphro*. In G. M. A. Grube, trans. and ed. *Plato: Five Dialogues*. Indianapolis: Hackett.

———. 1981c. *Meno*. In G. M. A. Grube, trans. and ed. *Plato: Five Dialogues*. Indianapolis: Hackett.

———. 1981d. *Phaedo*. In G. M. A. Grube, trans. and ed. *Plato: Five Dialogues*. Indianapolis: Hackett.

———. 1974. *Plato's Republic*. Trans. G. M. A. Grube. Indianapolis: Hackett.

———. 1892. *Menexenus*. In Benjamin Jowett, trans. and ed. *The Dialogues of Plato*. 3rd ed. Vol. 2. Oxford: Oxford University Press.

Plutarch. 1920. *Lives*. 11 vols. Trans. Bernadotte Perrin. Cambridge: Loeb.

Pocock, J. G. A. 1975. *The Machiavellian Moment: Florentine Political Thought and the Atlantic Republican Tradition*. Princeton: Princeton University Press.

Poli, Bernard. 1968. "The Hero in France and in America." *Journal of American Studies* 2: 225–38.

Pollack, Sir Frederick. 1882. "The Casuistry of Common Sense." In *Essays in Jurisprudence and Ethics*. London: Macmillan.

Polybius. 2011. *The Histories*. Vol. III. Trans. W. R. Paton, Rev. F. W. Walbank, and Christian Habicht. Cambridge: Harvard University Press.

Porpora, Douglas V. 1996. "Personal Heroes, Religion, and Transcendental Metanarratives." *Sociological Forum* 11: 209–29.

Pruyser, Paul W., and J. Tracy Luke. 1982. "The Epic of Gilgamesh." *American Imago* 39: 73–93.

Querbach, Carl W. 1985. "Hesiod's Myth of the Four Races." *Classical Journal* 81: 1–12.
Raaflaub, Kurt A. 1999. "Archaic and Classical Greece." In Kurt A. Raaflaub and Nathan Stewart Rosenstein, eds. *War and Society in the Ancient and Medieval Worlds: Asia, the Mediterranean, Europe, and Mesoamerica*. Cambridge: Harvard University Press.
Raaflaub, Kurt A., and Robert W. Wallace. 2007. " 'People's Power' and Egalitarian Trends in Archaic Greece." In Kurt A. Raaflaub, Josiah Ober and Robert Wallace, eds. *Democracy in Ancient Greece*. Berkeley: University of California Press.
Raglan, Lord. 1934. "The Hero of Tradition." *Folklore* 45: 212–31.
Rahner, Hugo. 1992. *Church and State in Early Christianity*. San Francisco: Ignatius.
Ramati, Ayval. 2001. "The Hidden Truth of Creation: Newton's Method of Fluxions." *British Journal for the History of Science* 34: 417–38.
Ramet, Sabrina P. 2011. "Dead Kings and National Myths: Why Myths of Founding and Martyrdom Are Important." In Ola Listhaug, Sabrina P. Ramet, and Dragana Dulić, eds. *Civic and Uncivic Values: Serbia in the Post-Milošović Era*. Budapest: Central European University Press.
Rank, Otto. 1914. *The Myth of the Birth of the Hero: A Psychological Interpretation of Mythology*. Trans. F. Robbins and Smith Ely Jelliffe. New York: Journal of Nervous and Mental Disease Publishing Company.
Rawlings, Louis. 2013. "War and Warfare in Ancient Greece." In Brian Campbell and Lawrence A. Tritle, eds. *The Oxford Handbook of Warfare in the Classical World*. Oxford: Oxford University Press.
Rawls, John. 1996. *Political Liberalism*. New York: Columbia University Press.
Reid, Thomas. 1785. *Essays on the Intellectual Power of Man*. Edinburgh: J. Bell and G. G. J.&J. Robinson.
Richmond, Scott C. 2012. "The Exorbitant Lightness of Bodies, or How to Look at Superheroes: Ilinx, Identification and Spider-Man." *Discourse* 34: 113–44.
Ripley, George. 1997. "Letter to the Church in Purchase Street." In Perry Miller, ed. *The Transcendentalists*. New York: MJF Books.
———. 1836. *Discourses on the Philosophy of Religion*. Boston: James Monroe and Company.
Risden, E. L. 1998. "Beowulf, Tolkien, and Epic Epiphanies." *Journal of the Fantastic in the Arts* 35: 192–99.
Robertson, D. W., Jr. 1968. "The Concept of Courtly Love as an Impediment to the Understanding of Medieval Texts." In Francis X. Newman, ed. *The Meaning of Courtly Love*. Albany: SUNY Press.
Rodgers, Daniel T. 1992. "Republicanism: The Career of a Concept." *Journal of American History* 79: 11–38.
Rohr, John von. 1965. "Covenant and Assurance in Early English Puritanism." *Church History* 34: 195–203.

Rollin, Roger R. 1983. "The Lone Ranger and Lenny Skutnik: The Hero as Popular Culture." In Ray B. Browne and Marshall Fishwick, eds. *The Hero in Transition*. Bowling Green: Bowling Green University Press.

Ronda, Bruce E. 2017. *The Fate of Transcendentalism: Secularity, Materiality, and Human Flourishing*. Athens: University of Georgia Press.

Roniger, Luis. 1983. "Modern Patron-Client Relations and Historical Clientelism: Some Clues from Ancient Republican Rome." *European Journal of Sociology* 24: 63–95.

Rosenstein, Nathan S. 1990. *Imperatores Victi: Military Defeat and Aristocratic Competition in the Middle and Late Republic*. Berkeley: University of California Press.

Rossel, Robert D. 1970. "The Great Awakening: An Historical Analysis." *American Journal of Sociology* 75: 907–25.

Rotundo, Anthony. 1993. *American Manhood: Transformations in American Masculinity from the Revolution to the Modern Era*. New York: Basic Books.

Rousseau, Jean-Jacques. 1923a. *A Discourse on the Arts and Sciences*. In *The Social Contract and Discourses*. Trans. G. D. H. Cole. London: Dent.

———. 1923b. *A Discourse on the Origin of Inequality*. In *The Social Contract and Discourses*. Trans. G. D. H. Cole. London: Dent.

———. 1896. *The Confessions of Jean-Jacques Rousseau*. Vol. 1. Trans. Anon. Edinburgh: Oliver and Boyd.

———. 1889. *Profession of Faith of a Savoyard Vicar*. Trans. Olive Schreiner. New York: P. Eckler.

Ruebel, James S. 1991. "Politics and Folktale in the Classical World." *Asian Folklore Studies* 50: 5–33.

Runciman, W. G. 1982. "Origins of States: The Case of Archaic Greece." *Comparative Studies in Society and History* 24: 351–77.

Russell, Jeffrey B. 1965. "Courtly Love as Religious Dissent." *Catholic Historical Review* 51: 31–44.

St. Augustine. 1887a. *City of God*. Trans. J. F. Shaw. In Philip Schaff, ed. *Nicene and Post-Nicene Fathers of the Christian Church*. Vol. II. Buffalo: Christian Literature Company.

———. 1887b. *On the Trinity*. Trans. Arthur West Haddan. In Philip Schaff, ed. *Nicene and Post-Nicene Fathers of the Christian Church*. Vol. III. Buffalo: Christian Literature Company.

———. 1887c. *Reply to Faustus the Manichean*. Trans. Richard Stothert. In Philip Schaff, ed. *Nicene and Post-Nicene Fathers of the Christian Church*. Vol. IV. Buffalo: Christian Literature Company.

Sallust. 1931. In John T. Ramsey and J. C. Rolfe, trans. and ed. *The War with Catiline. The War with Jugurtha*. Cambridge: Loeb.

Sandel, Michael J. 1984. "The Procedural Republic and the Unencumbered Self." *Political Theory* 12: 81–96.

Saxonhouse, Arlene W. 2012. "To Corrupt: The Ambiguity of the Language of Corruption in Ancient Athens." In Manuhuia Barchum, Barry Hindess and Peter Larmour, eds. *Corruption: Expanding the Focus*. Canberra: Australian National University EPress.

Schein, Seth L. 1984. *The Mortal Hero: An Introduction to Homer's Iliad*. Berkeley: University of California Press.

Schiller, Friedrich. 1884a. *Letters on the Aesthetical Education of Man*. In *The Works of Frederick Schiller. Vol. VIII. Aesthetical and Philosophical Essays*. Trans. Anon. Boston: S. E. Cassino.

———. 1884b. *The Moral Utility of Aesthetic Manners*. In *The Works of Frederick Schiller. Vol. VIII. Aesthetical and Philosophical Essays*. Trans. Anon. Boston: S. E. Cassino.

———. 1884c. *On the Sublime*. In *The Works of Frederick Schiller. Vol. VIII. Aesthetical and Philosophical Essays*. Trans. Anon. Boston: S. E. Cassino.

Schlenker, Barry R., Michael F. Weigold, and Kristine A. Schlenker. 2008. "What Makes a Hero? The Impact of Integrity on Admiration and Interpersonal Judgment." *Journal of Personality* 76: 323–55.

Schneewind, J. B. 1998. *The Invention of Moral Autonomy: A History of Modern Moral Philosophy*. Cambridge: Cambridge University Press.

Schofield, Malcolm. 1986. "*Euboulia* in the *Iliad*." *Classical Quarterly* 36: 6–31.

Seaver, Paul S. 1970. *The Puritan Lectureships: The Politics of Religious Dissent, 1560–1662*. Stanford: Stanford University Press.

Segal, Charles. 1978. "'The Myth Was Saved': Reflections on Homer and the Mythology of Plato's *Republic*." *Hermes* 106 Bd., H. 2: 315–36.

Sellers, Charles. 1991. *The Market Revolution: Jacksonian America, 1815–1846*. New York: Oxford University Press.

Shaffer, Thomas L. 1987. *Faith and the Professions*. Provo: Brigham Young University Press.

Shapin, Steven. 1994. *A Social History of Truth: Civility and Science in Seventeenth-Century England*. Chicago: University of Chicago Press.

Shelley, Mary Wollstonecraft. 1888. *Frankenstein: Or, the Modern Prometheus*. London: George Routledge and Sons.

Shelley, Percy Bysshe. 1915. *The Necessity of Atheism*. In Henry Stephens Salt, ed. *Selected Prose Works of Shelley*. London: Watts.

———. 1891. *A Defense of Poetry*. Boston: Ginn and Company.

Sherwin-White, A. N. 1956. "Violence in Roman Politics." *Journal of Roman Studies* 46: 1–9.

Shippey, Tom. 1995. "Tolkien as a Post-War Writer." *Mallorn* 30: 84–93.

Shipps, Kenneth. 1976. "The 'Political Puritan.'" *Church History* 45: 196–205.

Shklar, Judith. 1979. "Let Us Not Be Hypocritical." *Daedalus* 108: 1–25.

Sidney, Sir Philip. 1890. *The Defense of Poesy, Otherwise Known as an Apology for Poetry*. Ed. Albert S. Cook. Boston: Ginn and Company.

Sikorski, Wade. 1993. *Modernity and Technology: Harnessing the Earth to the Slavery of Man.* Tuscaloosa: University of Alabama Press.

Simonton, Dean Keith. 1994. *Greatness: Who Makes History and Why.* New York: Guilford Press.

Simpson, George. 1951. "Science as Morality." *Philosophy of Science* 18: 132–43.

Singer, Marcus G. 1986. "Ethics and Common Sense." *Revue Internationale de Philosophie* 40: 221–58.

Skinner, Quentin. 1990. "The Republican Ideal of Political Liberty." In Gisela Bock, Quentin Skinner and Maurizio Viroli, eds. *Machiavelli and Republicanism.* Cambridge: Cambridge University Press.

Skitka, Linda J., and Elizabeth Mullen. 2002. "The Dark Side of Moral Conviction." *Analyses of Social Issues and Public Policy* 2: 35–41.

Slotkin, Richard. 1998. *The Fatal Environment: The Myth of the Frontier in the Age of Industrialization, 1800–1890.* Norman: University of Oklahoma Press.

Smirnov, Oleg, Holly Arrow, Douglas Kennett, and John Orbell. 2007. "Ancestral War and the Evolutionary Origins of 'Heroism.'" *Journal of Politics* 69: 927–40.

Smith, Adam. 1982. *The Theory of Moral Sentiments.* Ed. D. D. Raphael and A. L. Macfie. Indianapolis: Liberty Fund.

Smith, Henry Nash. 1950. *Virgin Land: The American West as Symbol and Myth.* Cambridge: Harvard University Press.

———. 1948. "The Western Hero in the Dime Novel." *Southwest Review* 33: 276–84.

Smith-Rosenberg, Carroll. 2004. "Surrogate Americans: Masculinity, Masquerade, and the Formation of a National Identity." *PMLA* 119: 1325–35.

Smythe-Palmer, A. 1908. *The Ideal of a Gentleman; Or a Mirror for Gentlefolks.* London: George Routledge and Sons.

Snodgrass, Anthony M. 1980. *Archaic Greece: The Age of Experiment.* London: J. M. Dent.

———. 1965. "The Hoplite Reform and History." *Journal of Hellenic Studies* 85: 110–22.

Solon. 2008. "Solon." In M. L. West, trans. and ed. *Greek Lyric Poetry.* Oxford: Oxford University Press.

Somerville, James. 1986. "Moore's Conception of Common Sense." *Philosophy and Phenomenological Research* 47: 233–53.

Sophocles. 1893. *The Ajax of Sophocles.* Trans. Sir Richard C. Jebb. Cambridge: Cambridge University Press.

———. 1891. *The Antigone of Sophocles.* Trans. Sir Richard C. Jebb. Cambridge: Cambridge University Press.

———. 1887. *The Oedipus Tyrannus of Sophocles.* Trans. Sir Richard C. Jebb. Cambridge: Cambridge University Press.

Speck, Ernest B. 1981. "Mody Boatright's Cowboy as Hero." *Southwest Review* 66: 268–76.

Speier, Hans. 1935. "Honor and Social Structure." *Social Research* 2: 74–79.

Spenser, Edmond. 1903. *Spenser's* The Faerie Queene. Ed. George Armstrong Wauchope. New York: Macmillan.
Starke, Sue P. 2007. *The Heroines of English Pastoral Romance*. Woodbridge: Boydell and Brewer.
Stefanson, Dominic. 2004. "Man as Hero—Hero as Citizen: Models of Heroic Thought and Action in Homer, Plato and Rousseau." PhD diss., University of Adelaide.
Stephens, Ann S. 1862. *Esther: A Story of the Oregon Trail*. London: G. Routledge and Sons.
Stewart, Dugald. 1829. *Outlines of Moral Philosophy*. Edinburgh: Cadell & Co.
Stewart, Rev. Angus. 1999. "The Decline and Fall of New England Congregationalism." *Protestant Reformed Theological Journal* 32: 50–88.
Stone, Lawrence. 1996. *The Causes of the English Revolution, 1529–1642*. London: Routledge.
———. 1980. "The Results of the English Revolutions of the Seventeenth Century." In J. G. A. Pocock, ed. *Three British Revolutions: 1641, 1688, 1776*. Princeton: Princeton University Press.
Stout, Rex. 1979. *The Rubber Band*. New York: Jove.
Streetby, Shelley. 2002. *American Sensations: Class, Empire, and the Production of Popular Culture*. Berkeley: University of California Press.
Sullivan, Michael P., and Anré Venter. 2010. "Defining Heroes through Deductive and Inductive Investigations." *Journal of Social Psychology* 150: 471–84.
———. 2005. "The Hero Within: Inclusion of Heroes into the Self." *Self and Identity* 4: 101–11.
Sullivan, Roger J. 1974. "The Kantian Critique of Aristotle's Moral Philosophy: An Appraisal." *Review of Metaphysics* 28: 25–53.
Svoboda, Frederic. 1983. "The Snub-Nosed Mystique: Observations on the American Detective Hero." *Modern Fiction Studies* 29: 557–68.
Syme, Ronald. 1939. *The Roman Revolution*. Oxford: Clarendon.
Taylor, Charles. 2003. *The Malaise of Modernity*. Toronto: Anansi.
———. 1993. *Reconciling the Solitudes: Essays on Canadianism and Nationalism*. Ed. Guy Laforest. Montreal: McGill-Queen's University Press.
———. 1992. "The Politics of Recognition." In Amy Gutmann, ed. *Multiculturalism: Examining the Politics of Recognition*. Princeton: Princeton University Press.
———. 1991. *The Ethics of Authenticity*. Cambridge: Harvard University Press.
———. 1989. *Sources of the Self: The Making of the Modern Identity*. Cambridge: Harvard University Press.
———. 1985. "Atomism." In *Philosophy and the Human Sciences: Philosophical Papers 2*. Cambridge: Cambridge University Press.
Taylor, Lily Ross. 1971. *Party Politics in the Age of Caesar*. Berkeley: University of California Press.

———. 1942. "Caesar and the Roman Nobility." *Transactions and Proceedings of the American Philological Association* 73: 1–24.
Taylor, Nathaniel W. 1849. *Concio ad Clerum: A Sermon*. New Haven: A. H. Maltby and Homan Hallock.
Taylor, Richard. 2004. "Daniel Boone as American Icon: A Literary View." *Register of the Kentucky Historical Society* 102: 512–33.
Te Selle, Eugene, Jr. 1965. "The Problem of Nature and Grace." *Journal of Religion* 45: 238–49.
Tertullian. 1889. *The Apology of Tertullian and the Meditations of the Emperor Marcus Aurelius Antoninus*. Trans. W. M. Reeve and Jeremy Collier. London: Griffith, Farran, Okeden & Welsh.
Teschke, Benno. 2003. *The Myth of 1648: Class, Geopolitics and the Making of Modern International Relations*. New York: Verso.
Thomas, John L. 1965. "Romantic Reform in America, 1815–1865." *American Quarterly* 17: 656–81.
Thorslev, Peter L., Jr. 1963. "The Romantic Mind Is Its Own Place." *Comparative Literature* 15: 250–68.
———. 1962. *The Byronic Hero: Types and Prototypes*. Minneapolis: University of Minnesota Press.
Thucydides. 1998. *History of the Peloponnesian War*. Trans. Benjamin Jowett. Amherst: Prometheus.
Tillyard, E. M. W. 1966. *The English Epic and Its Background*. New York: Oxford University Press.
Tocqueville, Alexis de. 1941. *Democracy in America*. Vol. 1. Trans. Henry Reeve. New York: J. and H. G. Langley.
Trepavlov, Vadim V. 1995. "The Social Status of the Yakut Epic Hero." *Asian Folklore Studies* 54: 35–48.
Trevor-Roper, H. R. 1959. "The General Crisis of the Seventeenth Century." *Past & Present* 16: 31–64.
Trilling, Lionel. 1972. *Sincerity and Authenticity*. Cambridge: Harvard University Press.
Turner, Frederick Jackson. 1920. "The Significance of the Frontier in American History." In *The Frontier in American History*. New York: Henry Holt.
Tuttle, Darcy. 2021. "'Dutifully They Were Crucified': The Moral and Legal Redemption of the Sabine Women in Augustine's *City of God*." In Susanna Elm and Christopher M. Blunda, eds. *The Late (Wild) Augustine*. Leiden: Brill.
Twain, Mark. 1885. *Huckleberry Finn*. New York: Charles L. Webster.
Tweney, Ryan D. 1997. "Jonathan Edwards and Determinism." *Journal of the History of the Behavioral Sciences* 33: 365–80.
Tyerman, Christopher. 2006. *God's War: A New History of the Crusades*. Cambridge: Belknap Press.

Tyler, Royall. 2008. *The Contrast*. Project Gutenberg Ebook 554. Prod. Judith Boss at www.gutenberg.org/cache/epub/554/pg554-images.html.
Upton-Ward, J. M. 2008. *The Rule of the Templars: The French Text of the Rule of the Order of the Knights Templar*. Rochester: Boydell & Brewer.
Ustick, W. Lee. 1932. "Changing Ideals of Aristocratic Character and Conduct in Seventeenth-Century England." *Modern Philology* 30: 147–66.
Van der Leeuw, Gerardus. 1938. *Religion in Essence and Manifestation: A Study in Phenomenology*. Trans. J. E. Turner. London: George Allen & Unwin.
Vernant, Jean-Pierre. 1960. "Le Mythe Hésiodique des Races. Essai d'Analyse Structurale." *Revue de l'Histoire des Religions* 157: 21–54.
Vlastos, Gregory. 1947. "Equality and Justice in Early Greek Cosmologies." *Classical Philology* 42: 156–78.
———. 1946. "Solonian Justice." *Classical Philology* 41: 65–83.
Walker, Henry J. 1995. *Theseus and Athens*. Oxford: Oxford University Press.
Walker, Obadiah. 1673. *Of Education. Especially of Young Gentlemen. In Two Parts*. Oxon: At the Theatre.
Wallace, Anthony F. C. 1956. "Revitalization Movements." *American Anthropologist* New Series, 58: 264–81.
Wallace, Robert W. 2007. "Revolutions and a New Order in Solonian Athens and Archaic Greece." In Kurt A. Raaflaub, Josiah Ober, and Robert Wallace, eds. *Democracy in Ancient Greece*. Berkeley: University of California Press.
———. 2015. "Equality, the Dêmos, and Law in Archaic Greece." In Delfim F. Leão and Gerhard Thür, eds. *Vorträge zur Griechischen und Hellenistschen Rechtsgeschichte*. Vienna: Austrian Academy of Sciences Press.
Walzer, Michael. 1981. "Philosophy and Democracy." *Political Theory* 9: 379–99.
———. 1969. *The Revolution of the Saints: A Study in the Origins of Radical Politics*. New York: Atheneum.
Ward, Cynthia V. 1991. "The Limits of 'Liberal Republicanism': Why Group-Based Remedies and Republican Citizenship Don't Mix." *Columbia Law Review* 91: 581–607.
Warren, Robert Penn. 1972. "A Dearth of Heroes." *American Heritage* 23: 4–7, 95–99.
Webber, Charles W. 1848. *Old Hicks the Guide; or Adventures in the Camanche Country in Search of a Gold Mine*. New York: Harper and Brothers.
Werden, Douglas. 2002. "'She Had Never Humbled Herself': Alexandra Bergson and Marie Shabata as the 'Real' Pioneers of *O Pioneers!*" *Great Plains Quarterly* 22: 199–215.
West, M. L. 1978. "Commentary." In M. L. West, trans. and ed. *Hesiod: Works and Days*. Oxford: Clarendon.
Whitley, James. 1991. "Social Diversity in Dark Age Greece." *The Annual of the British School at Athens* 86: 341–65.
Whitman, Walt. 1860a. "Walt Whitman [Song of Myself]." In *Leaves of Grass*. Boston: Thayer and Eldridge.

———. 1860b. "Chants Democratic." In *Leaves of Grass*. Boston: Thayer and Eldridge.
Wiersma, S. 1990. "The Ancient Greek Novel and Its Heroines: A Female Paradox." *Mnemosyne* 4th 43: 109–23.
Wilkie, Brian. 1965. *Romantic Poets and Epic Tradition*. Madison: University of Wisconsin Press.
Williams, George Hunston. 1951. "Christology and Church-State Relations in the Fourth Century." *Church History* 20: 3–33.
Winship, Michael P. 2012. *Godly Republicanism: Puritans, Pilgrims, and a City on a Hill*. Cambridge: Harvard University Press.
Winthrop, John. 1996. "A Model of Christian Charity." In *The Journal of John Winthrop, 1630-1649* Abridged ed. Ed. Richard S. Dunn and Laetitia Yeandle. Cambridge: Belknap.
Wolf, Brian, and Phil Zuckerman. 2012. "Deviant Heroes: Nonconformists as Agents of Justice and Social Change." *Deviant Behavior* 33: 639–54.
Wood, Gordon S. 1993. *The Creation of the American Republic, 1776-1787*. New York: W. W. Norton.
Woodhouse, A. S. P. 1949. "Nature and Grace in the *Faerie Queene*." *English Literary History* 16: 194–228.
Wordsworth, William. 1979. *The Prelude 1850*. In Jonathan Wordsworth, M. H. Abrams and Stephen Gill, eds. *The Prelude 1799, 1805, 1850*. New York: W. W. Norton.
———. 1798. *Lines Written a Few Miles above Tintern Abbey*. In William Wordsworth and Samuel Coleridge Taylor, *Lyrical Ballads: With a Few Other Poems*. London: J&A Arch.
Wright, Will. 2001. *The Wild West: The Mythical Cowboy and Social Theory*. Thousand Oaks: Sage.
Young, Iris Marion. 2011. *Justice and the Politics of Difference*. Princeton: Princeton University Press.
Zagorin, Perez. 1970. *The Court and the Country: The Beginning of the English Revolution*. New York: Atheneum.
Zakai, Avihu. 1991. "Orthodoxy in England and New England: Puritans and the Issue of Religious Toleration, 1640–1650." *Proceedings of the American Philosophical Society* 135: 401–41.
Zaret, David. 1989. "Religion and the Rise of Liberal-Democratic Ideology in 17th-Century England." *American Sociological Review* 54: 163–79.
Zuckert, Michael. 2004. "Natural Rights and Protestant Politics." In Thomas S. Engeman and Michael Zuckert, eds. *Protestantism and the American Founding*. South Bend: Notre Dame University Press.
Zumbrunnen, John. 2004. "Elite Domination and the Clever Citizen: Aristophanes' *Archarnians* and *Knights*." *Political Theory* 32: 656–77.

Index

Achilles: actions of, 38, 40, 41, 44, 69, 71, 217n1, 217n3; as heroic example, 13, 14, 15, 17, 199
Aeneas, 11, 18, 38, 41, 50
Aeschylus, 48, 54, 74, 76
aesthetics, 134, 156; and magnanimous hero, 54, 70–75, 76; and Romantic hero, 126, 136–37, 139, 205, 208–9; and Romanticism, 121, 126, 129, 134. *See also* art
affect: and *Frankenstein*, 133–34; and Romantic hero, 116–18, 126–27, 137, 138–39, 208; and Romanticism, 117, 134, 136, 206, 207; and social identity, 132, 134, 135; and spirituality, 130
Agamemnon, 40–41, 44, 69, 71–72, 74, 217n1
alienation, 121, 133–34
American Revolution, 93, 102, 103, 113, 139, 151, 169
Andrew the Hebridean, xvi, 171, 173–74
Anglicanism. *See* Church of England
Antigone, xiv, 72–73
antihero: defined, 33–34; in Greek tragedy, 76; and heroism, 34–35, 114, 115, 118, 138, 186, 199
aristocracy, 169, 203; in Greece, 38, 42–48, 51–52; Roman, 82–83, 86, 87

Aristotle: and Christian republicanism, 94, 95, 114; on completeness, 63, 64, 66–67, 96, 163, 196; and the contemplative life, 64, 65–66, 67, 218n6; cycle of regimes, 196–97; on *eudaemonia*, 63–64, 65, 96; on first principles, 67, 218n7; the great-souled man, xiv, 19, 53, 63, 67–70, 200; institutionalism of, 3, 63, 76, 135, 215n3, 222n1; on just agency, 4, 64; on just balance, 65, 94, 95; and justice, 54, 63–66; on magnanimity, 54, 94, 195, 200, 203; on virtue, 63, 64, 65–66, 67, 68, 75, 218n6
art: and divinity, 130–31; in the Renaissance, 121; and Romanticism, 117–18, 123–27, 134, 205. *See also* aesthetics
Arthur, 11, 13, 17, 18, 20, 102
Augustine, xv, 93, 94, 95–98, 130, 220n2
authenticity, 156, 162; of Romantic hero, xv, 21–22, 28, 116–17, 119–20, 137, 139, 205–6, 208; and Romanticism, 117–18, 122, 130, 132, 138; and social identity, 134–35, 206–7. *See also* social identity

Baptists, 150, 152
Batman, 188, 226n16

Bergson, Alexandra, 23, 174, 220n6, 225n5
big man politics, 42, 43, 46, 51, 78, 88
Big Sleep, The, 186, 225n10, 226n11
boni, 11, 19, 79, 141. See also *optimates*
Boone, Daniel, 24, 164, 168, 171, 177–79, 182, 224n1
Boorstin, Daniel, 32–33, 193, 195, 208
Bumppo, Natty, 24, 164, 171, 175, 179, 182, 224n1, 225n6
Bunyan, John, 50, 109, 111
Byron: *Childe Harold's Pilgrimage*, 22, 128; *Manfred*, 10, 11, 15, 22, 122, 125; *Prometheus*, 10, 11, 22, 23, 125; as Romantic hero, 21, 124, 127

Caesar, 79, 84, 87, 89–90
capacity, 12–13, 14, 16, 18, 21, 112, 145. See also moral capacity, endogenous
Captain America, 187, 189, 226n14
Captain Marvel, 15, 190
Cather, Willa, 23, 174, 220n6, 225n5
celebrity hero, 33, 193, 195, 208
Chandler, Raymond, xvi, 183, 185–86, 192, 226n11
chauvinism, 203–4
chieftains, 42, 43, 52. See also clientelism
Childe Harold's Pilgrimage, 22, 128, 131
chivalric knight: code of, 94, 99–100, 101, 220n3; and courtly love, 50, 95, 100–101, 220n4; heroism of, xv, 9, 10, 16, 18, 38, 94–95, 100
chivalry, 101, 104, 105, 106, 113, 182. See also chivalric knight; cowboy
Christian, 16, 38, 109, 111
Christian hero: and common hero, 94, 95, 104; as epic hero, 94, 112; and goodness, 50, 94, 112; humanism of, 101, 102, 112, 113; magnanimity of, 94, 95, 112–13; medieval, 95–102; and republicanism, 93, 114; role of, 95, 100, 103, 108, 113; and Romantic hero, 94, 95, 114. See also chivalric knight; English country gentleman; magnanimous hero; Puritan saint
Christian republicanism, xiv–xv, 93–94, 102, 103, 113, 114. See also Christian hero
Church of England, xv, 102, 103, 106–9, 112, 139, 150, 153
Cicero, xii, 19, 20, 82, 219n2; civic humanism of, 78–80, 83, 84; on great goodness, 139, 193; on justice, 79, 84, 90; republicanism of, 77, 79, 80, 87, 88, 90
City of God, 97–98
class, 67, 104, 137; and Homeric hero, 38, 44; in Republican Rome, 9, 48, 83, 86–88; and social identity, 135–36
clientelism: defined, 219n5; in Greece, 42, 52; in Republican Rome, 9, 78, 84, 88–89. See also big man politics
common hero: and Christian hero, 94, 95; and citizenship, 141, 167, 168, 169, 190–91; and common sense, 145, 191, 209; corruption of, 192, 212–13; as defender, 8, 23–24, 141, 167, 168, 190; egalitarianism of, 139, 142, 163, 171, 209; emergence of, xv, 24, 28, 167–69, 171, 183, 187–88, 191; and English country gentleman, 104, 163; examples of, xvi, 23, 24, 141, 164, 210; in film, 179, 186, 189, 190, 226n15, 226n17; and goodness, 143, 146, 157, 160–61, 163, 164, 168, 191–92, 210; and greatness, 23, 25, 141, 161, 163, 164; heroic completeness of, 196, 204; individualism of, 141, 142,

144, 146, 151, 171, 191; just agency of, xvi, 23, 143, 144, 160, 168, 169; in literature, 168, 178–81, 183, 189, 190, 210, 224n1, 226n16; and magnanimity, 141, 142, 157, 161, 169, 190–91; and magnanimous hero, 143, 174, 209–10, 211; on morality, 23, 25, 27, 142–43, 160, 191, 209, 210–11, 222n1; as nation builder, 12, 24, 142, 167, 168, 190, 191; as redeemer, 141, 167, 168, 190; republican elements of, 141, 142, 163, 164–65, 167, 171, 191; and Romantic hero, 118, 139–40, 142–43, 164, 209, 211; rural/urban distinction, 174–75; scholarship on, 28–29; social virtues of, 209, 210–13; as steward, 23–24, 141, 167–69, 190–91; and the transcendent life, 23, 143, 161, 222n1; and transcendentalism, 24, 28, 157, 159, 160–61, 162–63, 209, 211; virtue of, 161, 162, 171, 191, 210

common sense: American emergence of, xvi, 146–47, 150–51, 154–55; and the common hero, 145, 171, 175, 180, 181, 183, 186, 191, 209; defined, 143–44; and moral competence, 143–45, 155, 156; principles of, 145–46; and reasonableness, 210; in the Second Great Awakening, 152, 153, 165

completeness: Aristotelian, 63, 64, 66–67, 96, 163, 218n4; heroic, xii, xvi, 196–97, 204–5, 213; Renaissance ideal of, 103, 105, 220n6

contemplative life, 65, 66. See also *eudaemonia*; good life; philosophical life

contextual authenticity, 134–35. See also social identity

Continental Op, xvi, 183–84, 186, 225n9

Contrast, The, 170–71

Cooper, James Fennimore, 24, 168, 180

corruption: in Archaic Age Greece, 46, 62; and common hero, 10, 168, 183–86, 192, 212–13; and epic hero, 199–200, 213; and heroism, 8, 9, 195, 196–97; and magnanimous hero, 54, 203–4, 213; of regime types, 3; in Republican Rome, 78, 79, 84–85, 87–88; and Romantic hero, 207–9, 213. See also clientelism

cosmic harmony, 55, 59, 126. See also just condition

cosmic justice, xii, 3–4, 63, 68, 101; and Christian republicanism, xiv, 93–94; in Greek tragedy, 71–72, 74; Hesiod on, 55, 75; and the republic, 42, 52, 54. See also just agency; just balance; just condition; justice

cosmic obligation, xv, 17, 19, 22, 118, 142. See also just agency; obligation; republican virtue

courtly love, 95, 100–101, 182, 220n4

cowboy, 24, 177, 181–83, 184, 186, 210

Creon, 72–73, 74

Crevecoeur, Hector St. John de, xvi, 168, 171, 173

Crusades, 98–99

culture of rectitude, 201, 202, 203–4

cycle of regimes, 196–97

Daly, Carroll John, xvi, 183, 226n11

defender: Christian hero as, 95, 100; common hero as, 8, 23–24, 141, 167, 168, 175–76, 179, 186, 187, 190; defined, 8; epic hero as, 18, 197; magnanimous hero as, 200;

defender *(continued)*
  republican hero as, 7, 195; in Republican Rome, 77, 90
depravity, 124–25
Diderot, 123–24
dignitas, 83, 123, 135, 137, 172, 219n3
dignity, 105, 142, 172, 219n3; and Romantic hero, xv, 119, 135, 136, 137, 138–39; and Romanticism, 22, 117, 118, 123–24, 126, 133
dime novels, 168, 179, 180–81

Edwards, Jonathan, 58, 144, 148, 149
efficacy, 198–200, 203
egalitarianism: and the American republic, 163, 167; and common hero, 139, 142, 163, 168, 171, 176; and Romanticism, 118, 208–9. *See also* equality
egoism, 117–18, 119, 128, 132
egoistical sublime, 127–28, 132, 208
Eleatic Stranger, 9, 61, 62
Emerson, Ralph Waldo, 130, 132, 145; and common hero, 24, 25, 28, 142, 160–63, 182, 183, 186, 189; and the over-soul, xvi, 25, 144, 189, 206, 223n6; and transcendentalism, 156–57, 162, 186
English Church. *See* Church of England
English Civil War, xv, 103, 110
English country gentleman: and common hero, 104, 163; as hero type, xv, 9, 95, 102–7; Puritanism of, 95, 102, 108, 110, 112, 114; as redeemer, 10, 95, 103; republican sentiments of, 102–4, 106, 111, 112, 114; and Romantic hero, 104, 115, 116
Enlightenment, the: and early America, 148, 150; and heroism, xv, 197, 213; moral philosophy of, xv, 6, 22, 33, 102, 111, 115, 116; Scottish, xvi, 6, 144, 150
epic hero: athletic competitions of, 44, 217n5; Christian hero as, 94, 112; and common hero, 174, 188; corruption of, 199–200, 213; as defender, 18, 197; defined, 16–17, 37, 197; estimability of, 17–18, 48, 50, 52, 197, 216n11; goodness and, xiv, 17–18, 38, 48–50, 52, 216n11; greatness and, 16–17, 27, 37, 38, 48–50, 52, 197; and magnanimous hero, 60, 77, 200; scholarship on, 26–27; social virtues of, 196, 198–200, 203. *See also* Homeric hero
equality: and common hero, 142, 144, 209; in early America, 150, 155; and ingenuity, 204; and Romantic hero, 23, 126, 137–38, 206, 207, 208–9; and Romanticism, xv, 118, 135–36. *See also* egalitarianism
essentialist communities, 134–36, 137
estimability: as attribute of hero, 12, 13–14, 15; and Christian hero, 97, 104; and common hero, 23; and epic hero, 17–18, 48, 50–52, 197, 216n11; and magnanimous hero, 53, 54, 63; and Romantic hero, 22, 116, 124, 128, 138. *See also* goodness
ethics: and aesthetics, 6, 126, 209; Aristotle on, 63, 65; and chivalry, 100; and common hero, 146, 181, 209–10, 211; in the Enlightenment, 33, 121; and magnanimity, 70, 76, 126, 203; and Romanticism, 115, 117, 121, 126, 205; virtue, 27, 52, 126
eudaemonia, 53, 63–64, 65, 96, 218n4, 218n6. *See also* contemplative life; good life; philosophical life
Euripedes, 48, 54, 71, 72, 76

evangelism, 148, 149, 152, 153–54, 155, 165
exemplar: Christian hero as, 95, 113; common hero as, 23, 190–91; examples of, 10–11; Homeric hero as, 17, 38; magnanimous hero as, 19, 20; republican hero as, 7, 195; in Republican Rome, 77, 79; Romantic hero as, 11, 22, 116

Faerie Queene, 11, 15, 18, 102
feminist movement, 136–37
Filson, John, 177–78
Finney, Charles Grandison, 144, 153
First Great Awakening, 144, 148–49, 152, 165
formal equality, 137, 207
Frankenstein, 10, 22, 121, 132, 133–34, 195
French Revolution, 9, 126, 133, 139, 208
frontier life, 168, 173–79, 184, 225n7

Galahad, 16, 18, 20, 50, 102
Gilgamesh, 38–39
Glorious Revolution, xv, 9, 103, 112
gods: and contemplative life, 65; and Hesiod's five ages, 54, 55–57; laws of the, 54, 71, 72, 73, 74; and mortals, 39, 40, 54, 57–58, 216n1
Goethe, 22, 121
Golden Fleece, 16, 49
good, the, 4, 5, 66, 118, 126, 127, 201. *See also* goodness
good life, 21, 30, 32, 63, 118, 206
goodness: Aristotle on, 64–65, 67, 70; Augustinian, 130; and Christian hero, 94, 112; and Ciceronian republicanism, 77, 79–80, 90; and common hero, 16, 25, 143, 146, 157, 160–61, 163–64, 168, 180, 185–87, 191–92, 210; and epic hero, xiv, 17–18, 38, 48–50, 52, 199, 216n11; and God, 95, 97, 98; and heroic capacity, 13, 16, 26–27, 216n8; Hesiod and, 55; and ingenuity, 201; in Jacksonian America, 158; and magnanimous hero, 16, 18–20, 53, 60, 62, 200, 216n11; modernity critics on, 29, 32; in Republican Rome, 77–78, 79, 84, 90, 139; and republicanism, xii, 52; and Romantic hero, 115, 119, 138, 216n11; Socrates on, 62, 70, 77, 117, 202. *See also* good, the; greatness; great-souled man; magnanimity
Gracchi assassinations, 86–87
grace, order of, 2, 19, 149, 216n13; Augustine on, xv, 96–97; and Christian hero, 93, 95, 100, 112, 113, 114; and modernism, xi, 30–31, 35; and Puritanism, 103, 107, 110, 112; and republicanism, 94, 102
Great Awakening, 114. *See also* First Great Awakening; Second Great Awakening
great man: and heroism, 25, 41, 52; role of, 28, 54, 84, 90, 112, 162
greatness: and Christian hero, 94, 112; and common hero, 23, 25, 141, 161, 163, 164; and epic hero, 16–17, 37–38, 39, 48–50, 52, 60, 197; and heroic capacity, 13, 16, 26–27; and Homeric hero, 30, 42, 47, 51; and magnanimous hero, 16, 18, 53, 60; and modernity, 29, 31, 32, 200, 211, 213; in Republican Rome, 77–78, 79, 84, 90, 98; and republican virtue, xii, 52; and Romantic hero, 116; and superhero, 188–89, 217n7. *See also* goodness; great-souled man

great-souled man, 19, 53, 63, 67, 68, 69–70, 76, 200. *See also* Aristotle
Greek tragedy, xiv, 10, 18, 20, 54, 70–76
Grey, Zane, 180, 182

Hammett, Dashiell, xvi, 183–84, 192, 225n9, 226n11
hard-boiled detective, xvi, 10, 24, 141, 168, 183–87, 189, 210
Hector, 40, 41
Hecuba, xiv, 71–72
hero: attributes of, 12–14; condition of, 12, 14–16; critics of modernity on, 29–33; cultural impact of, 7, 10–12; defined, 1, 12; Hesiodic age of, 56–57; institutional impact of, 7–10; market for, 78, 80–83; in Republican Rome, 77–78; scholarship on, 25–29; unsung, 14. *See also* antihero; celebrity hero; Christian hero; common hero; epic hero; heroine; Homeric hero; magnanimous hero; postheroism; Romantic hero
Herodotus, 39, 49
heroine, 15, 187–88, 215n5, 220n6. *See also* hero
Hesiod, xii, 46; five ages of, xiv, 55–57, 218n2; on heroes, 56–57, 17, 193, 194; on republican justice, 54, 55–58, 75
Hickock, Wild Bill, 179, 181
Holy Grail, 38, 102
Homer, xiv, 40, 44, 57. *See also* Achilles; Homeric hero
Homeric hero: and aristocracy of Archaic Age Greece, xiv, 38, 43–45; greatness of, 26–27, 40, 42, 47, 51, 60; honor and, 39–41, 49, 51, 60, 197; immortality quest of, 39–41, 197; and justice, 62, 75; as nation builder, 17, 38, 51; republican legacy of, 18, 38, 42, 51; virtues of, 42, 50, 51. *See also* Achilles; epic hero
homesteader, 174, 184, 210, 225n5
honor, 60, 68, 69–70, 71, 82–83, 175
Huckleberry Finn, 158–59, 171
humanism: Christian, xv, 20; and Christian hero, 101, 102, 104, 112, 113; and Christian republicanism, 94, 102; civic, 78–80, 84, 130; of Solon, 47–48, 58, 75

individualism: of common hero, 141–42, 144, 146, 151, 167, 171, 176, 182–83, 191; in early America, 150, 151, 154, 155, 165; of Romantic hero, 116
ingenuity, 201–2, 204
intersubjectivity, 41, 51, 132, 168, 177
Isles of the Blest, 56, 57, 178, 219n12

Jason, 16, 48–49
just agency, 5, 47, 80, 101, 155; Aristotle on, 4, 64; and common hero, xvi, 23, 143, 144, 160, 168, 169, 175, 183; and epic hero, 17, 38; and heroic qualities, xii, 12, 213, 216n8; Hesiodic, 55, 57; and magnanimity, 19, 70; and republicanism, 6–7, 52, 54, 93–94; and Romanticism, 22, 137, 138. *See also* cosmic justice
just balance: Aristotle on, 65, 94, 95; in chivalric code, 101; in heroism, xii, 38, 80; and magnanimity, 59, 70; and republicanism, xiv–xv, 3, 52, 54, 94; Solon on, 47, 54. *See also* cosmic justice; Solon
just condition: in chivalric code, 101; in heroism, xii, 38, 58, 59, 169, 183; and magnanimity, 58, 59, 70;

philosophy on, xv, 4, 55, 64, 96, 218n2; and republicanism, xiv–xv, 3, 5, 52, 54, 93, 94; Socrates on, 218n2. *See also* cosmic justice
just war, 98, 99
justice, 35, 39, 77, 87, 98, 155, 207; Cicero on, 79, 84, 90; and common hero, 181, 184; and Greek tragedy, 54, 70–75, 76; Hesiod and republican, xiv, 54, 55–58, 75; and magnanimous hero, 53, 54, 59, 62, 63–66, 200; and modernity, 31–32; and Romantic hero, 116, 124, 127, 209; Solon on, 38, 47, 52, 62, 75. *See also* cosmic justice

Kant, Immanuel, 142, 144, 222n4
Keats, John, 103, 127, 208. *See also* egoistical sublime
King, Martin Luther, Jr., 10, 20, 136, 201
knowledge, 59, 60, 62, 69. *See also* wisdom

Lancelot, 18, 102, 220n5
last man, 22, 29–30, 31, 32–33, 124, 199
Leatherstocking. *See* Bumppo, Natty
liberty, 6, 31, 145, 157; and common hero, 144, 180, 191, 210; corruption of, 208–9, 210, 212; in early America, 10, 139, 148, 150, 151, 153, 155, 191; and Romantic hero, 120, 206–7, 208–9; and Romanticism, xv, 117, 138
Livy, 78, 84, 90
Lone Ranger, 164, 189, 225n9
Long Goodbye, The, 185, 226n13

Madison, James, 78, 81, 91, 191
magnanimity, 52, 121, 135, 138, 203; asymptotic, 69, 78, 87, 90; and Christian hero, 95, 102, 103, 112–13; and common hero, 141, 142, 157, 161, 169, 176, 190–91; corruption of, 195, 209, 212; of God, 96, 98, 100, 113
magnanimous hero: Aristotle on, 54, 61, 67, 69, 94; and common hero, 143, 174, 185, 209–10, 211; corruption of, 202–5, 213; examples of, 19, 20–21, 53, 200, 201; and goodness, 18, 53, 60, 200, 216n11; and greatness, 18, 27, 53, 60; and Greek tragedy, 54, 70–76; and justice, 53, 54, 58, 59, 62, 63, 200; and modernity, 20, 200–201; philosopher as, 53, 60, 62–63, 75–76; as redeemer, 19, 20–21, 54, 63, 200; in Republican Rome, 77, 78, 80, 81, 86, 90; and Romantic hero, 122–23; social virtues of, 196, 201–5; and Socrates, 27, 53, 54, 58, 59–63, 67, 69, 75–76, 94, 202, 203; virtue of, 18–19, 53, 63, 123. *See also boni*; great-souled man; *optimates*; philosopher king
Manfred, 10, 11, 15, 22, 122, 125, 127, 131, 162
manliness, 168, 170, 171, 175, 188, 224n3, 225n5
Manly, Colonel Henry, xvi, 170–71, 224n2
Marius, 79, 83, 87, 88–89
Marlowe, Philip, xvi, 183–86, 225n10, 226n13
millennialism, xv, 94, 95, 102, 103, 107, 110
Milton, John, 124, 132, 133
modernity: and antiheroism, 33–34; criticism of, xi–xii, 20, 29–33, 35; and heroism, xii, xvi–xvii, 193–94, 213. *See also* Boorstin, Daniel; Nietzsche, Friedrich; Taylor, Charles

monomyth, 8, 15, 25, 189
moral agency, 7, 114, 152, 157; and common hero, 23, 25, 28, 143, 191; and the Enlightenment, xv, 111; and Romantic hero, 21, 23
moral capacity, endogenous, 6, 102, 200, 203, 211
moral competence: and common sense, 143–45, 155, 156; and heroism, xiv, 143, 173, 210
moral intuition: and common hero, 143, 157, 159, 162, 189, 191, 209; versus moral convention, 159–60; and transcendentalism, xvi, 7, 157, 159, 165, 191
moral obligation, 72, 74, 201, 212
moral order: and common hero, 184, 187, 191, 210–11, 212; and Romantic hero, 206, 209
morality: and common hero, 142–43, 160, 168, 175, 181–83, 185, 186, 222n1; and common sense, 145–46, 156; culture of rectitude, 201, 203–4; in early America, 147–48, 152, 153, 155, 158, 165; Enlightenment philosophy of, xv, 6, 22, 102, 111, 115, 116; in Republican Rome, 84–86; and Romantic hero, 21, 23, 27–28, 120, 122, 126–27, 135, 137–38, 206; and Romanticism, 102, 114, 115, 116, 117; and transcendentalism, 7, 144–45, 156–57, 159–60, 162
mos maiorum, 19, 78, 79, 81, 86, 89

nation builder: common hero as, 24, 142, 167, 168, 174, 175, 190, 191; epic hero as, 197; examples of, 11–12; Homeric hero as, 17, 38, 51; and Old West literature, 178, 179, 180; republican hero as, 7; in Republican Rome, 77, 90; Romantic hero as, 23
Native Americans, 177–78, 180, 225n7
nature: in frontier life, 173, 175–76, 178–79, 180, 183, 184; and Romantic hero, 21, 137; and Romanticism, 114, 115, 117, 118, 120–23, 132
nature, order of: Augustine on, xv, 96–97; and Christian hero, 93, 95, 100, 101, 110, 112, 114; in early America, 152, 165; and Greek tragedy, 54, 71; and magnanimous hero, 19, 200; and modernism, 30–31, 32–33, 35; and republicanism, 2, 94, 102, 114; and Romantic hero, 21
Nietzsche, Friedrich: as critic of modernity, 29–30, 31, 193; on the last man, 124, 199; on the overman, 119, 206
nihilism, 194–95, 208. *See also* modernity

obligation: defined, 4–5; culture of rectitude, 201; in Greek tragedy, 71, 72, 74; and hero types, 17, 19, 52; and Romanticism, xv, 128–32, 138; to self, 4, 128, 138; Solon on, 48. *See also* cosmic obligation; moral obligation; republican virtue; social obligation; virtue
Odysseus, 15, 38, 71, 72, 217n1
Oedipus trilogy, 15, 72–74
Old West: common hero in, xvi, 179–83, 224n1, 225n6; in film, 179, 189, 226n15, 226n17; Romanticism of, 174, 180, 182. *See also* cowboy; dime novels; frontier life; homesteader
oligarchy, 60, 82, 203

optimates, 79, 87, 89. *See also* boni
order of grace. *See* grace, order of
order of nature. *See* nature, order of
ordinary life: Aristotle on, 64; described by Charles Taylor, 4, 30, 31, 32; and heroism, 7, 13, 33, 53, 119, 144. *See also* transcendent life
overman, 29, 30, 119, 206
over-soul, xvi, 25, 144, 156, 189, 206, 223n6. *See also* Emerson, Ralph Waldo

Parks, Rosa, 10, 21, 136
Patroclus, 40, 41, 44, 45, 69, 217n3
Peloponnesian War, 61, 69, 222n1
"people like us," 7, 118, 132, 136, 204, 207. *See also* usness
Pericles, 61, 218n3, 222n1
philosopher: as magnanimous hero, 53, 60, 62–63, 75–76; Socratic, 67, 96. *See also* philosopher king
philosopher king: heroic completion in, 196; as magnanimous hero, 19, 127, 200–201, 202; in the modern era, 212; Socratic, xiv, 19, 59, 67, 68, 195
philosophical life, 64, 65, 66. See also *eudaemonia*; good life
pioneer, 174, 225n5. *See also* homesteader
placefulness, 135–36, 206
Plato, 48, 55, 118, 193, 200
Plutarch, 49, 69, 82, 133
poetry, 39, 116, 130–31
Polymestor, 71, 72
Pompey, 18, 79, 89
populism, 83, 84, 87, 89
postheroism, xi, xii, 196
Presbyterians, 150, 153
Priam, 41, 71
primary hero, 17–18, 27, 101–2

Prometheus: myth of, 57, 123, 124; as Romantic hero, 10, 11, 22, 23, 125, 128
Protestantism: early American, xvi, 94, 114, 150, 154, 167, 181; English, 11, 38, 107, 221n8; orders of nature and grace, 216n13. *See also* evangelism; Puritanism
prudence, 5, 67
public service, 77–78, 80–83, 87
Puritan republic, 95, 103, 108, 109, 110–12, 165
Puritan Revolution, 9, 93, 102, 109, 111, 112, 139, 152
Puritan saint: millennialism of, xv, 94, 95, 103, 107, 110; as redeemer, 10, 95; republicanism of, 103, 107–8, 109, 110–11, 114, 221n9; as steward, 9, 95
Puritanism, 220n1, 225n8; and the Church of England, xv, 107, 108, 109; in early America, 147–50, 151; ecclesiastical, 108–9, 111, 114; English country gentleman, 102, 108; failure of the Puritan republic, 95, 110–12; political, 108–9, 114

quests, 15–16, 49, 50. *See also* epic hero; Gilgamesh; Holy Grail; Homeric hero

Rameau's Nephew, 11, 123–24, 208
ranger, 179–80
Real Whigs, xv, 104, 110, 112, 114
reason: 4, 59, 67, 119, 129, 153; and affect, 126–27; and common hero, 143, 209; and *Frankenstein*, 133–34; and Romantic hero, 205, 207–8; and Romanticism, 123, 126
reasonableness, 201, 210–12

recognition: and estimability, 13, 14, 17; and hero types, 44, 113, 136, 151, 168, 175; social, 122, 137; and social identity, 207, 209

Red Harvest, 184, 186, 226n11

redeemer: Christian hero as, 95, 103; common hero as, 141, 167, 168, 186, 190; examples of, 9–10, 22–23; magnanimous hero as, 19, 20–21, 54, 63, 200; republican hero as, 7, 195; in Republican Rome, 77, 90; Romantic hero as, 22–23, 116, 119, 135, 136, 205

redemptive hero. *See* redeemer

republican hero: cultural impact of, 7, 10–12; functions of, 2, 7, 195; heroic completeness in, 16, 196–97, 200, 204–5, 213; institutional impact of, 7–10; and the modern age, xii, xvi–xvii, 2, 193–94, 213; types of, 16–25. *See also* Christian hero; common hero; epic hero; Homeric hero; magnanimous hero; republicanism; Romantic hero

republican virtue, xii, 153; and common hero, 171, 177, 191; and corruption, 208, 213; and epic hero, 17, 48; and obligation, xv, 5, 128, 138, 191; and Romantic hero, xv, 116, 118, 128, 132, 138, 208. *See also* obligation; virtue

republicanism: ancient, 25, 52, 54, 139, 172, 210; classical versus modern, 6–7, 93, 104, 112; and common hero, 167; defined, 3, 5–6; and English country gentleman, 102–4, 106, 111; and epic hero, 38, 47–48, 48–49; evolution of, xiii, 6–7, 52, 54, 75, 77, 90, 94, 102, 112, 114, 115, 139; and heroic qualities, xii–xiii, 13; and Homeric hero, 38, 42, 51; institutional structure of, 3–4; modern, 3, 6, 93, 95, 104, 114–15, 139, 183, 194, 213, 219n3; and the Puritan saint, 103, 107–8, 109, 110–11, 112, 221n9; and Romantic hero, 115, 127–28, 136, 139; Solonian, 47, 52, 59

revivalism, 148–49, 152, 153

Roland, 38, 50

role model, 141, 169, 187–88, 197

Roman Catholic Church, 98–99, 220n3

romance tales, 100–101, 220n4

Romantic hero: aesthetics of, 126, 136–37, 205; and affect, 116, 117, 126, 127, 137; as antihero, 114, 115, 118, 138; authenticity and, xv, 21–22, 28, 116, 126, 205–6, 208; and Christian hero, 94, 95, 104, 114, 115, 116; and common hero, 118, 139–40, 142–43, 164, 209, 211; corruption of, 207–9, 213; depravity of, 124–25; described, xv, 21, 115–16, 119–20, 137–38, 216n11; dignity of, xv, 119, 135, 136, 137, 138–39; and equality, 23, 115, 118, 126, 137–38, 139, 142, 209; estimability of, 22, 116, 124, 128, 132, 138; examples of, 10, 20–21, 136–37; and magnanimous hero, 122–23; in modern era, 205–6; morality and, 21, 23, 27–28, 120, 122, 126, 127, 135, 137, 138; as redeemer, 10, 22–23, 116, 119, 135, 136, 205; republicanism of, 114, 115, 127–28, 139; self-mastery of, 124–26, 127; social virtues of, 196, 204, 206–9; and the transcendent life, xv, 21, 28, 122, 143, 206. *See also* Romanticism

Romanticism, 50, 103, 156; and affect, 6, 138–39, 207; art, 117–18, 121, 123–27, 130; and authenticity, 117–

18, 119, 122, 130, 132, 138, 207; and common hero, 162, 163, 184, 186, 209; and dignity, 22, 117, 118, 126, 123–24; divinity and religion, 117, 128–30, 131, 132; and equality, 118, 135–36; and frontier life, 173, 174, 177, 178, 180, 182; morality of, 102, 114, 115, 116, 117; and nature, 114, 115, 117, 118, 120–23, 132; self-mastery of, 118, 124–26, 127; obligation of, 22, 128–34, 136, 138; transcendence in, 115–16, 117, 126; usness, 23, 118. See also *Frankenstein*; Romantic hero

Rousseau, Jean-Jacques, 21, 121, 122, 128, 129, 132

Sallust, xii, 78, 83, 85, 90, 193
sameness, 136, 204, 209, 212
Satan, 10, 11, 23, 124–25, 128, 225n8
Savoyard Vicar, 128, 130, 131
Second Great Awakening, 144, 148, 151–55, 165
secondary hero, 17–18, 27, 101–2, 188
self-made man, 168, 171–73, 174–75, 210
self-mastery: and common hero, 142, 163, 168, 173, 174; Renaissance, 2; and Romanticism, 21, 118, 124, 125–26, 127
self-reliance: and common hero, 11, 24, 163, 174, 175, 176, 183, 185, 189, 209; in early America, 155, 158; and Romanticism, 35, 209. See also Emerson, Ralph Waldo
self-sufficiency: and Christian hero, xv, 95, 105, 107, 111, 113, 115; and common hero, 142, 163, 171, 172, 176–77, 191; in early America, 151, 154; moral, xiii, 7, 222n1; of Oedipus, 73; and Romanticism, 115, 117

Shelley, Mary, 10, 22, 128, 132, 133, 195, 208, 222n3
Shelley, Percy, 22, 126, 128–31, 205
singular hero: common hero as, 23, 24, 160, 174, 189, 191; defined, 14, 216n9; historical, xii, xiii; magnanimous hero as, 23, 24, 53, 61, 62, 67, 69, 76, 174; in modern era, xvi, 194–96, 213
situational equality, 135–36, 137, 207, 222n6
social capital, 11, 23, 201–2, 203
social gospel, 152, 153, 154, 155
social groups, 206–7
social identity, 132, 134–36, 137, 206–7, 209, 222n5
social movements, 136–37
social obligation: defined, 4–5; and heroism, 13, 17, 118, 132; and Romanticism, xv, 22, 128, 132–34, 138. See also obligation; republican virtue; virtue
social recognition, 122, 137. See also honor
social solidarity, 11, 45, 136, 195, 201. See also social capital; usness
social virtues: of common hero, 210–13; correctives to, 203, 204–5; defined, 196–97; of epic hero, 198–200; of magnanimous hero, 201–5; of Romantic hero, 206–9
Socrates: on good men, 13–14; and heroic corruption, 199, 203; and magnanimous hero, 27, 54, 58, 59–63, 70, 75–76, 94, 202, 218n1; and philosopher king, xiv, 19, 195, 200; and the soul, 4, 18, 19, 26, 58, 59, 60, 75, 96, 117, 218n2; on virtue, 61, 75, 77, 78, 80; on wisdom, 5, 59, 60, 62. See also philosopher king
soldier of Christ, 95

Solon: Aristotle contrasted with, 68, 76; on balance, 64, 68; humanism of, 47–48, 58, 75; institutionalism of, xiv, 135; and justice, 3, 38, 47, 52, 62, 75; as redeemer, 9, 54; republicanism of, 47, 52, 59
sophistry, 60, 61
Sophocles, 48, 54, 72–73, 76. See also *Oedipus* trilogy
soul: Aristotle and, 67, 76; Socrates and, 4, 18, 19, 26, 58, 59, 60, 75, 96, 117, 218n2. See also great-souled man
Spade, Sam, xvi, 183, 226n12
Spenser, Edmund, 11, 15, 18, 20, 38, 50, 102
Spiderman, 15, 190
spiritual order. See grace, order of
statis, 38, 46–47, 87
steward: Christian hero as, 95, 100, 108; common hero as, 23–24, 141, 167–69, 187, 190–91; defined, 8–9; epic hero as, 18; magnanimous hero as, 19, 20, 54, 59, 63, 75; republican hero as, 7, 195; in Republican Rome, 77, 90
Sulla, 79, 84, 85, 89, 199
superhero: as common hero, 10, 11, 24, 141, 187–90, 226n16; emergence of, 168, 226n15; epic hero contrasted with, 188, 191, 217n7; heroic completeness in, xvi, 196
superheroine, 187–88
Superman, 15, 17, 187, 188–89, 190, 191

Taylor, Buck, 179, 181
Taylor, Charles, 4, 28, 30–32, 33, 193
Thebes, 72, 73, 74
thymos, 26, 44. See also soul
timocracy: and epic hero, 47, 49, 199; and Homeric hero, 18, 38, 42, 52, 60, 61, 71

tolerance, 201, 210–12, 212–13
transcendence: and authenticity, 137–38; and hero types, 33, 53, 113, 200, 206; and Romanticism, 115–16, 117, 118. See also transcendent life
transcendent life: and common hero, 23, 143, 161, 222n1; defined, 4–5; and ingenuity, 202; and Romantic hero, xv, 21, 28, 122, 126, 143, 206. See also ordinary life; transcendence
transcendentalism: and common hero, 24, 28, 157, 159, 160–61, 162–63, 186, 209, 211; in Jacksonian America, 158–59, 192; and morality, 7, 144–45, 156–57, 159–60, 162; principles of, xvi, 144, 155–58
Trump, Donald J., 199, 219n5
Tyler, Royall, xvi, 170, 224n2

urban man. See self-made man
usness: and hero types, 7, 45, 171, 189, 195; and nation building, 7, 11, 24; and Romanticism, 23, 118, 136; and sameness, 136, 204, 209. See also "people like us"

Van Rough, Mr., xvi, 170–71
virilis virtus, 8, 50, 100
virtue: active, 64, 65, 67, 218n6; affective, 70, 75; Aristotle on, 63, 64, 67, 68, 75, 215n3; and chivalry, 50, 101; and Christian hero, 95, 96, 101–2, 104, 105, 106; civic, 5, 108, 155, 167, 183; and common hero, 141, 142, 144, 161, 162, 173, 174, 183, 184, 210; contemplative, 64, 65–66, 67, 218n6; corruption of, 209, 213; defined, 4, 216n7; in early America, 169, 170–73; and epic hero, 17, 48, 52, 60; and heroism, 7, 8, 13, 80, 218n3; and magnanimous

hero, 18–19, 53, 60–61, 63, 75, 123; and modernity, 32; in Republican Rome, 77, 79, 82–83, 84–86, 87, 90, 219n2; and Romantic hero, 114, 116, 119, 208, 209; Socrates on, 61, 75, 77, 78, 80. *See also* justice; obligation; republican virtue; wisdom

virtues: of Christian hero, 99, 100, 101, 102; of hero types, 194–95; and heroic completeness, 196–97, 200, 204–5, 213; and of Homeric hero, 42, 50, 51; of magnanimous hero, 53, 59, 60–61, 200; virtue distinguished from, 216n7. *See also* social virtues; *virilis virtus*

vulnerability: of common hero, 24; as condition of hero, 12, 14–16; of epic hero, 17, 40, 197; of magnanimous hero, 75; of Romantic hero, 22, 116, 128

Werther, 11, 121, 133, 138, 162, 208
Whitman, Walt, 23, 142, 156, 157, 163, 225n5
Williams, Race, xvi, 183–84, 226n12
Winthrop, John, 147, 150
wisdom, 59, 60, 62, 64, 67. *See also* contemplative life
Wonder Woman, 13, 15, 17, 188, 190
woodsman, 176, 179, 210. *See also* frontier life
Wordsworth, William, 50, 103, 131

yeoman farmer, xvi, 11, 168, 173–75, 176, 210

www.ingramcontent.com/pod-product-compliance
Lightning Source LLC
Chambersburg PA
CBHW020642230426
43665CB00008B/278